TV
UNFORGETTABLES

TV UNFORGETTABLES

OVER 250 LEGENDS OF THE SMALL SCREEN

★★★★★★★

ANTHONY & DEBORAH HAYWARD

GUINNESS PUBLISHING

Editor: Paola Simoneschi
Design and Layout: Stonecastle Graphics Ltd, Marden, Kent

Copyright © Anthony and Deborah Hayward 1993

Published in Great Britain by Guinness Publishing Ltd, 33 London Road,
Enfield, Middlesex

Typeset in Galliard Roman by
Ace Filmsetting Ltd, Frome, Somerset
Printed and bound in Great Britain by
The Bath Press, Bath

'Guinness' is a registered trademark of Guinness Publishing Ltd
A catalogue record for this book is available from the British Library

ISBN 0-85112-594-8

Picture Credits
Arlington Enterprises Ltd, British Film Institute, Clifford Elson (Publicity)
Ltd, Howes & Prior Ltd, JRA Agencies Ltd, Layston Productions Ltd,
London Management, Popperfoto, Select Artists Representatives, Annette
Stone Associates, Thomas and Benda Associates Ltd.

Contents

****

Foreword

WELCOME to *TV Unforgettables*, a celebration of more than 250 stars from the Golden Age of Television. Since its birth in the 30s, television has become the world's most popular form of entertainment and many have contributed to its appeal. Some of them are still alive today but others have passed on, leaving behind everlasting memories of their days on the small screen.

Our aim in writing this book is to pay tribute to those who have made their names in TV's most popular programmes and as television stars in their own right. Although most come from the fields of drama and entertainment, factual television – in particular, the news – has produced its own personalities, whether it be Reginald Bosanquet bringing the stories of the day to viewers in his own, distinctive style or Armand and Michaela Denis enthralling everyone in documentaries showing their encounters with the world's wildlife.

When we started writing, our intention was to include only those who no longer appear on the small screen. As we progressed, we had to add to our roll of honour – with the deaths of favourites such as Benny Hill and Frankie Howerd – and found that others we intended to include were suddenly appearing on screen once again, although in this case we generally left them in as a mark of the contribution they have already made.

We hope this book will be read for enjoyment and as a reminder of those who shaped the first 50 years of television. We have also endeavoured to make it as fact-filled as possible so that it will serve as a reference work for those interested in the stars and the programmes.

Many people have given us help, including some of those stars still alive, and their agents, as well as relatives of personalities now dead, to whom we are particularly grateful for the time extended to us during our research. For general help, we would like to thank staff at the British Film Institute Library and the British Newspaper Library. For their patience, we also thank our children, Danielle, Clare and Alexander.

Anthony and Deborah Hayward

★★★★★★★★★★★★

Peter Adamson

b. 16 February 1930

AS Len Fairclough in *Coronation Street*, Peter Adamson was the hard-drinking, tough-talking, no-nonsense leading man in a serial dominated by strong women. It was the similar traits he exhibited off screen that led to his fall from grace.

Born in Liverpool at the start of the Depression, Peter was inspired as a schoolboy by the writing of Aldous Huxley and decided to create his own Brave New World by carving out a career in acting.

That came only after leaving school at 14 and working in a solicitor's office, until he was sacked for persistently drumming on a desk with pens and an inkwell. He also had a job as a commercial artist.

When, at the age of 17, his mother persuaded him to appear in a community-centre play, Peter caught the acting bug. He went to London in 1948, made his debut in theatre clubs and started training at the London Academy of Music and Dramatic Art, only to leave after two months because he refused to take the lessons seriously.

The high-spirited actor returned North to join a theatre in Sale, Cheshire, playing bit-parts. Then, in 1949, he joined the Fortescue Players in Bury, Lancashire, where he acted in and produced weekly melodramas for five years, before setting up his own repertory company as actor, manager and producer,

and staging summer shows at Weston-super-Mare, in Somerset.

It was during this time that Peter made his television debut in an early ITV music show, in 1956, followed by roles in the drama series *Skyport* and *Knight Errant*, both made by Granada Television shortly after it became the ITV contractor for the North of England.

When Granada was planning *Coronation Street*, Peter auditioned for the roles of Dennis Tanner and Ken Barlow but was considered too mature. In February 1961, two months after the programme began, he landed the part of Len Fairclough and soon became one of its most popular actors, fêted by public, politicians and royalty in Britain and around the world.

During his 23 years on screen, the character was married twice – to Nellie Briggs and Rita Littlewood – and had romances with Elsie Tanner, Janet Reid and Bet Lynch.

Off screen, Peter gained a reputation as a hell-raiser, admitting that he had a drink problem and getting involved in pub brawls. His salvation came from Alcoholics Anonymous, but worse was to come.

In 1983, Peter – a part-time swimming instructor – was accused of indecently assaulting two eight-year-old girls in a swimming pool. At the end of a well publicised case, at Burnley Crown Court, he was cleared of the charges. However, he had legal costs of £120 000 and his decision to sell 'inside stories' about his *Street* colleagues – who had stood by him throughout his ordeal – to *The Sun* newspaper for an alleged £60 000, led to Granada Television sacking him. The company had already given Peter a warning after he had sold stories to the same newspaper earlier that year. His exit from the *Street* was engineered to ensure no viewer sympathy, with Len Fairclough being killed in a motorway accident after apparently visiting a mistress.

Peter took a short break in the South Sea island of Bali, then returned to Britain to star as a detective in *Dial M for Murder* on the London West End stage. Down on his luck, he was later tracked down by the press and was found living in a caravan while on a stage tour. Peter decided to seek pastures new and emigrated to Canada, where he continued his acting career.

By then, his wife Jean – who suffered from chronic arthritis but had bravely attended every day of Adamson's trial – had died after a series of operations. The couple had two sons, Michael and Greig.

Ray Alan

b. 18 September 1930

TELEVISION ventriloquists come and go, but Ray Alan remains the doyen of the dummy handlers, with a range of characters that have included Lord Charles, Tich and Quackers, and Ali Cat.

Born in Greenwich, South London, son of a docks tally clerk and grandson of a rat-catcher, Ray won a talent contest at his local Gaumont cinema, aged five, and eight years later took to the stage as a call-boy at the old Lewisham Hippodrome, where he also operated the spotlight. It was there that he was taught to play the ukelele by none other than the legendary George Formby.

He developed an act as a comedian and impressionist at private concerts and dinner parties, soon adding ventriloquism to his array of skills. Entering an *Opportunity Knocks*-style talent show called *Speedway Revels* at the New Cross Empire, in London, Ray was asked about his act. With a host of magicians, impressionists and ukelele players already due to take part, he was persuaded to take on his home-made dummy and do the only three gags he knew, plus a rendition of 'We'll Meet Again'. Winning the contest, he was given a week's performances at the

theatre and was spotted by agents eager to book such an act, which meant turning professional as a ventriloquist.

Ray was soon getting laughs at Britain's leading variety theatres, performing in cabaret in India for eight months and touring with Laurel and Hardy, before playing a season at the Windmill Theatre, London.

When television sounded the death-knell for music-hall, Ray soon appeared in the new medium. He replaced his old faithful dummy – page-boy Steve, accompanied by a parrot – with his new creation, tipsy aristocrat Lord Charles, who made his debut at a Wormwood Scrubs concert, before being unleashed on the wider public in the BBC's *Good Old Days* variety show. The programme made him a household name and Ray holds the record for most appearances on it.

Later, he created Tich and Quackers for a children's television series of the same name, which ran for seven years. As well as making guest appearances on many shows, Ray presented *Ice Show* and *Magic Circle* – with a new doll, Ali Cat – and hosted the panel game *Where In the World* and the quiz shows *It's Your Word* and *Three Little Words*.

In 1985, he was one of the special guests to appear in *Bob Hope's Birthday Show*, staged

at the Lyric Theatre, London, in the presence of Prince Philip, to celebrate the legendary comedian's 82nd birthday, screened on ITV and throughout America. Ray also hosted the BBC Radio 2 series *The Impressionists*.

Less well known is the fact that, as a scriptwriter, Ray wrote 26 episodes of the classic comedy series *Bootsie and Snudge*, and has contributed to *The Dave Allen Show* and *The Two Ronnies*. He also devised, wrote and presented *A Gottle of Geer* and *Starmakers*, histories of ventriloquists and theatrical agents.

Ray has written two books, *A Gottle of Geer* and *Lord Charles' Wine Guide*, and continues to perform in cabaret around the world. He has married and divorced twice, with his second wife, Barbie, co-hosting *Three Little Words* with him. Ray and his third wife, Jane, live in Surrey.

Patrick Allen

b. 17 March 1927

IN THE 60s, the square-jawed, tough-looking Patrick Allen was the smuggler in the title role of *Crane* on television and was accustomed to playing villains and heroes on the cinema screen. Since then, his distinctive, resonant voice has been his fortune, providing countless TV commercials with authoritative tones behind the glossy images.

Born in Malawi, Patrick moved to Britain as a child and was evacuated to Canada during the Second World War. He attended McGill University, Montreal, gained experience as a local radio broadcaster and appeared on television in plays and documentaries, before returning to Britain in 1947 and acting in *The Survivors*, a series of four plays for the BBC.

Seven years later, he appeared in his first film, the Hitchcock classic *Dial M for Murder*, starring Ray Milland and Grace Kelly, and followed this with more than 30 films, including *High Tide at Noon*, *I Was Monty's Double*, *The Wilby Conspiracy*, *The Wild Geese* and *The Sea Wolves*. He also narrated half-a-dozen films.

Patrick made his stage debut in *Desperate Hours*, in 1955, and his subsequent theatrical appearances have included *The Flip Side*, *Present Laughter*, *Savages*, Harold Pinter's *The Lover* and, with the Royal Shakespeare Company, *The Island of the Mighty*, playing King Arthur.

Patrick's TV appearances were only occasional, but in 1963 he made his mark as Crane, the Briton who left his job to run a café in Morocco, indulging in more than a spot of smuggling in the process. *Crane* ran for two years and made him a household name.

He became King of the Voice-Overs, in commercials for products such as Barratt Homes, Anadin and Bold, and earned enough from TV commercials to have a stake in three businesses, including St John's Wood Studios, in North London, where many adverts are made.

Patrick was in front of the TV cameras again for an episode of *Van Der Valk*, before playing Gradgrind in Granada Television's four-hour production of the Dickens classic *Hard Times*, shown on ITV in 1977. Two years later, he appeared as Prestongrange, Lord Advocate of Scotland, in ITV's 13-part serial of Robert Louis Stevenson's *Kidnapped*, and as Auchinleck in the BBC's *Churchill and the Generals*.

He has subsequently acted in the BBC's *Hamlet*, *The Trial of Lady Chatterley*, *The Dick Emery Show*, Rowan Atkinson's comedy *Blackadder* and *Bergerac*, as well as in *The Return of Sherlock Holmes* and the American mini-series *The Winds of War*.

Patrick, who was also heard as the voice of the tug in an animated ITV children's series, *Tugs* – made by the same company that produced *Thomas the Tank Engine* – is married to actress Sarah Lawson, who appeared as the third prison governor in *Within These Walls*. The couple have two sons, Stephen and Stuart.

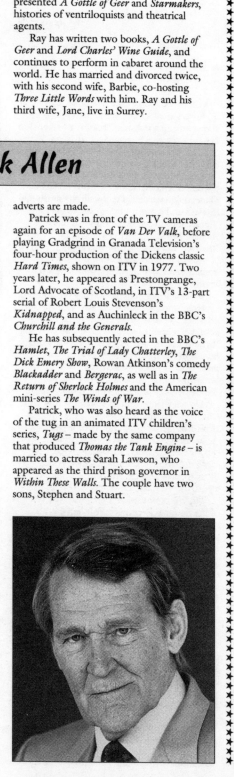

Ronald Allen

b. 16 December 1930
d. 18 June 1991

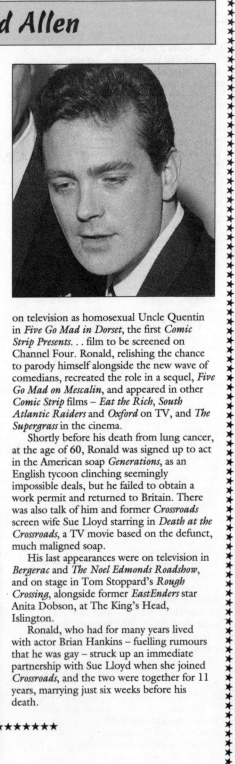

ALTHOUGH Hollywood had once beckoned, it was as the perennial soap star – playing a magazine editor, a soccer club boss and a motel manager – that Ronald Allen will be remembered, with his stiff suits and even stiffer acting.

Born in Reading, Berkshire, Ronald trained at RADA, where he won the John Gielgud Scholarship. He joined Salisbury Rep in 1953 and subsequently acted at the Old Vic, London, playing Mountjoy alongside Richard Burton in *Henry V* at the Old Vic, Benvolio alongside Claire Bloom and John Neville in *Romeo and Juliet* and Paris in *Troilus and Cressida*, which transferred to Broadway.

Ronald's matinée-idol looks were courted by Hollywood and he spent two years under contract to Twentieth Century-Fox, taking small parts in films such as *Cleopatra*, starring Richard Burton and Elizabeth Taylor. Later, he was in the British film *Hell Boats* and, more notably, he appeared as a honeymooning husband in *A Night To Remember*, about the sinking of the *Titanic*.

On television, Ronald starred as magazine editor Ian Harman in *Compact*, the squeaky-clean BBC serial created in 1962 by Hazel Adair and Peter Ling, who later came up with the idea for *Crossroads*. Ronald joined *Compact*, about a magazine aimed at the 'busy woman', six months into its three-and-a-half-year run and left before it ended.

He followed this, in 1966, with the role of the fictional Brentwich Football Club's new manager in *United!*, a year after the programme's launch. One year later, the BBC dropped the serial.

Then, in 1969, began his long-running role as David Hunter in *Crossroads*. Probably the dullest character in soap opera, motel manager Hunter survived the ordeals of having a gun-toting terrorist son and a drunken wife, who later shot him, only to end up as a hopeless gambler. Ronald himself survived the role until a new producer decided to axe him and second screen wife Sue Lloyd in 1985 – less than three years before the programme itself was dropped.

He went on to find a new career in alternative comedy, having already appeared on television as homosexual Uncle Quentin in *Five Go Mad in Dorset*, the first *Comic Strip Presents. . .* film to be screened on Channel Four. Ronald, relishing the chance to parody himself alongside the new wave of comedians, recreated the role in a sequel, *Five Go Mad on Mescalin*, and appeared in other *Comic Strip* films – *Eat the Rich*, *South Atlantic Raiders* and *Oxford* on TV, and *The Supergrass* in the cinema.

Shortly before his death from lung cancer, at the age of 60, Ronald was signed up to act in the American soap *Generations*, as an English tycoon clinching seemingly impossible deals, but he failed to obtain a work permit and returned to Britain. There was also talk of him and former *Crossroads* screen wife Sue Lloyd starring in *Death at the Crossroads*, a TV movie based on the defunct, much maligned soap.

His last appearances were on television in *Bergerac* and *The Noel Edmonds Roadshow*, and on stage in Tom Stoppard's *Rough Crossing*, alongside former *EastEnders* star Anita Dobson, at The King's Head, Islington.

Ronald, who had for many years lived with actor Brian Hankins – fuelling rumours that he was gay – struck up an immediate partnership with Sue Lloyd when she joined *Crossroads*, and the two were together for 11 years, marrying just six weeks before his death.

★★★★★★★★★★★★

Eamonn Andrews

b. 19 December 1922
d. 5 November 1987

To millions of television viewers, Eamonn Andrews was the man with the big red book. As host of *This Is Your Life*, the 6ft Irishman's mischievous grin and Gaelic charm never failed to keep audiences spellbound as he sneaked up on his latest 'victim'.

The show presented a condensed half-hour biography of a selected 'life', liberally sprinkled with anecdotes from long-forgotten relatives and friends, who were often flown in from far-flung corners of the globe for tearful reunions.

Born in Dublin, the son of a carpenter, the world of showbusiness seemed far away as the young schoolboy fought his way to the top to become the All Ireland Juvenile Boxing Champion. It was his love for this sport that gave Eamonn his first break in broadcasting when, at the tender age of 16, he became Radio Eirann's boxing commentator.

Because the job was on only a casual basis, Eamonn worked as a clerk in a Dublin insurance company and studied acting under Ria Mooney at the Abbey Theatre. He went on to take part in Radio Eirann plays and even wrote one himself – a sombre and rather unsuccessful tale entitled *The Moon is Black*.

Eamonn's career in radio went from strength to strength and it was not long before he left his clerk's job to become the *Irish Independent*'s radio critic. His programme, *Microphone Parade*, was packed with interviews and talks, and proved such a success that it ran for almost three years.

It was not until 1942 that Eamonn was first introduced to British audiences, when he arrived on a *Joe Loss Band Show* tour as chairman of a *Double Or Drop* quiz – which was later sold to the BBC and became part of *Crackerjack!*

The following year, he took over as presenter of the hit BBC radio quiz programme *Ignorance is Bliss* and, apart from a few boxing commentaries for television, Eamonn worked in radio over the next few years. He was known mainly for programmes such as *A Book at Bedtime* and *Housewives' Choice*, and for his skill at interviewing celebrities.

It was in July 1951, with *What's My Line?*, that Eamonn's television career really began, followed four years later by *This is Your Life*. He even dipped into children's programmes, taking part in such favourites as *Crackerjack!* and *Playbox*, and went on to win the TV Personality of the Year award four times. In 1960, Eamonn became chairman of the Irish station Radio Eirann and helped to set up RTE, the Irish television network.

Four years later, his contract with the BBC expired and *This is Your Life* was axed, much to the chagrin of Eamonn, who moved to ITV as presenter of *World of Sport* and, later, as host to celebrities in *The Eamonn Andrews Show*.

He finally left sports presenting in 1968 when, after the redistribution of ITV franchises, he became presenter of *Today*, Thames Television's regional news programme, staying with it for ten years.

This is Your Life was relaunched in 1969, on ITV, and continued to run, drawing ratings-topping audiences. In 1984, Eamonn became presenter of a revived *What's My Line?*, turning his television career full circle.

He was also the author of two books, his autobiography *This is My Life*, and *Surprise of Your Life*, about the programme that had made him a legend.

Eamonn never surrendered his Irish citizenship and was a man with considerable business interests, as well as being a devout Roman Catholic. He received a Papal Knighthood in 1964 for his charitable works, and was made a CBE in 1970.

After months of illness, he died from heart disease at the age of 64, in the private Cromwell Hospital, London. He left behind wife Grainne Bourke, whom he married in 1951, and their three adopted children, son Fergal and daughters Emma and Niamh.

Harry Andrews

b. 10 November 1911
d. 6 March 1989

ALTHOUGH dividing his career mainly between films and Shakespearean theatre, Harry Andrews brought his charm, authority and talent for underplaying to television in various productions.

Born in Tonbridge, Kent, the son of a Scottish doctor, Harry enjoyed amateur dramatics. Casting aside ideas of becoming a cricketer or policeman, he decided on a career in acting, securing repertory work at the Liverpool Playhouse, where he made his debut in *The Long Christmas Dinner*, in 1933.

Catching the eye of John Gielgud in London, Harry took over the role of Tybalt in John Gielgud and Laurence Olivier's production of *Romeo and Juliet*. He followed it in 1937 with appearances in Gielgud's Shakespeare-Sheridan-Chekhov season, playing both Horatio and Laertes to the star's Hamlet.

During the Second World War, Harry served in the Royal Artillery, rising to the rank of acting major. On being demobbed, he joined the Shakespeare Memorial Theatre company at Stratford-upon-Avon, under director Anthony Quayle, playing 27 roles in 14 years there and in London – at the Old Vic and in the West End.

After criticism of his performance as Othello at Stratford, Harry switched almost completely to films, although he resisted the lure of Hollywood when one studio wanted

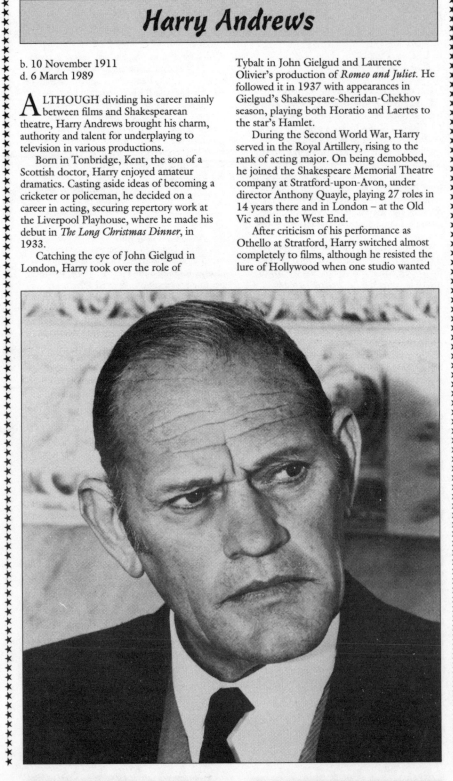

to operate on his protruding ears.

Making his debut as a Scottish sergeant-major in *The Red Beret*, in 1953, Harry's stern looks brought similar roles in many of his 80 pictures. They included *Alexander the Great*, *The Charge of the Light Brigade*, *Entertaining Mr Sloane*, *Death on the Nile* and *Superman*. He even provided the voice of General Woundwort in the animated feature *Watership Down*.

His television appearances included roles in *Clayhanger*, *Edward the Seventh*, *A J Wentworth, BA* – the gentle comedy starring Arthur Lowe – *Dynasty*, *The Return of Sherlock Holmes* and *Jack the Ripper*.

In one of his last TV roles, as the elderly admirer of the widow Wendy Hiller in *All Passion Spent*, he brought to bear all the qualities of warmth, charm and pathos that lay behind his best performances.

Harry, who never married, was honoured with a CBE. He died aged 77.

Desi Arnaz

b. 2 March 1917
d. 2 December 1986

PERHAPS most famous for being the husband of Lucille Ball, Cuban-born bandleader Desi Arnaz was nevertheless a first-class entertainer in his own right. As half of the world's most popular husband-and-wife team, in the *I Love Lucy* shows, he enjoyed the public's adoration for almost a decade.

Born Desiderio Alberto Arnaz y de Acha III, his grandfather was one of the founders of Bacardi Rum. However, any wealth that the family had was lost during the Cuban revolution of 1933. Desi fled the country and arrived in America, where he scraped a living by cleaning bird cages in Florida.

Five years later, he formed his own band, appearing at La Conga Club, Miami, where he found himself on the brink of fame and fortune, introducing the world to a whole new dance craze – the conga.

Having moved to New York, he was cast in the Broadway musical *Too Many Girls* and was subsequently signed by RKO to perform in a 1940 film version of the show. It was here that he met and fell in love with Lucille Ball, who starred alongside him. The romance moved at a dramatic pace and the pair were married in the same year, shortly after the film was completed.

Work seemed to keep the newlyweds apart for a great deal of time as Lucille continued with her film career and Desi went on the road with his own band, until his career was put on hold for three years while he served in the US Army during the Second World War.

Back in civvy street, he proceeded to form another band, as well as becoming musical director on Bob Hope's radio show.

However, when the couple were given the opportunity to star in their own television show together, they eagerly grabbed it. *I Love Lucy*, which was loosely based on the couple's previous hit radio show, *My Favourite Husband*, began in October 1951 and went on to become more popular than anyone could have predicted, with Desi playing Ricky Ricardo and Lucille his crazy wife. The couple also starred in *The Lucille Ball and Desi Arnaz Show*.

By 1955, they had bought out RKO – allowing Desi to demonstrate what an astute businessman he really was – and, as owners of the station, they became not only two of the most successful entertainers, but also two of the most formidable comedy producers on the small screen.

They were the pioneers of making programmes before a studio audience and, with their own company, Desilu, were able to control all distribution and rights. The couple seemed to have a finger in every pie – they were Hollywood's own royalty. However, the Arnaz marriage seemed to be fraught with problems from the outset and, even before the *I Love Lucy* series, Lucille had filed for divorce. She later withdrew the complaint and the pair had a second wedding in church after a dramatic reconciliation.

As the golden couple's marriage began to tarnish again, Lucille divorced her husband in 1960, after 179 episodes of *I Love Lucy*, then married nightclub comedian Gary Morton in the following year. Desi sold his share of Desilu to Lucille, who later sold out to Paramount.

The couple had two children, daughter Lucie and son Desi Arnaz Jr, who both appeared with their mother as Kim and Craig Carter in her subsequent series, *Here's Lucy*, before moving on to follow their own careers.

Desi retired, married Edith Mack Hirsch in 1963, wrote an autobiography – *A Book*, published 13 years later – and died at the age of 69. A 1990 TV movie, *Lucy and Desi: Before the Laughter*, traced the couple's stormy life together before international fame came their way.

James Arness

b. 26 May 1923

AS Marshal Matt Dillon in the long-running American series *Gunsmoke*, 6ft 6in James Arness was one of ITV's first stars. He also made his mark in the 70s as Zeb Macahan in *How the West Was Won*.

Born in Minneapolis, Minnesota, real name James Aurness and brother of *Mission Impossible* actor Peter Graves, James took an interest in acting at school, performing in plays and operettas. On leaving, he worked as a lumberjack and seaman, then served in the US Army in Italy during the Second World War, and was wounded on the Anzio beach-head.

Discharged in 1945, he worked in advertising and real estate before becoming a radio announcer. It wasn't long before he was landing roles in radio dramas and decided on a career in acting.

In 1947, James made his film debut in *The Farmer's Daughter*, alongside Loretta Young, Joseph Cotten and Ethel Barrymore. He made a further eight films under the name Aurness, before changing it in 1950.

Although he appeared in more than 30 films in all, it was on television that he became a major star, as Matt Dillon in *Gunsmoke*, which ran in Britain under the title *Gun Law*, for 20 years (633 episodes). It began in 1955, the year that ITV started, and became one of the many Western series that were flooding into Britain from America.

Gunsmoke, set in Dodge City, Kansas, had been a hit on radio, starring William Conrad, who went on to take the title role of *Cannon* on TV. Its first television episode was introduced by John Wayne, who had turned down the lead role. After its long run, seeing his character rise from sheriff to marshal, James – who had become producer of the programme – starred in the 1976 TV movie *The Macahans: How the West Was Won*, as mountain scout Zeb Macahan, guiding his brother's family on a westward trek from Bull Run, Virginia, to avoid the Civil War.

It was William Conrad who narrated the TV movie, which later became a mini-series and then a full-blown series. However, James was not to find such success in the title role of *McClain's Law*, which was dropped after only one series, in 1981.

Since then, he has tried to revive his fame as Matt Dillon with three TV movies: *Gunsmoke: Return To Dodge* (1987), *Gunsmoke: The Last Apache* (1990) and *Gunsmoke III: To the Last Man* (1991).

After James's divorce from his first wife, actress Virginia Chapman, who later died of a drugs overdose, he married another actress, Janet Surtees. He has one daughter, Jenny – who also died of a drugs overdose, after splitting up with rock star Gregg Allman – and two sons, Craig and former world surfing champion Rolf, all from his first marriage.

Dame Peggy Ashcroft

b. 22 December 1907
d. 14 June 1991

UNDOUBTEDLY the *grande dame* doyen of British theatre, Peggy Ashcroft commanded a talent of such indefinable quality that, to this day, it has remained unsurpassed.

For more than 50 years, she enthralled audiences with performances as diverse as Cleopatra, at the Old Vic, and Barbie in the classic ITV series *The Jewel in the Crown*.

Edith Margaret Emily Ashcroft was born in Croydon, Surrey, daughter of an estate agent and a keen amateur actress. At the age of 16, she enrolled at the Central School of

Speech and Drama in London, before making her professional debut in 1926, in J M Barrie's *Dear Brutus*, at the Birmingham Repertory Theatre. A year later, she made her first London appearance in *One Day More*.

A stream of theatrical successes followed and the young actress held London in the palm of her hand, with outstanding performances in productions such as *Jew Suss*, in 1929, and *Othello*, in which she played Desdemona.

The theatre continued to be Dame Peggy's one true passion and the 30s took her career through an entire gamut of roles, including Juliet – with Gielgud and Olivier alternating as her Romeo – at the New Theatre, Oxford, and Rosalind and Imogen at the Old Vic. The 50s saw an extension in Peggy's already prolific repertoire, with performances as Hedda Gabler at The Lyric, Hammersmith, Beatrice in *Much Ado About Nothing* at the Shakespeare Memorial Theatre, Stratford-upon-Avon, and Miss Madrigal in *The Chalk Garden* at the Haymarket Theatre, London.

Peggy was an actress held in high esteem by both her adoring audiences and those in the profession for which she lived.

It was through her stage roles that she was introduced to television, making her debut in *Shadow of Heroes*, in 1956, and following it with *The Wars of the Roses*, *Days in the Trees* and *The Cherry Orchard*.

In 1978, she was cast as Queen Mary in ITV's controversial but popular series *Edward and Mrs Simpson*, and appeared in *Cream in My Coffee*.

But it was her memorable performances in ITV's major series of 1984, *The Jewel in the Crown*, and the David Lean film *A Passage to India*, released in the same year, that brought her to the attention of a wider audience, at the age of 76. Both productions were based in India and required Peggy to give performances of humility and consideration. The TV series won her a BAFTA award and the film both Academy and BAFTA Awards, but Peggy acted in films only occasionally, having made her debut in *The Wandering Jew*, in 1933. Her other pictures included *The 39 Steps*, *Quiet Wedding*, *Sunday, Bloody Sunday* and *Joseph Andrews*. She also provided the voice of Hilda Bloggs in the animated feature *When the Wind Blows*, based on the Raymond Briggs book.

The actress, who was made a CBE in 1951 and a dame five years later, was married and divorced three times, to Old Etonian Rupert Hart-Davis, actor-turned-publisher Theodore Komisarjevsky and barrister Jeremy Hutchinson, who went on to become Lord Hutchinson of Lullington. She died leaving a daughter, Aliza, and a son, Nicholas. In 1962, the Ashcroft Theatre, Croydon, was opened and named in her honour.

Arthur Askey

b. 6 June 1900
d. 16 November 1982

WHAT Arthur Askey lacked in inches he certainly made up for in talent. This 5ft 3in comedian was the original mini-dynamo. He could do it all – variety, pantomime, revue and radio. Frequently billed as 'Big-hearted Arthur', the Liverpool-born comic is remembered with affection by the millions who laughed along with him.

He didn't even have to open his mouth before they were rolling in the aisles – one look was enough. With his stick-like frame, red hair and large, horn-rimmed spectacles, he was a born funnyman.

The only son of a sugar factory book-keeper, Arthur spent most of his childhood involved in church activities and was a keen member of the choir. He was even chosen to sing solo in front of the Archbishops of Canterbury and York when they visited Liverpool Cathedral.

As a schoolboy, his holidays were spent in the North Wales resort of Rhyl, and it was there that he first fell in love with light entertainment. Every day, without fail, he would rush down to the sands to watch a pierrot troupe perform. He never missed a show, so by the end of the holiday he knew their routine off by heart.

At 16, Arthur began work at Liverpool Education Office for the princely sum of £10 a month and, apart from a brief spell in the Army, he stayed behind his desk until 1924, when his skill as an amateur singer and entertainer won him a place in the *Song Salad* concert party at the Electric Theatre, Colchester.

Arthur learned his craft the hard way – years of touring the provinces and taking part in summer concerts. All the work eventually paid off when the new radio show *Band Waggon*, which started in 1938 and spawned a film spin-off the following year, established

him as a national figure. A string of other radio shows followed, including *Arthur's Inn*, *Hello Playmates* and *Askey Galore*, all popular after the War.

Arthur was also a hit in variety, farce and 40s films, such as *Charley's (Big-Hearted) Aunt*, *The Ghost Train* and *King Arthur Was a Gentleman*. His first television series, in 1953, was *Before Your Very Eyes* and was followed by a new series every year.

In his later years, Arthur suffered muscular problems in his legs – but, being the little fighter that he was, he overcame a series of falls and a severe heart attack to top the bill in his tenth Royal Variety Performance, before the Queen Mother in 1978.

He thrived on hard work and wrote an autobiography, *Before Your Very Eyes*, published in 1975. To mark the 50th anniversary of radio, Arthur appeared with Richard Murdoch in a revival of *Band Waggon*. Both these were in the same year that he had his legs amputated.

He was awarded an OBE in 1969 and was made a CBE in 1981, and was featured, on two separate occasions, as the subject of the TV programme *This Is Your Life*.

Arthur, who in 1925 married concert party singer Miss May Swash (Elizabeth May Swash), had a daughter, Anthea, who followed in her father's footsteps, appearing in several shows with him. His wife died in 1974, eight years before his own death at the age of 82.

Pam Ayres

b. 14 March 1947

AS pop poets go, Pam Ayres was unique in television, finding fame as a winner of the talent show *Opportunity Knocks* and then presenting her own series.

Born in Stanford-in-the-Vale, Oxfordshire, daughter of an electricity board worker, Pam left school at 15 and worked as a Civil Service clerical assistant, before joining the WRAF. While in Singapore, she took up amateur dramatics, appearing in plays such as *Boeing-Boeing* and *Collapse of Stout Party*.

On her return to Britain, Pam became a Redcoat at Butlin's, before settling down to life as a secretary. In her spare time, she read her own poems in an Oxfordshire folk club.

Failing to find a publisher for her works, she put out her own book, *The Entire Collection (Eight) of Masterpieces By Pam Ayres, Famous Poet and Washer of Jamjars*, which sold 7000 copies – more than a modest success in publishing terms.

She also broadcast her poems on BBC Radio Oxford and Radio 4's *Woman's Hour*, then landed her big chance on *Opportunity Knocks*, in 1975. The instant fame won Pam her own shows, *The World of Pam Ayres* and *Pam Ayres' Hong Kong Christmas*, as well as an appearance in the 1977 Silver Jubilee Royal Variety Performance, in front of the Queen.

There were also guest spots on *The Black and White Minstrel Show* and *What's On Next?*, as well as best-selling books of poetry and two 1976 Top 30 albums, *Some of Me Poems and Songs* and *Some More of Me Poems and Songs*.

In 1981, Pam married theatre producer Dudley Russell and let her career take a back seat while bringing up two sons, William and James.

Pam has since returned to showbusiness, touring the country with her own stage show – recorded by BBC television in 1987 – appearing on radio reading children's stories in *Listening Corner*, and on television with her *Piggo* stories in *Playdays*. She has also been the resident humourist in HTV's weekly programme *It's Nearly Saturday*.

Her five books of poems were followed by a 1992 compilation, *The Works*, and her books for children include *The Bear Who Was Left Behind*, *Jack Crater* and a series of three *Piggo* stories. Pam and her family live in the Cotswolds.

Angela Baddeley

b. 4 July 1904
d. 22 February 1976

AS the little, round dumpling Mrs Bridges in ITV's hugely popular series *Upstairs, Downstairs*, actress Angela Baddeley looked almost as wholesome as the tasty treats served up at the Bellamys' Eaton Square home.

Elder sister of film and stage actress Hermione Baddeley, Angela was born in London and appeared on the stage from childhood. She made her debut at the age of 11, as the Little Duke of York in *Richard III* at the Old Vic. She subsequently appeared in productions such as *The Beggar's Opera*, *The Wild Duck* and *Henry VIII*, before leaving for a tour of Australia.

On her return, Angela succeeded in establishing herself as one of the most popular young theatre actresses, with roles in *The Rising Stud* and *Marriage à la Mode*.

In 1931, she appeared in two popular films, the Sherlock Holmes tale *The Speckled Band*, featuring Raymond Massey as Sir Arthur Conan Doyle's sleuth, and a big-screen version of the hit stage thriller *The Ghost Train*.

Throughout the 40s, she played many strong female roles on stage, including Miss Prue in *Love for Love* and Nora in *The Winslow Boy*.

As she grew older, Angela became more of a matronly figure and was consequently cast in such parts. Her television role as the cook Mrs Bridges in *Upstairs, Downstairs* was a prime example.

The programme, which began in 1971, portrayed life above and below stairs in Edwardian England. Scenes often centred around the huge kitchen where Mrs Bridges cooked sumptuous meals for her rich employers, the Bellamys.

As cook, she would often be seen huffing and puffing along, cheeks blown out with effort. However, a less pudding-shaped cook you could not have found because Angela weighed only seven-and-a-half stone, so she had to be specially padded out for the role.

The series proved so successful that it ran for five years and launched many of the cast's careers, including those of Pauline Collins, Simon Williams and Lesley-Anne Down.

Angela, who died soon after the series finished, was married twice. Her marriage to director Stephen Thomas was dissolved, after which she wed actor and director Glen Byam Shaw. She had three children, a daughter from her first marriage and a son and a daughter from the second.

Hylda Baker

b. 4 February 1908
d. 3 May 1986

HYLDA Baker specialised in impersonating women full of malapropisms and camp mannerisms and it was with them that the diminutive Lancashire actress made her name.

She was born in Farnworth, near Bolton, the first of painter and signwriter Harold Baker's seven children. The tough Lancashire man also worked the music halls as a part-time comedian, so it seemed perfectly natural that his daughter should take to the stage.

At the age of ten, she made her debut at the Opera House, Tunbridge Wells, and continued to tour as a single variety act, singing, dancing and performing hilarious impersonations.

By the age of 14, Hylda had become a leading lady, before going on to write, produce and perform in her own touring shows. During the Second World War, she staged many shows, with titles such as *Meet the Girls* and *Bearskins and Blushes*. After 15 years, tired of playing second fiddle to stars such as Johnny Ray and Guy Mitchell, she finished touring and embarked on a solo career.

It was not until the age of 47, however, that Hylda became a television phenomenon, after a brief appearance in the BBC music-hall show *The Good Old Days*, and she subsequently created her 'Cynthia' routine, for which she was to become best known.

Littered with such snappy catchphrases as "she knows, y'know", the stage act was a sensation. Standing alongside her silent stooge Cynthia – played by a burly man in drag – Hylda would dissolve her audiences into helpless laughter as Cynthia triggered the funny lady's frequent asides.

During the 50s, Hylda had her own

seaside show at Blackpool for three consecutive seasons, before making her London West End stage debut in 1956, topping the bill at the Prince of Wales Theatre.

Five years later, she starred in her own television show, *Our House*, followed by *Best of Friends*. But Hylda's greatest screen success was the ITV situation-comedy series *Nearest and Dearest*, which started in 1968 and featured her with Jimmy Jewel as Nellie and Eli Pledge, a brother and sister who were heirs to a Lancashire pickle factory. The earthy Northern humour helped the show to run for nearly 50 episodes and spin off into a 1972 film. Hylda then went on to play landlady Nellie Pickersgill in another sitcom,

Not On Your Nellie, set in a Northern pub.

A good character actress, she gave a fine performance as a backstreet abortionist in director Tony Richardson's 1960 film *Saturday Night and Sunday Morning*. Her other films included *Up the Junction* and *Oliver!*

Hylda returned to the West End in 1968 to act in *Fill the Stage with Happy Hours* and, a year later, she appeared in a short-lived musical, *Mr & Mrs*, based on Noël Coward's *Brief Encounter* and *Fumed Oak*, and performed at the Palace Theatre.

She married an advertising salesman at the age of 24 but divorced eight years later and never revealed her husband's identity. The couple had no children.

Richard Baker

b. 15 June 1925

BRITAIN'S first television newsreader, Richard Baker represented the old school of news presentation in Britain that was challenged by the coming of a commercial rival. He was one of those who survived the transition from radio and, as well as coping with the hustle and bustle of news broadcasting, went on to become a much respected host of music programmes in both mediums.

Born Richard Douglas James Baker in Willesden, London, he excelled in music as a child, learning the piano from the age of seven and playing the cello in his school's orchestra, spurred on by his father, who was an amateur singer, and his mother, a pianist. But it was an interest in acting that led him to perform with the ADC and the Marlowe Society, as well as to play piano for *Footlights* revues, while studying history and modern languages at Peterhouse, Cambridge.

His studies were interrupted by the end of the Second World War, when he was called up to serve in the Royal Navy, where he rose to the rank of sub-lieutenant, but he completed his university education and, after two years acting in repertory theatre and six months as a teacher of English in a South London grammar school, he went into broadcasting.

Richard joined the BBC in 1950 as an announcer for the Third Programme and moved to television four years later as the BBC's first newsreader, his voice originally being heard behind still pictures of the latest events, followed by the traditional newsreels.

The first *News and Newsreel*, broadcast from Alexandra Palace in North London, was broadcast at 7.30pm on 5 July 1954. Richard opened the ten-minute bulletin with the words, "Here is an illustrated summary of the news. It will be followed by the latest film of events and happenings at home and abroad."

It was the following year, two weeks before ITN was launched on the new Independent Television, that the BBC launched a 15-minute news programme with its newsreaders in vision – although they could be seen only during the headlines. Another year on, Richard, Robert Dougall and Kenneth Kendall were chosen to be the BBC's answer to ITN's 'personality' newscasters.

From 1970, he was also presenter of the Radio 4 current affairs series *Start the Week with Richard Baker*.

He retired from newsreading in 1982 but has continued broadcasting as a presenter of music programmes, mainly on radio. His is a familiar voice in *Melodies for You*, *Richard Baker Compares Notes*, *Music for a While* and, occasionally, *Mainly for Pleasure*. On television, he was a regular panellist in *Face the Music* and he still presents coverage of the first and last nights of the Proms. His voice was also heard in the animated children's series *Mary, Mungo and Midge*, in the 70s.

Since 1987, Richard has presented many of the Philomusica of London's concerts and he enjoys staging his own shows: *Richard Baker's Grand Tour to Melody*, about operetta, *The Best of British*, about British musicals, and his autobiographical *Music in my Life*.

As a writer, he has penned seven books – *Here is the News*, *The Terror of Tobermory*, *The Magic of Music*, a biography of Mozart, two naval biographies and *Richard Baker's London* – and theatre shows about Gilbert and Sullivan, Verdi and Noël Coward.

Richard, who was awarded an OBE in 1979 and the Reserve Decoration after many years' service in the Royal Naval Reserve as a lieutenant-commander, lives in Hertfordshire with his wife, Margaret. They have two sons, Andrew and James.

Lucille Ball

b. 6 August 1911
d. 26 April 1989

AS a performer, Lucille Ball was known for her boundless energy and raucous sense of comedy, in which subtlety played no part. She was America's original funny girl and, with her long-running television show *I Love Lucy*, she enjoyed international stardom.

Born in Jamestown, New York State, daughter of a telephone engineer, Lucille was stage-struck from an early age, but suffered bitter disappointment when she was unsuccessful at drama school, turning to modelling instead.

However, she had more than just good

looks and it was not long before her shining talent was spotted by Goldwyn talent scouts, who took her to Hollywood, where she made her film debut as a chorus girl in *Roman Scandals*.

Surrounded by a world of glitz and glamour, Lucille felt insecure and self-conscious and she seemed most at ease when playing comic or frumpy roles.

After a string of bit-parts, she switched to radio and, by 1938, was a regular comedienne on Jack Haley's programme.

It was not until the 40s that Lucille's film career began to pick up, playing the title role in *DuBarry Was a Lady*, opposite Red Skelton, and towards the end of the decade she made two successful films with Bob Hope, *Sorrowful Jones* and *Fancy Pants*.

Lucille was also asked by Cecile B. DeMille to star in *The Greatest Show on Earth* but had to drop out after discovering she was pregnant with daughter Lucie, who was born in the summer of 1951.

In 1940, she had married Cuban-born singer and band leader Desi Arnaz, who was her co-star in the film musical *Too Many Girls*. Although the marriage was fraught with problems from the early days, it went on to become one of the most successful television partnerships ever.

In the *I Love Lucy* series, loosely based on their previous hit radio show, *My Favourite Husband*, and first broadcast on TV in October 1951, the couple created the characters of Lucy and Ricky Ricardo. The show was fast-moving and unsophisticated, but very professional. Audiences couldn't get enough, and it became a universal hit.

They followed it with *The Lucille Ball and Desi Arnaz Show*, and the couple's production company, Desilu, prospered and even bought out the former RKO studios, where Lucille had once worked in B-movies.

However, in 1960, Lucille divorced her husband and, only a year later, was walking down the aisle again, to marry nightclub comedian Gary Morton. The dizzy TV character of Lucy continued in *The Lucy Show* and *Here's Lucy*, with the red-haired actress going on to make a total of more than 500 shows.

Films had taken a back seat during her 20 years of TV success and, slipping into semi-retirement, Lucille was coaxed out only briefly in 1974 to take the title role in a film version of *Mame*, which was badly received. Eleven years later, she staged an unsuccessful comeback playing a Manhattan bag-lady in a TV movie, *Stone Pillows*, and a year later tried again with a new situation-comedy series, *Life With Lucy*, which was later axed because of poor ratings.

Lucille's two children, Lucie and Desi Arnaz Jr – both from her first marriage – appeared with their mother in *Here's Lucy*, before following their own careers. Lucie Jr has had her own series, *The Lucy Arnaz Show*.

The much-loved actress died at the age of 77, after heart surgery. A TV movie, *Lucy and Desi: Before the Laughter*, released in 1990, traced the stormy couple's life together before they found international fame.

Ronnie Barker

b. 25 September 1929

THE rotund half of *The Two Ronnies*, Ronnie Barker, became a household name alongside Ronnie Corbett, with the unlikely pair acting out sketch upon sketch of hilarious routines, but Ronnie was also the versatile star of a string of hit situation-comedies, with *Porridge* becoming a classic of the genre.

Born Ronald Barker in Bedford, the son of an oil company clerk, Ronnie caught the acting bug through his involvement with amateur dramatics. After only a year, he decided to leave his job as a bank clerk and turn professional.

Repertory theatre beckoned and the young Ronnie was soon treading the boards in Aylesbury, Manchester and Oxford. He made his London debut in *Mourning Becomes Electra* at the Arts Theatre, before acting in five plays at the Royal Court.

He then switched to radio, changing his name from Ronald to Ronnie, thinking listeners would find it less formal. In 1966 came his part in *The Frost Report*, a satirical television show starring David Frost and the team who went on to found *Monty Python's Flying Circus*.

It was the turning point in Ronnie's career, for it was here that he met diminutive, Edinburgh-born raconteur Ronnie Corbett and the two of them also appeared in the sequel, *Frost Over England*. They hit it off instantly and it was from this rapport that their award-winning show, *The Two Ronnies*,

was born in 1971. It ran for 17 years.

Ronnie was also a solo success as a comedy actor in situation-comedies such as *Hark at Barker, His Lordship Entertains, Open All Hours* – as Northern shopkeeper Arkwright, with David Jason co-starring – and, most popular of all, *Porridge*, in which he played prison lag Norman Stanley Fletcher. So successful was the series that there was a 1979 film spin-off and a TV sequel, *Going Straight,* featuring Ronnie and co-star Richard Beckinsale struggling to adapt to life back in civvy street. His final sitcom part, screened in 1988, was the title role in *Clarence,* playing a short-sighted removal man.

His films, starting in 1953 with the short *The Silent Witness,* included *Doctor In Distress, The Bargee, A Home of Your Own, A Ghost of a Chance, Futtock's End, The Magnificent Seven Deadly Sins* and *Robin and Marian.*

In January 1988, aged 58 and dogged with high blood pressure, Ronnie decided to retire after doctors advised him to avoid all stress, leaving behind him a glittering career.

Awarded an OBE in the 1988 New Year's Honours List and winner of BAFTA awards as Best Light Entertainment Performer in 1971, 1975 and 1977, Ronnie now has the time to indulge his passion for Victoriana, collecting postcards, illustrated books and prints. He is married to Joy Tubb, who runs an antiques shop in Oxfordshire, and the couple have three children, daughter Charlotte and sons Larry and Adam.

Lady Isobel Barnett

b. 30 June 1918
d. 20 October 1980

ONE of the small screen's most elegant and well-known faces during the 50s, Lady Isobel Barnett was most famous for her role as a panellist in the massively popular quiz programme *What's My Line?*

The show's popularity was largely a result of the skill and professionalism of its participants, and Lady Isobel was no exception. With her charming manner and shrewd way of getting to the heart of the matter, she would often discover the challenger's hidden occupation.

A doctor's daughter, born in Aberdeen, she followed in her father's footsteps by studying medicine at Glasgow University. She qualified as a doctor in 1940 and, the following year, married solicitor and company director Sir Geoffrey Barnett, who was knighted for political and public services to Leicester in 1953. He was also Lord Mayor of the city and an alderman of Leicestershire County Council.

Lady Isobel spent some years after her marriage working as a general practitioner but gave up her medical career in 1948 and, for the next 20 years, was a Justice of the Peace.

In 1953, she arrived on BBC television as one of the original panel of *What's My Line?* and stayed for ten years. She was also on radio, in *Any Questions?* and *Twenty Questions.*

The discreet charm, crystal-clear voice and engaging smile also made Lady Isobel a much-in-demand after-dinner speaker, a role into which she slipped confidently, always delivering a highly amusing and perfectly polished, professional speech.

Sadly, in 1980, Lady Isobel committed suicide in the bathroom of her 18th-century home in Cossington, Leicestershire, only one week after she had been found guilty at Leicester Crown Court of stealing one tin of tuna fish and a carton of cream, valued at 87p.

Lady Isobel – whose autobiography, *My Life Line,* was published in 1965 – had one son, Alastair, with her husband, who died ten years before her.

Michael Barratt

b. 3 January 1928

FROM the late 60s and through the 70s, *Nationwide* bumbled through early evenings on BBC1, watched by many viewers keen to see just how many technical breakdowns could be achieved in a single programme, held together throughout most of its run by the gruff Michael Barratt.

Born in Leeds, Michael entered journalism as a reporter for Kemsley Newspapers in 1945, becoming editor of the *Nigerian Citizen* 11 years later and working for the Nigerian Broadcasting Service.

Back in Britain, he joined the BBC's current affairs flagship, *Panorama*, as a reporter in 1963 and, two years later, became a presenter of *24 Hours*, the nightly show that replaced the legendary *Tonight*.

He stayed until 1969, when *Nationwide* was launched as the BBC's new early-evening news magazine, intended to link all parts of the country. But, with the frequent hitches, it was the ability of the apparently grumpy, mawkish Michael and other presenters – including Frank Bough and Sue Lawley – that was critical in keeping the programme afloat.

Riding high on his fame, Michael hosted *Gardeners' Question Time* on radio and even appeared in two films, *The Magic Christian* – with Peter Sellers – and *Percy's Progress*.

Before the BBC finally dropped *Nationwide*, Michael left in 1977 and was given a royal-style send-off, with a train hired to take him all around the country.

Since then, he has presented *Songs of Praise* and Thames TV's weekly regional current affairs programme *Reporting London* – spending five years on each – and worked in America and Australia, as well as acting as a consultant and running a public relations business.

He has written four books: his 1973 autobiography *Michael Barratt*, *Down To Earth Gardening Book*, *Michael Barratt's Complete Gardening Guide* and *Golf With Tony Jacklin*.

Michael has been married twice. His first wife, Joan Warner, was a fellow reporter on a Loughborough newspaper during his early days in journalism. They had six children – sons Mark, Andrew and Paul, and daughters Eve, Jane and Rachel – but the couple divorced after 24 years. Michael then married one of his *Nationwide* co-presenters, Dilys Morgan, and has since had two sons, Oliver and Barnaby, and a daughter, Jessica.

Ray Barrett

b. 2 May 1927

AS Dr Don Nolan in *Emergency – Ward 10* and go-getting oil executive Peter Thornton in *The Troubleshooters*, tough guy Ray Barrett became one of the heart-throbs of 60s television.

Born in Brisbane, Australia, he had his own radio breakfast show at the age of 16 and moved to Sydney in the 50s to follow a singing career, under contract to Philips Records and releasing several records.

Ray also acted on stage and radio with Spike Milligan, Richard Murdoch and Kenneth Horne, and toured with Margaret Rutherford in *The Happiest Days of Your Life*. He became the first actor to be put under contract by the Australian Broadcasting Corporation, appearing in many plays and series.

In 1959, a year after moving to Britain, Ray appeared in the revue *One To Another*, alongside Beryl Reid, Patrick Wymark and Sheila Hancock. He was also on radio in *Educating Archie* and in the revue *Don't Shoot, We're English*, with Dick Emery, Clive Dunn and Michael Bentine.

When television success came, in 1961, it was in one of Britain's top programmes, *Emergency – Ward 10*, which also made stars of John Alderton, Desmond Carrington and Richard Thorp, and he stayed in the role of Dr Nolan until the following year.

In 1965, after appearances in *Z-Cars*, *Ghost Squad*, *The Brothers Karamazov* and *Doctor Who*, Ray took one of the lead roles in a series called *Mogul*, about an oil company. A year later, the programme changed its name to *The Troubleshooters* and kept viewers hooked with its true-to-life stories of Mogul Oil – from the boardroom to the bedroom – until 1971.

His was also one of the voices in Gerry Anderson's sophisticated puppet series *Stingray* and *Thunderbirds*, and the spin-off film *Thunderbirds Are Go*.

He made further TV appearances in *Black Beauty*, *Barlow*, *Dixon of Dock Green* and *Colditz*, as well as acting in the films *The Sundowners*, *Time to Remember*, *Just Like a Woman*, *Jigsaw*, *The Reptiles*, *Revenge*, *Hostages* and *Touch of Death*.

In 1974, Ray returned to his native Australia to make a cigarette commercial and resettled there two years later. He has appeared in a dozen films since then, including *The Chant of Jimmie Blacksmith*, winning an Australian Film Industry Best Supporting Actor award for his role as a sadistic police chief in the story of a half-white Aborigine's rampage against the country's whites.

His other films there have included *Don's Party*, which he originally performed on

stage, *The Earthling*, with William Holden, and *A Dangerous Summer*, with James Mason.

Ray won the AFI Best Actor award for his role in the 1982 film *Goodbye Paradise* – as well as the same award from the Sydney Film Critics' Circle – and the Television Society of Australia's Best Actor In a Supporting Role award for *The Last Bastion*, three years later.

He was also in the TV drama *Golden Soak*, starring as a mining engineer facing financial problems, faking his death on a Cornwall cliff and fleeing Down Under.

Ray, who lives in Queensland, has two sons, Reginald and Jonathan, by British-born first wife Miren, a former BBC production assistant. Following their divorce, he married second wife Gaye.

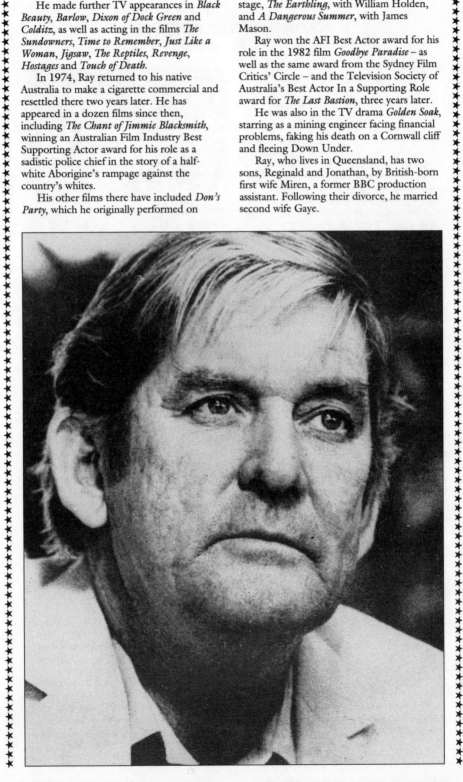

Richard Basehart

b. 31 August 1914
d. 17 September 1984

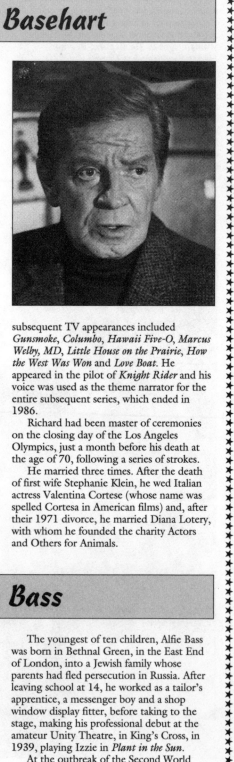

TO many, American actor Richard Basehart will always be the admiral of the glass-nosed submarine in television's popular nautical adventure series *Voyage to the Bottom of the Sea*. His powerful voice and rugged good looks made him an obvious choice for the role – although, as an introvert, he felt more at home playing characters in mental turmoil.

Born in Zanesville, Ohio, Richard was the son of a local newspaper editor and he, too, entered journalism, first as reporter and then as a radio announcer, before eventually moving into acting.

He gained stage experience working in stock companies, before appearing in several Broadway shows, winning the New York Critics' Award for his performance in *The Hasty Heart*.

In 1946, Richard made his film debut in *Cry Wolf* and went on to make more than 80 pictures, including *The House on Telegraph Hill*, *Canyon Crossroads*, *The Satan Bug*, *Mansion of the Doomed* and *The Island of Doctor Moreau*.

During the 50s, many of his films were made in Europe, most notably two for Italian director Federico Fellini, *La Strada* and *Il Bidone*. Back in America, in 1962, he played the title role in *Hitler*.

On television, Richard appeared in episodes of series such as *Rawhide*, *The Alfred Hitchcock Hour*, *The Naked City*, *Ben Casey* and *The Twilight Zone*, before landing the role of Admiral Nelson in *Voyage to the Bottom of the Sea*, which was screened for four years from 1964 and has recently enjoyed a re-run in Britain on Channel Four. His many subsequent TV appearances included *Gunsmoke*, *Columbo*, *Hawaii Five-O*, *Marcus Welby, MD*, *Little House on the Prairie*, *How the West Was Won* and *Love Boat*. He appeared in the pilot of *Knight Rider* and his voice was used as the theme narrator for the entire subsequent series, which ended in 1986.

Richard had been master of ceremonies on the closing day of the Los Angeles Olympics, just a month before his death at the age of 70, following a series of strokes.

He married three times. After the death of first wife Stephanie Klein, he wed Italian actress Valentina Cortese (whose name was spelled Cortesa in American films) and, after their 1971 divorce, he married Diana Lotery, with whom he founded the charity Actors and Others for Animals.

Alfie Bass

b. 8 April 1921
d. 17 July 1987

IT WAS television, and in particular *The Army Game* and its sequel, *Bootsie and Snudge*, that made diminutive East End comic Alfie Bass a household name. Irrepressible, infinitely funny and completely likeable, Alfie was a natural comic and, as Private 'Excused Boots' Bisley – Bootsie, for short – he was hilarious.

The youngest of ten children, Alfie Bass was born in Bethnal Green, in the East End of London, into a Jewish family whose parents had fled persecution in Russia. After leaving school at 14, he worked as a tailor's apprentice, a messenger boy and a shop window display fitter, before taking to the stage, making his professional debut at the amateur Unity Theatre, in King's Cross, in 1939, playing Izzie in *Plant in the Sun*.

At the outbreak of the Second World

War, Alfie was called up into the Middlesex Regiment as a despatch rider, but even this did not stop him from acting. He dived into concert parties and took part in documentaries for the Army Film Unit.

After the War, Alfie resumed his stage career, playing Abel Drugger in *The Alchemist* at the Liverpool Playhouse, in 1945, and starring as Og the leprechaun in the American musical *Finian's Rainbow* at the Palace Theatre, two years later.

In 1953, he starred as the ghost in Wolf Mankowitz's Jewish fantasy *The Bespoke Overcoat* and repeated the role in a film short of the same name. He had made his film debut in the 1943 production *The Bells Go Down* and followed it with many pictures, often playing cockneys or Jews.

Alfie's first *major* role was in *The Lavender Hill Mob* and his later big-screen appearances included *Doctor in Clover*, *Alfie* – opposite Michael Caine – *A Funny Thing Happened on the Way to the Forum*, *Up the Junction*, *Revenge of the Pink Panther* and *Moonraker*.

On television, Alfie was a hit as Private 'Excused Boots' Bisley in *The Army Game*. The series, which ran for three years from 1957, also featured Bill Fraser, William Hartnell and Bernard Bresslaw. Alfie's character had a total aversion to wearing regulation Army footwear, preferring to slouch around in unlaced plimsolls and uttering "Never mind, eh?" at every opportunity. Needless to say, this soon became the actor's much-used catchphrase.

The Army Game was modelled on the 1956 film *Private's Progress* and portrayed a gang of conscripts doing their utmost to avoid potential hazards and responsibilities. Audiences fell in love with the chaotic rabble and a 1958 film spin-off, *I Only Arsked!*, was made, as well as the TV sequel *Bootsie and Snudge*, with Alfie and Bill's characters back in civvy street, struggling to work in a rather dire gentlemen's club.

The meticulous comedy actor subsequently appeared on television in series such as *Till Death Us Do Part* and *Are You Being Served?*

Alfie, who died at the age of 66, was married to actress Beryl Bryson, with whom he had a son, Julian, and a daughter, Gillian.

Faithful to his Jewish roots, Alfie was always there when morals and rights were at stake. He took part in the historic fracas in Cable Street, when he helped to prevent a mob of Oswald Mosley's Fascists marching through the East End, and he worked all his life to help boys' clubs and spastic children.

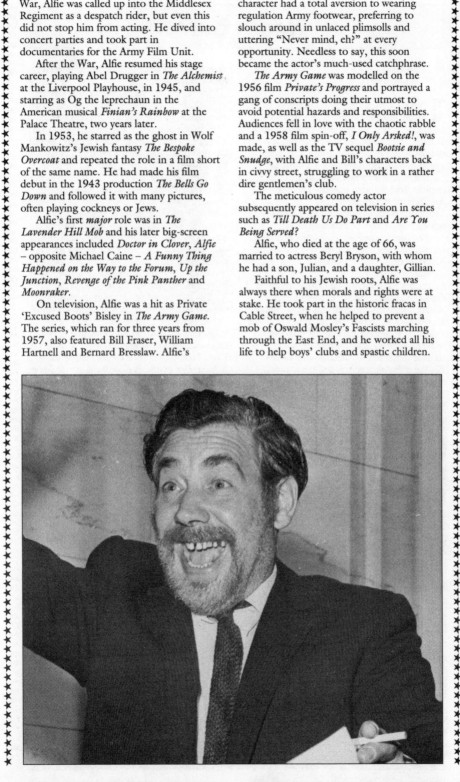

Ralph Bates

b. 12 February 1940
d. 27 March 1991

TWO TV roles that could not have been more different made Ralph Bates a star: he starred first as heart-throb villain George Warleggan in *Poldark* during the 70s and then as lonely heart John Lacey in the classic situation-comedy *Dear John* a decade later.

Ralph, a descendant of Louis Pasteur, was born in Bristol and at one time held dual Anglo-French nationality. He read French at Trinity College, Dublin, before winning a scholarship to Yale Drama School.

The course completed, Ralph returned to Ireland to make his stage debut in Shaw's *You Never Can Tell*, at The Gate Theatre, Dublin, in 1963.

A career in repertory theatre followed and the young actor gained experience in productions ranging from classics, such as *Hedda Gabler*, to raucous comedies.

Later, Ralph carved a niche in the world of Hammer horror films, playing spine-chilling characters in pictures such as *The Horror of Frankenstein* and *Dr Jeykll and Sister Hyde*, in which he played a deranged

doctor who mistakenly transforms himself into a shapely siren.

On television, Ralph had already starred as Caligula in the ITV series *The Caesars* and alongside Cyd Hayman in a passionate French tale of murder and mystery, in ITV's *Crime Of Passion* series, when he was offered the role of Ross Poldark's enemy, George Warleggan, in *Poldark*, which ran for 29 episodes, starting in 1975.

It looked, for a while, as if he might remain typecast as the archetypal mean-and-moody hunk. But then along came John Sullivan's farcical comedy series *Dear John*, which saw Ralph as the loveable but loveless central character set among a singles group, with each member searching for that perfect but elusive partner. Ralph also appeared in the TV movie *Minder on the Orient Express*.

The actor died of cancer at the age of 51. He was married twice, first to actress Joanna Van Gyseghem, then to former actress Virginia Wetherall, with whom he had two children, actress daughter Daisy – seen in the second series of *Forever Green*, alongside John Alderton and Pauline Collins – and son William, who played his son in *Dear John*.

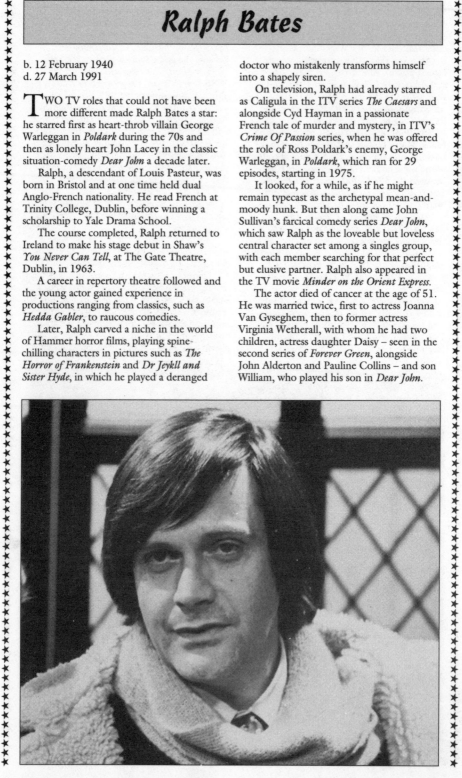

Raymond Baxter

b. 25 January 1922

THE authoritative and distinctive style of presentation that Raymond Baxter gave to *Tomorrow's World* for its first 13 years helped to give the BBC science series both a credibility and popularity that it has lacked since. His voice has also been one of those heard on television and radio during coverage of major state occasions, such as the Queen's Coronation and Remembrance Day services.

Born Raymond Frederic Baxter in Ilford, Essex, he joined the RAF in 1940 and served as a Spitfire fighter-pilot, flying across Europe, the Mediterranean and the Middle East. After the Second World War, he flew Mustangs and Dakotas for a year, before joining Forces Broadcasting in Cairo.

In 1947, he became deputy station director of the British Forces Network, in Hamburg, and three years later joined the BBC in London as motoring correspondent and a presenter of outside broadcasts. He commentated on many events transmitted live for the first time, such as the first Telstar satellite link with America, the first television transmission between Britain and Australia, and the first live pictures from the moon.

Specialising in science, technology and aviation, Raymond's first TV series was *Eye on Research*, which ran for four years from 1959. He was one of the original presenters of *Tomorrow's World* when it began in 1965 and his slightly robotic but eloquent style has been much imitated since, but to lesser effect.

He left the BBC in 1967 to become Director of Motoring Publicity for the British Motor Corporation, although he continued on *Tomorrow's World*, before returning to broadcasting as a freelance less than two years later.

Raymond left the programme in 1977, after bitter disagreements with the new editor, Michael Blakstad – who described him as 'the last of the dinosaurs' – and presented a new series, *The Energy File*, which ran for a year.

Since then, his television appearances have been less regular, although he has been a permanent fixture at State Openings of Parliament, Festivals of Remembrance, Battle of Britain displays, Royal Tournaments and, between 1950 and 1984, Farnborough Air Shows.

Special events commentated on by Raymond include the 1952 Coronation, Princess Margaret's wedding, the funerals of Sir Winston Churchill, General de Gaulle and Lord Mountbatten, the Investiture of the Prince of Wales, the Queen's Silver Jubilee celebrations and the Royal Fireworks at the Prince and Princess of Wales's wedding.

As well as occasional work for the BBC, such as writing and presenting a feature on transport and technology during the Queen's reign as part of the celebrations to mark her 40 years on the throne, Raymond has appeared as himself on TV in the 1954 BBC pantomime – as the coachman, alongside announcers McDonald Hobley and Sylvia Peters – and with Tony Hancock in *Hancock's Half Hour*, Michael Bentine in *It's a Square World* and Spike Milligan in two series, as well as an episode of *The Goodies* and *The Generation Game*, in which he, Henry Cooper and Terry Wogan dressed up as Ugly Sisters and the audience had to guess the stars under the disguises.

He has co-written two *Tomorrow's World* books, was general editor of *The Library of Motoring* and author of *Farnborough Commentary*.

Raymond is Vice-President of the RNLI, a Freeman of the City of London and co-founder and Honorary Admiral of the Association of Dunkirk Little Ships. He and his wife Sylvia – an American nurse whom he met during the War – have a son, Graham, and a daughter, Jennifer, and live in Henley-on-Thames, in Oxfordshire.

Stanley Baxter

b. 24 May 1926

THE films of Fred Astaire and Ginger Rogers took the young Stanley Baxter into another world, fuelled his desire to go into showbusiness and were typical of the era to which he paid tribute in his spectacular TV shows.

Born in Glasgow during the 20s, Stanley impersonated friends and teachers from an early age. His mother, who loved vaudeville, wanted him to go into variety. They put an act together, with him singing and her playing the piano, and at the age of seven he appeared on a church-hall stage.

Seven years later, Stanley began broadcasting in children's programmes and clocked up a hundred shows before being called up for the Army towards the end of the Second World War.

On being demobbed, he went straight to Edinburgh to appear in celebrated director Tyrone Guthrie's production of the Scottish stage classic *The Thrie Estaites*, following it with other Guthrie productions, such as *The Atom Doctor*, *The Queen's Comedy*, *Douglas* – alongside Dame Sybil Thorndike and Sir Lewis Casson – and the première of Guthrie's own play *Top of the Ladder*.

Leaving straight theatre, Stanley acted in Howard and Wyndham's summer revue *Five Past Eight*, in Glasgow, and in London's West End in *The Amorous Prawn*, with Evelyn Laye, and the revue *On the Brighter Side*, with Betty Marsden. Stanley and his co-star transferred the revue to television in 1959, retitled *On the Bright Side*, sending up Hollywood films and TV programmes and winning him the Guild of Television Producers and Directors Award for Light Entertainment Personality of the Year. Returning to Scotland, he made another series, *The Stanley Baxter Show*.

Subsequent West End stage shows included Joe Orton's *What the Butler Saw* and the title role in *Phil the Fluter*.

Stanley had already appeared in Frank Launder and Sidney Gilliat's film comedy *Geordie*, in 1955, but had to wait six years before his next big-screen role, starring in *Very Important Person*, then *Crooks Anonymous*, *The Fast Lady*, *And Father Came Too* and *Joey Boy*.

Back on television, he made three series of *The Stanley Baxter Picture Show* for ITV, starting in 1972, and followed it with *The Stanley Baxter Big Picture Show* and *The Stanley Baxter Moving Picture Show* – a series that won seven awards, including four from the Society of Film and Television Arts.

His other ITV programmes included *Stanley Baxter's Christmas Box*, *Merrie Old Christmas*, *Stanley Baxter on Television* and *The Stanley Baxter Series*, before he moved to the BBC in 1985 to make *Baxter's Christmas Hamper*, followed by *The Stanley Baxter Picture Annual* and *The Hogmanay Show*. He also played the title role in the ITV children's series *Mr Majeika*.

Stanley's voice is one of those putting words into the mouths of the chimps in the Brooke Bond PG Tips TV adverts and, in 1989, he won the Golden Break Award for the best voice-over in a commercial.

Every Christmas, he loved to take part in pantomime, but in 1992 – in his mid-60s – he decided to do no more because of the numerous costume changes and energy required. Early the following year, he was heard playing Noël Coward in *Marvellous Party*, on Radio 4.

Stanley is married to former actress Moira Robertson, whom he met when they were both 'extras' in a comedy called *Bunty Pulls the Strings*. The couple live in Highgate, North London.

Richard Beckinsale

b. 6 July 1947
d. 19 March 1979

EVER-youthful Richard Beckinsale, whose career was tragically cut short by a fatal heart attack at the age of 31, was one of television comedy's most loved young stars, making his mark in four hit series as the genial young man going slightly off the rails.

Born in Nottingham after the Second World War, son of a legal executive, Richard became an apprentice upholsterer on leaving school, then an inspector of spun iron pipes in a factory and a clerk in a gas-board accounts department.

However, intent on acting as a career, he took a drama course at college, then attended RADA. His first professional work was with

Crewe Rep, where his many appearances included the title role in *Hamlet*.

Richard's first TV role was as PC Wilcox of Tile Street Police Station, who arrested Ena Sharples in *Coronation Street*, in 1969. She had organised a sit-in against plans to demolish the pensioners' club-room to make way for a car park, but he let her off with a caution.

After failing an audition for another Granada Television programme, *A Family at War*, he was offered the lead role as Geoffrey in the Jack Rosenthal-scripted comedy series *The Lovers*, alongside Paula Wilcox.

His character was forever trying to get girlfriend Beryl into bed, but she was determined not to give in to 'Percy Filth'. The programme soon rocketed him to stardom, and he left behind rep work for £150 a week on the small screen. There was also a film spin-off of the same name.

He followed this in 1974 with another ITV series, playing medical student Alan in *Rising Damp*, alongside the irrepressible Leonard Rossiter – who, as landlord Rigsby, kept a watchful eye on the goings-on of his two male tenants.

Richard sported long, flowing locks in this role, for both the TV series and the 1980 film spin-off, but for his biggest hit they were to be chopped off.

Porridge was Dick Clement and Ian La Frenais's classic prison comedy, featuring Ronnie Barker as wily old Fletcher and Richard as his cell-mate, Godber. It became one of television's most popular comedy series, with Christmas specials, a spin-off film of the same name and a sequel, *Going Straight*, with Fletcher and Godber facing life in civvy street.

It was as he was about to complete a new BBC comedy series, *Bloomers*, in which he played an out-of-work actor who became a partner in a florist's shop, that Richard collapsed at his home, in Sunningdale, Berkshire, from a heart attack.

He had appeared in many stage plays, including 19 months in the London West End hit *Funny Peculiar* as a promiscuous North Country grocer, and he had played the starring role in the London production of the Broadway musical *I Love My Wife*, proving that he could sing and dance as well as act.

Richard also appeared at the Royal Court Theatre in *Mrs Grabowski's Academy*, but never achieved his ambition to perform at the National Theatre.

Married to Nottingham secretary Margaret Bradley at the age of 18, Richard had a daughter – actress Samantha, of *London's Burning* fame – although the marriage was dissolved in 1971. By then, he had met Judy Loe, who had acted with him at Crewe Rep, and they lived together for eight years before marrying, in 1977. The couple had a daughter, Kate.

Jill Bennett

b. 24 December 1931
d. 4 October 1990

AN unconventional and seemingly vulnerable beauty, Jill Bennett was one of the finest comediennes of her generation. Many television viewers will remember her for the marvellously funny series *Poor Little Rich Girls*, in which she co-starred with Maria Aitken.

Born in Penang, Malaya, of wealthy Scottish parents, this elegant actress entered the cut-throat world of showbusiness at the age of 18, making her professional debut at the Shakespeare Memorial Theatre, Stratford-upon-Avon, in 1949.

It was there that she experienced her first real love, when she fell passionately under the spell of the theatre's leading man, Sir Godfrey Tearle. She was only a teenager and he was a performer of 60. With such an age difference, controversy followed and the couple's relationship created a great scandal.

Jill remained unbowed and, when Tearle died four years later, it was in her arms, the end of what she claimed to have been one of the most exhilaratingly happy and fulfilled periods of her life.

A year after first treading the boards, she was spotted by Laurence Olivier, who invited her to join his company at St James's Theatre, in London, where she flourished in productions such as *Captain Carvallo*.

Both her talent and beauty shone and, after her 1951 film debut in the British picture *The Long Dark Hall*, Jill was whisked away to Hollywood at the age of 22 and appeared in such films as *Moulin Rouge* and *Lust for Life*.

But the theatre remained the medium that seemed to give her that extra zest for life and help to chase away the melancholy moods which frequently ensnared her.

The mid-50s saw her touring in repertory theatre, where she gave fine performances in *The Seagull*, as Marsha, and *Time Present*, written for Jill by her second husband, John Osborne, telling the story of an alcoholic actress remembering life with her dying father.

The role, which Osborne felt inspired to write when Jill told him of her memories of life with Tearle, won her both the London *Evening Standard* and Variety Club of Great Britain Best Actress awards.

On television, her plays included *The Heiress*, *A Midsummer Night's Dream*, *The Three Sisters*, *Design for Living*, *The Parachute* and *Rembrandt*. But she will be best remembered as Maria Aitken's upper-crust cohort in the 1984 ITV series *Poor Little Rich Girls*. Two years later, Jill appeared in John Mortimer's *Paradise Postponed* series.

One of her last performances was in London's West End, where she starred with Sir John Mills in a revival of Terence Rattigan's *Separate Tables*.

Jill, who never had children, married and divorced twice – both her husbands (Willis Hall and John Osborne) were playwrights. After their separation, Osborne publicly referred to her as 'Adolf'. Although Jill never married again, she was linked until her death with city stockbroker Thomas Schoch.

Jack Benny

b. 14 February 1894
d. 26 December 1974

A vaudeville and radio comedian of superstar status, American Jack Benny hosted his own television show for 20 years, with Hollywood's greatest vying for his attention – even Marilyn Monroe made her small-screen debut on the show, in 1953.

Born Benjamin Kubelsky, in Chicago, Jack's father was a haberdasher in Waukegan, Illinois, where he was brought up. The young boy studied the violin and, when he was only 13, played in the Waukegan dance orchestra.

The violin was to remain dear to him for the rest of his life – he once even played in a serious concert with the New York Philharmonic, although a critic wrote, 'Last night Jack Benny played Mendelssohn, and Mendelssohn lost.'

Teaming up with Cora Salisbury at the age of 17 and calling himself Benny K Benny, he took to the road, performing a serious music routine for the next two years.

Leaving this act in 1911, Jack joined pianist Lyman Woods and the pair made their debut in Britain the following year, at the Palace Theatre, London, as the start of a 12-week tour.

The partnership broke up, however, in

1917, when Jack was enlisted into the US Navy during the First World War, when he entertained the troops in a services revue that toured training camps.

Back in civvy street, he returned to the theatre as a stand-up comic and, in 1921, appeared at Proctor's Music Hall, New York, a well-known venue for rising stars.

In 1928 Jack made his film debut in the short *Bright Moments* and followed it with 50 pictures, including *Mr Broadway*, *Broadway Melody of 1936*, *Buck Benny Rides Again*, *Charley's Aunt* and *It's a Mad, Mad, Mad, Mad World*.

In 1931, he made his first solo appearance at the London Palladium, which was to be the first of many, with his radio partners Phil Harris, Mary Livingstone and Eddie 'Rochester' Anderson frequently starring in his stage productions, which included several Royal Variety Shows.

For 18 years Jack, along with a group of tremendously talented entertainers, ruled the airwaves, with many of their programmes broadcast by the BBC World Service during the Second World War.

The po-faced comic, who feigned meanness and bad-temperedness, and posed as a cheapskate, made his first television appearance in March 1949, with the opening of the first Hollywood television station.

One year later, at the age of 56 – although professionally he was 'always 39' – he hosted various variety specials, which evolved into the half-hour *Jack Benny Show*, which began in 1952 and ran for 13 years. It won Emmy awards in 1957 and 1958.

His presence on British TV became an annual event, his last appearance at the London Palladium in 1973.

Jack was married to Mary Livingstone (real name Sadye Marks), who appeared with him in both his radio and TV shows, and the couple had an adopted daughter, Joan. He died of stomach cancer at the age of 80 while planning a film with Walter Matthau, based on Neil Simon's Broadway hit *The Sunshine Boys*.

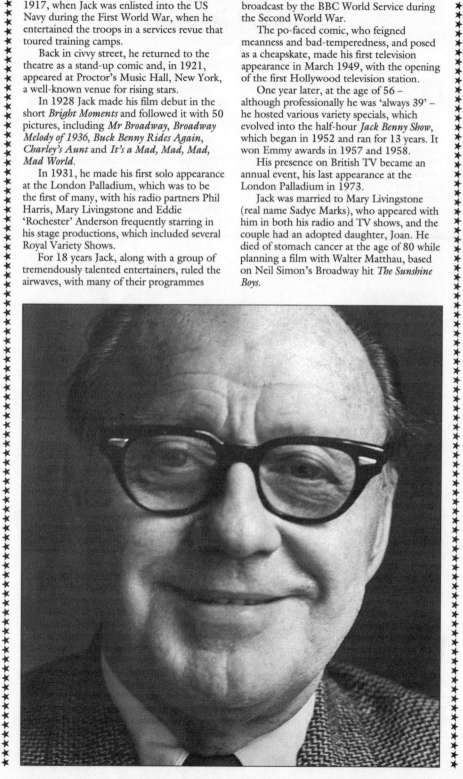

Michael Bentine

b. 26 January 1922

ONE of the infamous Goons on radio and television, actor, comedian and writer Michael Bentine found his biggest solo successes with programmes that used animation, such as *The Bumblies*, *It's a Square World*, *All Square* and *Michael Bentine's Potty Time*.

Born in Watford, Hertfordshire, of a Peruvian father who came to Britain at the turn of the century, Michael is an Old Etonian who began his career as the juvenile lead in *Sweet Lavender*, in Cardiff in 1940, before joining Robert Atkins's Shakespearean company in Regent's Park, London.

Volunteering for RAF service during the Second World War, Michael worked on intelligence operations with Polish squadrons. After the War, he performed at the Windmill Theatre and in various revues, before branching out into radio, where he became one of the founders of The Goons, with Peter Sellers, Spike Milligan and Harry Secombe.

The programme started as *Junior Crazy Gang*, in 1951, before changing its name to *Those Crazy People*, *The Goons* and then *The Goon Show*. Its anarchic humour worried some executives, but radio listeners loved it and future generations, such as the Monty

Python team, acknowledged it as an influence on their work.

Michael left The Goons in 1954, before it had really reached its peak, and made an animated children's TV series, *The Bumblies*, set around pear-shaped beings from the planet Bumble. It was his first venture into a more visual style of comedy.

After working in American and Australian television, Michael created a new, madcap series in Britain called *It's a Square World*, which also featured Dick Emery, Clive Dunn and Frank Thornton.

Starting in 1960, it again included animation, with sequences such as the fictional sinking of the Woolwich ferry and a Chinese junk sailing up the Thames to attack the Houses of Parliament, which was banned by the BBC because it was considered too political at the time of a general election.

Michael left for ITV in 1966 to launch a follow-up, *All Square*, and – six years later – another children's television series, *Michael Bentine's Potty Time*, featuring puppets with constantly changing wigs and moustaches.

Since then, he has done little television work and has concentrated on developing his interest in the paranormal and supernatural, which began as a child.

Michael was in the film *The Sandwich Man* – which he co-wrote and also starred Dora Bryan, Harry H Corbett, Diana Dors and a host of other British comedy actors – and *Bachelor of Arts*.

After getting divorced from his first wife, he married former ballet dancer Clementina Stuart. Sadly, his children have been beset by tragedy: son Gus, from his first marriage, died in a small aircraft crash in 1972, while the other child of his first marriage, Elaine, died of cancer in 1983. Four years later, Fusty – a daughter by his second wife – also died of cancer. Michael has two other children from his second marriage, daughter Suki and son Peski (Richard).

He has written three autobiographies, *The Long Banana Skin*, *The Door Marked Summer* and *The Reluctant Jester*; his other books include *Doors of the Mind* and *Lords of the Levels*.

John Bentley

b. 2 December 1916

FIRST making his name on stage and in films, John Bentley switched to television to star as the white hunter in the 50s series *African Patrol* and went on to play Hugh Mortimer in the ITV serial *Crossroads*.

Born in Sparkhill, Birmingham, during the First World War, John began broadcasting at the age of 16 in a musical. He had the joint lead, sang two solo songs, two duets and in a quartet – all backed by the BBC Midland Orchestra and Chorus. He was an announcer for Radio Luxembourg before the Second World War, then made his London stage debut in *New Faces*, in 1940.

His first film appearance, at the age of 30, was in the 1947 picture *The Hills of Donegal*, and he followed it with more than 30 pictures.

John acted various fictional detectives, including the title roles in the Paul Temple series of films – *Calling Paul Temple*, *Paul Temple's Triumph* and *Paul Temple Returns* – and in *Salute the Toff* and *Hammer the Toff*.

He also made several American films in the 50s, such as *Istanbul* – alongside Errol Flynn – and *Submarine Seahawk*, but the Hollywood contract came too late to catapult him out of the general run of second-feature stars.

Television beckoned and, in 1958, having already appeared in *Strictly Personal*, John landed the starring role of Patrol Inspector Paul Derek in the ITV series *African Patrol*, which ran over the next few years for 39 episodes.

In 1965, after his film career had finished, he joined the ITV serial *Crossroads* as millionaire businessman Hugh Mortimer, who romanced Meg Richardson, only to lose her to another man – but he eventually won her back years later.

Their 1975 TV wedding – with a blessing filmed at Birmingham Cathedral and Larry Grayson chauffeuring the happy couple – was one of the television events of the year. Thousands of fans flocked to the Cathedral for the recording and brought the centre of Birmingham to a halt.

The screen marriage lasted just three years, with Hugh dying of a heart attack after being kidnapped by terrorists, in a serial pilloried by critics for its outrageous storylines and poor acting.

John's other TV appearances have included *Armchair Theatre*, *Time Out of Mind*, *Misfire* and *Any Other Business*. His sonorous voice has also been heard in TV commercials for products such as Super National Petrol, Timex and Cadbury's Flake. John's marriage to wife Joyce was dissolved in 1955 and the couple had one son. John lives in Sussex.

Katharine Blake

b. 4 April 1928
d. 1 March 1991

A shining light both on and off screen, Katharine Blake was a hugely talented actress and television writer. Many will remember her in ITV's popular series *Within These Walls*, in which she played prison governor Helen Foster, during the 70s.

Born in Johannesburg, South Africa, to an Irish mother and English father, she first visited Britain at the age of 11. During the holiday, war broke out and, instead of returning home, she went to live with her aunt in Perth, Scotland.

Educated at a nearby convent, Katharine felt a calling to become a nun, until the Reverend Mother decided that this career choice was no more than a theatrical aspiration.

Leaving the convent at 16, her first job was as an assistant stage manager at Perth Repertory Theatre, where she was often given small parts in performances. Gaining in experience, she moved to Amersham and Windsor repertory companies, before making her West End debut in *A Man About the House*.

In 1948, she was acclaimed for her starring role as Cathy in an early television version of *Wuthering Heights*.

Four years later, Katharine travelled to America with Laurence Olivier's company to appear on Broadway in *Antony and Cleopatra* and *Caesar and Cleopatra*.

Katharine fell in love with the country and decided to stay, acting on the stage and appearing on Canadian television, with her screen performances winning her that country's Best Television Actress award for three successive years, from 1957.

She worked with a group of talented television and stage people, including writer Arthur Hailey and producer Sydney Newman, whom she followed back to London in 1959. Newman had been invited to make the *Armchair Theatre* series for ITV and Katharine became the star of many episodes.

Over the next decade, she could be seen in many plays and dramas on both BBC and ITV, and in 1964 won the Television Actress of the Year award for her fine performance in *The Rose Tattoo*.

At around this time she appeared in several films, including *Anne of the Thousand Days*, which starred Richard Burton and Genevieve Bujold.

Katharine was also a clever writer and, under the pen name of Ursula Gray, she wrote such memorable adaptations as Brecht's *Galileo* and Brigid Brophy's *The Snow Ball*, in which she played the lead.

Her acting career came to an end after she suffered a debilitating spine condition for which she underwent surgery. This came at the time when she was established in her starring role in the 70s ITV prison series *Within These Walls*, which she took over from Googie Withers.

Katharine was married and divorced three times, the last marriage to British-born director Charles Jarrott, and had two daughters.

Colin Blakely

b. 23 September 1930
d. 7 May 1987

C OLIN Blakely was one of the finest classical actors of his generation, enjoying a career that was rich in both passion and diversity. Over 30 years, he performed with the Royal Shakespeare Company, the English Stage Company and the National Theatre, as well as appearing on television and in films.

Colin George Blakely was born in Bangor, County Down. His family ran a sports retailing business, in which he worked on leaving Sedbergh School, in Yorkshire.

Keen on amateur dramatics, Colin's experience with the Bangor Operatic Society stood him in good stead when he subsequently turned professional as an actor.

He made his stage debut in 1958, at the age of 27, with the Ulster Group, Belfast, as Dick McCardle in *Master of the House*.

Within a year, he had moved to the Royal Court Theatre, London, taking small roles in *Cock-a-Doodle-Dandy* and *Serjeant Musgrave's Dance*.

In 1961, he joined the Royal Shakespeare Company at the Shakespeare Memorial Theatre, Stratford-upon-Avon, playing such parts as Touchstone in *As You Like It*.

Colin moved to the National Theatre on its opening, two years later, and started off with small parts, before moving up the ranks to play important characters such as Ben in *Love for Love*, the title role in *Volpone*, and Creon in Peter Brook's production of Seneca's *Oedipus*.

One of the most sought-after leading actors of the day, he rejoined the RSC in 1972 to perform in Harold Pinter's *Old Times*, before going on to act in many West End productions.

Colin's most memorable television role was his controversial portrayal of Jesus Christ in Dennis Potter's *Son of Man*. He also starred in many other programmes, including *Peer Gynt*, *The Birthday Party*, John Mortimer's *Paradise Postponed* and *Drums Along Balmoral Drive*.

He appeared in 30 films, making his debut in *Saturday Night and Sunday Morning* in 1960 and following it with pictures such as *This Sporting Life*, *A Man for All Seasons*, *Charlie Bubbles*, *Young Winston*, *The National Health*, *Murder on the Orient Express* and *The Pink Panther Strikes Again*.

He and his actress wife Margaret Whiting – whom he married in 1961, after playing Phil Hogan opposite her in *A Moon for the Misbegotten* – had three sons, Cameron, Hamish and Drummond. Colin died from leukaemia at the age of 56.

Jasmine Bligh

b. 29 May 1913
d. 21 July 1991

ONE of the most familiar faces on BBC television before and after the Second World War was Jasmine Bligh, TV's first female announcer.

Descended from Captain Bligh of the *Bounty* and a niece of the ninth Earl of Darnley, Jasmine Lydia Bligh ignored her mother's opposition to a career in acting to become a Charlot showgirl at the Cambridge Theatre, London, aged 17.

Five years later, the struggling actress answered a BBC advertisement for female television 'hostess-announcers' – unmarried and without red hair. Elizabeth Cowell and Jasmine were picked from 1122 applicants across the British Empire. Along with fellow-announcer Leslie Mitchell, they were seen during test transmissions from Alexandra Palace in 1935.

Her theatrical experience proved useful, having to learn 400 words a day to speak direct to the camera. She earned £350 a year and had an annual dress allowance of £25 to buy two evening dresses, two skirts and two blouses. The press described Elizabeth Cowell and Jasmine as 'Twin Paragons', and Jasmine continued when the BBC began its regular television service a year later.

She became a personality in her own right and, amongst other things, she was seen being given a fireman's lift and hurtling about in a motorcycle sidecar.

Television transmissions were closed down during the Second World War, but when they returned, on 7 June 1946, Jasmine was the first announcer to be seen, first in full view, then in close-up, with the words, "Hello, do you remember me?"

Missing the pioneering spirit of the old days, she left the BBC and moved to Ireland to live a rural existence with her second husband, Frank Fox, and daughter Sarah. Like her first marriage, to John Johnson, it ended in divorce and Jasmine returned to Britain and the BBC, taking part in programmes for the deaf and reading for the *Noddy* series.

She was married a third time, to broadcaster Howard Marshall, and his illness in 1967 led her to look for a new way of earning money. She set up a travelling second-hand clothes shop called Bargain and sold her wealthy friends' cast-offs at country fairs.

After Howard's death, in 1973, Jasmine presented a series of the Thames Television women's magazine *Good Afternoon*. In 1981, a stroke left her speaking with difficulty and she died ten years later.

Dan Blocker

b. 1929
d. 13 May 1972

SLOW-thinking Hoss Cartwright in the 60s Western series *Bonanza* made a star of Dan Blocker, the giant 6ft 3 in, 20-stone actor known as 'the big 'un'.

Born in Texas, he had reached 6ft by the age of 12 and, while studying for a drama and physical education degree college in Abilene, made his stage debut in *Arsenic and Old Lace*. He later returned to Abilene to take a masters degree after service in the Korean War.

Dan was at UCLA (the University of California, Los Angeles) when he won his first TV role, in *Gunsmoke*, and followed it with other Western series.

His biggest break came with the part of Eric Cartwright, known as 'Hoss', in *Bonanza*, which began on American television in 1959.

The programme made millionaires of Dan and the programme's other stars, who were paid the then phenomenal sum of £7500 per episode, with additional earnings from foreign screenings and personal appearances.

Throughout the 60s, it was the most popular programme on American television and ran for just one more series after Dan died from a blood clot in the lung, in 1972. He had appeared in more than 300 episodes.

At the time of his death, Dan was due to star in the film *The Long Goodbye*, opposite Elliott Gould. His previous big-screen appearances included *The Errand Boy*, *Lady in Cement* and *The Cockeyed Cowboys of Calico County*.

Ward Bond

b. 9 April 1903
d. 5 November 1960

AS the veteran of more than 200 Hollywood Westerns, warm-hearted Ward Bond was well qualified to play Major Seth Adams in the 50s TV series *Wagon Train*.

Born in Denver, Colorado, he attended USC (the University of Southern California) and began his career as an American footballer. He switched to acting and became a much-in-demand character player, especially in director John Ford's Westerns.

Ward's many films, beginning in 1929 with *Salute*, included *The Oklahoma Kid*, *The Maltese Falcon*, *Gentleman Jim*, *Fort Apache*, *The Quiet Man* and *Dakota Incident*.

It was on John Ford's 1950 film *Wagonmaster*, in which Ward appeared, that the TV series *Wagon Train* was based. Set around a westward pilgrimage from Missouri to California, the big-budget programme began in 1957 and featured different guest stars each week – even John Wayne and Ronald Reagan – as the trek continued.

With a long history of heart problems, Ward had to leave the series for a short time the following year but battled on until 1960, when he suffered a heart attack in his shower on location in Dallas, Texas, and died. The series continued until 1965, with John McIntire taking over the lead role.

Ward, who was married to Mary Lou, was one of John Wayne's fellow actors on the American Right politically, outspoken against Communism and a board member of the Screen Actors Guild.

Reginald Bosanquet

b. 9 August 1932
d. 28 May 1984

THE son of Middlesex and England cricketer B J T Bosanquet, who invented the 'googly' bowl, newscaster Reginald Bosanquet delivered his own 'googly' every night on *News At Ten*, his lop-sided grin and idiosyncratic pronunciation imploring viewers to hold on to his every word. The news was always unpredictable and, with Reggie presenting it, never dull.

Born in Chertsey, Surrey, Reggie was the grandson of a successful Fleet Street editor. He was orphaned at the age of seven, evacuated to Canada during the Second World War and attended Winchester public school, before doing national service in the Green Jackets and studying history at New College, Oxford.

As ITN was gearing up to provide the news service for the forthcoming ITV network in 1955, Reggie landed a job there as a trainee. After learning the business as a sub-editor, he reported from around the world and was diplomatic correspondent, presenter of *Roving Report* and the news magazine *Dateline*, and one of the newscasters who launched *News at Ten* in July 1967.

Reggie became well known for his screen partnership with Andrew Gardner and, later, with Anna Ford. In 1979, after an 11-week strike by ITV technicians had kept ITN off the air, he resigned amid a blaze of publicity.

News had become showbusiness with Reggie in front of the camera, donning a hairpiece – the result of suffering from dermatitis, a recurring inflammation of the scalp, which meant he had to shave off some of his hair occasionally – and presenting stories in a manner that at times made viewers wonder whether he had indulged in a small tipple before entering the studios.

In fact, the precarious delivery and contorted smile were the result of being paralysed down the left-hand side of his body at birth.

With Reggie's reputation for partying, the satirical magazine *Private Eye* immortalised the much loved newscaster as 'Ronnie Beaujolais' in its *After the Break* cartoon strip.

Reggie had two daughters, Abigail and Delilah, from two marriages that both ended in divorce – to Karin Lund and Felicity Fearnley-Whittingstall – and he wed his third wife, Joan Adams, in 1983.

His autobiography, *Let's Get Through Wednesday*, was published in 1980, a year after he left ITN. He was Rector of Glasgow University for three years and died in 1984 after a battle against cancer.

William Boyd

b. 5 June 1895
d. 12 September 1972

WESTERNS had already become big business in the cinema by the time television was moving into its 'Golden Age', so it seemed natural that *Hopalong Cassidy* star William Boyd and his horse Topper should switch to the small screen.

Born in Hedrysburg, Ohio – although some sources say it was in Cambridge, in the same state – William was the son of a farm labourer who moved to Oklahoma when William was seven. When his parents died, he worked in the flourishing oil fields there, before making his way to Hollywood.

He began his screen career as a romantic actor in silent films, making his debut in the 1918 picture *Old Wives for New*, and he later starred in Cecil B DeMille classics such as

King of Kings and, as Feodor, in *The Volga Boatmen*.

In the early 30s William's career appeared to be over when another actor of the same name, William 'Stage' Boyd, was arrested after a bar-room brawl and a newspaper carried the wrong photograph.

For several years, he acted under the name of Bill Boyd but changed his name back to William when the other actor died, in 1935.

In that same year, William – who had been silver-haired from the age of 19 – first played the limping cowboy who rarely shot to kill in the film *Hop-a-long Cassidy*, repeating the role in 65 further films of the 30s and 40s.

He portrayed the hero of Clarence E Mulford's stories – originally a mean, sweating, hard-drinking cowboy with a limp – as a good Samaritan who personified law, order, honour and bravery.

The shrewd star acquired the rights to the pictures and, from 1949, they were edited into TV episodes and shown in America on Sunday afternoons, establishing the Western on the small screen. When they were used up, William made 52 new half-hour episodes for television, in 1952 and 1953.

The programme – shown around the world – was the first to have supporting merchandise, such as a Hoppy's Troopers club for children, hats, guns, spurs, T-shirts and confectionery.

William made a final 'Hopalong' feature film, the 1951 short *Hopalong in Hoppyland*, and a year later the last of his more than 130 films, with a cameo in Cecil B DeMille's Oscar-winning *The Greatest Show on Earth*. By 1954, he had earned enough from his Hopalong Cassidy role to retire.

Married four times, although some sources suggest it was five, William divorced actresses Ruth Miller, Elinor Fair and Dorothy Sebastian, before marrying another actress, Grace Bradley, who survived his death from a combination of Parkinson's disease and congestive heart failure at the age of 77. The actor had only one child, a son who died at the age of nine months.

Bernard Braden

b. 16 May 1916
d. 2 February 1993

CREDITED with bringing Esther Rantzen to television, Bernard Braden was one of the TV stars of the 60s, famous for his part in such shows as *Braden's Week* and *On the Braden Beat*, and following a career in acting by being seen as the consumer's champion.

Born and educated in Vancouver, he appeared on the stage as a child at the Kelowna Theatre, playing a goblin in *Springtime*.

Although he successfully auditioned for the Metropolitan Opera, in New York, tuberculosis ended his hopes of becoming a singer and Bernard went into radio as an engineer for the Canadian Broadcasting Corporation, subsequently moving on to announcing, singing and acting, until he moved to Britain in 1949.

Bernard acted in many London West End plays, making his debut that year as Harold Mitchell in Laurence Olivier's production of *A Streetcar Named Desire*, at the Aldwych Theatre, and subsequently appearing in *The Biggest Thief in Town*, *The Man*, *No News from Father*, *Anniversary Waltz*, *Period of Adjustment* and *Spoon River* – at the Royal Court. He also directed *Angels in Love* and landed his own BBC radio programmes, *Breakfast with Braden* and *Bedtime with Braden*.

Moving into television, he presented the BBC's first broadcast for schools, then *The Brains Trust* – from 1957 – and an ITV Saturday-afternoon sports magazine called *Let's Go* from 1959.

With his wife Barbara Kelly, a fellow-Canadian, he starred in the situation comedy *The Bradens* and followed it with *Early to Braden*, *On the Braden Beat* and *Braden's Week*. The latter, a consumer programme that began on the BBC in 1968, included Esther Rantzen as a researcher and reporter, and was a model for her subsequent hit series *That's Life!*

However, when Bernard made an ITV commercial for 'Stork' margarine, the BBC sacked him, adjudging that he could not be seen to endorse a product while presenting a consumer programme.

In 1973, he revived *Braden's Week* on Canadian television and subsequently presented a British series called *Celebrity Sweepstakes*, as well as the weekday programme *After Noon Plus* and revived ITV series *All Our Yesterdays*.

His films in Britain included *Love in Pawn*, *Jet Storm*, *The Day the Earth Caught Fire*, *All Night Long* and *The War Lover*.

In more recent years, Bernard made industrial and training films through his own company, Adanac Productions.

He and Barbara Kelly had one son, Christopher, and two daughters, Kelly and actress Kim. Bernard wrote a book entitled *These English* and, in 1990, his autobiography, *The Kindness of Strangers*, was published. He died three years later, aged 76.

Wilfrid Brambell

b. 22 March 1912
d. 18 January 1985

AS rag-and-bone man Albert Steptoe in *Steptoe and Son*, Wilfrid Brambell's performances were legendary. His brilliant caricature of the dirty, pathetic father will always be remembered as classic.

Wilfrid was born in Dublin, where his father was a Guinness brewery worker and his mother an opera singer. His first public performance was entertaining wounded soldiers from the First World War at the tender age of two.

On leaving school, Wilfrid worked as a cub reporter for *The Irish Times* and, at the same time, worked part-time as an actor at the Abbey Theatre, Dublin, where he received the princely sum of ten shillings a week.

After falling in love with the world of entertainment, he left his newspaper job to become a professional actor at the Gate Theatre, Dublin.

During the Second World War, the young actor toured with the entertainment organisation ENSA and, after being demobbed, appeared in repertory theatre in Swansea, Bristol and Chesterfield.

His London stage appearances included *The Canterbury Tales*, at the Phoenix Theatre, in which he acted three parts, and *The Ghost Train*, at the Old Vic. In 1965, he made his Broadway debut in *Kelly*, which closed after only one show.

Although Wilfrid considered himself a straight actor, comedy was the vehicle to his dramatic success and he appeared in many such roles on television, in series such as *Life with the Lyons* and Arthur Askey's shows.

His straight roles included a part in the 50s science-fiction series *The Quatermass Experiment*, and an old tramp in *No Fixed Abode*. It was the latter programme that brought him to the attention of the scriptwriting partnership of Ray Galton and Alan Simpson when they were writing *Steptoe and Son*, and he was cast as the dirty old man.

So successful was the programme, which started as an episode of the experimental *Comedy Playhouse* in 1962, that it began as a series two years later and ran until 1973, that it regularly attracted 15 million viewers.

The often cutting banter between the bony old man and his son, Harold, played by Harry H Corbett, was compulsive viewing. Who could fail to laugh as Harold, weighed down with middle-class aspirations, cringed in disgust while his old dad sat scrubbing his back in the kitchen sink?

Wilfrid also starred in two disappointing film spin-offs, *Steptoe and Son* and *Steptoe and Son Ride Again*. His other 40 films, many in the roles of old codgers, included *The 39 Steps*, *Dry Rot*, *The Three Lives of Thomasina*, *A Hard Day's Night* – a Beatles picture in which he played Paul McCartney's grandfather – and *Carry On Again Doctor*.

Wilfrid, who threw his wife Molly out of their home after discovering she had become pregnant by a lodger, divorced her for adultery in 1955 and she died a year later. The actor claimed to have then remained celibate for ten years.

In his will, he left £170 000 to his Chinese-born companion, Yussof Ben mai Saman, who had lived with him for 15 years. His autobiography, *All Above Board*, was published in 1976.

Bernard Bresslaw

b. 25 February 1934

BY the time hulking, 6ft 7in comedy star Bernard Bresslaw became a regular in more than a dozen of the *Carry On* films, he had already made his name on television as Private 'Popeye' Popplewell in *The Army Game*.

Born in Stepney, East London, son of a tailor's cutter and a mother who took in sewing to make ends meet, Bernard was intent on a career in acting after many trips to the Hackney Empire. Winning a London County Council scholarship to train at RADA, he won the Emile Littler Award for Most Promising Actor while studying there and was picked by Laurence Olivier to play an Irish wrestler in his production of *The MacRoary Whirl*, at the Duchess Theatre.

He followed it with *The Bad Seed*, at the Aldwych Theatre, and was in the legendary radio series *Educating Archie*, before finding fame on television in *The Army Game*, alongside Alfie Bass and Bill Fraser, in 1957, and appeared in the spin-off film, *I Only Arsked!* (his character's catchphrase), the following year.

Bernard took part in a stage tour of *The Army Game* and was on the record of the programme's signature tune, which reached no. 5 in the British singles chart. He then made his own single, *Mad Passionate Love*, which reached no. 6 in 1958.

He had already made his film debut, in the 1954 Robin Hood picture *Men of Sherwood Forest*, and his new-found stardom gave him the chance to star in *The Ugly Duckling*, five years later, as the son of Dr Jekyll who discovers his father's secret formula.

Unfortunately, the film was a disappointment and Bernard's career fell into a lull, with occasional TV appearances – in series such as *Danger Man* and *Z-Cars* – but he soon bounced back, performing Shakespearean roles at the Open Air Theatre, Regent's Park, and winning the Variety Club of Great Britain's Most Promising Newcomer award.

Then, in 1965, Bernard was cast in *Carry On Cowboy* and stayed with the famous team to make another 13 *Carry On* films over ten years – reviving his Popeye catchphrase, "I only arsked!", which had previously been a millstone round his neck.

Bernard's other films include *Spring and Port Wine*, *Up Pompeii*, *One of Our Dinosaurs is Missing*, *Joseph Andrews*, *Jaberwocky* and *Krull*. On television, he has acted in *The Onedin Line*, *Secret Army*, *Emmerdale Farm*, *Androcles and the Lion*, two series of *Mann's Best Friends*, *The Book Tower* and *Terry and June*.

He frequently returns to the stage, performing in pantomimes and West End shows such as *Charley's Aunt*, *Run for Your Wife* and *Me and My Girl*. But he particularly enjoys acting in the classics, having played Bottom in *A Midsummer Night's Dream*, the title role in *Falstaff*, Mephistopheles in *Dr Faustus* and the Boris Karloff role in *Arsenic and Old Lace*.

Bernard has performed with the National Theatre, the Royal Shakespeare Company, the English Stage Company and the Young Vic Company. He and his wife Liz have three sons.

Coral Browne

b. 23 July 1913
d. 29 May 1991

A striking actress of immense style and personality, Coral Browne was triumphant playing herself in Alan Bennett's BAFTA award-winning television drama *An Englishman Abroad*.

The saga, set in Moscow during the 50s recounted the real-life tale of Coral encountering spy Guy Burgess during her visit there with the Old Vic to perform *Hamlet*.

Burgess, played by Alan Bates, had burst into her dressing-room, invited her out to dinner and requested that she arranged for some clothes to be made for him by a London tailor.

Born in Melbourne, Australia, daughter of restaurateur Leslie Brown, Coral Edith Brown was educated at Claremont Ladies' College, Melbourne, before going on to study painting. At the age of 17, she took to the stage, appearing in a range of both farce and classics.

In 1934, along with a group of other

young, hopeful Australians, she travelled to Britain in the hope of finding stage success. After seven years understudying, Coral hit on success in the role of Maggie Cutler in *The Man Who Came to Dinner* and as Mrs Cheyney in *The Last of Mrs Cheyney*, alongside British song-and-dance man Jack Buchanan – whom Coral came close to marrying.

For the next 20 years, her career continued with a glittering array of classical theatre performances, including Helena in *A Midsummer Night's Dream*, and Emilia in *Othello* – both at the Old Vic – and Zabina in Tyrone Guthrie's New York production of *Tamburlaine the Great*.

This elegant and sophisticated actress began making films in 1936, with an appearance in *The Amateur Gentleman*, and continued to do so for the next 50 years. Of all her screen work her most controversial picture was undoubtedly *The Killing of Sister George*, in which she shocked cinema audiences with a lesbian scene she shared with Susan George.

Her other big-screen appearances included *The Courtneys of Curzon Street*, *Auntie Mame*, *The Roman Spring of Mrs Stone* and the horror-comedy *Theatre of Blood*, in which she met her second husband, actor Vincent Price. Coral used to delight in telling friends that she had met him in a graveyard.

She also gave a brilliant performance in the 1985 film *Dreamchild*, as 80-year-old Mrs Alice Hargreaves, visiting New York for author Lewis Carroll's centenary, having been the model for his *Alice in Wonderland* story.

On television, Coral – whose first husband was actor Philip Pearman, who later became an agent and died in 1964 – had already acted in *Eleanor: First Lady of the World* and *Time Express*, before she starred in *An Englishman Abroad*. She died in 1991.

Jill Browne

b. September 1937
d. 5 December 1991

AS Nurse Carole Young in television's long-running hospital drama *Emergency – Ward 10*, Jill Browne increased the pulse rate of Britain's male viewers. In fact, appearing for seven years in the ITV series, which was rife with doctor-nurse romances, made her a household name.

Only 19, with petite, blonde good looks and an above-average acting ability, Jill was an instant success as the trainee nurse who eventually became a sister.

So popular was the weekly saga, which began in 1957, that 10 million viewers regularly tuned in and Jill found herself with sackloads of fan-mail.

But it was not only the public that had fallen for her charms, for love had blossomed between Jill and actor John Alderton, who played Doctor Richard Moore. The couple were married four days after she was dropped from the series, in 1964, but six years later they were divorced.

After such instant stardom, Jill found it very difficult ever to scale such dizzy heights again. New television work arrived, including *Stars and Garters*, a serial set in a pub, but it flopped.

During her marriage to John Alderton, the pair formed a company, Altinger Productions, which staged a tour of the hit TV comedy *Doctor in the House*.

The last years of Jill's acting career were spent touring the provinces and Canada in such productions as Noël Coward's *The Marquise* and *Rattle of a Simple Man*.

After marrying her second husband, theatre producer Brian Wolfe, in 1971, she retired from the world of showbusiness and took various jobs, ranging from telephonist and receptionist to tour guide. Jill died of cancer at the age of 54.

★★★★★★★★★★★★

Margot Bryant

b. 1898
d. 1 January 1989

Minnie Caldwell of *Coronation Street*, who sat in the Rovers Return snug with Ena Sharples and Martha Longhurst, was far removed from the more temperamental Margot Bryant, who played the character for 16 years.

Born in Hull, East Yorkshire, the daughter of a doctor, Margot was still a child when her family moved to London. She took to the stage in her teens, as a chorus girl in pantomime, before progressing to musical comedy.

Her biggest stage success was in London's West End, dancing in the Fred Astaire hit *Stop Flirting*.

Margot made her television debut in the play *My Mother Said*. Then, in 1960, she joined the new serial *Coronation Street*, first acting put-upon Minnie Caldwell in the third episode.

Minnie and her cat, Bobby, became part of the furniture and fittings of the programme, but viewers would never have guessed that the sweet, butter-wouldn't-melt-in-her-mouth character was nothing like the actress.

Former *Street* producer Bill Podmore recalled that Margot could be quarrelsome in the studio and that her language was often 'unladylike'. Towards the end of her time in the serial, Margot suffered from amnesia, finding it difficult to remember her lines.

She finally left in 1976 through ill health, after acting in 560 episodes, and returned to her home in Hove, East Sussex, for a while, before spending the last years of her life in a Manchester nursing home.

Margot, who died on New Year's Day 1989, had never married.

Alfred Burke

b. 28 February 1918

THE role of seedy detective Frank Marker in *Public Eye*, usually down on his luck and struggling to make ends meet, made Alfred Burke a major star of the 60s small screen, for a full seven series.

Born in Peckham, South London, he worked as an office boy in a railway repair firm on leaving school. A year later, he became a steward in a businessmen's club, before working in a silk warehouse.

Throughout this time, Alfred acted with a local amateur dramatic society and, in 1937, he won a scholarship to RADA. His first professional work was at the Barn Theatre, Shere, in Surrey.

As a conscientious objector, he worked as an agricultural labourer during the Second World War. Afterwards, he was in repertory theatre in Farnham and acted in an Arts Council tour, before joining the Young Vic theatre company in 1947.

After more rep, in Manchester and Nottingham, Alfred made his West End debut in Picasso's *Desire Caught by the Tail*, in 1950, then returned to rep, in Birmingham, for three years.

Back in London, he was in *Sailor Beware* and, alongside Vanessa Redgrave and Jonathan Pryce, in *The Seagull*.

Before finding fame in television, he wrote an ITV play called *Where Are They Now?*, under the pen-name of Frank Hanna. He started playing Frank Marker in *Public Eye* in 1965, showing the less than glamorous side of private detectives who operate from rundown offices and struggle to make enough money to earn a living.

After the ITV series finally ended, Alfred

won acclaim for his television role as the Reverend Patrick Brontë in *The Brontës of Haworth* series, in 1973, and five years later played the Nazi Richter in *Enemy at the Door*, an ITV series set in the wartime Channel Islands.

He also acted a rather eccentric Long John Silver in a BBC adaptation of *Treasure Island* and has appeared in *Tales of the Unexpected*, *The Borgias*, *No 10* – as Pitt the Elder – *The Glory Boys*, *Bergerac* and *Sophia and Constance*.

Alfred's 30 films, beginning with *The Constant Husband* in 1955, include *Yangtse Incident*, *The Trials of Oscar Wilde* and *The House on Garibaldi Street*.

His recent stage appearances, with the Royal Shakespeare Company, have included those in *Troilus and Cressida*, *Two Shakespearean Actors*, *The Seagull*, *As You Like It*, *All's Well That Ends Well* and *Antony and Cleopatra*.

Alfred is also co-writer with Leeds University lecturer Brian Wilks, of a one-man show about the life of Rev. Patrick Brontë and his three literary daughters.

He is married to former stage manager Barbara and the couple have two sets of twins, Jacob and Harriet, and Kelly and Louisa.

Sir Alastair Burnet

b. 12 July 1928

THE doyen of British newscasters, often likened to America's Walter Cronkite, Alastair Burnet was largely responsible for making *News at Ten* an ITV institution and became the authoritative anchorman for the channel's coverage of General Elections, Budgets, royal weddings and other major events.

Born James William Alexander Burnet in Sheffield – where his mother went for the birth on the instructions of his father, in the hope that the child might one day be good enough to play cricket for Yorkshire – the future newscaster was brought up in Glasgow, graduated from Worcester College, Oxford, and started his journalistic career on the *Glasgow Herald*, eventually becoming a leader writer.

He joined ITN as political editor in 1963. Although becoming editor of *The Economist* two years later, he was able to continue as a newscaster at ITN and was one of the two who fronted the first *News at Ten*, which was launched in July 1967.

Five years later, Alastair left ITN for the BBC – presenting *Panorama* and the two 1974 General Election programmes – but moved on to become editor of the *Daily Express*. He was one of a string of editors of the paper after it went tabloid, most of whom never managed to give it a clear identity.

In 1976, after two years at the *Express*, he returned to ITN to launch *News at 5.45*, giving the early-evening bulletin its own, distinctive flavour. He later moved to *News at Ten* as senior newscaster and, in 1982, also became the programme's associate editor.

Throughout his years at ITN, Alastair was presenter for coverage of ITV's major political events, bringing his enthusiasm and encyclopaedic knowledge to bear – and winning the coveted BAFTA Richard Dimbleby Award for television journalism a record three times, in 1966, 1970 and 1979.

For a while, he combined his newscasting duties with presenting the current affairs programme *This Week*, and he had a Sunday-morning phone-in show on the London news and information radio station LBC.

Alastair, who was knighted in 1984, retired from ITN six years later and is now a director of Times Newspapers. He married Maureen Sinclair in 1958 and the couple live in Glasgow and London.

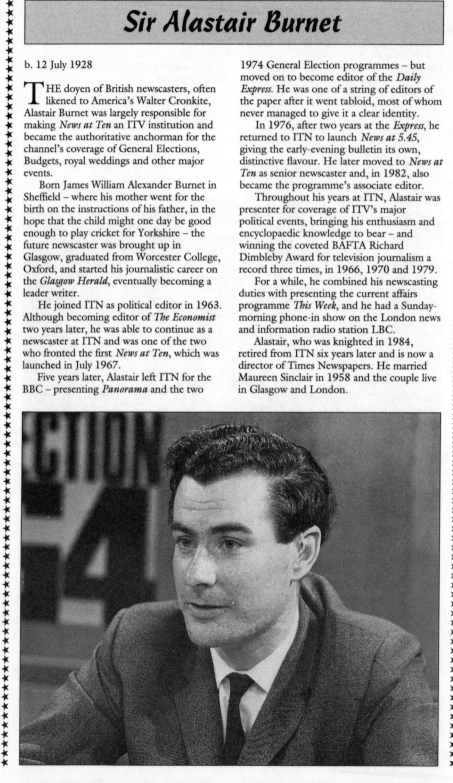

Raymond Burr

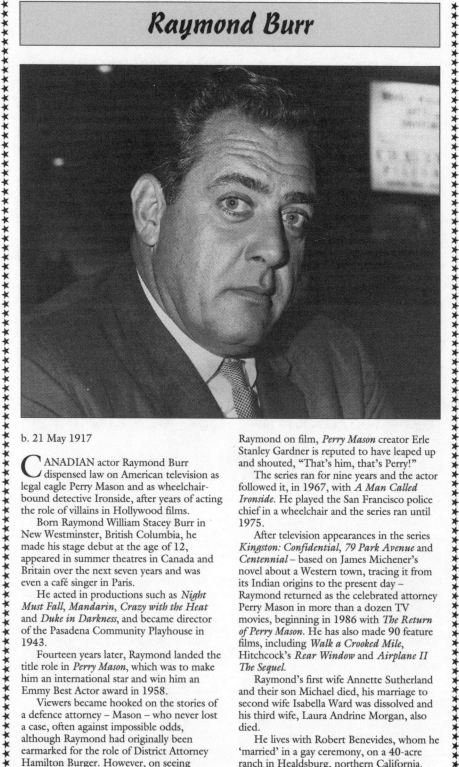

b. 21 May 1917

CANADIAN actor Raymond Burr dispensed law on American television as legal eagle Perry Mason and as wheelchair-bound detective Ironside, after years of acting the role of villains in Hollywood films.

Born Raymond William Stacey Burr in New Westminster, British Columbia, he made his stage debut at the age of 12, appeared in summer theatres in Canada and Britain over the next seven years and was even a café singer in Paris.

He acted in productions such as *Night Must Fall*, *Mandarin*, *Crazy with the Heat* and *Duke in Darkness*, and became director of the Pasadena Community Playhouse in 1943.

Fourteen years later, Raymond landed the title role in *Perry Mason*, which was to make him an international star and win him an Emmy Best Actor award in 1958.

Viewers became hooked on the stories of a defence attorney – Mason – who never lost a case, often against impossible odds, although Raymond had originally been earmarked for the role of District Attorney Hamilton Burger. However, on seeing

Raymond on film, *Perry Mason* creator Erle Stanley Gardner is reputed to have leaped up and shouted, "That's him, that's Perry!"

The series ran for nine years and the actor followed it, in 1967, with *A Man Called Ironside*. He played the San Francisco police chief in a wheelchair and the series ran until 1975.

After television appearances in the series *Kingston: Confidential*, *79 Park Avenue* and *Centennial* – based on James Michener's novel about a Western town, tracing it from its Indian origins to the present day – Raymond returned as the celebrated attorney Perry Mason in more than a dozen TV movies, beginning in 1986 with *The Return of Perry Mason*. He has also made 90 feature films, including *Walk a Crooked Mile*, Hitchcock's *Rear Window* and *Airplane II The Sequel*.

Raymond's first wife Annette Sutherland and their son Michael died, his marriage to second wife Isabella Ward was dissolved and his third wife, Laura Andrine Morgan, also died.

He lives with Robert Benevides, whom he 'married' in a gay ceremony, on a 40-acre ranch in Healdsburg, northern California.

Peter Butterworth

b. 4 February 1919
d. 17 January 1979

THE tubby figure, wonderfully mobile face and potty mannerisms of kind-hearted actor Peter Butterworth brought some of the finest comedy acting to the famous, typically British *Carry On* films, but his own sensitivity and generosity were particularly apparent in the television programmes and films he made for children.

Born in Bramhall, Cheshire, he appeared in camp shows when he was held as a prisoner-of-war while serving in the Fleet Air Arm during the Second World War, after being shot down by the Germans.

In the camp, scriptwriter Talbot Rothwell persuaded Peter to take part in concerts, which were intended to drown out the noise of prisoners trying to escape. His first performance was singing a duet of 'The Letter Edged in Black' with Rothwell, often followed by a witty repartee.

After the War, Peter appeared in revues and summer shows, as well as acting in repertory theatre, before appearing in children's television programmes and as a guest in shows with Ted Ray and Frankie Howerd.

Later, he mixed comedy with straight acting on television, appearing in *The Fishing Match, The Odd Man, Hugh and I, Danger Man, Doctor Who, Emergency – Ward 10, Love Story, Public Eye* and *Bless This House.* Stage success came in farces such as *Uproar In the House*, with Brian Rix's company at the Whitehall Theatre.

He made his film debut in *William Comes to Town*, in 1948, and his subsequent pictures included *Murder at the Windmill, The Prince and the Pauper, Live Now – Pay Later, Doctor in Distress, A Funny Thing Happened on the Way to the Forum, A Home of Your Own, The Amorous Adventures of Moll Flanders, Robin and Marian* and *The First Great Train Robbery.*

But it was as a member of the *Carry On* team, starting with the 1965 film *Carry On Cowboy*, that Peter is best remembered by cinema audiences, appearing in 16 of their productions in all, right up to the last of the original team's pictures, *Carry On Emmannuelle*, in 1978.

Peter, who died of a heart attack in 1979, was married to actress-comedienne Janet Brown and they had two children, actor son Tyler and daughter Emma – both appeared in an episode of the 70s children's series *Catweazle*, before Tyler went on to find success as an adult in TV comedies such as *Home to Roost* and *The Darling Buds of May*, continuing the family tradition.

Max Bygraves

b. 16 October 1922

SINGING, acting, comedy, all-round entertaining – Max Bygraves has done it all in showbusiness, starting in music-hall, moving through radio and films, hosting his TV musical specials and releasing hit singles and 'singalong' albums.

Born Walter William Bygraves in Rotherhithe, part of London's East End, 'Wally' grew up during the Depression, living in a one-bedroom council flat with his mother, dock worker father, grandfather and six brothers and sisters.

The family lived on the breadline, and the young Max learned shoemaking and carpentry at a local evening institute and mended shoes to earn extra money for the family. He was already interested in entertainment and won a talent contest in 1935.

On leaving school at the age of 14, he was apprenticed to a carpenter, singing in an amateur group called The Happy Crew in his spare time.

While serving in the RAF during the Second World War, Max took part in a camp show on his first day as an airman fitter, doing an impersonation of Max Miller. He was immediately nicknamed Max and the name stuck.

On being demobbed in 1945, Max took a £6-a-week job as a carpenter, but continued performing in London pubs and clubs. He went professional the following year after successfully auditioning for a show that BBC radio was putting together with former servicemen.

The late bandleader Jack Payne heard the broadcast and booked Max for a roadshow that also included Frankie Howerd. Wearing a loud check suit and billing himself as 'The

Lazy Comic', he fine-tuned his act and, three years later, was performing at the London Palladium.

Shortly afterwards, Max appeared on stage with Judy Garland at the London Palladium and the Palace, in New York.

Continuing his radio work, he was in *They're Out*, then the celebrated *Educating Archie*, written by Eric Sykes and featuring Peter Brough and the ventriloquist's dummy, as well as stars such as Benny Hill, Beryl Reid and Hattie Jacques during its run.

By then, Max was also appearing in films. Having made his debut in the 1949 picture *Bless 'Em All*, he followed it with features such as *Skimpy in the Navy*, *Nitwits on Parade*, *Charley Moon* and *The Alf Garnett Saga*, which was the second film spin-off from the *Till Death Us Do Part* TV series.

He also brought his act to television in *Max Bygraves*, *Max*, *Singalongamax*, *Max Rolls On* and his *Max Bygraves – Side By Side With* series, each show featuring him with a different star.

He was less successful as presenter of the game show *Family Fortunes*, having taken over from slick Bob Monkhouse, but he later brought his nostalgia trip back to television in a special, *Max Bygraves – Singalongawaryears*.

His 'singalong' LPs have won him three platinum, 31 gold and 15 silver discs, and his hit singles include the double-A-side 'You Need Hands'/'Tulips from Amsterdam', 'Fings Ain't Wot They Used T'Be' and 'Deck of Cards', 'Meet Me on the Corner', 'Cowpuncher's Cantata' and 'Mr Sandman'.

Max, who has performed in 19 Royal Variety Performances, married Mabel Gladys – known as 'Blossom' – when he was 19. They have two daughters, Christine and Maxine, and a son, Anthony, who appeared in Max's act for a while.

The all-round entertainer has written three volumes of autobiography, *I Wanna Tell You a Story*, *After Thoughts* and *I Wanna Tell You a Funny Story*, as well as a novel, *The Milkman's on His Way*.

Phyllis Calvert

b. 18 February 1915

FORTIES film star Phyllis Calvert gained a whole new following when she starred in the title role of *Kate*, ITV's series about a large-circulation magazine's agony aunt.

Born Phyllis Bickle in London, she trained at the Margaret Morris School of Dancing and performed from the age of ten. Just two years later, she was appearing in the film *The Land of Heart's Desire*, also known as *The Arcadians*.

Deciding on acting as a career, Phyllis performed in repertory theatre and in several films, before making her London stage debut in *A Woman's Privilege*, in 1939.

During the following decade, she starred in many film romances – including *Fanny by Gaslight*, alongside James Mason and Stewart Granger, and *My Own True Love* – and became one of Britain's highest-paid stars, although three Hollywood films failed to make her in demand with studios there.

Her later films included Richard Attenborough's musical *Oh! What a Lovely War* and *The Walking Stick*, notable less for its dramatic content than for Stanley Myers's theme music, 'Cavatina', later used in *The Deer Hunter*.

Phyllis had already appeared on television in the Sunday-afternoon serials *Little Women, Parnell, You'll Know Me by the Stars in My Eyes* and *Love Story* when, in 1970, she landed the part of an agony aunt with problems of her own in *Kate*.

Since then, she has made many TV appearances, in programmes such as *Crown Court, Ladykillers, Tales of the Unexpected, A Month in the Country, Cover Her Face, A Killing on the Exchange, Boon, The Woman He Loved, After Henry, Woof!* and *The Lime Grove Story*.

Her only subsequent film appearance has been in *The Death of the Heart*, in 1986, but the actress's London West End stage appearances include *It's Never Too Late, Mènage à Trois, Portrait of a Murder, Scent of Flowers, Present Laughter* and *Before the Party*.

She acted at the Royal Court Theatre in *Love From Margaret*, at the Chichester Festival in *The Heiress* and on tour in *The Hot Tiara, Hay Fever* and *The Reluctant Debutante*.

Phyllis was married to actor, and later antiquarian bookseller, Peter Murray Hill, who is now dead.

Patrick Campbell

b. 6 June 1913
d. 9 November 1980

LOVED by many as the stammering star of the weekly series *Call My Bluff*, humorous writer and broadcaster Patrick Campbell succeeded in turning his speech impediment into his trademark.

Patrick Gordon Campbell, the third Baron Glenavy, was the elder son of Lord Glenavy, the Secretary of the Department of Industry and Commerce in the Irish Free State from its foundation, in 1922, for ten years. His mother, Beatrice Elvery, was an artistic woman who studied sculpture at the Dublin School of Art, before turning to painting.

Patrick was educated at Rossall and Pembroke College, Oxford, but left without taking his degree. Uninterested in following his father's profession, he decided to work in journalism. So, after a short time in Germany, he began work on *The Irish Times*, where his hidden talents came to the fore.

He later joined the staff of the London *Evening Standard*, where he remained until the outbreak of the Second World War, when he served in the Irish Marine Service.

Back in Ireland, he wrote a column for *The Sunday Dispatch* and was assistant editor of the short-lived magazine *Lilliput* during the late 40s, as well as being a columnist on *The Sunday Times* for 18 years.

It was not until 1964 that Patrick's own brand of idiosyncratic humour reached television audiences with the BBC satirical show *Not So Much a Programme, More a Way of Life*, in which he sparred with such small-screen heavyweights as David Frost and Norman St John-Stevas, and later as a member of the panel on *Call My Bluff* – based on an American show. It started in 1965 and his weekly confrontations with Frank Muir made compulsive viewing.

He wrote a dozen published books, including such titles as *A Long Drink of Cold Water*, in 1950, and *35 Years on the Job*, in 1973. His autobiography, *My Life and Easy Times*, was published in 1967.

Patrick, who also co-scripted films such as *Lucky Jim* and *Go to Blazes*, was married three times, the last to scriptwriter Vivienne Knight. His first two marriages – to Sylvia and Cherry – were dissolved and he had a daughter from the second one. He died in 1980, aged 67.

Patrick Cargill

b. 3 June 1918

AS the suave writer of pulp thrillers, who struggled to bring up two lazy, man-mad teenaged daughters while fending off his ex-wife, Patrick Cargill became a household name in the comedy series *Father, Dear Father*.

Born in London, into a military family, he went to Sandhurst to train as an officer and served in the Indian Army, but resigned his commission to return home and become an actor, learning the ropes at Bexhill Rep in 1939.

With the outbreak of war, Patrick was back in the Army but, on being demobbed, he took to the boards in repertory theatre at Buxton, Croydon and Windsor. Since then, his West End stage appearances have included the revue *High Spirits, Say Who You Are, Two and Two Makes Sex, Blithe Spirit, Sleuth* and more than 1500 performances, over three years, in *Boeing-Boeing*.

Before success came in *Father, Dear*

Father, Patrick tended to play sinister roles on TV – drawing swords with Richard Greene in *The Adventures of Robin Hood* and acting an Argentine 'businessman' in the 1961 crime series *Top Secret* and both Thorpe and Number Two in the cult 60s series *The Prisoner*. He was also the doctor in the classic 1961 *Hancock's Half Hour* episode *The Blood Donor* and also co-wrote, with Jack Searle, the West End play *Ring for Catty*, which was adapted into the film *Carry On Nurse*.

Patrick's own film appearances include *Carry On Regardless, Carry On Jack*, the Beatles' *Help!*, *The Magic Christian* and *Father, Dear Father*, a spin-off from the TV series, which ran for five years from 1968, and was screened in more than 30 countries. He subsequently made a sequel to the series, *The Many Wives of Patrick*, and an Australian version of *Father, Dear Father*.

Since then, Patrick has acted mostly on the stage, in West End plays.

He is single and lives in Henley-on-Thames, Oxfordshire.

Ian Carmichael

b. 18 June 1920

THE Hooray Henry of many mid-20th-century British film comedies, Ian Carmichael also excelled on the small screen as Lord Peter Wimsey and P G Wodehouse's Bertie Wooster.

Born in Hull, the son of an optician, Ian was intent on a career in either the theatre or music. Acting won and he trained at RADA, then made his debut as a robot in *RUR*, at the People's Palace, in Mile End, East London, in 1939. He then played Claudius in *Julius Caesar* at the Embassy Theatre,

London, before touring in the Farjeon revue *Nine Sharp*.

He was called up for military service during the last week of the tour, in September 1940. After joining the Royal Armoured Corps, he went to Sandhurst and came out with a commission in the 22nd Dragoons, serving in Europe.

Resuming his career after the War, Ian gained more stage roles – becoming a regular revue artist – and eventually starred in plays in London's West End and on Broadway.

Augie Poole in *Tunnel of Love*, at Her Majesty's Theatre in 1957, remains his

favourite stage role. He made his first New York appearance as Robert in *Boeing-Boeing*.

Ian's film debut was in *Bond Street*, in 1948, but it was seven years and more than half-a-dozen films later that he made his first real impression on the big screen, in *Simon and Laura*, alongside Peter Finch and Kay Kendall, recreating the role of a TV producer from a straight play in which he had starred on stage.

This made him a screen name – and he soon found out the two sides of fame. Rank cast him as the lead character in *The Big Money*, a comedy so bad that it was not seen by the public for several years, when the studio decided to cash in on Ian's subsequent stardom.

Fortunately, the Boulting Brothers cast him in the role of Army recruit Stanley Windrush in *Private's Progress* and it was the beginning of a long association with them.

Ian then played a naïve young barrister in *Brothers in Law*, a working-class university lecturer in *Lucky Jim*, and was particularly memorable when resurrected as Stanley Windrush in the trade unions satire *I'm All Right, Jack*, with Peter Sellers in the role of the militant shop steward and Ian playing the university-educated management trainee caught in the crossfire between the shop floor and the boardroom.

Ironically, Sellers was to take over his mantle as Britain's top box-office comedy star when Carmichael left the Boulting Brothers for British Lion, although he made little impression in their films. In 1963, he returned to the Boultings for a cameo appearance in *Heavens Above!* – starring Peter Sellers – but his popularity had peaked and he has made only eight films in the 20 years since.

However, television gave Ian a new platform, and in 1965 he made the role of P G Wodehouse's Bertie Wooster his own in *The World of Wooster*. Seven years later, he did the same with the part of Dorothy L Sayers's debonair detective Lord Peter Wimsey in a series of the same name.

Between the two, he had starred as father Peter Lamb bringing up children by himself in three series of *Bachelor Father*. He has also made guest appearances in *The Morecambe and Wise Show*, *Father, Dear Father* and *Just a Nimmo*, narrated a *Survival* documentary and starred in *Down at the Hydro* – a play in the ITV series *All for Love*.

More recently, Ian starred with Deborah Kerr in Peter Ustinov's *Overheard* at the Theatre Royal, Haymarket, and with Stewart Granger in a national tour of *The Circle*. He was also in the film *Diamond Skulls* and on television in *All for Love*, *A Day in Summer*, the BBC play *Obituaries* and, as Sir James Menzies, in *Strathblair*.

Ian went into semi-retirement in 1977, returning to his native Yorkshire, but he increased his workload after the untimely death of his wife 'Pym' (Sheila Pyman Maclean), aged 61, in 1983. The couple had two daughters, Lee and Sally. His autobiography, *Will the Real Ian Carmichael . . .*, was published in 1979.

Lynne Carol

b. 29 June 1914
d. 30 June 1990

SHARP-tongued Martha Longhurst of *Coronation Street* was eldest of the three gossips who held court in the Rovers Return snug in the 60s and the first to die, but in real life Lynne Carol was the youngest actress and last to go to her grave.

Born in Monmouthshire of a theatrical family – boasting six generations of actors – Lynne started her own stage career there at the age of three.

She worked in provincial theatre for many years, before landing the role of Martha in *Coronation Street* when it began, in 1960.

As cleaner of the Rovers Return, she could also be found giving it her custom, drinking milk stouts, along with friends Ena Sharples and Minnie Caldwell. She could hold her own against the fearsome Ena.

When the scriptwriters decided that one of the trio should be killed off, it was Martha they chose to axe – thinking Lynne was most likely to find other acting jobs – and a heart attack in the snug duly followed, in May 1964.

Viewers responded by complaining in their thousands and, later, the writers acknowledged that they had made a mistake.

Lynne later appeared in the short-lived 60s BBC serial *The Newcomers* – alongside Wendy Richard, who went on to play Pauline Fowler in *EastEnders*, and Alan Browning, who was later in *Coronation Street* as Elsie Tanner's third husband – and the 1979 film *Yanks*, starring Richard Gere.

Married to the late character actor Bert Palmer, who appeared in the *Street* as Walter Biddulph, who sold The Kabin to Len Fairclough, Lynne had a son and a daughter, and died in 1990 at the age of 76.

Leo G Carroll

b. 1892
d. 16 October 1972

A S spymaster Mr Waverly in the gadget-clad cult series of the 60s, *The Man from U.N.C.L.E.*, British-born Leo G Carroll was the father figure to action-men Robert Vaughn and David McCallum.

Born in Weedon, Northamptonshire, of Irish parents, Leo performed in school productions of Gilbert and Sullivan, acted in *The Prisoner of Zenda* on the London stage at the age of 11, and made his professional debut at the age of 18 in *Liberty Hall*.

Shortly afterwards, in 1912, he went to America as stage manager and actor in *Rutherford and Son*, but his career was interrupted by the First World War, during which he was wounded while serving in the British infantry.

Settling in America in 1924, Leo appeared in more than 300 stage plays, and his Broadway appearances included those in *Angel Street*, *The Late George Apley* – which he also performed on TV in *Kraft Television*

Theater – and *The Druid Circle*. He made his big-screen debut in *What Every Woman Knows*, in 1934, and followed it with 60 more films, including *The Barretts of Wimpole Street*, *A Christmas Carol*, *Wuthering Heights*, *Rebecca*, *Suspicion*, *North by Northwest* and, Alfred Hitchcock's *Spellbound*, in which he played the villain.

Small-screen success came in the role of befuddled urban banker Cosmo Topper, whose house was inhabited by the ghosts of its former owners, in the 50s series *Topper*, TV's first fantasy comedy, based on the films of the 30s and 40s starring Roland Young.

In 1965, Leo landed the role of Mr Waverly, head of the United Network Command for Law Enforcement organisation, in the spoof spy series *The Man from U.N.C.L.E.* Mr Waverly and his top agents, Napoleon Solo and Illya Kuryakin, saved the world from deadly enemies such as THRUSH and KAOS. The hit series recently enjoyed a re-run in Britain on BBC2.

Leo died at the age of 80. He was married with a daughter.

Violet Carson

b. 1 September 1898
d. 26 December 1983

AS Ena Sharples, *Coronation Street*'s hairnetted harridan, Violet Carson became the ITV serial's first big star. She appeared in its first episode, in December 1960, and stayed with the programme for 20 years and more than 2000 episodes.

Born in a *Coronation Street*-style two-up, two-down terrace in the Ancoats district of Manchester at the end of the 19th century, Violet grew up with music, her mother being an amateur singer.

Having played the piano from the age of two, Violet and her sister Nellie performed a singing act as children. As the Carson Sisters, they sang at church functions and wedding receptions, earning two guineas a time. At the age of 15, Violet became a relief pianist at the Ambassador Cinema, in Pendleton, Manchester, accompanying silent films for £2 5s a week.

At the age of 28, Violet married road contractor George Peploe in Manchester Cathedral, but tragedy struck two years later when he died. She never wed again, saying that she was a one-man woman. Instead, she immersed herself in work, which she had given up during her marriage.

She became known on radio as the voice of 'Auntie Vi' in *Children's Hour* and, for six years, she was the pianist in the Wilfred Pickles quiz show *Have a Go!*, as well as being a presenter and interviewer on *Woman's Hour* for five years and acting in many radio dramas. On stage, she played the Duchess of York in *Richard III*.

When Granada Television was having difficulty in finding an actress to play Ena Sharples in its new serial *Coronation Street*, creator Tony Warren remembered the fearsome 'Auntie Vi' with whom he had worked as a child actor on radio in *Children's Hour*.

On his telling Violet about the part of Ena, she commented that she amounted to 'nothing more than a back-street bitch'. When Warren suggested that maybe she thought the role was too difficult, she retorted, "Don't be ridiculous! I have lived with this woman all my life. There is one in every street in the North of England."

The part was hers, although she had no inkling that it would last so long, having already turned down a role in the 50s BBC serial *The Grove Family* on the grounds that she did not want to act in a long-running programme.

Ena Sharples, the God-fearing, outspoken battleaxe, was an immediate hit with viewers, often seen setting the world to rights. She was the matriarchal figure who epitomised the programme's tough, gritty, Northern character.

As *Coronation Street* became internationally popular in the 60s, Violet herself became famous around the world and was one of the serial's stars who flew all over the globe on promotional trips. By the end of the programme's first year, Ena Sharples was introduced at Tussaud's Blackpool waxworks. In 1965, Violet was awarded an OBE in the Queen's Birthday Honours and, eight years later, an honorary degree by Manchester University.

Her only regret about this success was that it did not allow her the time to do other work – especially acting in the classics on stage, which she enjoyed. But she became a frequent guest on the popular religious programme *Stars on Sunday*, giving viewers a chance to hear her fine singing voice.

Violet took time off from *Coronation Street* in 1973 after suffering a nervous breakdown and left through ill health seven years later. She died on Boxing Day 1983, aged 85, having suffered pernicious anaemia during her last years.

The pleasure she had brought to millions was rewarded with a memorial service at Manchester Cathedral. She was last seen in the serial in February 1980, the character of Ena leaving for Lytham St Anne's to look after an elderly relative.

Donald Churchill

b. 6 November 1930
d. 29 October 1991

A fine writer and actor, Donald Churchill was the man behind the popular ITV series *Moody and Peg*.

Born in Southall, Middlesex, the son of an engine driver on the old Great Western Railway, he finished his education at the age of 14, after attending 13 different schools because his family had moved around a great deal.

He entered films and television in 1956 and wrote many successful scripts, including 40 plays for television. His television writing credits included *The Cherry on Top*, for the *Armchair Theatre* series in 1964, the comedy *Never a Cross Word* and, in 1974, another comedy series, *Moody and Peg*, the tale of spinster Judy Cornwell and divorcé Derek Waring, who decide to share a flat. Both comedies were written with Julia Jones.

Donald subsequently played the title role in the comedy series *Spooner's Patch*, wrote (with Joe McGrath) and starred in *Good Night and God Bless*, playing a TV quiz show host who humiliated the contestants, and appeared in *C.A.T.S. Eyes*, *Bergerac* and *Don't Wait Up*, as well as adapting *Our Mutual Friend*, *Mr Pye* and *Echoes* (all with Julia Jones) for television.

His film screenplays included *Victim*, *The Wild Affair* and *My Family and Other Animals*, and for the stage he wrote *Under My Skin* and, with Peter Yeldham, *Fringe Benefits*.

At the time of his death in Fuengirola, southern Spain, Donald was filming for the ITV series *El C.I.D.* and shortly afterwards was seen on TV in *Stanley and the Women*.

He was married to actress Pauline Yates, and the couple had two daughters, Jemma and Polly.

Kenneth Clark

b. 13 July 1903
d. 21 May 1983

WITH his TV series *Civilization*, Kenneth Clark became a well-known face throughout the land. Viewers thrilled to his exciting accounts of West European art through the centuries, hanging on to his every knowledgeable word.

Born Kenneth Mackenzie Clark, he was educated at Winchester School, where he won an award for his drawing, and Trinity College, Oxford.

His first official role in the art world was as one of the team of organisers of a major exhibition of Italian art at the Royal Academy, in 1930. A year later, he was made Keeper of Fine Art at the Ashmolean Museum, before he went on to become the Director of the National Gallery, at the unusually young age of 31, although his job finished when the art collection was 'evacuated' to Wales during the Second World War.

Kenneth then found a new position as the Ministry of Information's first director of the Film Division and, subsequently, controller of Home Publicity.

At the end of the War, he gave in his resignation and not until 1953 did he take another administrative post, when he became chairman of the Arts Council. A year later, he was appointed chairman of the newly formed ITA, which started in 1955, but four years later, he gave up both posts.

Kenneth had already made his name by then, first as the extremely eloquent writer of such acclaimed books as *Clark's Landscape into Art*, *The Nude* and *Rembrandt and the Italian Renaissance*, then, in 1969, the £200 000 BBC series *Civilization* gave him the opportunity to bring art culture to the man in the street. During two years of filming, Kenneth and his production crew travelled 80 000 miles, went to 117 locations, and visited 118 museums and 18 libraries.

Kenneth – who wrote two autobiographies, *Another Part of the Wood*, in 1974, and *The Other Half*, three years later – was married three times, first to Jane, who died, second to Elizabeth Martin, with whom he had two sons and a daughter before their divorce, and third to Mme Nolwen de Janze-Rice.

He received many honours, degrees and international awards, being made a KCB in 1938, a Companion of Honour in 1959 and a life peer in 1969. Kenneth was awarded the Order of Merit in 1976.

Maurice Colbourne

b. 24 September 1939
d. 4 August 1989

AS yacht-builder Tom Howard, Maurice Colbourne was the backbone of the seafaring soap *Howards' Way*, Britain's nearest equivalent to the gloss and glamour of American serials such as *Dallas* and *Dynasty* – and it was almost like going back to his youth.

Born Roger Middleton in Sheffield, South Yorkshire, at the beginning of the Second World War, his mother died when he was seven and he left school with the idea of going to sea. So, after breaking an apprenticeship with a stonemason, he set off for Liverpool, only to find it in the middle of a depression and with no jobs.

He turned up in Manchester and landed a job as a fairground roustabout, working on the ghost train at Bellevue, before moving on to the travelling fairs.

With thoughts of becoming a writer, he went down to London and worked as a waiter to earn money. He had the idea of acting when another waiter landed a role in the film *The Loneliness of the Long-Distance Runner* and its star, Tom Courtenay, dropped in for a chat with his colleague.

Encouraged by Courtenay to try for the stage, he successfully auditioned for a place at the Central School of Speech and Drama and it was while there that he changed his name to Maurice Colbourne, having seen an obituary of a Shakespearean actor of that name.

On leaving drama school, Maurice went into repertory theatre in Leicester and Birmingham. In 1968, he joined the Portable Theatre Company, a new touring group founded by playwright David Hare, and he joined the Arts Lab in Drury Lane, London – where actors, singers, dancers and mime artists shared their skills – and worked in fringe theatre, becoming a founder-director of the Half Moon Theatre, in East London, one of the centres of new writing for the stage.

Maurice came to prominence on television as John Kline, an ex-convict who helped the police, in *Gangsters*. The two series, beginning in 1977, resulted from a *Play for Today* about Birmingham gangsters that Philip Saville had directed, although it had taken much persuasion on his part to get Maurice to agree to star in it.

Afterwards, the actor appeared on the small screen in *Van Der Valk*, *The Return of The Saint*, *The Day of the Triffids*, *Doctor Who*, *Armchair Thriller* and *The Onedin Line* – often typecast as villains – before getting the lead role of Tom Howard in *Howards' Way*.

The *Barracuda* and her crew set sail in 1985, although most of the action was set on dry land. Tom Howard was a redundant aviation designer who sank his golden handshake into an ailing boatyard on the South Coast.

It was in the classic boardroom-to-bedroom style television drama about the business world. Tom was having an affair with Avril Rolfe and his wife Jan was doing the same with Ken Masters – and everyone else seemed to be playing a similar game.

The programme ran for six series, although Maurice died during the making of the fifth series, which hastened the serial's demise. His death, from a massive heart attack at the age of 49, occurred during a stay at his Brittany farmhouse.

The actor was married twice, with two daughters – Ingaliza from his marriage to Icelandic writer Bibi Jonsdóti, and Clara by second wife Jeannie (Chan Lian Si), a Malay Chinese nursing sister.

Chuck Connors

b. 10 April 1921
d. 10 November 1992

DOZENS of attempts at making it big in films never seemed to work for macho 6ft 5in American actor Chuck Connors, but he finally made his mark in television as Lucas McCain, wandering star of *The Rifleman*, at the turn of the 50s.

Born Kevin Joseph Connors in Brooklyn, New York, he served in the US Army for three years, before launching his career as a basketball player with the Boston Celtics, then switching to baseball with the Brooklyn Dodgers and Chicago Cubs.

He is said to have made his film debut in a 'blue' production, but Connors found his route into more demanding 'acting' when real sportsmen were invited to audition for small roles in the Katharine Hepburn-Spencer Tracy movie *Pat and Mike*, about a sportswoman's affair with her manager. He played a police captain to whom director George Cukor gave a few lines.

Chuck seized on the opportunity and was soon appearing regularly in films, but stardom never quite came to him. His most notable performance was as the star of *Geronimo*, in 1962, and the following year he appeared in *Flipper*, a big-screen version of the later TV series.

By then, he had already become a TV star in *The Rifleman*, firing his Winchester faster than the bad guys could reach for their .45s. The series ran for five years from 1958 and he followed it with another Western series, *Branded*, and the 70s series *Police Story*.

Chuck also had guest roles in *The Six Million Dollar Man*, *Fantasy Island*, *Love Boat* and *Murder, She Wrote*, as well as appearing in the mini-series *Roots* and TV movies such as *The Capture of Grizzly Adams*.

His later films included a memorable performance as a tough, ex-army mechanic in the disaster spoof *Airplane II The Sequel*, in 1982.

Chuck, who appeared on the Chicago stage in *My Three Angels* and *Mary, Mary* in the 70s and publicly supported Ronald Reagan as American President, was married and divorced three times and had four sons. He died of lung cancer at the age of 71.

William Conrad

b. 27 September 1920

AS private eye Frank Cannon in the 70s, William Conrad proved that you do not have to be young, slim and fit to make it as a TV detective.

Born in Louisville, Kentucky, he was the son of a theatre-owner who moved to southern California, where William excelled at drama and literature while at school.

He began his career as a writer, director and announcer for Los Angeles radio station KMPC, before becoming a Second World War fighter-pilot in 1943.

Two years later, he left the air force with the rank of captain, having finished his time in it as producer-director of the Armed Forces Radio Service.

Back in civvy street, William acted in many radio dramas and was the original Marshal Matt Dillon in *Gunsmoke*, which ran for 11 years on CBS, before it switched to television, with James Arness taking over the lead role.

William entered films in 1946 with *The Killers* and followed it with pictures such as *Sorry, Wrong Number*, *East Side, West Side*, *Lone Star*, *The Desert Song* and *The Naked Jungle*. As a producer for Warner Brothers, he made a string of feature films, including *Brainstorm*, *Two on a Guillotine*, *An American Dream*, *A Covenant With Death*, *First to Fight*, *The Cool Ones* and *The Assignment*.

On television, he directed 35 episodes of the series *True*, produced and directed *Klondike* and *This Man Dawson*, and produced *77 Sunset Strip*. His voice was one of those heard in the classic American children's series of the 50s *Rocky and His Friends*, which appealed just as much to adults. He also narrated the hit 60s series *The Fugitive* and *The Invaders*, and the 1976 TV movie *The Macahans: How the West Was Won*, which starred James Arness.

But it was as the fat, balding detective Frank Cannon that William found small-screen fame. *Cannon*, which started in 1970 with a TV movie of the same name, ran for five series and was one of the most successful programmes of its genre. Ten years after it began, William revived the character in the

TV movie *The Return of Frank Cannon*. There was no room for another series, but William came back with a new character in *Jake and the Fatman*, first in a 1987 TV movie, then in a moderately successful series. He and his wife live in California.

Peter Cook

b. 17 November 1937

FROM his performances in *Beyond the Fringe* and at The Establishment club, Peter Cook joined Dudley Moore to make one of the most celebrated satirical series of the 60s, *Not Only . . . But Also*.

Born Peter Edward Cook in Torquay, Devon, before the Second World War, with a father in the British colonial service, he found an outlet for his acting and writing skills at Cambridge University, where he performed in *Footlights* revues. At the 1960 Edinburgh Festival, he wrote and starred in *Beyond the Fringe*, which was such a success that it transferred to London's West End the following year. Peter, with fellow Cambridge graduate Jonathan Miller and Oxford graduates Dudley Moore and Alan Bennett, went with it.

In the same year, Peter co-founded The Establishment club in London and the satirical magazine *Private Eye*. Anti-establishment feelings ran high in the Swinging 60s and Peter was one of those to exploit the opportunities.

His character E L Wistey, introduced at the 1959 *Footlights* revue, complete with raincoat and hat, first appeared on television in Bernard Braden's 1964 series *On the Braden Beat*, philosophising about the ways of the world.

Dudley Moore was spotted by the BBC playing with his own jazz trio at The Establishment and was offered his own, one-off TV special. He asked Peter to be his guest and Peter wrote two sketches, one of them about two cloth-capped characters called, of course, Dud and Pete, who – like E L Wistey – philosophised about life.

Pete and Dud became their most popular characters when the pair were given their own BBC2 show, *Not Only . . . But Also*, in 1965, and it ran for four series, becoming a classic of its kind.

Peter also appeared regularly in the ITV pop show *Revolver* as a foul-mouthed dance-hall manager, for six years, from 1965. He had his own show, *Peter Cook & Co*, on American TV, in 1980, and teamed up there with Dudley Moore again for the series *The Two of Us*.

Since then, he has appeared on television in the 1992 ITV series *Gone to Seed*, as a ruthless property developer.

Peter made his first film, *Bachelor of Hearts*, in 1955 and has appeared in a further 20, including *The Bed Sitting Room*, *The Adventures of Barry McKenzie*, *The Secret Policeman's Ball*, *Yellowbeard*, *Supergirl* and *The Princess Bride*.

With Dudley Moore, he has made *Derek and Clive* records, with legendary bad language, and appeared in various films, including *The Wrong Box*, *Bedazzled*, *Monte Carlo or Bust*, *Hound of the Baskervilles* and *Derek and Clive Get the Horn*.

Peter, whose books include *Dud and Pete* and *The Dagenham Dialogues*, has been married and divorced twice. He has two daughters, Lucy and Daisy, from his first marriage to Wendy Snowden, but no children by his second wife, Judy Huxtable.

Pat Coombs

b. 27 August 1930

WHENEVER a dithering, giggling slice of the female race was needed in British TV comedy, Pat Coombs would be there. She was a foil to comedians such as Eric Barker, Eric Sykes, Terry Scott, Marty Feldman, Reg Varney and Dick Emery, before moving on to more restrained, elderly characters.

Born in Camberwell, London, her first job was teaching in a kindergarten, but she won a scholarship to train at LAMDA and subsequently taught drama there. She started her stage career at Scunthorpe Rep and then went on to work with other companies around the country.

Like many comedy actors of her generation, Pat first became a hit on radio, playing Nola in Arthur Askey's show *Hello Playmates*. But it was on television, alongside Peggy Mount in *Lollipop Loves Mr Mole* and Reg Varney, Peter Jones and June Whitfield in *Beggar My Neighbour*, that she reached a wider audience.

She also appeared on TV in *The Dick Emery Show* and in Marty Feldman's series *Marty*, then later in the situation comedies *Don't Drink the Water!*, *You're Only Young Twice* – again with Peggy Mount – *The Lady is a Tramp*, *Till Death Us Do Part* and its sequel, *In Sickness and In Health*. More recently, she was in the children's series *Ragdolly Anna*, as well as *Roy's Raiders* and *An Actor's Life for Me*. She also played Brown Owl Marge Green in *EastEnders*.

Pat, who was in the Dick Emery film *Ooh... You Are Awful* and *Adolf Hitler – My Part in his Downfall*, is single and lives in Harrow-on-the-Hill, Middlesex.

Tommy Cooper

b. 19 March 1922
d. 15 April 1984

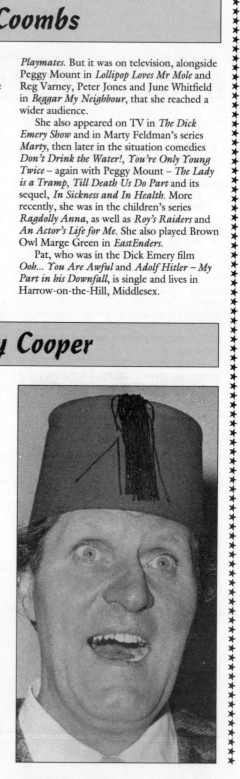

WITH his red fez, face-splitting grin and 'Just Like That' catchphrase, Tommy Cooper was one of television's favourite funnymen. He didn't have to work at it – he was a born comedian.

His physical presence, all 6ft 4in and 15 stone of him, was magnetic. People loved to be near him, watching his disastrous conjuring tricks as he feigned an air of bemused innocence, then stared in total bewilderment as his audience rolled round the aisles in unsuppressed laughter.

Although he became famous for his inability to pull off a trick, Tommy was in actual fact a fine magician and a member of the prestigious Magic Circle. However, once he realised that people preferred things to go wrong, there was no stopping him.

Born in Caerphilly, Mid Glamorgan, but brought up in Exeter and Southampton, Tommy worked as an apprentice shipwright and spent seven years in the Horse Guards, before making his showbusiness debut in the forces during the Second World War.

It was during a NAAFI concert in Cairo that his famous Egyptian fez was introduced, by chance, when the pith helmet that Tommy had planned to wear was mislaid and he borrowed the waiter's hat instead.

Demobbed in 1947, he performed in variety theatres and at London's famous Windmill Theatre, where he once did 52 shows in a week.

In 1952, he appeared at the London Palladium for the first time, before he moved into the television shows for which he was to become best known.

His first series, *Cooper*, in 1957, was followed by *Cooper's Capers*, *Cooperama*, *Life with Cooper*, *Cooper at Large* and *Cooper*

King Size. In 1969, he was voted ITV Personality of the Year by the Variety Club of Great Britain.

The 60s were the Tommy Cooper years – his popularity was at its peak and his vast following was to hold him in its affection for the next 20 years, continuing after his death in 1984, when the burly comedian suffered a heart attack on stage while appearing in the TV show *Live from Her Majesty's*.

He and his wife Gwen had two children.

Harry Corbett

b. 28 January 1918
d. 16 August 1989

To his army of young followers, Harry Corbett was the kindly, old gentleman who took care of Sooty, Sweep and Soo. He captivated his audiences with this trio of furry glove puppets for more than 30 years, with several generations of children growing up with them.

Born in Bradford, West Yorkshire, Harry left school at 16 and served an apprenticeship as an electrical engineer, then spent five years as an engineer surveyor, before he bought the yellow-and-black bear glove puppet through which he was to find fame and fortune. Costing only 7s 6d (37½p) from a toyshop on the North Pier, Blackpool, Sooty was to become one of his best bargain buys ever.

A part-time amateur magician and pianist, he turned professional after winning a talent contest. He was subsequently offered a series of six fortnightly programmes by the BBC, called simply *Sooty*, and became an overnight success.

Sooty first appeared in 1952, joined five years later by Sweep to create a hilarious double-act that had the kids rolling around in stitches as the naughty twosome grappled with their disastrous magic tricks and played out their pranks on their doting master, who – in the early days – was paid £10 per programme.

Other characters followed hot on Sweep's heels and soon the show had become quite a family, with Kipper the cat, Butch the dog and Ramsbottom the snake, who spoke with a heavy Northern accent.

Harry and his loveable characters won international recognition. Sooty-mania took over and children throughout the land had Sooty glove puppets, books and, later, videos. There is even a Sooty Museum in Shipley, West Yorkshire.

The show became one of television's longest-running programmes and Harry, realising that his fingers were his fortune, reportedly had them insured for £20 000.

He set himself up as the puppets' straight man, frequently taking a dousing in a water-pistol fight or being coshed over the head with one of Sweep's infamous sausages. Even royalty failed to avoid the terrible twosome when Prince Philip took a complete soaking from them.

The introduction of Sooty's friend Soo – a prettily-dressed female panda – brought a storm of outrage from parents who thought she brought a sexual element to the show, and indignant feminists protested that she was always seen carrying out the chores.

Harry left the BBC in 1968, when television chiefs decided the show could continue but that he himself should not appear in the programme. Packing up his puppets, Harry moved to ITV with *The Sooty Show*. In 1975, he suffered a severe heart attack, prompting his son Matthew – previously his assistant – to take over.

Harry, who was a member of the Institution of Electrical Engineers, a governor of the National Children's Home and a member of the International Brotherhood of Magicians, gave a lifelong commitment to charity work, which was recognised in 1976 with an OBE. He and his wife Marjorie had two sons, Peter (Matthew) and David.

★★★★★★★★★★★★

Harry H Corbett

b. 28 February 1925
d. 21 March 1982

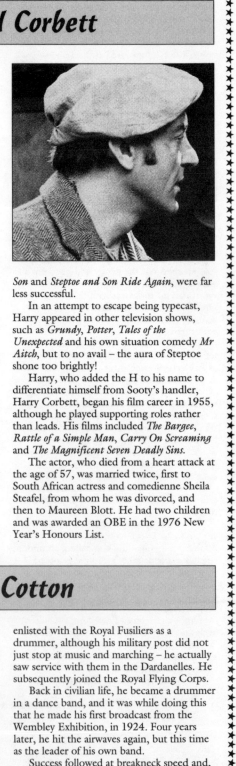

LOVED by millions for his role as rag-and-bone man Harold Steptoe in the classic comedy series *Steptoe and Son*, Harry H Corbett spent the rest of his acting career trying to break free from the role.

The son of an Army officer, he was born in Rangoon, Burma, but raised by his aunt in Manchester after his mother died when he was only three years old. During the Second World War, he served in the Royal Marines and trained as a radiographer, before becoming an understudy with the Chorlton Repertory Company.

After gaining experience, he moved to Joan Littlewood's Theatre Workshop, in East London, where, during the 50s, he played parts in Shakespeare, Ibsen and Jonson plays, as well as appearing in *Hamlet*, *The Power and the Glory* and *The Way of the World* in the West End.

In 1964, *Steptoe and Son* – which had begun as a pilot programme in the 1962 *Comedy Playhouse* season – started, featuring Harry and Wilfrid Brambell, who played his possessive father. The acid banter between the two scrap merchants was classic comedy and a hilarious study of human interaction. The father and son quarrelled about anything and everything in their love-hate relationship, Brambell trying desperately to contain his erstwhile son, who was full of middle-class aspirations.

So successful was the series that it ran for ten years, at its peak bringing in an audience of 22 million viewers, including the Queen Mother, who was reputedly an ardent fan. However, the two spin-off films, *Steptoe and Son* and *Steptoe and Son Ride Again*, were far less successful.

In an attempt to escape being typecast, Harry appeared in other television shows, such as *Grundy*, *Potter*, *Tales of the Unexpected* and his own situation comedy *Mr Aitch*, but to no avail – the aura of Steptoe shone too brightly!

Harry, who added the H to his name to differentiate himself from Sooty's handler, Harry Corbett, began his film career in 1955, although he played supporting roles rather than leads. His films included *The Bargee*, *Rattle of a Simple Man*, *Carry On Screaming* and *The Magnificent Seven Deadly Sins*.

The actor, who died from a heart attack at the age of 57, was married twice, first to South African actress and comedienne Sheila Steafel, from whom he was divorced, and then to Maureen Blott. He had two children and was awarded an OBE in the 1976 New Year's Honours List.

Billy Cotton

b. 6 May 1899
d. 25 March 1969

DURING the 50s, larger-than-life Billy Cotton and his dance band had the nation swaying to their big-band sound in *The Billy Cotton Band Show*. It was the first and last of its kind, a racy, hilarious compilation of music, mirth and energy.

Billy, who was born in Westminster, London, took the first steps along the path of his musical career when, at the age of 15, he enlisted with the Royal Fusiliers as a drummer, although his military post did not just stop at music and marching – he actually saw service with them in the Dardanelles. He subsequently joined the Royal Flying Corps.

Back in civilian life, he became a drummer in a dance band, and it was while doing this that he made his first broadcast from the Wembley Exhibition, in 1924. Four years later, he hit the airwaves again, but this time as the leader of his own band.

Success followed at breakneck speed and,

by the early 30s, he was topping the bill at Ciro's Club and The Alhambra, in Leicester Square.

Specialising in hilarious songs and sketches, he was one of the most popular broadcasters during the Second World War. His catchphrase opening cry of "Wakey-wakey" and his theme song, 'Somebody Stole My Gal', made him a national hero.

In 1956, he played his way on to television sets and caught the public's imagination with *The Billy Cotton Band Show* and, later, *Wakey-Wakey Tavern*.

These shows gave Billy the opportunity to clown around and display his remarkable sense of theatre, as he cartwheeled his 17st frame around the studio. So successful were the shows that, at their peak, they attracted 15 million viewers.

Even though they were made on low budgets and could never compete with the likes of *Sunday Night at the London Palladium*, there were still star guests such as Tom Jones, Hugh Lloyd and Cliff Richard.

Billy was a man who loved speed, and motor racing was one of his life-long passions – he even bought Sir Malcolm Campbell's first *Bluebird*.

Not content with just watching the sport, he himself took part and was a familiar figure at the old Brooklands track. He raced at every opportunity and did not give up until he was 50, when he came sixth in the British Grand Prix, at Silverstone.

In 1962, Billy was named Showbusiness Personality of the Year by the Variety Club of Great Britain, shortly before he was taken ill and had to take three months off work.

Six years later, he hosted another series, *Billy Cotton's Music Hall*, but his last performance on BBC television, in 1969, was in Cilla Black's series *Cilla*, only weeks before he was due to have been in his own new series.

Billy was married and had two sons, one of whom, Bill Cotton Jr, produced his father's show before becoming controller of BBC1.

Jacques Cousteau

b. 11 June 1910

THE mysteries of the deep were unravelled for many television viewers when French marine explorer Jacques Cousteau began filming his underwater documentaries in the 60s, explaining his findings in distinctive nasal tones.

Born Jacques-Yves Cousteau in St André de Cubzac, he attended Brest Naval Academy, served as a gunnery officer, commanded the French naval base at Brest and was a lieutenant in the French Navy during the Second World War, becoming partly responsible for the invention of the aqualung in 1943. This enabled him to pioneer new methods of underwater exploration, using free-swimming divers.

Jacques founded the Undersea Research Group in 1946 and the Campagnes Oceanographiques Françaises four years later. Then, in 1951, he set off around the world on the first of more than 30 voyages on his converted minesweeper *Calypso*.

When he began filming his adventures, Jacques showed the undersea world in vivid detail. His early films were documentary features shown in the cinema, the first – *The Silent World*, in 1956 – winning top prize, the Palme d'Or, at the Cannes Film Festival and a Hollywood Oscar. He also won Oscars for *The Golden Fish* and *The World Without Sun*.

Jacques' first television series, *The World of Jacques-Yves Cousteau*, began in 1966 and he followed it, two years later, with *The Undersea World of Jacques Yves-Cousteau*, which ran until 1976.

A dozen more one-off documentaries followed, plus the series *Oasis in Space*, *The Cousteau Odyssey*, *The Cousteau Amazon*, *Cousteau Mississippi* and *Cousteau's Rediscovery of the World*.

All of these aimed to show people the link between the sea and the human world, and in recent years Jacques has campaigned vigorously on environmental matters – against nuclear waste and oil slicks, for example.

He is also the author of 20 books, including *Captain Cousteau's Underwater Treasury*, *The Living Sea*, *Life and Death in a Coral Sea*, *Diving for a Sunken Treasure*, *The Ocean World of Jacques Cousteau* and *The Cousteau Almanac*, and they have won 20 international prizes.

He has been accompanied on many of his adventures by his wife Simone, with whom he had two sons, one of whom died. He was director of the Oceanic Museum of Monaco until his retirement in 1988, but was less successful with the subsequent opening of the Cousteau Oceanic Park in Paris, which was declared bankrupt two years after its 1989 opening.

Fanny Cradock

b. 1909

USUALLY partnered by her husband, Johnny, Fanny Cradock was the first cook to become a TV star, discarding an apron and showing off her culinary skills while wearing an evening gown.

Unintentionally funny, she was once described as "an enchanting cross between Barbara Cartland and Danny La Rue". To her, a whisk was "a thing Johnny and I picked up in Jersey for half-a-crown 20 years ago".

Phyllis (her real name) and her third husband, monocled, Harrow-educated, former Royal Artillery major John Cradock, together wrote the famous *Bon Viveur* column in *The Daily Telegraph* and were joint food and wine editors of *Esquire* magazine.

In 1955, BBC television producer Henry Caldwell brought them to the small screen in the series *Kitchen Magic*. Their eccentric style was hugely popular and the idea that a husband and wife could work as a team in the kitchen was revolutionary, although Fanny was the bossy, sharp-tongued one who was clearly in charge, with jolly Johnny always standing in the background.

When ITV began, in the same year, it lured the pair across to present *Fanny's Kitchen*, with Phyllis and John becoming Fanny and Johnny, a mark of the less stuffy approach taken by the new channel.

The couple made more series for the BBC in the 60s and early 70s, but Johnny died in 1987, at the age of 80, and Fanny now lives on an estate for the elderly in Stockbridge, Hampshire.

Broderick Crawford

b. 9 December 1911
d. 26 April 1986

A stocky American actor with a pudgy broken nose, Broderick Crawford was best known for his role as Dan Matthews, chief of California's mobile force in the popular *Highway Patrol* series of the 50s.

Born William Broderick Crawford into a theatrical family, in Philadelphia, his mother, Helen Broderick, was one of the best-known comediennes of her time, while his father, Lester Crawford, was a vaudeville performer.

Broderick began his career in radio and vaudeville and made his first serious character debut playing a footballer in *She Loves Me Not* at the Adelphi Theatre, London, in 1932. Although the play ran for only three weeks, it was long enough for Broderick's obvious talents to be spotted by Noël Coward, who found him a role in his 1935 Broadway production of *Point Valaine*.

He continued on the Broadway stage in various shows, until he made his Hollywood film debut in *Woman Chases Man*, in 1937, playing a comic butler. This was to be the start of a film career that lasted more than 40 years and included such notable pictures as *I Can't Give You Anything But Love Baby*, *The Time of Your Life*, *All the King's Men* – for which he won an Oscar – *Born Yesterday*, *The Mob* and *Human Desire*. One of his most famous later films was *The Private Files of J Edgar Hoover*, a controversial picture in which he portrayed the FBI chief.

During the Second World War, Broderick had served with the United States Air Force, but he came to Britain as a sergeant in 1944, acting as compere with the Glenn Miller American Band.

Although, for many, Broderick is thought of primarily as a film star, he did appear in several popular TV programmes, the most famous of which was the American series *Highway Patrol*, which began in 1956, launching him in the role of bulldog cop Dan Matthews.

His radio call-signs, "Ten-Four" (message received and understood) and "Ten-Twenty" (report your position), went on to become catchphrases around the world.

His other small-screen appearances included *King of Diamonds* and *The Interns* and in the late 70s he appeared as guest host on *Saturday Night Live*, taking part in a skit of *Highway Patrol*.

Married four times, with two sons, Chris and Kelly, from his marriage to actress Kay Griffith, Broderick died at the age of 74 and was survived by his last wife, Alice.

Leslie Crowther

b. 6 February 1933

WITH the catchphrase "Come on down!", Leslie Crowther hit the top of the popularity stakes as the host of *The Price is Right*, which brought the frenzied type of American TV game show to Britain for the first time.

Born in Nottingham, the son of stage actor Leslie Crowther Sr, he trained as an actor at the Arts Educational School. His mother was also involved in theatre – she claimed to be the first woman stage manager – so Leslie was encouraged to take his place in the world of entertainment.

A keen pianist, he had originally intended, as a child, to take up a career in music, although he began broadcasting in BBC radio children's programmes while still at school.

A talented actor, Leslie appeared in repertory at The Open Air Theatre, in Regent's Park, made his London West End debut in *High Spirits* and acted in *Babes in the Wood* at the London Palladium.

His television career, however, was far more extensive. He spent eight years, from 1960, as a presenter of the children's show *Crackerjack* and this led to his screen and stage appearances in *The Black and White Minstrel Show*.

Later, he starred with Sylvia Syms in the situation-comedy *My Good Woman* and played Chesney Allen to Bernie Winters' Bud Flanagan, both in *Bud 'n' Ches* on television and the stage musical *Underneath the Arches* at the Prince of Wales Theatre.

In *The Price is Right*, which started on ITV in 1984, Leslie's slick patter, permanent grin and flawless appearance endeared him to the millions who tuned in for their weekly dose of hysteria. The game was based on the competitors' skill in correctly costing a selection of shop goods – collecting prizes ranging from garden furniture to exotic holidays as they screamed, waved and generally made fools of themselves.

Leslie subsequently presented two series of the impressionists' talent show *Stars in Their Eyes* and appeared as himself in the comedy series *Birds of a Feather*.

On radio, he presented shows such as *Accent on Youth*, *Crowther's Crowd* and *Family Favourites*.

He underwent brain surgery after a car crash in 1992 and lives near Bath with his wife Jean. The couple have four daughters – twins Lindsay and Elizabeth (an actress), and Charlotte and Caroline – and one son, Nicholas. Caroline was married to Thin Lizzy singer Phil Lynott, who died from kidney and heart failure after a drugs overdose in 1986.

Andrew Cruickshank

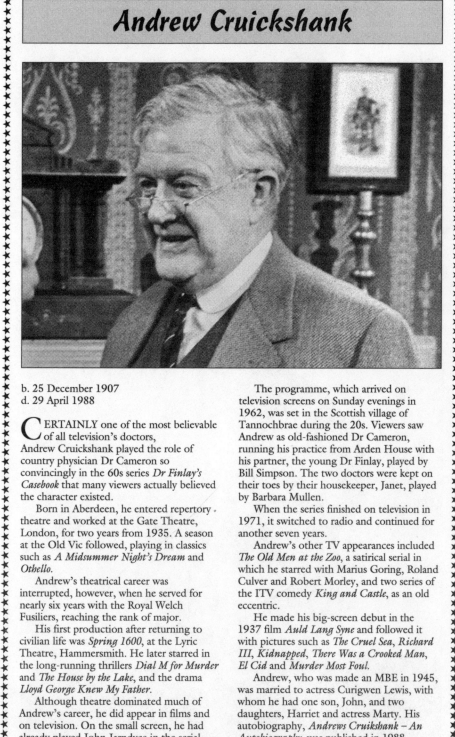

b. 25 December 1907
d. 29 April 1988

CERTAINLY one of the most believable of all television's doctors, Andrew Cruickshank played the role of country physician Dr Cameron so convincingly in the 60s series *Dr Finlay's Casebook* that many viewers actually believed the character existed.

Born in Aberdeen, he entered repertory theatre and worked at the Gate Theatre, London, for two years from 1935. A season at the Old Vic followed, playing in classics such as *A Midsummer Night's Dream* and *Othello*.

Andrew's theatrical career was interrupted, however, when he served for nearly six years with the Royal Welch Fusiliers, reaching the rank of major.

His first production after returning to civilian life was *Spring 1600*, at the Lyric Theatre, Hammersmith. He later starred in the long-running thrillers *Dial M for Murder* and *The House by the Lake*, and the drama *Lloyd George Knew My Father*.

Although theatre dominated much of Andrew's career, he did appear in films and on television. On the small screen, he had already played John Jarndyce in the serial *Bleak House*, when he was cast in *Dr Finlay's Casebook*.

The programme, which arrived on television screens on Sunday evenings in 1962, was set in the Scottish village of Tannochbrae during the 20s. Viewers saw Andrew as old-fashioned Dr Cameron, running his practice from Arden House with his partner, the young Dr Finlay, played by Bill Simpson. The two doctors were kept on their toes by their housekeeper, Janet, played by Barbara Mullen.

When the series finished on television in 1971, it switched to radio and continued for another seven years.

Andrew's other TV appearances included *The Old Men at the Zoo*, a satirical serial in which he starred with Marius Goring, Roland Culver and Robert Morley, and two series of the ITV comedy *King and Castle*, as an old eccentric.

He made his big-screen debut in the 1937 film *Auld Lang Syne* and followed it with pictures such as *The Cruel Sea*, *Richard III*, *Kidnapped*, *There Was a Crooked Man*, *El Cid* and *Murder Most Foul*.

Andrew, who was made an MBE in 1945, was married to actress Curigwen Lewis, with whom he had one son, John, and two daughters, Harriet and actress Marty. His autobiography, *Andrews Cruikshank – An Autobiography*, was published in 1988, shortly after his death, in 1988, from heart failure.

Allan Cuthbertson

b. 7 April 1920
d. 8 February 1988

OFTEN seen as the villain of the piece in films, Allan Cuthbertson revealed his double-edged talent when he stooged for some of showbusiness's favourite funnymen on television.

Born Allan Darling Cuthbertson in Perth, Western Australia, he performed on both stage and radio from an early age. Arriving in Britain in 1947, he made his debut as Romeo in *Romeo and Juliet* at the Boltons, before moving on to London's West End to play in classics such as *Hamlet*, *The Beaux' Stratagem* and *Man and Superman*.

Allan's almost military bearing and ability to seem blustering to the point of pomposity often saw him cast as commanding officers. He made his film debut in *The Million Pound Note*, in 1953, followed a year later by *Carrington VC*, which saw him as a conniving colonel in the big-screen version of one of his stage shows.

The industrious actor made more than 40 films, including *The Guns of Navarone*, *Term of Trial*, *Half a Sixpence* and *The Sea Wolves*. In *Room at the Top*, in 1958, he played a pompous, goading rival to Laurence Harvey's working-class character and subsequently appeared in the sequel, *Life at the Top*.

It was television that allowed Allan to crack the mould and break free from the villains, snobs and highfalutin military men. Acting as the perfect foil to comedians such as Tommy Cooper and Morecambe and Wise, he displayed previously untapped talent.

He also appeared in several TV comedy series, including *Ripping Yarns* and *Fawlty Towers*, and Michael Palin's TV movie *East of Ipswich*, as the arrogant father of a teenaged daughter.

Allan was married to Czech-born Dr Gertrude Willner and the couple had an adopted son.

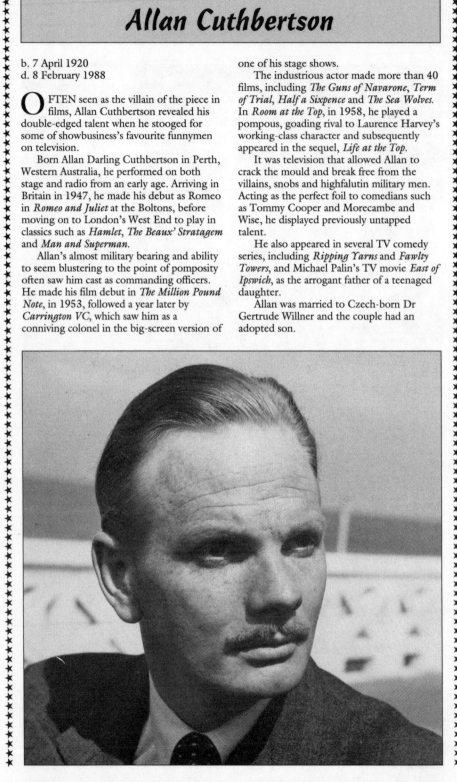

Billy Dainty

b. 1927
d. 19 November 1986

BRASH, gaudy and infinitely hysterical – Billy Dainty's yearly pantomime performance of Widow Twankey was legendary. His skilful comic timing and vaudevillian routines made him a family favourite for more than 30 years.

He first appeared on stage at the age of 12, before winning a scholarship to RADA, where the young Billy skipped a few lessons to appear in the chorus line of the show *Strike a Note*.

When the Second World War broke out, the promising young actor was called up for National Service but, once finished, he was back out and performing in concert parties and summer shows.

It was not until 1974 that Billy's television career really began, following his appearance in the Royal Variety Performance. So impressive was his act that ITV created the series *Billy Dainty Esquire* for him.

This versatile performer also had a large following of radio listeners, who loved his shows, which included *Stick a Geranium in Your Hat*.

Billy, who died at the age of 59, left a widow and one son.

Rupert Davies

b. 22 May 1916
d. 22 November 1976

WITH his battered trilby and his pipe, actor Rupert Davies was the definitive TV 'Maigret'. So popular was the series that it ran for 52 episodes and viewers would eagerly tune in every week to watch stocky Chief Inspector Maigret solving his latest case.

Born in Liverpool, Rupert joined the merchant navy on leaving school, before becoming an observer in the Fleet Air Arm.

During the Second World War, he was held for five years in a German prisoner-of-war camp after he was picked up by a tanker when he was shot down over enemy lines and his plane crashed into the sea.

On his release, Rupert resumed his acting career almost immediately, appearing in an ex-POW show, *Back Home*, at the Stoll Theatre, London.

The acting bug stuck and he joined the Company of Four, at the Lyric Theatre, Hammersmith, before appearing at the Young Vic and eventually moving on to the Old Vic.

His days there brought many interesting and challenging roles, including Williams in *Henry V* and Snout in *A Midsummer Night's Dream*.

Rupert made his television debut in 1945 and went on to play Count Rostov in the BBC's adaptation of the Tolstoy novel *War and Peace*, as well as appearing in *Sailor of Fortune* and, as Inspector Duff, in *The New Adventures of Charlie Chan*.

His first film was *Private Angelo*, in 1949, and he followed it with pictures such as *The Spy Who Came In From the Cold*, *Witchfinder-General* and *Zeppelin*.

In 1960, *Maigret* arrived on TV and viewers saw Rupert as the shrewd French detective in a series based on the Georges Simenon novels. So successful was it that he played the character for four years, his performance honoured when he was named Television Actor of the Year in 1963.

Rupert, who died at the age of 60, was survived by wife Jessica and their two sons, Timothy and Hogan.

Sir Robin Day

b. 24 October 1923

THE Grand Inquisitor of television, Robin Day was for more than 30 years the interviewer whom politicians most feared. His abrasive style made him one of the pioneers of such interviewing, from his early days at ITN to his later work presenting *Panorama* and *Question Time* for the BBC.

Born in London, Robin served in the Army during the Second World War, before studying law at Oxford University, where he was president of the Student Union. After being called to the Bar, in 1952, and practising for a year, he served with British Information Services in Washington, then became a radio talks producer with the BBC.

Joining ITN shortly before it was due to go on the air as the new ITV channel's news service, in September 1955, he became one of its first two newscasters, with former athlete Chris Chataway.

Alongside the handsome, young sports star, Robin was seen by some colleagues as blunt at the microphone and unphotogenic. But he soon showed his mettle, presenting the 7pm news programme in the revolutionary style that ITN was introducing to British television, with its presenters putting themselves across as personalities – in contrast to the BBC's po-faced, robotic newsreaders – and reporters and interviewers not being subservient to politicians and actually asking them the questions that needed to be put.

Robin quickly made a name for himself, not only as a newscaster but as parliamentary correspondent and the presenter of ITN's current affairs programmes *Roving Report* and *Tell the People*.

After ITN's first editor, Aidan Crawley, resigned in January 1956 – following a lost battle for extra time on the ITV network – Robin conducted his first live interview, cross-examining Independent Television Authority chairman Kenneth (now Lord) Clark.

For the first time, the public were seeing the head of an organisation being grilled by one of its staff, and Clark, under interrogation from Robin, affirmed his belief in the news service and confirmed that it would not be cut, gaining the interviewer a stature on which he continued to build.

In June 1957, Robin showed that ITN meant business in its approach to news when he interviewed President Nasser of Egypt, just six months after the end of the Suez crisis, when Britain was still technically at war with Egypt.

"Is it right that you now accept the permanent existence of Israel as an independent sovereign state?" he asked. "Well, you know, you are jumping to conclusions," answered Nasser, to which Robin retorted, "No, I am asking a question."

During the interview, the President made clear his wish for a return to friendly relations with Britain, and Robin brought to bear the qualities that had previously led him to start a career in law.

However, six months before the 1959 General Election, he left ITN to seek a political career, standing as Liberal candidate for Hereford. When he failed to take the seat, he joined *Panorama*, helping it to become the flagship of BBC current affairs programmes, and became its presenter for five years from 1967. He was also frequently seen on other BBC programmes, including General Election night coverage.

Unusually for a broadcaster who has made it in television, Robin was also the regular presenter of a daily radio programme, recalling his ITN newscasting days by hosting *The World at One*, on BBC Radio 4, from 1979 to 1987.

However, it was as presenter of *Question Time* – which also started in 1979 – for which he will be best remembered in his later broadcasting years. The idea was simple: to make a television version of the radio programme *Any Questions?*, with a panel of four politicians, or other leading figures, questioned by an audience made up of members of the general public.

It was a measure of the esteem in which Robin was held that, on his retirement in

1989, there was much debate about who should take over his mantle, with newscaster Peter Sissons eventually becoming the controversial choice.

The programme won Robin a Broadcasting Press Guild Award in 1980. Also winner of the coveted BAFTA Richard Dimbleby Award, in 1974, and the Royal Television Society Judges' Award, for recognition of his 30 years in TV journalism, in 1985, he was knighted in 1981 and has more recently presented a political programme for Central Television.

Robin was divorced from his wife Katherine in 1986, after 21 years of marriage, and has two sons, Alexander and Daniel. His books include *Television: A Personal Report*, *The Case for Televising Parliament* and two autobiographies, *Day By Day* (1975) and *Grand Inquisitor* (1989). A collection of his political interviews, ... *But With Respect*, was published in 1993.

Yvonne De Carlo

b. 1 September 1922

FILM star Yvonne De Carlo became 156-year-old Lily Munster in the 60s TV series *The Munsters* when she needed extra money – and is probably more famous for that role than any she played on the big screen.

Born Peggy Yvonne Middleton in Vancouver, Canada, she joined the city's Little Theatre Group on leaving high school and played a variety of roles, from comedy to stage hand.

Saving enough to buy a one-way ticket to Hollywood, and having trained at the Vancouver School of Dance as a child, 17-year-old Yvonne travelled south and enrolled at the Fanchon and Marco Dancing School. Her first professional work was dancing at the Florentine Gardens and the Earl Carroll Theater, in Hollywood.

Yvonne's first film part was in the 1941 short *I Look at You* and she became noted for her Western and comedy roles, although it was as an exotic dancer-turned-Mata Hari spy that she had her first starring part, in the 1945 picture *Salome Where She Danced*. Her more than 80 films also include *For Whom the Bell Tolls*, *Hotel Sahara* and *The Captain's Paradise*.

It was while making *The Ten Commandments*, alongside Charlton Heston, that Yvonne met stuntman Bob Morgan and they subsequently married. He narrowly escaped death when a load of logs fell on him while filming *How the West Was Won* and he had to have his left leg amputated.

Inevitably, Morgan – who was in hospital for more than a year – found very little work afterwards and it was left to Yvonne to earn money. She took the role of vampire Lily, with the whiter-than-white face, in *The Munsters* to help to pay the bills and, alongside Fred Gwynne as Herman, made the series a worldwide success, running for two years (70 episodes).

The programme also meant a return to Universal City Studios, in Hollywood, which had signed her for *Salome Where She Dances* almost 20 years earlier. She also appeared in the spin-off film *Munster Go Home!*

Yvonne's subsequent television appearances have included *The Virginian*, *Bonanza*, *Murder, She Wrote* and the TV movies *The Mark of Zorro* and *The Munsters' Revenge*.

On stage, she starred in *Enter Laughing* with Alan Arkin, on Broadway and in Los Angeles, *Pal Joey* and *Little Me* in Las Vegas, *No, No Nanette* in Australia, a tour of *Hello, Dolly!* and took the lead role in *Applause* for the San Bernardino Civic Light Opera.

Stephen Sondheim composed 'I'm Still Here' for her in the critically acclaimed Broadway hit *Follies*, in which she starred.

Yvonne – whose autobiography, '*I'm Still Here*', published in 1986, told of her romances with Howard Hughes and Errol Flynn – is divorced from Bob Morgan, with whom she has two sons, writer Bruce and musician Michael.

Armand and Michaela Denis

Armand Denis, b. 1897, d. 15 April 1971
Michaela Denis, b. 1914

INTREPID travellers Armand and
Michaela Denis were the husband-and-wife team who scoured Africa, South America and the Far East to bring the animal world into people's homes for the first time, via the TV screen.

Born in Belgium, the son of a judge, Armand Denis was evacuated to Britain during the First World War and studied chemistry at Oxford University. He emigrated to America, became an American citizen and started a career in chemical research as a Research Fellow at the Californian Institute of Technology.

Finding an interest in radio, he helped to develop an automatic volume control device, but it was another interest, photography, that led him into filming animals.

Armand first met London-born Michaela in New York, then again in Ecuador, where she was on a solo safari and he on an expedition. She became his assistant and, when he proposed in the Andes, the couple married in Bolivia.

Michaela was a dress designer when they met. Her father, an archaeologist, had died when she was only three months old and she had written a book called *Maid of Money*, about a poor girl who becomes an inventor and makes a fortune.

Soon, Armand and Michaela were making television documentaries in their own, inimitable style, narrating alternately, he in his distinctive accent and she in the dialect she had developed through conversing in three languages as a child. Michaela, who was often pictured with a leopard, also became a pin-up, with her shining blonde hair and good looks. The pair's exploits, from tracking down sea-cows and armadillos to rescuing baby spring hares, were seen all over the world.

Their first programmes, for the BBC in 1954, were *Filming Wild Animals* and *Filming in Africa*, which was named Best TV Documentary of the Year. In 1955, they moved to the new ITV network to make *Michaela and Armand Denis*, before returning to the BBC three years later for their popular *On Safari* series, which ran for 11 years and 105 half-hour episodes.

Armand also made full-length films, including *Savage Splendour*, and wrote two books, his autobiography *On Safari*, published in 1963, and *Cats of the World*, a year later. After giving up film-making, he and his wife settled in Kenya to devote their lives to game conservation. He died there of Parkinson's disease in 1971.

Michaela later married Sir William O'Brien Lindsay, the last English Chief Justice in the Sudan, but he died only weeks after the wedding. She now runs a spiritual healing clinic in the Kenyan capital, Nairobi, and still enjoys going on safari.

Michael Denison

b. 1 November 1915

IT seemed like perfect casting when Michael Denison was cast as elegant, gentle barrister Richard Boyd in *Boyd QC* in the 50s, after almost 20 years on stage and in films.

Born in Doncaster, South Yorkshire, Harrow-educated Michael studied modern languages at Oxford University and, while there, appeared with Vivien Leigh in John Gielgud's production of *Richard III*. The experience convinced him that acting was for him and he trained at the Webber Douglas Academy.

His first role was as Lord Fancourt Babberley in *Charley's Aunt*, at Frinton-on-Sea, in 1938. He made his London debut the same year, in *Troilus and Cressida*, and followed it with repertory theatre work in Edinburgh, Glasgow and Birmingham.

The Second World War interrupted Michael's career and, serving in the Intelligence Corps, he went to Northern Ireland, Egypt, Greece and Russia.

He had already made his big-screen debut in the 1939 film *Inspector Hornleigh on Holiday* when, nine years later, he played opposite Dulcie Gray – by then his wife – in *My Brother Jonathan*. His subsequent films included *The Franchise Affair*, *Angels One Five* and *The Importance of Being Earnest*.

On stage, Michael performed in a season at the Shakespeare Memorial Theatre in Stratford-upon-Avon in 1955, along with Laurence Olivier and Anthony Quayle.

Between 1956 and 1963, much of Michael's time was spent in the title role of the TV series *Boyd QC*, which ran for more than 80 episodes.

Subsequently, he appeared on television as Captain Percival in *Blood Royal* and in many episodes of *Crown Court*, as well as in *Private Schultz*, *The Agatha Christie Hour*, *Rumpole of the Bailey* and *Howards' Way*, in which Dulcie Gray was a regular. Michael was also the subject of *This Is Your Life*, in 1977.

His work in the theatre has been prolific, with notable roles as Professor Higgins in *My Fair Lady*, in Australia, Captain Hook to Susan Hampshire's *Peter Pan*, and Pooh-Bah in *The Black Mikado*.

He performed a year of Shakespeare, Fry and Chekhov for the Prospect Theatre Company at the Old Vic, and had London West End roles in *A Coat of Varnish*, *The School for Scandal*, *The Apple Cart* – with Peter O'Toole – *Court in the Act* and *You Never Can Tell*. He has also acted alongside Dulcie in many plays.

The couple were both made CBEs in 1983 and live in part of an early Adam house in Buckinghamshire.

The actor wrote about their early years together in *Overtures and Beginners*, published in 1973, and brought their story up to date in *Double Act*, 12 years later.

Richard Dimbleby

b. 25 May 1913
d. 22 December 1965

THE founder of British broadcast journalism, Richard Dimbleby later brought the world's state occasions, with all their pomp and ceremony, live into the public's front rooms for the first time, with his authoritative commentaries on great events such as the Queen's coronation and Sir Winston Churchill's funeral. His flair, self-assurance and driving ambition made him a true pioneer of the 20th-century news media.

Born in Richmond-upon-Thames, Richard was educated at Mill Hill School and, in 1931, went to work for the family newspaper, *The Richmond and Twickenham Times*. The paper, now run by his son David, was then edited by Richard's father, Frederick J G Dimbleby, before he became political adviser to Lloyd George.

After a time on the *Bournemouth Echo* and as news editor for *Advertisers Weekly*, Richard became one of the BBC's first news reporters, in 1936. Three years later, after experience reporting on the Spanish Civil War, he was sent out with the British Expeditionary Force to France as the BBC's first war correspondent.

So successful was Richard that he proceeded to cover campaigns in the Middle East, East Africa, the Western Desert and Greece, until he was recalled to London, in 1942.

The first reporter to fly with Bomber Command – he subsequently flew 20 missions with them – Richard was fired with a sense of justice and possessed a burning desire to reveal the atrocities of war that he witnessed. He was, however, frustrated by the restrictions and cloying censorship that the BBC placed on its war reports.

Although he felt suffocated by this, he did not let his feelings mar his work and it was during the Second World War that he submitted his memorable report on Belsen, being the first reporter to arrive at the German concentration camp.

During this busy time, he still managed to write several books and contribute to periodicals and newspapers.

The War over, Richard came back from the front to become the BBC's definitive anchorman – one on whom it could always depend to give a glowing commentary on televised state occasions, his greatest day being the Queen's coronation, in 1953.

He is also remembered for his contribution to political programmes such as *Panorama*, which he presented from September 1955, when it was relaunched as a weekly 'window on the world'.

It was here that Richard pulled off one of television's most famous hoaxes, fooling many viewers with his mock, but authoritative report on the Swiss spaghetti harvest.

Although having made the move from radio to television, he continued to work for BBC radio, as chairman of *Twenty Questions* and the interviewer in *Down Your Way*, as well as an *Off the Record* series of talks for the North American Service.

Despite his exhausting schedule of work for the BBC, by then as a freelancer, he still found time for interest in the family paper, as Managing Director from 1954.

Richard died shortly before Christmas 1965, at the age of 52 after battling silently against cancer for five years.

A memorial service held at Westminster Abbey was rather like one of the state occasions on which he himself had often commentated. His dignity and courage created such sympathy among the public that funds flooded in to set up a fellowship of cancer research.

Richard, awarded the OBE in 1945 and made a CBE in 1959, had been married to his wife Dilys since 1937, after they had met while she was working as his father's personal assistant. They had three sons, broadcasters Jonathan and David, and Nicholas, as well as one daughter, Sally.

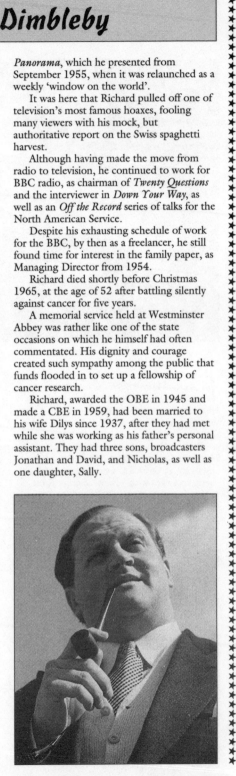

Ken Dodd

b. 8 November 1927

WITH a tickling stick in his hand, hair pointing heavenward and two protruding front teeth, 'comedian's comedian' Ken Dodd has had audiences in stitches for more than 50 years, although it was in the 60s that he made his biggest impression on television, supported by the Diddymen.

Born Kenneth Arthur Dodd in the Knotty Ash area of Liverpool, which he has immortalised in his act, the diddy Doddy 'adjusted' his teeth at the age of 12, when he fell off his bike and went crashing head first to the pavement.

On leaving school, he worked for his coal merchant father for a while, then hawked pots and pans around the Liverpool backstreets on a barrow. His first attempt at entertaining was when he gave a ventriloquist show with his dummy, Charlie Brown, at the Knotty Ash orphanage, aged just 14.

Ken continued as an amateur, performing in concert halls and billing himself as Professor Yaffle Chuckabutty – Operatic Tenor and Sausage Knotter, until 1954, when he performed his first show as a professional, at the Nottingham Empire. At the London Palladium, 11 years later, *Ken Dodd's Laughter Show* ran for 42 weeks and created new box-office records.

His stage act owes much to music hall and he has undertaken lengthy seasons and tours around the country, only occasionally appearing on television, but always with maximum impact.

The Good Old Days provided a natural showcase for his talents, but it was *The Ken Dodd Show*, which started in 1959 and ran throughout the 60s, complete with 'Diddy' David Hamilton and the Diddymen – characters such as Dicky Mint, Nigel Ponsonby Smallpiece and Mick the Marmaliser – that brought him to a wide audience.

He also had success with *Ken Dodd's World of Laughter* and enjoyed chart success as a ballad singer with 19 hit singles, including 'Love is Like a Violin', 'Happiness' and the number one 'Tears'. He has also had four hit albums, *Tears of Happiness, Hits for Now and Always, For Someone Special* and *20 Golden Greats of Ken Dodd*.

A collector of thousands of books about the art of comedy and in *The Guinness Book of Records* for telling 1500 jokes non-stop in three-and-a-half hours, Ken has also performed as a straight actor on stage, playing Malvolio in Shakespeare's *Twelfth Night*, at the Royal Court Theatre, Liverpool.

Awarded an OBE in 1982, Ken was the subject of a one-hour *This is Your Life* special, in 1990, shortly after being cleared of tax evasion charges. He was found not guilty on four counts of false accounting and four of cheating the Inland Revenue.

Although he has never married, Ken has had two long engagements. His fiancée of 24 years, Anita Boutin, died in 1977 and he subsequently became engaged to former Bluebell dancer Anne Jones. They live in the Georgian farmhouse in Knotty Ash, Liverpool, in which Ken was born.

★★★★★★★★★★★★★

Diana Dors

b. 31 October 1931
d. 4 May 1984

WITH her hour-glass figure and platinum blonde hair, Diana Dors was Britain's answer to Marilyn Monroe. And, like her American counterpart, tragedy and drama seemed to dog her for most of her life as she battled against ill health, bankruptcy and broken romances.

Born Diana Mary Fluck, in Swindon, Wiltshire, the only child of a railway clerk and a former Army captain, she was plucked from the relative obscurity of being a 15-year-old student at RADA to make her film debut in the 1946 thriller *The Shop at Sly Corner*.

After a string of pictures, she was finally offered a contract by the Rank Organisation, which ran the famed Rank Charm School, grooming British actors and actresses for the silver screen.

Diana was to be seen in the Dickens classic *Oliver Twist*, followed by two of the hilarious *Huggett* films, *Here Come the Huggetts* and *Vote for Huggett*, which allowed her tremendous flair for comedy to shine through. However, her film career failed to advance and the Rank contract ended in 1950, with quality work then seeming hard to come by.

Diana Dors, as she was by then known – after dropping the Fluck and taking her maternal grandmother's name – appeared in two second-rate films and took to the London West End stage.

The Blonde Bombshell show was on the road and gathering in speed. The public loved her – men lusted after her gravity-defying bosom and women tried hard to emulate her scarlet pout. She became hot property and everything she did – both on and off screen – became public knowledge, and continued to grab the public's attention for more than 30 years.

Realising her popularity, Rank offered Diana another contract, which she delighted in turning down, preferring to work with director Carol Reed on his film *A Kid for Two Farthings*, in 1955. A year later, she decided to make a stand by moving away from glamour-puss parts to star in *Yield to the Night*, a rather grey and serious tale set in a prison cell, but the film did not bring her credibility as a serious actress, as she had wished, and the bright lights and lightweight roles of Hollywood beckoned.

However, by the end of the 50s, Diana's place as the British screen goddess was beginning to disintegrate, along with her shapely figure, and – although she continued to work in films – she was no longer the leading lady.

Ironically, her private life triggered more interest than her films, with every sordid detail splashed across the tabloids. In 1960, she was paid £35 000 by *The News of the World* for her memoirs. The Archbishop of Canterbury waded in to condemn the venture, but the saucy revelations attracted a large swell of readers.

Separated in 1957 from her first husband, Dennis Hamilton, Diana went on to marry American comedian Dickie Dawson, with whom she had two sons, Mark and Gary. The marriage ended after eight years, with Diana losing custody of her sons. But happiness followed when she married her third husband, actor Alan Lake, in 1968, and the couple had a son, Jason.

From then on, the pair seemed dogged by trouble. In that same year, Diana was declared bankrupt, with a £48 413 tax bill, and in 1970 Lake was jailed for 18 months after taking part in a pub brawl.

In 1974, the actress had a brush with death when she contracted meningitis. Eight years later, she underwent surgery for cancer.

As her film star days disappeared, television beckoned and gave Diana an interesting collection of meaty character roles, such as Mrs Bott in the *Just William* series and a part written specially for her in *Queenie's Castle*, in 1970.

One of her last television appearances, in 1983, saw the bloated actress – who tipped the scales at well over 14 stone – hosting a regular slimming feature on *Good Morning Britain*, for the then ITV breakfast station TV-am.

Diana lost her brave battle against cancer when she died five days after undergoing major abdominal surgery. Her third husband, Alan Lake, committed suicide five months later.

Robert Dougall

b. 27 November 1913

ONE of the BBC's first television newsreaders, Robert Dougall was respected for his diction and professionalism throughout his 20 years on screen, and he later reappeared to present a Channel Four series for the elderly.

Born in Croydon, Surrey, he began his working life in accountancy with the London firm of Deloitte, Plender, Griffiths, before joining the BBC accounts department. He became an Empire Service announcer at the age of 20, in the days when even radio presenters wore evening dress, and served with the Royal Naval Volunteer Reserve during the Second World War, when he was an interpreter with Russian convoys in Murmansk.

Returning to the BBC in 1946, Robert worked as a reporter for the European Service and the Far Eastern Broadcasting Service in Singapore, before becoming an announcer for the Light Programme.

He moved into television in 1954, as one of the BBC's first three newsreaders, with Richard Baker and Kenneth Kendall. At first, all three simply read the news behind pictures of the day's events, but the following year they were actually seen on screen during the headlines – a move hastened by the imminent arrival of ITN on the commercial channel – and a year later they were seen reading the news stories as well.

After almost 40 years with the BBC, Robert retired from newsreading in 1973 and wrote an autobiography, *In and Out of the Box*. He also presented the religious series *Stars On Sunday* for two years and wrote six more books, four of them fuelled by his interest in birds, as well as an anthology of poetry called *Now for the Good News*, and a book on retirement, *Years Ahead*, to tie in with his Channel Four series of the same name aimed at the elderly, which ran for five series from 1982.

During his years as a public figure, he was honoured as a subject of *This is Your Life* and made guest appearances on programmes such as *The Generation Game*, *The Russell Harty Show* and *Celebrity Squares*.

Robert, who was made an MBE in 1965 and was president of the Royal Society for the Protection of Birds for five years in the 70s, is now happy to lead a quiet retirement in a 17th-century farmhouse on the Suffolk coast, near Aldeburgh, spotting bearded tits, marsh-harriers and other rare birds. He married his wife, Nan, in 1947 and has a son, Alastair, and a step-daughter, Michele.

Colin Douglas

b. 28 July 1912
d. 21 December 1991

ALTHOUGH a solid character actor on stage and television throughout a long career, Colin Douglas will always be remembered best as Edwin, father of the Ashtons of Liverpool, in *A Family at War*.

Born in Newcastle upon Tyne, Colin emigrated to New Zealand at the age of 16 but returned to Britain five years later to train as an actor at RADA. He went into repertory theatre, but his career was halted by the outbreak of war. He trained at Catterick and Sandhurst, becoming a captain and adjutant in the Border Regiment and served in the First Airborne Division.

Later, in the theatre, Colin made his mark in Alan Plater's mining play *Close the Coalhouse Door*, which opened in Newcastle and transferred to London's West End. It was while appearing in it that he was chosen by Granada Television to star in *A Family at War*, the ITV series that ran for 52 episodes from 1970.

It followed the working-class Ashton family as they coped with the trials and tribulations of the Second World War, and was an instant hit with viewers, earning a re-run on Channel Four in the 80s.

Colin's other television work included *Bonehead*, *Dick Barton – Special Agent*, *Follyfoot*, *Love Story*, *The Sweeney*, *The Omega Factor*, *Telford's Change* and *Nanny*. His last screen role, in 1991, was as Labour Party traditionalist and coach firm owner Frank Twist in Alan Bleasdale's classic series *G.B.H.*

He and his actress wife, the late Gina Cachia, had four sons – Timothy, Angus, Blaise and Piers – and a daughter, Amanda, who died before her father.

Charlie Drake

b. 1925

ROLY-poly comedian Charlie Drake charmed audiences with his welcome, "Hello, my darlings," and daring sight gags, scoring his biggest TV hit in the 60s with *The Worker*.

Born Charles Springall in the Elephant and Castle, London, he was one of seven children, of whom only four survived. He grew up in poverty and his father, although a trapeze artist, scraped money together by selling newspapers and collecting bets on the streets while his wife went out cleaning.

Charlie himself sang at the South London Palais at the age of eight to bring in extra money and left school two years later, taking various jobs, before becoming an electrician's mate, often causing explosive disasters during the course of his work.

Turned down by the Royal Navy, he served in the RAF during the Second World War, performed in shows and met comic Jack Edwardes, whom he bumped into again several years after the War.

Both struggling to earn a living as comics – Charlie had appeared on BBC TV in *The Benny Hill Show* but at one time was even driving a tractor to earn a living – the chalk-and-cheese pair teamed up as comedy duo Mick and Montmorency, Charlie 5ft 1½in and Jack 6ft 6in.

By 1950, they had become stars of children's variety shows on BBC television, appearing in *Jobstoppers*, *Jolly Good Time* and *Mick and Montmorency*, but eight years later Charlie decided to go solo.

He had already appeared in Bob

Monkhouse and Denis Goodwin's comedy series *Fast and Loose*, having his left ear literally blown off by Monkhouse, who as a Russian spy in one sketch shot blanks from a pistol, hitting Drake's ear and causing it to sever. Fortunately, a doctor was on hand to stitch it.

On going solo, Charlie had an immediate TV hit with the appropriately titled *Drake's Progress*. The slapstick of his double-act had turned to even wilder stunts, with plenty of jumping, falling and swinging.

But it was being thrown through a bookcase, then out of a window, in his next series, *Bingo Madness*, that caused Charlie a fractured skull and two years out of the business. The show was broadcast live and the director blacked out TV screens when he realised that Drake had smashed his head against a stage weight. The rest of the series was cancelled and its star announced his retirement, taking up oil-painting and even having exhibitions of his work.

Charlie returned, in 1965, with his greatest success, *The Worker*, which ran for three years. He played a totally unemployable man trooping along to the job centre every week for a new job. Henry McGee, one of the great straight men in TV comedy, was the job centre manager, Mr Pugh, whom Charlie referred to as Mr 'Poo'.

After another period of 'retirement', he returned in *The Charlie Drake Show*, but his comedy peak was past and – after being banned by the actors' union Equity from appearing in provincial theatres for employing a talent contest winner in his 1974 Christmas pantomime – he switched to straight acting.

Charlie won a Best Actor award for his role in Harold Pinter's *The Caretaker*, at the Royal Exchange, Manchester, and was in *As You Like It*, at the Ludlow Festival. On television, he appeared in Samuel Beckett's *Endgame*, the *Great Writers* episode featuring Dostoyevski's *Crime and Punishment*, and the BBC serial *Bleak House*, as well as the TV movies *Mr H is Late* and *Filipina Dreamgirls*.

His films, after a big-screen debut in the 1954 picture *The Golden Link*, were mostly made at the height of his comedy success and included *Sands of the Desert*, *Petticoat Pirates*, *The Cracksman* and *Mister Ten Per Cent*.

Charlie has had five hit singles, 'Splish Splash', 'Volare', 'Mr Custer', 'My Boomerang Won't Come Back' and 'Puckwudgie', and admitted gambling away millions of pounds.

Married and divorced twice, to Heather Barnes and dancer Elaine Bird, he has three sons – Christopher, Stephen and Paul – from his first marriage and lives in South London.

Clive Dunn

b. 9 January 1922

LANCE Corporal Jones, the butcher who implored his colleagues in the Home Guard, "Don't panic! Don't panic!" when he was the only one panicking, was the masterly creation of Clive Dunn in the hit comedy series *Dad's Army*.

Born in London, with two generations of his family already in the theatre, Clive trained at the Italia Conti Stage Academy and made his professional debut as a dancing frog and a flying dragon in *Where the Rainbow Ends*, at the Holborn Empire, in 1936.

During the Second World War, he served in Greece in the 4th Hussars, was captured by the Germans and became a prisoner-of-war in Austria.

Leaving the Army in 1947, Clive returned to showbusiness, performing in summer shows, pantomimes, ice shows and variety. He first made his name on television in 1960, as Old Johnson in *Bootsie and Snudge*, follow-up to the hit ITV series *The Army Game*, with stars Alfie Bass and Bill Fraser facing life on civvy street.

Then, Clive played a panoply of character roles in Michael Bentine's zany BBC series *It's a Square World* – which also featured Dick Emery and Frank Thornton – and he appeared in Spike Milligan's series *The World of Beachcomber*.

In 1968, he was cast as Corporal Jones in *Dad's Army*, the situation-comedy written by David Croft and Jimmy Perry about a Home Guard platoon in the fictional South Coast town of Walmington-on-Sea during the Second World War.

Clive's character – much older than himself – was supposed to be a veteran of wars fought with bayonets and would exclaim, "They don't like it up them!" as he advocated their use.

Trying to win favour with commanding officer Captain Mainwaring, Jones in his civvy street role would offer him under-the-counter sausages. On parade, he would simply ask, "Permission to speak, sir?" – another of his catchphrases.

The series ran for nine years and was one of the most successful comedies ever, making stars of the entire cast, who also appeared in a 1971 film spin-off.

By then, Clive had already starred in the title role of a children's series, *Grandad*, in 1970, and enjoyed a number one single with the theme song, which he performed himself. He also starred in the ITV comedy *My Old Man*, which began in 1974.

One of his notable stage roles was as Frosch in an English National Opera Company production of *Die Fledermaus*. His other films include the army comedy *You Must Be Joking* and *Just Like a Woman*.

Clive, who was awarded the OBE in 1975, is married to actress Priscilla Morgan and has two daughters, Polly and Jessica. He is now semi-retired and lives in Portugal.

Buddy Ebsen

b. 2 April 1908

TELEVISION fame came late to Buddy Ebsen. Just when he was thinking about retiring, he landed the role of Jed in *The Beverly Hillbillies*, then he scored another hit as elderly detective Barnaby Jones.

Born Christian Rudolph Ebsen in Belleville, Illinois, he went to Orlando, Florida, as a child when his father moved his dancing school there. He was a natural dancer but gave up at the age of 13, thinking it a cissy thing to do. Planning a career in medicine, he entered the University of Florida, but during his first year the Florida real estate bubble burst and the Ebsen family's finances disappeared.

Looking for a job, he eventually found work in a soda fountain at the Pennsylvania Railroad Terminal in New York. Broadway producer Florenz Ziegfeld spotted him there and cast him as a dancer in *Whoopee*, whose star was Eddie Cantor, in 1928.

A year later, Buddy's sister Vilma joined him and they performed routines together on Broadway for almost ten years and appeared on stages around the world, and in the film *Broadway Melody of 1936*.

Buddy drifted into solo roles, in subsequent MGM pictures such as *Born to Dance* and *Broadway Melody of 1938*, alongside Judy Garland, although he missed the opportunity to appear with her as the Tin Man in *The Wizard of Oz* when he suffered a particularly nasty reaction to the aluminium-based make-up.

After serving for two years in the US Navy at the end of the Second World War – rising to the rank of lieutenant – Buddy picked up his career on the stage, starring in the Broadway revival of *Show Boat*. Then, a play he wrote, *Honest John*, was produced at Las Palmas Theater, in Hollywood.

He also wrote and acted in a TV pilot, *Elmer Fox*. Republic Studios saw it and signed him up to act in a series of Westerns. Although he had appeared in 13 films before war service, his big-screen career had subsequently faltered, but he went on to appear in pictures such as *Under Mexicali Stars*, *Silver City Bonanza* and *Rodeo King and the Senorita*.

Then, in 1954, he co-starred as George Russell, sidekick to the Alamo defender in *Davy Crockett*, in the *Disneyland* TV series. Fess Parker played the king of the wild frontier and two feature films, *Davy Crockett, King of the Wild Frontier* and *Davy Crockett and the River Pirates*, were put together from the series, each comprising three episodes.

Buddy then appeared in television Western series such as *Maverick*, *Bonanza*, *Rawhide* and *Gunsmoke*.

He also started writing songs, published by Walt Disney's music publishing company. He penned the lyrics for *Wild Card* and *The Handsome Stranger*, and later wrote *Snowshoe Thompson*, *Behave Yourself* and *Pretty Little Girl with the Red Dress On*.

His subsequent films included *Breakfast at Tiffany's* and *Tom Sawyer*, but it was as widower Jed Clampett in *The Beverly Hillbillies*, on television from 1962, that he became a star. Buddy played the head of a family of rustics from the Ozark mountains who struck oil – and 25 million dollars – and moved to Beverly Hills.

The series ran for nine years and more than 200 episodes, and he also starred in a TV movie, *The Return of the Beverly Hillbillies*, in 1981.

By then, he had already played the lead role in another series, *Barnaby Jones*, this

time playing it straight as a private detective appearing to be past his sell-by date. The series ran from 1973 to 1980 and Buddy also played the character in two TV movies, *Final Judgment* and *Nightmare In Hawaii*.

The private eye was particularly popular with older viewers, who formed the Barnaby Jones Luncheon Club. One of the programme's biggest fans was former American President Richard Nixon, who once addressed the club.

Since then, Buddy – whose other TV appearances include those in *Hawaii Five-O*, *Alias Smith and Jones* and *Hardcastle and McCormick* – has produced the play *Turn to the Right* and the comedy *Division Street*, which was directed by his second wife, Nancy Wolcott, and featured their daughter, Bonnie.

Buddy's first marriage, to Ruth Cambridge – by whom he has two daughters, Libby (Elizabeth) and Alix – ended in divorce. He has four daughters, Susannah, Cathy, Bonnie and Kiersten, and one son, Dustin, by his second wife. They have an ocean-front home in Newport Beach, California, and a ranch in Malibu Canyon.

Jimmy Edwards

b. 23 March 1920
d. 7 July 1988

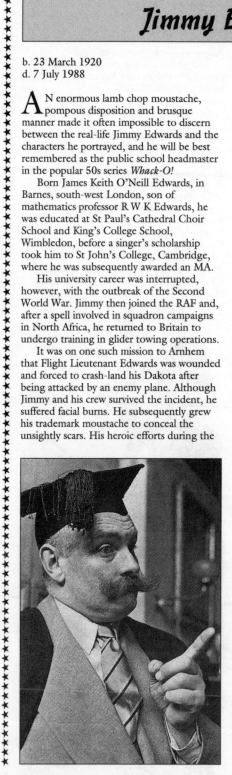

A N enormous lamb chop moustache, pompous disposition and brusque manner made it often impossible to discern between the real-life Jimmy Edwards and the characters he portrayed, and he will be best remembered as the public school headmaster in the popular 50s series *Whack-O!*

Born James Keith O'Neill Edwards, in Barnes, south-west London, son of mathematics professor R W K Edwards, he was educated at St Paul's Cathedral Choir School and King's College School, Wimbledon, before a singer's scholarship took him to St John's College, Cambridge, where he was subsequently awarded an MA.

His university career was interrupted, however, with the outbreak of the Second World War. Jimmy then joined the RAF and, after a spell involved in squadron campaigns in North Africa, he returned to Britain to undergo training in glider towing operations.

It was on one such mission to Arnhem that Flight Lieutenant Edwards was wounded and forced to crash-land his Dakota after being attacked by an enemy plane. Although Jimmy and his crew survived the incident, he suffered facial burns. He subsequently grew his trademark moustache to conceal the unsightly scars. His heroic efforts during the War were acknowledged when he was decorated with the Distinguished Flying Cross.

Jimmy was one of the many entertainers of his generation who first made their mark in radio before moving to the small screen. In 1947, he was instrumental in the revival of the wartime comedy programme *Navy Mixture*.

One segment of the show featured the Glum family and, a year later, they were given their own spin-off, *Take it From Here*, with Jimmy as Pa Glum, alongside Dick Bentley and June Whitfield (taking over the part previously played by Joy Nichols) as Ron and Eth in writers Frank Muir and Denis Norden's much-loved series. *The Glums* became a national institution. It ran for 12 years and Jimmy repeated his role in a 70s TV version.

For many, Jimmy's larger-than-life appearance and eccentricities lent themselves perfectly to television. He appeared as 'Professor' Jimmy Edwards, headmaster of Chislebury School, in *Whack-O*, which ran from 1957 to 1961, with a further series in the late 70s, and in 1966 he appeared in the title role of the BBC series *John Jorrocks Esq*.

Jimmy's small-screen career was supplemented with both film and theatre performances, although his character and appearance created difficulties for film-makers, who did not know which pigeon-hole to place him in.

However, after his big-screen debut in *Trouble in the Air*, in 1948, he made 16 pictures, including *Murder at the Windmill*, *Bottoms Up!* – the 1959 film version of the TV hit *Whack-O!* – *The Bed Sitting Room* and Eric Sykes's silent comedies *The Plank* and *Rhubarb*.

He had more success with plays, making his stage debut after the War, at the Windmill Theatre, London. He later appeared with Eric Sykes in *Big Bad Mouse*, which they performed in the West End and around the world, and created theatrical history when the two actors tired of the script and decided to ad-lib.

Jimmy, who died of bronchial pneumonia, was a complex man. He was fond of polo and fox-hunting – he was a Master of the Foxhounds – and in 1964 he had stood unsuccessfully for Parliament, as a prospective Conservative candidate for North Paddington.

A homosexual, he was divorced from Valerie Seymour 11 years after their 1958 wedding.

Denholm Elliott

b. 13 May 1922
d. 6 October 1992

ONE of the few true-blue gentleman film stars, Denholm Elliott carved a niche for himself playing sinister, rather menacing men on both the cinema and television screens.

Born Denholm Mitchell Elliott in London, he went on to train at RADA but left after only a year and enlisted in the RAF during the Second World War. He served as a radio operator and gunner, until he was shot down over Denmark and imprisoned in Germany for three years.

During his time in captivity, he became interested in amateur dramatics and, once the War was over, he decided – against his family's wishes – to make acting his career.

They had hoped that he would follow in the family tradition and go to the Bar, like his grandfather, a well known QC.

Starting with Amersham Rep in 1945, Denholm was quick to learn and his theatrical career began to develop rapidly. He subsequently appeared in tours and in London's West End, in productions such as the Christopher Fry comedy *Venus Observed*, in 1950, chosen by Sir Laurence Olivier to play his son.

Denholm made his film debut as a civil servant in *Dear Mr Prohack*, in 1949, and followed it with pictures such as *The Cruel Sea*, as a two-timing Naval officer, *The Heart of the Matter*, as a civil servant who cuckolds Trevor Howard, and *Pacific Destiny*, based on the autobiography of Sir Arthur Grimble.

He also appeared in *Zulu Dawn*, *A Private Function*, *Maurice*, *Raiders of the Lost Ark*, *Indiana Jones and the Last Crusade*, *A Room With a View* – as Mr Emerson, a part which won him an Oscar nomination as Best Supporting Actor – and *Defence of the Realm*, as an ageing ex-Fleet Street hack.

His television performances were equally prolific, ranging from that in *Blade on the Feather* – for which he won a BAFTA Best Actor award in 1980 – to the thriller series *Codename Kyril*.

His small-screen work centred on quality dramas and TV movies, perhaps the most famous being the award-winning *Hôtel du Lac*, also starring Anna Massey.

The bisexual actor, who was made a CBE in 1988 and died of AIDS at the age of 70, was married twice. His first marriage, to actress Virginia McKenna, ended in divorce and he subsequently wed actress Susan Robinson, with whom he had a son, Mark, and a daughter, Jennifer.

Dick Emery

b. 19 February 1917
d. 2 January 1983

PERHAPS best known for his catchphrase "Ooh, you are awful – but I like you", Dick Emery became a household name with his hilarious range of characters, from the toothy vicar to peroxide bombshell Mandy.

Born Richard Gilbert Emery in Bloomsbury, London, to theatrical parents who had a double-act known as Callan and Emery, showbusiness seemed an inevitable career choice.

He was taken on tour from the age of three weeks and became a member of his parents' routine while still a young child.

However, with a rich tenor voice, he showed interest in opera before moving towards variety.

Like so many entertainers of his generation, Dick's blossoming career suffered a temporary hiccough when the outbreak of the Second World War saw him serving in the RAF, although he became a member of Ralph Reader's famous Gang Show.

The War over, he left the RAF and made regular appearances with Tony Hancock at the Windmill Theatre, London, but it was in radio that Dick first made his name.

His big break came in the 50s with the popular *Educating Archie* show – featuring Peter Brough and his ventriloquist's dummy, Archie Andrews – in which Dick demonstrated his brilliant capacity for comedy, and he followed it with his own series, *Emery at Large*.

His earliest television appearances were in *Two's Company*, with Libby Morris, *It's a Square World* and the hit situation-comedy *The Army Game*, at the end of the 50s.

In 1963, Dick was given his own BBC television programme, *The Dick Emery Show*, enabling him to present a showcase of hilarious and ingenious sketches that endeared him to audiences for the next 20 years.

Later, the programme became a comedy-thriller – an unusual form in television – under the title *Emery*!

He won the BBC Television Personality Award from the Variety Club of Great Britain in 1972, but missed the ceremony when he was rushed to hospital.

Dogged by illness throughout his later years, Dick suffered from a heart complaint, stomach disorders and an eye problem for which he had undergone a series of operations.

He was married five times – to Zelda, Irene, Iris, Victoria and dancer Josephine Blake – and had four children.

At the time of his death, Dick had left his last wife for showgirl Fay Hillier, 30 years his junior.

Marty Feldman

b. 8 July 1934
d. 2 December 1982

WITH his huge bug eyes, gangly limbs and a shock of uncontrollable, frizzy hair, Marty Feldman was a strange sight to behold. But it was perhaps because of his offbeat appearance, coupled with his outrageous comic talent, that he was such a success.

Although later lost to the cinema, many television viewers will remember him in such comedy classics as the 1967 satirical series *At Last the 1948 Show*, alongside John Cleese, Tim Brooke-Taylor and Graham Chapman, and for his own series, *Marty*.

Born to a poor Jewish family in Canning Town, East London, Marty played jazz in the city's clubs as a child, before becoming the trumpeter in a variety act called Maurice, Marty and Mitch. After doing the usual round of music-halls and clubs, he left the trio and teamed up as a scriptwriter with Barry Took, who was just another aspiring comedian at that time.

During their ten-year partnership, they wrote radio hits such as *Round the Horne* and TV shows that included *The Army Game* and *Bootsie and Snudge*.

After appearing in *At Last the 1948 Show* with stars who went on to form the Monty Python team and the Goodies, Marty really made a name in his own series, co-written with Barry Took and screened on BBC2.

Marty provided the actor with the ideal vehicle to reveal his talent to the nation. Relying heavily on visual humour, it was an instant success, and it was his strong visual sense that, a decade later, led him away from the small screen and into the cinema full-time.

Marty made his film debut with a small part in the 1969 black comedy *The Bed Sitting Room*, alongside Peter Cook, Dudley Moore and Spike Milligan. His next picture, *Every Home Should Have One*, failed miserably and it was not until he began appearing in Mel Brooks and Gene Wilder movies that his Hollywood career really took off.

Forming an instant rapport with Brooks, he starred in such pictures as *The Young Frankenstein*, a splendid spoof of the classic monster tale, and *Silent Movie*.

He subsequently directed two of his own films, *The Last Remake of Beau Geste* and *In God We Trust*.

In 1980, when his Tinseltown career seemed to be dwindling slightly, Marty seemed to go off the rails – he became involved in the drugs scene and made a suicide attempt.

At the time of his premature death from a heart attack in Mexico City, while filming the pirate comedy *Yellowbeard*, he had been considering a return to the small screen.

Marty was married to Lauretta Sullivan, and his sister, actress Fenella Fielding, is the star of many films and television programmes.

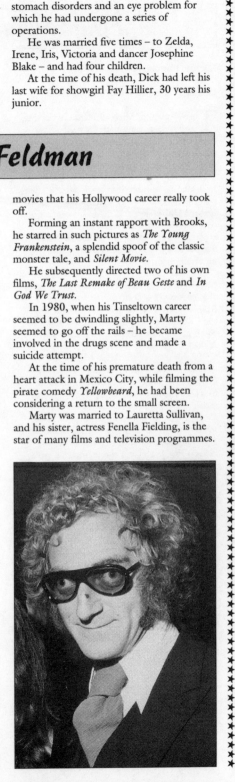

Flanders and Swann

Michael Flanders, b. 1 March 1922
d. 15 April 1975
Donald Swann, b. 30 September 1923

THE fusion of Michael Flanders's acting and lyric-writing with Donald Swann's composing skills created a dazzling double act that brought pleasure to television and theatre audiences throughout the world.

Michael, born in Hampstead, North London, his mother a professional musician, was educated at Westminster School and Oxford University, and made his professional debut at the Oxford Playhouse in 1941, appearing as Valentine in *You Can Never Tell*, as well as acting and directing many university productions.

He left Oxford to join the RNVR (Royal Naval Volunteer Reserve), serving first as an able-seaman in a destroyer on convoys to Russia and Malta, and later as an officer in the Coastal Forces. He contracted polio when his ship was torpedoed during the African landings of 1943.

Wishing to return to his studies, he was devastated when his application to rejoin Oxford University was declined and spent much of the next ten years performing in musical evenings at his parents' house.

In 1951, he began to carve out a niche for himself as a songwriter, penning music and lyrics for impresario Laurie Lister's revues. Five years later, he teamed up with Donald Swann, with whom he was to find fame and fortune on the British stage.

Donald, born in Llanelli, Dyfed, had also attended Westminster School, before going on to the Royal College of Music, where he studied Greek and Turkmenistan folk music. His talent lay in writing music and, teamed with Michael's ability as a lyricist, a brilliant partnership was born.

The pair decided to write a show together, using songs they had previously

written but nobody had wanted to sing. The completed show, *At the Drop of a Hat*, opened at a small fringe theatre in Kensington, West London, in 1956. It was so popular that it soon transferred to the Fortune Theatre, in the West End, where it ran for 759 shows before Flanders and Swann took it to Broadway.

For the first time, the public was able to hear the pair's delightful songs, such as *The Hippopotamus* and *The Honeysuckle and Bindweed*. Flanders's often acidic lyrics and Swann's tuneful melodies made them such a success – theatres swelled with throngs of fans determined to sample a taste of their infectious humour.

After a tour of Canada and America, the pair returned to Britain for a national tour of the show, until in 1963 its successor, *At the Drop of Another Hat*, was unveiled at the Globe Theatre, London.

During the late 60s, Michael wrote the libretto for a cantata for Joseph Horowitz, *Captain Noah and His Floating Zoo*. He was frequently seen on television conducting such musical works as *Peter and the Wolf* and *Façade*. He also narrated many documentaries, was heard on numerous radio shows and, as an actor, made several films, the most notable being *The Raging Moon*.

Michael, who was awarded an OBE in 1964, died from a cerebral haemorrhage while on holiday in Wales. He was married to American Claudia Davis, with whom he had two daughters.

Like Michael, when their touring days were coming to an end, Donald leaned more towards the small screen, where he made many appearances, including those in *Sunday Best*. He also displayed his exceptional talents on record and has composed a musical autobiography entitled *The Space Between Bars*. He and his wife, Janet, were divorced in 1983.

Cyril Fletcher

b. 25 June 1913

IT took Esther Rantzen and *That's Life!* to bring Cyril Fletcher and his 'Odd Odes' back to television – although the popular comedian from variety and radio days had been an early star of the small screen.

Born in Watford, Hertfordshire, where his

father was a solicitor and town clerk, Cyril began writing odes about his teachers, then his first boss.

Cyril began his working life as an insurance clerk but wanted to become a classical actor. Spotted reciting one of his odes by Greatrex Newman, he joined her *Fols de Rols* concert party in 1936 and made his debut at the White Rock Pavilion, Hastings, subsequently appearing in London, at the Holborn Empire.

In the same year, Cyril appeared on the BBC's new, regular television service from Alexandra Palace, acting in its first pantomime, *Dick Whittington*, and reciting his 'Odd Odes' in what was considered to be a perfect piece of presentation for the TV cameras because he managed to keep still.

He also landed his own radio show, *Dreaming of Thee*, and his many radio roles included schoolgirl 'Aggie' in the weekly series *Thanking Yew*.

Cyril loved appearing in pantomime, playing every role from Buttons in *Cinderella* to dames, and even branched out into films such as the wartime melodrama *Yellow Canary*, the Ealing Studios version of *Nicholas Nickleby*, and *A Piece of Cake*.

For many years after the Second World War, Cyril and his actress wife Betty Astell – another performer from the early days of television, whom he met during the recording of a *Henry Hall Guest Night* on radio – staged the seasonal show *Summer*

Masquerade in the theatre on Sandown Pier, on the Isle of Wight, which in 1949 was broadcast on BBC television for six consecutive weeks as the *Saturday Night Attraction*, with then 'unknown' Harry Secombe as Cyril's second comedian.

Cyril has performed in London West End revues and at the London Palladium, but it was in the classic television panel game *What's My Line?*, television's first religious series, *Sunday Story*, and, later, with his 'Odd Odes' revived in *That's Life!* – for eight years from 1972 – that he reached a wide audience.

Since his stint on *That's Life!*, he has indulged his love of gardening in front of the cameras, presenting *Gardening Time* for ATV and its successor Central Television in the Midlands ITV region for 14 years, and *Cyril Fletcher's Lifestyle Garden* on the now-defunct satellite channel Lifestyle, from 1990.

He also appeared in the chorus line of the 1980 Royal Variety Show, singing Flanagan and Allen's 'Strollin'' in front of the Queen Mother.

Cyril and his wife, Betty, live in Jersey and have one daughter, actress-comedienne Jill.

Harry Fowler

b. 10 December 1926

CHEERFUL cockney Harry Fowler has enjoyed a film career that stretches back to the early 40s and brought his chirpy manner to television in comedy series such as *The Army Game* and *Our Man at St Mark's*.

Born in Lambeth Walk, South London, Henry James Fowler was just two months old when his parents split up and he was brought up by his grandmother, who died in the Blitz, leaving Harry to fend for himself from the age of 13.

It was while working as a newspaper-seller that he was interviewed on the radio programme *In Town Tonight* at the age of 15. His potential for playing cockney roles was spotted and he made his debut in the 1942 film *Salute John Citizen*.

He showed great screen presence as leader of a gang of street kids in *Hue and Cry* and followed it with more than 80 films, including *The Pickwick Papers*, *Lucky Jim*, *Lawrence of Arabia*, *The Longest Day*, *Doctor in Clover*, *George and Mildred* – the big-screen version of the TV hit – and, more recently, *Chicago Joe and the Showgirl*.

On television, Harry first made his name as Corporal Flogger Hoskins in the 50s comedy series *The Army Game*, alongside Alfie Bass and Bill Fraser, taking over the role from Michael Medwin. He subsequently played the verger in the clerical comedy *Our Man at St Mark's*, joining it in its second series as a burglar of the church given a chance to reform by the programme's star, Donald Sinden.

Harry and Kenny Lynch later presented a children's series called *Going a Bundle*, a forerunner of *Record Breakers*, featuring the longest, tallest and fastest of everything and adding a bit of history not usually found in the facts-and-figures reference books. Another series in the same vein was *Get This*, which Harry presented with James Villiers.

He has since made guest appearances in *Minder*, *Scarecrow & Mrs King*, *Supergran*, *Davro's Sketch Pad*, *In Sickness and In Health*, *Big Deal*, *Casualty*, *All in Good Faith*, *The Bill* and *Love Hurts*.

Harry, who was made an MBE in 1970, has appeared in many TV commercials and has done voice-overs for dozens more. In 1951, he married actress Joan Dowling, who died three years later. He and his second wife, Catherine, live in Chelsea.

Raymond Francis

b. 6 October 1911
d. 24 October 1987

AS Detective Superintendent Tom Lockhart in the 60s, Raymond Francis became one of the most popular small-screen policemen of the day in the crime series *No Hiding Place*.

The London-born actor, who claimed that he had no education, learned acting the hard way – touring in repertory theatre – through which he emerged with an air of confidence and a controlled grasp of stage performance.

After six years in the Army, he returned to acting, appearing in plays such as *The Deep Blue Sea*, at The Duchess Theatre.

During the mid-50s, Raymond entered British films, taking character roles in such memorable pictures as *Reach for The Sky*, *Carve Her Name with Pride* and *Carrington VC*.

But it was in television that he really made his name, making his debut as Dr Watson in a BBC Sherlock Holmes series, in 1950, and appearing in small-screen plays such as *Laburnum Grove*, *The Devil's Disciple* and *The Deep Blue Sea*.

Raymond really found stardom as Detective Superintendent Lockhart, a character he played for ten years, first given an airing in *Murder Bag*, a 1957 half-hour ITV series that proved so popular it went on to spawn both *Crime Sheet* and the long-running *No Hiding Place*, each starring the snuff-loving detective.

The programme was broadcast live every week and Raymond's habit of hiding his lines in discreet nooks and crannies on the set often created a spot of potentially hilarious viewing.

No Hiding Place, which ran from 1959 to 1966, was a major triumph for him, but in a way he also became a victim of his own success, when he subsequently suffered typecasting for the rest of his career and, after the series finished, it was several years before he returned to television.

He later played Dr Fuller in *Together*, a short-lived daytime soap, and appeared in *Edward and Mrs Simpson*, *Thomas and Sarah*, *Play for Today*, *Agatha Christie's Miss Marple*, *Drummonds* and *Me & My Girl*, as well as playing Colonel Bosworth in the 1976 feature film *It Shouldn't Happen to a Vet*, the sequel to the big screen version of *All Creatures Great and Small*.

In 1982, Raymond returned to the role of detective as a spoof Lockhart character seen arresting baddie Ronald Allen in *Five Go Mad in Dorset*, the first *Comic Strip Presents . . .* film to be shown on Channel Four.

The actor, who died at the age of 76, was married to Margaret. The couple had two daughters, Caroline and Frances, and one son, Clive.

William Franklyn

b. 22 September 1926

DESPITE a television career that goes back to the earliest days of ITV, when he appeared in the channel's first play, William Franklyn is destined to be known as the actor in the "Schhh! You know who" commercials for Schweppes.

Born in Kensington, West London, he spent ten years in Australia, where his actor father, Leo Franklyn – who later appeared in Brian Rix's Whitehall farces – was working and travelled around in a Pullman car.

On returning to Britain, William appeared on stage in *My Sister Eileen*, at the age of 15, served with the paratroops during the Second World War and resumed his career in *Arsenic and Old Lace*, on Southsea Pier in 1946.

He worked in repertory theatre in Ryde and Margate, and made his London West End debut in *The Love of Four Colonels*, following it with shows such as *There's a Girl in My Soup*, *Death Trap*, *In Praise of Love*, *Dead Ringer* and *Touch of Danger*.

The first of his 20 films was an Ealing Studios political melodrama, *The Secret People*, in 1951. His other pictures include *Above Us the Waves*, *Quatermass II*, *Danger Within*, Morecambe and Wise's *The Intelligence Men* and *Ooh . . . You Are Awful*, starring Dick Emery.

William appeared in ITV's first play, *Mid-Level*, in 1955, and many of the commercial channel's early series, such as *Douglas Fairbanks Jr Presents*, *The Count of Monte Cristo*, *International Detective* and *Sir Lancelot*, before starring in the 1961 series *Top Secret*, as British agent Peter Dallas, teaming up with Argentine 'businessman' Patrick Cargill in Buenos Aires.

Subsequent TV appearances included those in *Public Eye*, *The Avengers*, *The Baron*, *Maigret*, *What's on Next?*, *The Steam Video*

Company and, more recently, *G.B.H.*, *Moon and Son* and *The Upper Hand*.

William also made 50 Schweppes commercials over nine years and chaired the TV quiz series *Masterspy*, as well as directing various stage plays, such as *Same Time, Next Year*, *Rope*, *That's No Lady* (retitled *The Bedwinner*) and the first Italian production of *There's a Girl in My Soup*.

William has an actress daughter, Sabina, from his first marriage to actress Margot Johns, which ended in divorce, and two more daughters – Francesca and Melissa – by his second wife, actress Susanna Carroll.

★★★★★★★★★★★★

Bill Fraser

b. 5 June 1908
d. 5 September 1987

AS Sergeant Major Claude Snudge in the popular series *The Army Game* and its sequel, *Bootsie and Snudge*, Bill Fraser was irrepressible and, with the catchphrase, "'Ave no fear, Snudge is 'ere," he became an instant star.

Born in Perth, Tayside, Bill started his working life as a bank clerk in his home town, before travelling to London in his 20s to try his luck as an actor.

In those early days, when work was scarce, necessity forced him to sleep on the city's Embankment, but his raw determination won through and the young Scot spent many hours learning to speak with an English accent.

In 1933, only two years after entering the world of theatre, he formed his own repertory company at the Connaught Theatre, Worthing, which ran until the outbreak of the Second World War, when he served in the RAF as a signals officer.

It was 1946 before he walked the boards again, in a revue at the Playhouse, followed by supporting roles in the West End.

During the mid-60s Bill performed at the Chichester Festival Theatre, in *The*

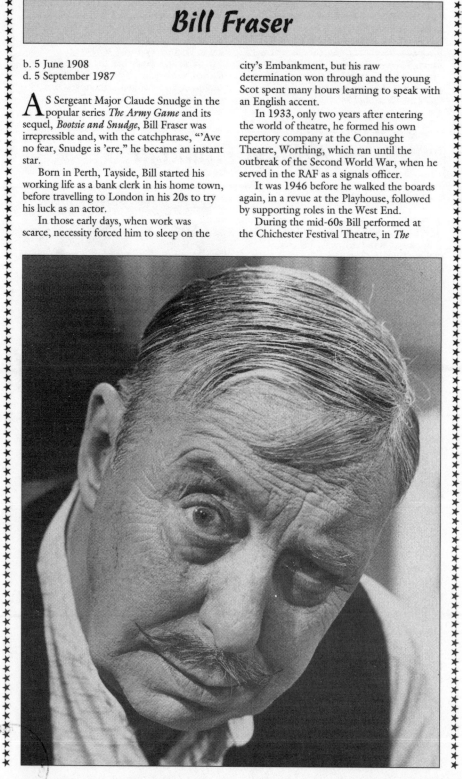

Clandestine Marriage and *The Cherry Orchard*, and roles followed at both the Royal Shakespeare Company, in Stratford-upon-Avon, and The National Theatre, in plays such as *Mrs Warren's Profession* and *The Good-Natured Man*.

He also appeared in several films, including *A Home of Your Own*, *Doctor at Large*, *Up Pompeii* and *Up the Chastity Belt*, *Wagner* and some of the *Carry On* sagas.

But it was on the small screen that Bill will be best remembered, for his role as Sergeant Major Snudge, alongside Alfie Bass's Private 'Excused Boots' Bisley, in *The Army Game*, which started in 1957 and ran for three years.

Based in Hut 29 of Nether Hopping Army Camp, the series was very much in the style of the *Carry On* films, revelling in the calamitous antics with the most unruly bunch of soldiers anyone is ever likely to see.

Such a hit was the programme that there was a 1958 film version, *I Only Arsked!*, and a TV sequel, *Bootsie and Snudge*, in 1960, with the two favourite characters marched into their own series and seen fending for themselves back in civvy street.

The actor's many other television roles included Judge Bullimore in *Rumpole of the Bailey* and Mr Micawber in the BBC's production of *David Copperfield*, as well as appearances in *The Comedians* and the serial *Flesh and Blood*.

Bill, who died at the age of 79, was married to actress Pamela Cundell, by whom he had a stepdaughter.

Sandy Gall

b. 1 October 1927

FOR 20 years, Sandy Gall saw more frontline action than any of his contemporary British newscasters, returning to the action that he had seen as a foreign correspondent in Vietnam and other war zones.

Born Henderson Alexander Gall in Penang, Malaya, where his Scottish father was a rubber planter, he went to school in Scotland, served as a corporal in the RAF after the Second World War and gained an MA at Aberdeen University.

Starting his career on the Aberdeen *Press and Journal*, Sandy became a trainee with the news agency Reuters in 1953 and subsequently worked as a correspondent in Berlin, Nairobi, Geneva and Johannesburg, and covered Budapest after the Hungarian revolution and the Congo wars of 1960–63.

In 1963, he joined ITN and continued as a foreign correspondent, reporting from the world's major trouble spots – from Cyprus to the Middle East, China to Pakistan.

But his most daring assignments were in dictator Idi Amin's Uganda, where he was arrested and jailed in 1972, and in Vietnam, on and off for ten years, courageously staying on at the end of the war to see North Vietnamese troops capture Saigon after the American evacuation.

Sandy had become a regular *News at Ten* presenter in 1970 but continued to cover hostilities around the globe, taking several trips to Afghanistan after the Russian invasion.

He also made seven TV documentaries while with ITN, including three on

Afghanistan – *Behind Russian Lines*, *Allah Against the Gunships* and *Agony of a Nation*.

He drew on his experiences in a Ugandan jail to write his first novel, *Gold Scoop*, published in 1977. He has since written seven books: *Chasing the Dragon*, his memoirs *Don't Worry About the Money Now*, *Behind Russian Lines*, *An Afghan Journal*, *Afghanistan: Agony of a Nation*, *Salang* and *George Adamson: Lord of the Lions*.

Made a CBE in 1988, Sandy retired from ITN four years later. He and his wife, Eleanor, have one son, Alexander, and three daughters, Fiona, Carlotta and Michaela.

Dustin Gee

b. 1942
d. 3 January 1986

IT WAS as a member of the hugely successful television comedy show *Russ Abbot's Madhouse* that Dustin Gee first found fame and fortune. He and stage partner Les Dennis had the ability to make audiences fall around the aisles as they decked themselves out in wigs and flowery frocks to become, most famously, *Coronation Street's* Vera and Mavis.

Born Gerald Harrison in York, but brought up in Manchester, Dustin studied at art college, before taking a job as an artist working with stained glass and playing in a rock band in the evenings.

The group worked as Gerry B and the Hornets, before changing their name to Gerry B and the Rockafellas. When they split

up, he became a compere, then comedian, but it took 20 years in showbusiness before he reached the pinnacle of his career, with Les.

The successful comedy duo first met in 1975, when they both appeared on the impressionists' show *Who Do You Do?*

From then on, it seemed that there was no stopping them. They created an original and funny repertoire of acts, impersonating stars such as Robert Mitchum, Mick Jagger and Boy George.

After *Russ Abbot's Madhouse*, which was without doubt their launchpad to the top, they went on to their own programmes, *Go for It* and *The Laughter Show*.

The pair were even appearing together at the time of Dustin's tragic death when he collapsed with a heart attack, while appearing in the pantomime *Cinderella*. He was 43.

Ann George

b. 5 March 1903
d. 8 September 1989

AS bossy Brummie Amy Turtle in *Crossroads*, Ann George helped to give the ITV serial a character that was lampooned by critics but later paid homage to by Victoria Wood in her 'Acorn Antiques' sketches. Ann – who frequently forgot her lines – represented the golden days of *Crossroads*, laughed at by the critics, but lapped up by millions of viewers.

Born in Smethwick, Birmingham, she entered showbusiness as a singer, appearing on stage in the musicals *The Belle of New York* and *The Desert Song*, and in D'Oyly Carte Gilbert and Sullivan productions.

She also sang as a soloist in Handel's *Messiah*, at Birmingham Town Hall, and had her own cabaret act, singing and telling jokes.

Ann, who took her first husband George Snape's forename as her stage name, worked by day as a secretary with a firm of Birmingham architects after his death.

She joined *Crossroads* as absent-minded Amy Turtle in 1965, only a few months after it began, having written to producers ATV complaining that none of the cast spoke in a true Birmingham accent.

After appearing as a customer in the shop owned by Meg Richardson's sister, Kitty Jarvis, Amy worked in the shop until Kitty's

death, then became the Motel's cleaner.

In 1976, Ann married her second husband, Gordon Buckingham, a fan of the serial who wooed her with letters for nearly a

year. Danny La Rue gave her away at the wedding ceremony and Peter Brookes – who played postman Vince Parker in the serial – was best man.

In the same year, Ann was axed from *Crossroads*, with the character of Amy despatched to Texas to visit a nephew.

She continued working in clubs and acting in pantomimes, then returned to her famous TV role 11 years later, written into the script as a friend of the Motel's last manager, Tommy Lancaster, and his wife.

For many years, she revelled in the trappings of stardom, wearing fur coats and renting a suite at the Holiday Inn, Birmingham.

After a long fight against cancer, Ann died in 1989, at the age of 86, leaving widower Gordon Buckingham and a son, George Jr, by her first marriage. The Noele Gordon and Crossroads Appreciation Society recalled her as the Queen Mum of the serial.

Peter Gilmore

b. 25 August 1931

AS Captain James Onedin of the *Charlotte Rhodes* schooner, Peter Gilmore became a TV heart-throb of the 70s but then almost completely disappeared from the public eye.

Born in Leipzig, Germany, he came to Britain at the age of six and was brought up by relatives in Nunthorpe, North Yorkshire. Leaving school at 14, he went to London and worked in a factory.

Intent on acting as a career, Peter attended RADA but was thrown out and went off to do his National Service in the Army. Afterwards, finding he had a good singing voice, he joined the George Mitchell Singers, then became a stooge to stars such as Frank Sinatra and Danny Kaye.

His stage appearances include *Grab Me a Gondola*, *Valmouth*, *Love Doctor*, *Follow That Girl* and *Lock Up Your Daughters*. Although he made a dozen appearances in London West End musicals, they were all flops.

Intent on acting, Peter gave up singing and started by making TV commercials in Germany, Ireland and America.

Eventually, he appeared in films such as *The Dress Factory*, *Doctor in Clover* and nine *Carry On* films – including *Cabby*, *Follow That Camel*, *Don't Lose Your Head* and *Henry*, in which he played the King of France.

He was also on television as MacHeath in *The Beggars Opera* and in *Hugh and I* – starring Terry Scott and Hugh Lloyd – and *The Doctors*, before finding fame as the star of *The Onedin Line*, complete with long, bushy sideburns.

The series, which began in 1971, followed the fortunes of Captain James Onedin as he tried to strike a balance between ruthlessly running a shipping line and keeping his two wives happy. It was one of BBC1's most popular period dramas, running for nine years.

In 1978, during the programme's run, the actor released a record album, *Peter Gilmore Sings Gently*. Peter subsequently starred on television in *A Man Called Intrepid* and played safari park boss Ben Bishop in the zoo series *One By One*.

His two marriages, to actresses Una Stubbs – with whom he adopted a son, Jason – and Jan Waters, both ended in divorce.

★★★★★★★★★★★★

Noele Gordon

b. 25 December 1923
d. 14 April 1985

KNOWN as the Queen of the Soaps in the 60s and 70s, Noele Gordon became a national institution as Meg Richardson in *Crossroads* – and no one was more shocked than the actress herself when she was axed from the serial after 17 years.

Born on Christmas Day 1923 in East Ham, London, the daughter of a merchant navy engineer who earned just £11 a month, Noel – as she was christened – started dancing lessons at the age of two with 'Madame Maud' Wells and made her first public appearance at the East Ham Palace.

Shortly afterwards, she showed another side to her flourishing talents, singing *Dear Little Jammy Face* at the Holborn Restaurant, in London. Noele's mother, Johanna ('Jockie'), and her Aunt Bunty were keen for her to have a stage career, but the dancing lessons stopped when the family moved to Westcliff-on-Sea, in Essex.

The acting bug hit Noele again when they moved to Ilford, nearer London, and she attended a convent school that frequently performed plays.

After training at RADA, she joined the Brandon Thomas Players, in Edinburgh, and later performed in rep at the Theatre Royal, Birmingham.

Shortly before that, in 1938 – two years after the BBC launched its regular television service – Noele had made her small-screen debut as Norah, the Irish maid, in Eugene O'Neill's *Ah Wilderness!*

Television pioneer John Logie Baird then chose her to take part in his first colour experiment, transmitted from Crystal Palace shortly before the Second World War.

After a huge Union Jack was shown, Noele was seen sitting on a chair trying on an array of different-coloured hats.

Back on the stage, she toured in *Black Velvet* during 1940 – replete with a Norman Hartnell dark-red satin dress – and made her London West End debut in *Let's Face It*, at the Hippodrome a year later.

Noele's appearance in *The Lisbon Story*, at the same theatre, led to her first film role, in a big-screen version of the musical, in 1945. She also starred on stage in *Diamond Lil*, with Mae West.

Four years later, while beginning an acclaimed two-year, 1000-performance stage run as the village whore in *Brigadoon*, Noele was invited to appear in the Royal Variety Performance, doing a medley of Harry Lauder songs, which she dedicated to him at the time he was dying.

While touring in a stage production of *Call Me Madam* in the 50s, she realised the increasing popularity of television and went to New York University to study the medium in America. On returning to Britain in 1955, she joined ATV – the newly formed ITV company for the Midlands – as an adviser on women's programmes.

Noele was soon appearing on screen as a presenter, first in an advertising magazine called *Fancy That*. Her other programmes included *Week-End*, *Tea with Noele Gordon*, *Midland Profile*, *Midland Sports*, *Noele Gordon Takes the Air*, *Hi-T!* and, most notably, the chat-show *Lunch Box*, which began in 1957.

She became the first woman to interview a Prime Minister on television when Harold Macmillan agreed to appear on *Lunch Box*. It was the time of a General Election, but they discussed haggis and black pudding.

When ATV boss Lew (now Lord) Grade wanted to broadcast a daily serial like those in America, he asked *Lunch Box* producer Reg Watson to come up with an idea. The result was *Crossroads*, which started in November 1964 and featured Noele as motel owner Meg Richardson.

She stayed with the role for 17 years and 3521 performances – winning the *TVTimes* readers' award for Favourite Female Personality on TV eight times – until being sensationally sacked when Central Television, which took over the ITV Midlands franchise from ATV, tried to revamp the soap, which had been under fire from the critics ever since it began, despite winning up to 16 million viewers.

In the storyline, the Motel was razed in a fire, but Meg escaped and was seen leaving on the *QEII* from Southampton, to make a new life for herself in America.

Noele, who was once the subject of *This Is Your Life*, reappeared in the role briefly two years later, when screen daughter Jill married Adam Chance. She met them in Venice while they were honeymooning there.

In the meantime, she had carved out a new stage career for herself, starring in *Gypsy* at the Haymarket, Leicester, in 1981, a Middle and Far East tour of *The Boy Friend*, a London West End production of *Call Me Madam* and a tour of the 20s musical *No No Nanette*.

Noele, who died from stomach cancer in 1985, was due to make another brief return to *Crossroads*, but Edward Clayton – who

played her son-in-law, Stan Harvey – stepped in to discuss the sale of Motel shares instead.

Never married, although jilted at the age of 18, Noele had a 20-year relationship with showbusiness impresario Val Parnell and a brief but close friendship with Birmingham fish merchant Tony Walters, who tried to launch a singing career on the TV talent show *New Faces*. Her autobiography, *My Life at Crossroads*, was published in 1975.

Marius Goring

b. 23 May 1912

AFTER making his name as that master of disguise the Scarlet Pimpernel in the 50s, veteran actor Marius Goring – famed for his Continental roles in films – returned to TV screens a decade later as a pathologist in *The Expert*.

Born in Newport, on the Isle of Wight, the doctor's son was educated at universities in Frankfurt, Munich, Vienna and Paris, acquiring the accents and mannerisms that have won him so many roles as foreigners during his career.

Marius started acting at the Old Vic Dramatic School and later performed with the company in classical productions, making his London stage debut in 1927. Four years later, he toured France and Germany with the English Classical Players and he made his first London West End appearance as Hugh Voysey in *The Voysey Inheritance*, at the Shaftesbury Theatre, in 1934.

A year later, he took the title role in *Hamlet* at the Old Vic, then utilised his linguistic skills to tour France, Belgium and Holland with the Compagnie de Quinze, performing in French. He also starred in a play in Berlin, opposite Lucie Mannheim, whom he subsequently married.

During the Second World War, Marius joined the army and served in intelligence, before being seconded to the BBC as supervisor of productions in the Propaganda Broadcasting Service to Germany.

The actor played Hitler in BBC radio's first war programme, *The Shadow of the Swastika*, in 1939, and also broadcast to Germany under the name of Charles Richardson.

Marius had made his film debut in *The Amateur Gentleman*, in 1935, and appeared regularly on the big screen – even during the War, when one of his films was a short called *The True Story of Lilli Marlene*.

After the War, he starred with Anton Walbrook in the celebrated fairytale *The Red Shoes* and followed it with pictures such as

The Magic Box, The Adventures of Quentin Durward, The Barefoot Contessa, I Was Monty's Double and the Marianne Faithfull 60s film *Girl on a Motorcycle*.

Marius had already appeared on television before the War, making his debut in Chekhov's *The Bear*, in 1938. Later, he became the master of disguise in the 1955 series *The Adventures of the Scarlet Pimpernel* and starred as police pathologist Dr John Hardy, a forensic scientist, in *The Expert*, running for three years from 1968 and returning for another series in 1976.

He also made guest appearances in programmes such as *Man in a Suitcase, Wilde Alliance* and *Edward and Mrs Simpson*, and he, Andrew Cruickshank, Roland Culver and Robert Morley were acclaimed for their performances in the satirical serial *The Old Men at the Zoo*, in 1983.

More recently, his stage appearances have included *The Mystery Plays*, in Canterbury Cathedral, and *Beyond Reasonable Doubt*, at the Queen's Theatre, London.

Marius, made a CBE in 1991, has been married three times. His first marriage, to Mary Westwood Steel – by whom he has a daughter, Phyllida – ended in divorce and he subsequently wed German-born actress Lucie Mannheim, in 1936, the couple later appearing together in the films *So Little Time* and *Beyond the Curtain*. The actress died in 1976 and, a year later, he married Prudence FitzGerald.

Larry Grayson

b. 31 August 1923

FORMER drag artist Larry Grayson brought high camp to television in the 70s with his "Shut that door!" catchphrase and references to characters such as Everard, Slack Alice and Apricot Lil.

Born William White out of wedlock, his mother Ethel travelled to Banbury, Oxfordshire, for the birth because she was so scared of her family's reaction in Nuneaton, across the border in Warwickshire.

He grew up back there with foster parent friends of his mother, who as 'Aunt' Ethel was a regular visitor, but he never met his father, William Sully.

At the age of 14, Larry took to the stage as female impersonator Billy Breen and for 30 years worked in pubs, clubs, works canteens and in summer seasons. He once toured with Harry Leslie and his Tomorrow's Stars, but could only keep wishing that his own tomorrow would finally come.

Larry added stand-up comedy to his act and appeared in London at the Metropolitan and the Finsbury Park and Chiswick Empires during the last days of variety.

By the 60s, he accepted that his tomorrow would probably *never* come and returned to the Midlands, getting work around his native Nuneaton.

In 1969, theatrical agent Peter Dulay – who later became known to TV viewers as a presenter of *Candid Camera* – persuaded Larry to do a week's performances at the Theatre Royal, Stratford East, in London.

His music-hall patter went down so well that the show ran for seven weeks and impresario Paul Raymond cast him in his all-male revue *Birds of a Feather*, which opened at the Royalty Theatre the following year.

'England's Comedy Sensation', as Larry was billed in the show, won acclaim and was booked for a summer season in Brighton, variety at the London Palladium, a *Goldilocks and the Three Bears* pantomime with Dora Bryan in Brighton and a cabaret season at Danny La Rue's London club.

In 1972, his limp-wristed act proved a hit during his television debut in the ATV show *Saturday Variety* and he was given his own, 16-part series, *Shut That Door!*

He was the Variety Club of Great Britain's Showbusiness Personality of the Year in 1973 and, in the same year, performed in front of the Queen at the Royal Variety Gala, in aid of the Olympics Fund, at the London Palladium.

Larry did two summer seasons of *Grayson's Scandals*, in Margate and Blackpool, before taking the show to the London Palladium.

In 1974, he starred in a TV special, *Larry Grayson's Hour of Stars*, and the following year chauffeured Noele Gordon and John Bentley in his white Rolls-Royce for the TV wedding of Meg and Hugh Mortimer in *Crossroads*. He had previously appeared in the serial two years earlier, as a guest at the famous television motel.

When Bruce Forsyth left the BBC in 1978, Larry Grayson took over as host of *The Generation Game*, forming a screen partnership with Isla St Clair and taking the programme to new heights of popularity.

Unfortunately, his next game show, *Sweethearts* – which revolved around whether couples were telling the truth about their romances – was a flop and proved to be Larry's last series.

Hughie Green

b. 2 February 1920

TALENT-spotter Hughie Green gave dozens of showbusiness hopefuls their first step on the ladder to stardom in his show *Opportunity Knocks!* "And I mean it most sincerely," he would intone as he wished them luck.

London-born of a Scottish father and an Irish mother, Hughie was brought up in Canada and remains a citizen of that country. Back in Britain, he was discovered at the age of 14 by child talent-spotter Bryan Michie, who gave him his own BBC radio show with a concert party in tow, *Hughie Green and His Gang*, which he wrote and produced. He and the youngsters also toured music-halls.

Hughie immediately made his film debut in *Midshipman Easy*, in 1935, and followed it with *Little Friend*, before moving to Hollywood to appear in *Tom Brown's Schooldays* and to perform his cabaret act with the Benny Goodman Orchestera at the famous Coconut Grove Restaurant.

Serving in the Royal Canadian Air Force during the War, Hughie was first an instructor, then pilot of a Catalina flying boat over the North Atlantic. Posted to RAF Ferry Command, he became one of the first four pilots to command a Russian-crewed Catalina from America to Russia.

When peace came, he returned to showbusiness, presenting *The Hughie Green Show* on radio in Canada, performing on the Broadway stage and making the Hollywood film *If Winter Comes* – alongside Walter Pidgeon, Deborah Kerr and Janet Leigh – and a Lassie picture, *Hills of Home*, with Edmund Gwenn.

After facing £14 000 legal costs following an unsuccessful action against the BBC, he was declared bankrupt and worked as a Hollywood stunt pilot and ferrier of transport aircraft across the Atlantic to gain his discharge.

Hughie ferried Europe's first post-War passenger planes for Belgium Airlines and Air France. His business activities flourished as, in the mid-50s, he negotiated for the French Air Force a deal for seven A26 Attack Bombers from California and sold the Grumman Gulfstream Executive Turbo Prop to Agneli of Fiat. By royal command, he also flew the Duke and Duchess of Kent on their honeymoon.

By then, his talent show *Opportunity Knocks!* had already been born on BBC radio. It started in 1949, switched to commercial television seven years later and ran for 21 years, launching acts such as Les Dawson, Mary Hopkin, Freddie Starr, Frank Carson and Little and Large.

Hughie's other big TV success, the quiz show *Double Your Money*, began on Radio Luxembourg and moved to ITV when the commercial channel opened, in 1955.

The series ran for 13 years but was dropped when companies changed in the franchise reshuffle of 1968.

A subsequent ITV quiz, *The Sky's the Limit*, in 1972, failed to make the same impact, and his other TV appearances include being one of the first comperes of *Sunday Night at the London Palladium*.

In the late 70s, Hughie formed London Independent Television in a bid to win an ITV franchise, but failed. His famous talent show was revived by Bob Monkhouse in 1987, under the title *Bob Says Opportunity Knocks!*

Hughie, who is divorced from his childhood sweetheart Claire, has a daughter, Linda, and a son, Christopher, and lives in central London.

Lorne Greene

b. 12 February 1915
d. 11 September 1987

THE role of patriarch Ben Cartwright, a widower bringing up his three sons in the Western series *Bonanza*, made silver-haired Lorne Greene a worldwide star – and a fortune.

Born in Ottawa, Canada, Lorne planned a career as a chemical engineer but began broadcasting on radio while studying at Queen's University, in Kingston, Ontario. On leaving, he was soon the Canadian Broadcasting Corporation's chief newscaster and became known as 'The Voice of Canada'.

After serving with the Canadian Air Force in the Second World War, he returned to radio, before moving to New York in the early 50s to train as an actor. He appeared in TV productions and on the Broadway stage with Katharine Cornell in *Prescott Proposals*.

Moving back to Toronto, Lorne co-founded the Jupiter Theatre and the Academy of Radio Arts, but it was in the USA that he made his film debut, in *The Silver Chalice*, in 1954, and followed it with appearances in pictures such as *Autumn Leaves*, *Peyton Place* and *The Buccaneer*.

The role that was to change Lorne's career was in television. After starring in the British series *Sailor of Fortune* with Rupert Davies (who was later to play the title role in *Maigret*) and making guest appearances in *Alfred Hitchcock Presents*, *Cheyenne* and *Wagon Train*, Lorne was cast as Ben Cartwright in *Bonanza*, the first colour Western series on TV, which blended soap opera with melodrama and comedy.

Ben presided over the Ponderosa Ranch in Nevada and was the father of three sons, each by different wives who had left him widowed.

The saga began in America in 1959 and on British TV a year later. It ran until 1972, had 400 million viewers in 80 countries and was the most popular programme in America from 1964 to 1967.

Bonanza also brought Lorne and his co-stars riches, with earnings of £7500 per episode, plus royalties from repeat screenings and large fees for personal appearances at rodeos and various conventions.

Lorne's standing, combined with his rich, deep voice, made him much in demand. He was master of ceremonies at a Royal Command Performance given for the Queen during a trip to Canada, and presided over a televised national tribute to President John F Kennedy after his assassination. Lorne also topped the bill at the London Palladium in 1966 and was narrator and executive producer of his own documentary series, *Lorne Greene's Wilderness*.

Bonanza continued for one series after the death of Lorne's co-star Dan Blocker but finished shortly after he himself suffered a mild heart attack.

Lorne subsequently appeared in the films *Earthquake* and *Tidal Wave*, and found another starring role on TV in *Battlestar Galactica*, as Commander Adama in a spaceship taking survivors of a doomed planet on a journey to find a new home, although the series was short-lived. His other TV appearances included *The Trial of Lee Harvey Oswald*, the epic saga *Roots* and the *Empire Inc* series. He was reunited with *Bonanza* co-star Michael Landon in an episode of the younger actor's *Highway to Heaven* series.

In later years, the wealthy actor did TV commercials for Alpo dog food and medical insurance plans, and invested much of his money in real estate and a stable of thoroughbred racehorses.

He had two children from his first marriage and one by his second wife Nancy, and died at the age of 72, after developing pneumonia in the wake of an operation for a perforated ulcer. At the time, he was due to re-create the role of Ben Cartwright in a TV movie, *Bonanza: The Next Generation*, which was never made.

Richard Greene

b. 25 August 1918
d. 1 June 1985

AS television's definitive Robin Hood, Richard Greene won the hearts of the nation. An elegant and versatile actor, he was also popular as the chisel-jawed hero in many films in Britain and Hollywood.

Born in Plymouth, Richard was a descendent of British film pioneer William Friese-Greene, so it seemed inevitable that he would turn to the stage. He learned his trade in repertory theatre with the Brandon Thomas Company, in Scotland.

He made his screen debut in the 1934 Gracie Fields film *Sing As We Go*, although his brief appearance was not included in the final, edited version. Consolation came while touring in the stage play *French Without Tears*, when at the age of 20 he was spotted by a talent scout and whisked off to Hollywood, where he appeared in director John Ford's *Four Men and a Prayer*, in 1938.

As a result, Richard was offered a studio contract by Twentieth Century Fox, which saw him as its rival to MGM's leading man, Robert Taylor. There followed a string of successes, such as *The Hound of the Baskervilles* and *Stanley and Livingstone*, in which he supported Spencer Tracy and Cedric Hardwicke.

However, Richard's career in Tinseltown suffered a slight hiccough when he was called back to Britain at the outbreak of the Second World War. He served in the Forces for a time, until he was invalided out and made his London stage debut in *The Desert Rats*.

Returning to Hollywood a year later, he found himself regarded more for his handsome looks than for the quality of his acting, playing mediocre romantic and swashbuckling roles in films such as *Forever Amber* and *Lorna Doone*.

By the mid-50s, after making more than 30 films, Richard found the offers dwindling and his attempt to stage a play intended for London's West End failed miserably.

Desperation set in and in, 1955, the actor even modelled for a haircream commercial on the newly launched ITV channel.

In the same year, one of England's folklore heroes came to the rescue in the form of a new half-hour series, *The Adventures of Robin Hood*, British television's first costume series made on film.

Richard seemed perfect for the part and the action-packed stories, where good always triumphed over evil, were an instant success, in Britain and America. The 143 episodes, shown over four years, made him a family favourite and were repeated and enjoyed by a new generation in the 60s. He also made a spin-off film, *Sword of Sherwood Forest*.

This single character made Richard a fortune, enabling him to go into semi-retirement and buy a 370-acre farm in County Wexford, Ireland, where he bred horses to such a standard that within three years he had reached eighth place in the list of top breeders.

After making occasional appearances in television programmes such as *The Doctors* and the ITV play *A Lovable Man*, Richard suffered a brain tumour in 1982 and died three years later. He wed actress Patricia Medina in 1941. They were divorced ten years later and, in 1960, he married Beatrice Summers.

John Gregson

b. 15 March 1919
d. 8 January 1975

HOME-grown film star John Gregson found small-screen fame as top cop Commander George Gideon in the popular police series *Gideon's Way* after more than a decade in films.

Born in Liverpool of Irish descent, John began acting in amateur productions, before training as a professional at the Liverpool Old Vic and Perth Repertory Company.

Turning to films in 1948, he made his debut in *Saraband for Dead Lovers*, a tear-jerking romance starring Joan Greenwood and Stewart Granger. He went on to make 40 films, including *Scott of the Antarctic*, *The Lavender Hill Mob*, *The Titfield Thunderbolt* and, perhaps most famous of all, *Genevieve*. This 1953 comedy saw John starring alongside Kenneth More, Kay Kendall and Dinah Sheridan, and dashing around in a London-to-Brighton vintage car race.

John appeared to specialise in shy, handsome, soulful heroes filled with inner turmoil, but at the drop of a hat he could turn his hand to most roles and, during the 50s, his popularity was at its peak.

However, when the tide turned in the film industry and audiences demanded a new realism, he found his career beginning to fade, so turned to television, where he rediscovered an enormous following when he starred in the police series *Gideon's Way*, based on the John Creasy novels and beginning in 1965. The actor also appeared alongside Shirley MacLaine in her television series *Shirley's World*, in 1971.

John, who died from a heart attack at the age of 55 while on holiday in Somerset, had been married for 30 years to actress Thea Gregory, with whom he had six children.

The family lived in an 18th-century mansion in Shepperton, Middlesex.

Deryck Guyler

b. 29 April 1914

AS a regular in Eric Sykes's long-running TV show and the caretaker in the chaotic classroom comedy *Please Sir!*, Deryck Guyler was one of those character actors who provided the backbone of comedy series.

Born in Wallasey, Cheshire, shortly before the First World War, Deryck began acting professionally with Liverpool Rep and later found fame as Frisby Dyke in Tommy Handley's Second World War radio series *ITMA* (*It's That Man Again*), the first time a Liverpool accent had been used by an actor on the air.

He took part in a Royal Command Performance of *ITMA* for King George VI and Queen Elizabeth in December 1947. His other radio shows included *Just Fancy* and *Men from the Ministry*.

It was radio comedian and writer Eric Sykes's move into television that first brought Deryck recognition on the small screen, as friendly neighbourhood policeman Corky in the series *Sykes*, which ran for 20 years from 1960. He joined the show after Richard Wattis, who played a neighbour, left the series.

In 1970, he was also a regular as old Desert Rat Norman Potter, grumpy caretaker of Fenn Street Secondary Modern School, in *Please Sir!*, trying to tumble the horrendous pupils' latest schemes in the face of ineffectual teachers.

His subsequent TV appearances include those in *Three Live Wires*, *That's My Boy!* – the comedy series starring Mollie Sugden and Christopher Blake – and *Best of Enemies*. He was also in the film *Carry On Doctor*, as a doddery surgeon.

Deryck, a devotee of washboard playing since his schooldays, who has a collection of thousands of toy soldiers, is married to former singer Paddy Lennox – from the three-sister music-hall act The Lennox Three – and they have two sons, Peter and Christopher. Now retired, he lives in London.

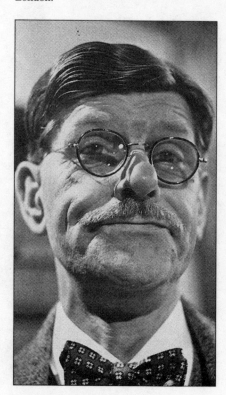

Fred Gwynne

b. 10 July 1926

POLICE officer Muldoon and Herman Munster were two of the great characters in American situation-comedies of the 60s, and Fred Gwynne was the 6ft 5in star who made them both larger-than-life.

Born in New York City, he spent his childhood in South Carolina, Florida and Colorado because his father travelled extensively. Leaving high school in 1944, he joined the US Navy as a radioman third class on a sub-chaser in the Pacific.

Fred then spent a year at art school, before studying English literature at Harvard University, where he became involved with the Brattle Theater, a professional repertory company founded by ex-GI graduates.

As a writer and illustrator since his teenage years, he had contributed stories and cartoons to *The Harvard Advocate*, which helped him to land a copywriting job with the giant J Walter Thompson advertising agency. This gave him the financial stability he needed to act in his spare time.

He starred in *The Winter's Tale* at the Stratford, Connecticut, Shakespeare Festival and in *Who Was That Lady I Saw You With?*, opposite Betty White, in Detroit.

But it was Fred's successful portrayal of Bottom in *A Midsummer Night's Dream* that gave him the confidence to move to New York, first landing the part of the Stinker in the Mary Chase fantasy *Mrs McThing* off-Broadway, alongside Helen Hayes, then playing the French gangster Poloyte-Le-Mou in the hit Broadway musical *Irma La Douce*, which made him a star.

In the middle of its successful run, Fred was cast as Officer Francis Muldoon in the comedy series *Car 54, Where Are You?*, which began in 1961. His comic talents, already recognised, had been used in *The Phil Silvers Show*, and now he had his own situation-comedy, with Joe E Ross co-starring as Officer Gunther Toody.

After the programme's two-year run, Fred was cast as Herman Munster in *The Munsters*, the character who resembled Frankenstein's monster, with a bolt through his neck. The series proved to be an even bigger success, running for two years and 70 episodes. He also appeared in the film spin-off *Munster Go Home!* and the 1981 TV movie *The Munsters' Revenge*.

He moved back to the East Coast of America after the series finished and joined a repertory company in Stratford, Connecticut, before more success on Broadway, appearing as Big Daddy in Tennessee Williams's *Cat on a Hot Tin Roof*, starring in the thriller *Whodunnit* and winning an Obie award for his performance in *Grand Magic*.

Having earlier appeared in films such as *On the Waterfront*, *Luna* and *Simon*, Fred returned to the cinema in 1984, as Frenchy in *The Cotton Club*, and followed it with roles in *The Boy Who Could Fly*, *Ironweed* and *Fatal Attraction*. His other TV appearances include *The Lesson* – for which he won an Emmy award – and the mini-series *Kane and Abel*.

Fred, who has written or illustrated a dozen children's books – including *The Battle of the Frogs and Mice*, *A Little Pigeon Toad*, *The King Who Rained*, *A Chocolate Moose for Dinner* and *Sixteen Hand Horse* – has two children, Kerion and Gaynor, with his wife, Jean.

Jack Haig

b. 1913
d. 4 July 1989

A talented character actor, Jack Haig was truly memorable as the bungling French Resistance worker Le Clerc in BBC television's popular comedy series *'Allo 'Allo*. A member of the cast since the programme began in 1984, he appeared in every episode and attracted a large fan-following over the following five years.

Born John Coppin in Streatham, South London, he was in showbusiness for most of his life, starting as a comedian in touring revues, musicals and pantomimes. The transition into the world of entertainment was an easy one for the young performer because the smell of grease paint was in the family – his mother and father had their own comedy act, in which they enacted a hilarious cross-talk sketch in variety theatre.

In the late 50s, Jack appeared on Tyne Tees Television, ITV's company in the North East, as the popular children's character Wacky Jacky, which he also played in *Crackerjack!* It was through the original Tyne Tees series that he later found himself in *'Allo 'Allo* – the prop man on the show, David Croft, went on to write and produce the spoof Resistance farce. Remembering Jack's wonderful comic ability, he cast him as Le Clerc.

But the actor's longest-running role on the small screen had been that of motel gardener Archie Gibbs in *Crossroads*, for 15 years. He also appeared in many supporting roles, in programmes such as *All Creatures Great and Small*.

Jack's London West End theatre roles included Sir January in *Canterbury Tales* and he performed in the stage version of *'Allo 'Allo* at The Prince of Wales Theatre and the London Palladium, and in a 1988 New Zealand tour.

During his career, he also had minor parts in a handful of films, including *Oliver!* and *Superman*.

In 1989, after becoming too ill to work, Jack died of cancer. His wife was revue actress Sybil Dunn, who had died the previous year, just two days before their golden wedding anniversary. The couple, who had often shared the bill during their early days in entertainment, left a daughter.

Tony Hancock

b. 12 May 1924
d. 25 June 1968

TO the public, Tony Hancock was a comic of great genius, but away from the spotlight he was very much the tragic clown. Hailed as the greatest comedian of the time for his radio and television show *Hancock's Half Hour*, and named Comedian of the Year in 1957 and 1959, he seemed to have it made, but his bouts of depression and heavy drinking ended with his own suicide in Australia, where he was trying to make a TV comeback.

Anthony John Hancock, born in Small Heath, Birmingham, moved to Bournemouth at the age of three when his father became a publican and part-time entertainer there. Attending boarding school, then public school, he made his acting debut at the age of 16, appearing as Anthony Hancock, The Confidential Comic, at The Theatre Royal, Bournemouth, and a year later he recited a monologue, 'The Night the Opera Caught Fire', in a BBC radio talent show.

In 1942, he joined the RAF and made a disastrous attempt to enter the forces entertainment organisation ENSA, drying up before he could get past the opening words of the audition. Instead, he joined Ralph Reader's Number Nine Gang Show, performing for the troops in North Africa, Italy, Malta, Yugoslavia, Greece, Crete and Gibraltar.

After being demobbed, in November 1946, Tony joined another of Reader's Gang Shows, called *Wings* and featuring 300 former RAF servicemen. Two years later, he appeared as resident comic at the famous Windmill Theatre, in London, doing impressions of the famous, and in 1949 he was in B C Hilliam's *Flotsam's Follies*, in Bognor Regis, before trying his hand in variety at the Empress Theatre, Brixton.

Tony became renowned for his remarkable ability to impersonate the impersonators, two of the most memorable being Charles Laughton as the Hunchback of Nôtre Dame and Henry Irving as Mathias in *The Bells*. In 1950, he made his mark on BBC radio in *Variety Bandbox* and, with pantomime always holding a special place in his heart, appeared that Christmas opposite Julie Andrews in Nottingham. His other early radio programmes included *Workers' Playtime*, *Happy-Go-Lucky* and *All-Star Bill*.

But it was his two years in the radio series *Educating Archie*, written by Eric Sykes, that made him top of the popularity stakes,

succeeding Robert Moreton in 1951 as the teacher who felt that instructing a ventriloquist's wooden dummy (Archie Andrews) was beneath him. His catchphrase, "Flippin kid", became a cult and he was constantly in demand.

In the same year, he appeared at the Prince of Wales Theatre in a stage adaptation of the show, and was in the Val Parnell revue *Peep Show*.

Tony's first Royal Variety Performance was in 1952, when he also starred in Jack Hylton's revue *London Laughs*, at the Adelphi Theatre, subsequently appearing there in *Talk of the Town*. Jimmy Edwards topped the bill with him in both productions.

On 2 November, 1954, the first *Hancock's Half Hour* was broadcast on BBC radio. Such a success was the show that two years later it switched to television and Tony became a household name.

Written by Ray Galton and Alan Simpson, whom Tony had met while broadcasting in *Happy-Go-Lucky* and *All-Star Bill*, the show featured Anthony Aloysius St John Hancock of 23 Railway Cuttings, East Cheam, complete with his megalomania, delusions of grandeur and capacity for self-deception – as well as a black homburg and shabby, over-long black raincoat – and Sid James giving a superb performance as his foil.

Once the programme transferred to television, Tony concentrated all his energies on it and it remains one of the greats of TV comedy. He dropped James for his last BBC series, in 1961, and proved that he could work without such a foil. One of the classic episodes, *The Blood Donor*, was featured in that final series.

In all, *Hancock's Half Hour* ran for 101 radio episodes and 59 television programmes, enjoying repeat runs years later, without the comedy seeming dated to its new audience.

However, the star's ventures into films proved a failure. He had already made his debut as a bandmaster in the 1954 Army comedy *Orders are Orders* when he looked for big-screen success after his hit TV series finished. He made four further films, *The Rebel*, *The Punch and Judy Man*, *Those Magnificent Men in Their Flying Machines* and *The Wrong Box*, but failed to make an impact on the big screen. His decision to switch his small-screen persona to ITV in 1963 for a new series, *Hancock*, also proved a disaster, with writers Galton and Simpson replaced by *Doctor Who* creator Terry Nation and the programme not having the impact or style of the original.

A year later, Tony topped the bill in *Sunday Night at the London Palladium*, the ITV variety show then at the height of its popularity. Ironically, his own popularity was already waning and a 1965 cabaret season at the Talk of the Town and another series of *Hancock* two years later did nothing to help boost the morale of a star who was by now drinking too much and frequently seeking psychiatric help. Perhaps running away from the scene of his problems, Tony travelled to Australia in 1968 to make a new series of 13 programmes for Channel 7, in Sydney. He was to feature as a pompous, whingeing 'Pom', but he had completed only three episodes when he returned to his flat at the end of a day's work and committed suicide by taking an overdose of drugs, washed down with vodka.

Serious and introspective, the actor was twice married and divorced, first to Cicely Romanis, then to his public relations agent, 'Freddie' Ross, who was granted a divorce a week before his death.

Irene Handl

b. 27 December 1901
d. 29 November 1987

THE grand dame of cheeky cockneys, Irene Handl succeeded in charming a chuckle from every viewer. Her roles were as diverse as her talent and many television viewers will remember her in the series *For The Love Of Ada*, with Wilfred Pickles, and the children's comedy *Metal Mickey*.

Although Irene specialised in playing Londoners, and she herself was born in the city's Maida Vale district, her background could not have been more cosmopolitan – her father was a Viennese banker and her mother was French.

Irene, who did not turn to acting until she was 40, travelled extensively on leaving school and returned home to look after her father after her mother died.

After training for a career on the stage at the Embassy School, which was run by the sister of Dame Sybil Thorndike, she made her London stage debut in 1938, in a poorly received play that closed after only two weeks.

But every cloud has a silver lining and her next role as Beer the maid in the West End comedy *George and Margaret* set her up for a long and successful acting career.

She went on to play many of the classic female comedy parts on the British stage, in plays such as *Goodnight Mrs Puffin* and Noël

Coward's *Blithe Spirit*. Her film debut was in the 1937 picture *Missing – Believed Married* and, after many years playing only small parts on screen, she found herself in such comedy classics as *The Belles of St Trinian's*, *I'm All Right, Jack*, *Morgan*, *A Suitable Case for Treatment*, *Carry On Nurse*, *Carry On Constable*, *The Last Remake of Beau Geste* and *Hedda Gabler*.

Irene was also a familiar voice on radio, with Arthur Askey in *Hello Playmates* and with Tony Hancock in *Hancock's Half Hour*.

But it was her television appearances that were to make Irene a household name. In 1970, she starred with Wilfred Pickles in the comedy series *For The Love of Ada*, a funnily romantic tale of twilight love.

The programme was such a success that it ran for three years, even prompting a 1972 film spin-off, although it was not as well received as the TV programme.

Irene continued to perform on television, in films and pantomime until well into her 80s. On TV, she starred with Julia McKenzie in the comedy *Maggie and Her*, and appeared in the children's series *Metal Mickey* and *Supergran*, as well as appearing as a medium in the Channel Four comedy *Never Say Die*.

Irene, who wrote a novel entitled *Sioux* in 1965, and followed it up with *The Gold Tip Pfitzer*, eight years later, died in her sleep a few weeks before her 86th birthday. She had never married.

Jimmy Hanley

b. 22 October 1918
d. 13 January 1970

FILM star, circus performer, disc jockey, children's author – you name it, Jimmy Hanley had more than likely done it. For more than 50 years this remarkable all-rounder commanded the public's attention and loyalty.

Born in Norwich, Norfolk, the star-struck young actor attended the Italia Conti Stage Academy and, while still a student there, made his stage debut at the London Palladium, as John Darling in *Peter Pan*.

Four years later, at the tender age of 16, he began his career in films, starring in pictures such as *The Way Ahead*, *The Gentle Sex*, *Henry V*, *The Captive Heart*, *The Blue Lamp* and *Look This Way*.

One of his most successful films in, 1947, was *Holiday Camp*, which introduced the Huggett family to the big screen. He also appeared in *Here Come the Huggetts* and *The Huggetts Abroad*, as well as the radio serial *Meet the Huggetts*, which ran from 1953 to 1962.

His career was interrupted briefly by the outbreak of the Second World War, in which he served in the King's Own Light Infantry, before being invalided out in 1942, after being wounded in a commando raid in Norway.

The early days of ITV saw Jimmy co-hosting *Jim's Inn*, an advertising magazine programme, with his second wife Maggie. The show was seen as an alternative form of advertising and had commercials slotted within it. Locals were filmed propping up the bar, discussing the latest bargains, but the show was brought to an abrupt end after eight years, when Parliament outlawed ad-mags.

Off screen, Jimmy decided to become a real-life landlord and took over The Plough, in Effingham, Surrey.

As well as being a star of the small screen, this versatile actor was quite a hit on radio with his weekly programme *Start the Day Right*, which attracted massive audiences.

He was a keen fisherman and would travel the world to take part in sea fishing competitions. In fact, he was such an expert that he was an adviser to the Ireland, Iceland and Egyptian fishing authorities.

Jimmy, who died of cancer at the age of 51, was married twice. He and his first wife, actress Dinah Sheridan, had two children, actress daughter Jenny and son Jeremy. After their divorce, Jimmy married Margaret Avery, with whom he had three children.

Susan Hanson

b. 2 February 1943

POOR 'Miss Diane' of *Crossroads* suffered more than most from the scriptwriters' highly imaginative minds. An illegitimate son kidnapped by his father, a second husband who was a terrorist, and a brain haemorrhage shortly before the serial finished were her lot in over 22 years in the serial.

Born in Preston, Lancashire, Susan appeared in BBC radio plays from the age of

eight, travelling to studios in Manchester most Saturdays and rubbing shoulders with *Children's Hour* presenter Violet Carson – later Ena Sharples of *Coronation Street* – and other child hopefuls such as Robert Powell, Nerys Hughes and Judith Chalmers.

Joining Preston Drama Club at the age of 11, Susan appeared in a production of *The Chalk Garden* alongside another future *Coronation Street* star, Roy Barraclough.

Turning professional after leaving school,

she worked in repertory theatre in Edinburgh, Bristol and Newcastle, and acted at the Mermaid Theatre, London. Her plays included *The Boy Friend*, *Private Lives* – with Paul Eddington – *Inadmissable Evidence*, *The Proposal* and a special bicentenary production at the Bristol Old Vic that stars such as Peter O'Toole flocked to see.

Susan made her film debut in John Schlesinger's classic *A Kind of Loving*, in 1962, starring Alan Bates and June Ritchie, and followed it with an appearance in *Catch Us If You Can*, with the Dave Clark Five.

Before joining *Crossroads* as Diane Lawton in 1965, Susan was on television alongside Cherie Lunghi in an episode of the children's serial *The Valiant Varneys*, featuring Reg Varney, and in a *Theatre 625* production called *Bruno*, directed by Ronald

Eyre. Ronnie Barker was also in the cast.

During her long stint in *Crossroads*, she was allowed breaks to do other work. On television, she appeared in episodes of the comedy *Nearest and Dearest* and the Arthur Negus programme *Going for a Song*, in which – as an avid collector of antiques – she won a competition to guess the value of an item.

Since leaving *Crossroads* in 1987, shortly before its demise, Susan has appeared in the Channel Four film *Out of Order* – playing the mother of subsequent *Minder* star Gary Webster – a tour of the Anthony Schaffer play *Widow's Weeds* and a production of *Just Between Ourselves*, at Watford.

She and her husband, singer Carl Wayne, who made his name in the 60s pop group The Move and appeared as milkman Colin in *Crossroads* for a while, have one son, Jack.

Gilbert Harding

b. 5 June 1907
d. 16 November 1960

A popular choice for the television panel game *What's My Line?*, Gilbert Harding entertained viewers with his sharp wit and short temper.

Born in Hereford, Gilbert Charles Harding went to Cambridge University, before teaching English in Canada and France. Returning to Britain, he joined the police force in Bradford, West Yorkshire, but was forced to retire as the result of a broken knee.

Gilbert then travelled to Cyprus, where he returned to teaching and became the *Times* correspondent on the island.

Back in Britain in 1936, he began reading for the Bar at Gray's Inn but, with his talent for languages, joined the BBC monitoring service at the outbreak of war. He later worked in the BBC's Toronto office and, after the War, was appointed Overseas Director.

He was back in Britain in 1947 as questionmaster in the radio shows *Round Britain Quiz*, *The Brains Trust* and *Twenty Questions*, before joining the celebrated *What's My Line?* team on television, when the series began in 1951.

Gilbert had initially been earmarked to chair the TV panel game alternately with Eamonn Andrews but, after mixing up a contestant's occupation in the first programme, he was happy to become a regular member of the panel and let Andrews keep order.

Over the next 12 years, *What's My Line?* became an institution on British television and Gilbert usually appeared alongside panellists such as Barbara Kelly and Lady Isobel Barnett. Together, they became legends of the small screen.

However, sudden stardom appeared to cause Gilbert some emotional distress and he was often seen to be irritable with contestants. He let slip his insecurities in a highly personal interview with John Freeman during a *Face to Face* interview on TV, in September 1960, breaking down while discussing the then recent death of his mother.

For once, he attracted public sympathy but, just two months later, he was dead. Gilbert, who never married, was rumoured to be a homosexual. He wrote two volumes of autobiography, *Along My Line* and *Master of None*.

Doris Hare

b. 1 March 1905

A S Reg Varney's long-suffering mother in the comedy series *On the Buses*, Doris Hare reached a wider audience than a lifetime in the theatre, going back to the time of her birth in Bargoed, Mid Glamorgan.

Her parents had a portable theatre in South Wales and it seemed inevitable that Doris would become a part of it, making her debut at the age of three in *Current Cash* and appearing in juvenile troupes all over Britain as a child, before going solo as 'Little Doris Hare'.

Appearing in music-hall, variety, cabaret, revues and pantomimes, she has also acted in plays by all the great writers, from Shakespeare to George Bernard Shaw, Noël Coward to Alan Bennett, Pinero to Harold Pinter.

In 1930, the actress toured in *The Show's the Thing*, taking the part made famous by Gracie Fields.

Doris was on radio during the BBC's early days at Savoy Hill and was hostess of *Shipmates Ashore*, the BBC's programme for the Merchant Navy, earning her an MBE in 1947.

In the 60s, she spent a year with the National Theatre, three years with the Royal Shakespeare Company and was with the Chichester Festival Theatre company for several seasons.

A performer on television during the pioneering days after the BBC launched the world's first regular service at Alexandra Palace, in 1936, Doris came to national attention more than 40 years later in her small-screen role as Stan Butler's widowed mother in *On the Buses*, taking over the part from Cicely Courtneidge in the raucous ITV comedy, which started in 1969.

It ran until 1975 and spawned three spin-off films, *On the Buses*, *Mutiny On the Buses* and *Holiday On the Buses*, in which Doris recreated her small-screen role. The cast also performed a stage version of the television hit in Vancouver, Canada, in 1988. At the height of the programme's popularity, Doris joined the cast of the London West End show *No Sex, Please – We're British*.

In the 60s, she appeared on TV as Alice Pickens in *Coronation Street* and since her success in *On the Buses*, she has appeared on screen in *Diamonds*, in the 1990 film *Nuns on the Run* and, two years later, on stage in the West End farce *It Runs in the Family*.

Doris, who won a Variety Club of Great Britain Special Award for her contribution to showbusiness in 1982, has two daughters, Susan and Catherine, by her marriage to Dr J Fraser Roberts, which ended in divorce.

Jack Hargreaves

b. 31 December 1911

THE leisurely countryside series *Out of Town* brought to television the gentle, nostalgic tones of Jack Hargreaves, who combined his enthusiasm for the country with being a television executive and a presenter of the children's series *How?*

Born into a Yorkshire farming family, Jack studied at London University and began his career as a vet's assistant, before entering journalism.

During his distinguished career, he was editor of the magazine *Lilliput* and managing editor of the legendary *Picture Post*, as well as writing and producing for radio, and working as the National Farmers' Union information officer.

He made his TV debut in a short series called *Gone Fishing*, for Southern Television, and it led to the long-running *Out of Town* series, with Hargreaves reminiscing about old countryside ways and customs. His hallmark was his ability to talk naturally to the camera and he managed to resist the use of teleprompters even when their use became almost universal throughout television.

Out of Town finished when Southern lost its ITV franchise in 1981, although it was later revived, less successfully, on Channel Four under the title *Old Country*. Jack and Fred Dinenage were among the quartet who presented the popular ITV children's series *How?*, although Dinenage was the only survivor when it was remade as *How 2* in the early 90s.

As well as being a popular broadcaster, Jack – who was awarded the OBE – was deputy programme controller of Southern Television from 1964 to 1976. Married several times, he now lives near Blandford Forum, in Wiltshire.

Gerald Harper

b. 15 February 1931

SUAVE, elegant James Hadleigh brought a touch of class to ITV in the series about an aristocratic landowner fighting to make his estate profitable – and actor Gerald Harper was well qualified for the role.

Born in Barnet, Hertfordshire, son of a City broker, he attended Haileybury public school and planned to be a doctor, but the acting bug hit him when his school performed plays on the Continent.

After National Service with the Army in Norfolk, during which he was a second lieutenant and heavyweight boxing champion of the Army's Eastern Command, Gerald trained at RADA and made his professional debut at the Arts Theatre, London, in a 1951 Festival of Britain season of all Bernard Shaw's one-act plays. There followed a year of repertory work at Liverpool Playhouse, before returning to the Arts Theatre in Strindberg's *The Father*, then acting in a London West End revival of *Charley's Aunt*,

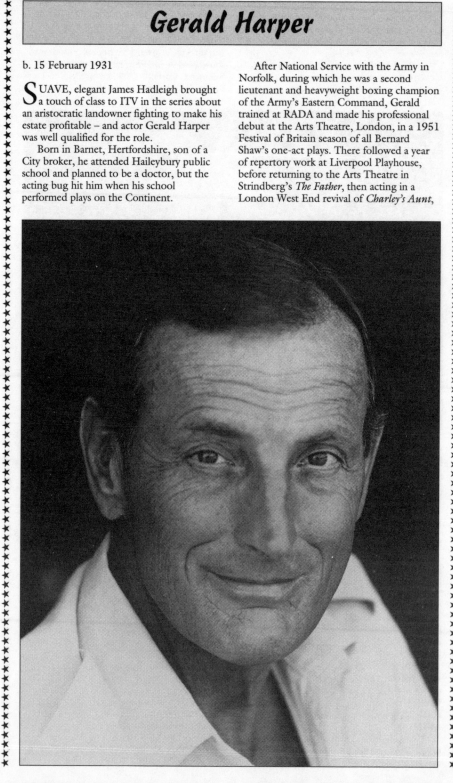

alongside Frankie Howerd, and singing in the musical *Salad Days*.

He appeared in West End productions of *Ross*, *Suddenly at Home*, *Baggage* and *The Little Hut*, toured America with the Old Vic Company in *Hamlet*, *Twelfth Night* and *Henry V*, and starred on Broadway with Ian Carmichael in *Boeing-Boeing*. His films include *The Admirable Crichton*, *Tunes of Glory*, *The Punch and Judy Man*, *The League of Gentlemen*, *Wonderful Life*, *Shoes of the Fisherman* and *The Lady Vanishes*.

In 1966, after TV appearances in *Skyport*, *The Sleeper*, *The Rolls-Royce Story*, *A Man Called Harry Brent*, *The Corsican Brothers* and *The Game of Murder*, Gerald starred in *Adam Adamant Lives!*, as the Edwardian hero taking on modern evils in the 60s.

Three years later, he became the country squire in *Hadleigh*, with the arduous task of maintaining his stately home, Melford Hall. Gerald had already played the character in a series called *Gazette*, in which Hadleigh – a former civil servant fresh up from London –

inherited a Yorkshire weekly newspaper from his father.

Riding high on the success of *Hadleigh*, which ran for seven years, Gerald presented his *Sunday Affair* programme on the newly launched Capital Radio, in London, and has more recently hosted his own show on BBC Radio 2.

His subsequent acting roles have been exclusively in the theatre, playing Sherlock Holmes and appearing in *House Guest*, *A Personal Affair* and *Murder by Misadventure* in the West End, and touring as Elyot Chase in *Private Lives*.

Gerald, who also toured in his one-man show *The King's Trumpeter*, based on the works of Rudyard Kipling, has directed plays, too, including a production of *Blithe Spirit* in Hebrew at the Israeli National Theatre, in Tel Aviv.

He has one daughter, Sarah Jane, by his first wife, actress Jane Downs, from whom he is divorced, and a son, Jamie, by his second wife Carla.

Kathleen Harrison

b. 23 February 1892

HOMELY Kathleen Harrison made a career out of playing cockney mothers, maids and charwomen and, after fame as cleaner Ma Huggett in the series of *Huggetts* film comedies, she found a new audience on television with the hugely successful series *Mrs. Thursday*, in the 60s.

Born in Blackburn, Lancashire, Kathleen trained at RADA, married J H Black and then went abroad to Argentina and Madeira.

On her return to Britain, she made her stage debut as Mrs Judd in *The Constant Flirt*, at the Pier Theatre, Eastbourne, in 1926, and appeared in London's West End for the first time the following year as Winnie in *The Cage*, at the Savoy Theatre. Her subsequent West End plays included *A Damsel in Distress*, *Happy Families*, *The Merchant and Venus*, *Lovers' Meeting*, *Line Engaged*, *Night Must Fall* – also acting in the film version – *The Winslow Boy* and *Watch It Sailor!*

Kathleen had already made her film debut with a small role in *Our Boys*, in 1915, when she appeared in the 1931 picture *Hobson's Choice*. Another 50 films followed, including *Gaslight*, *Kipps*, *In Which We Serve* and *Caesar and Cleopatra*, before she first played London East End charwoman Ma Huggett, in the 1947 picture *Holiday Camp*.

The actress continued with the role,

alongside Jack Warner as her screen husband, in *Here Come the Huggetts*, *Vote for Huggett* and *The Huggetts Abroad*, as well as a radio serial, *Meet the Huggetts*, which ran from 1953 to 1962.

Her other films included *Oliver Twist*, *The Winslow Boy*, *The Magic Box*, *Scrooge*, *The Pickwick Papers* and *The Fast Lady*.

As her cinema appearances became less frequent, Kathleen turned to television, finding massive success as the star of the comedy *Mrs. Thursday*, in 1966. The series was panned by the critics, but viewers loved it and immediately made *Mrs. Thursday* the most popular programme on TV at the time.

In the programme, Kathleen played a charwoman who inherited £10 million and the controlling interest in a company, with Hugh Manning – later the Rev Donald Hinton in *Emmerdale Farm* – as her co-star.

Five years later, she turned down the title role in writer Jeremy Sandford's acclaimed BBC play *Edna the Inebriate Woman*, which won Patricia Hayes a Best Actress On TV award.

Her other television appearances include *Shades of Greene*, *Danger UXB* and two BBC productions of Charles Dickens novels, *Our Mutual Friend* and *Martin Chuzzlewit*, Dickens being her favourite author.

Kathleen reached the grand old age of 100 in February 1992, making her one of Britain's oldest living actresses.

William Hartnell

b. 8 January 1908
d. 24 April 1975

AS television's original Doctor Who, William Hartnell thrilled and chilled an audience of young viewers with his battles against the evil Daleks and battalions of silver-painted Cybermen.

Born in London, William was a jockey's apprentice, before turning to acting with Sir Frank Benson's company in 1924 and touring for the next two years. He went on a tour of Canada in *A Bill of Divorcement*, in 1929, and made his London debut three years later, as Erik in *The Man I Killed*, at the Apollo Theatre.

After appearing in crowd scenes in films at the beginning of the 30s, William – who acted under the name Billy Hartnell for many years – made his big-screen acting debut in *Say It With Music*, in 1931, and made more than 60 films, including *Brighton Rock*, *The Magic Box*, *The Pickwick Papers*, *Private's Progress*, *Hell Drivers* and *The Way Ahead*, a tribute to the British Army by director Sir Carol Reed.

But it was another Army film, *Carry On Sergeant* – the first *Carry On* comedy – that brought him widespread recognition, as Sergeant Grimshaw, an NCO with the thankless task of knocking a bunch of raw recruits into shape. He also appeared as Sergeant Major Bullimore, in the ITV comedy series *The Army Game*, which began in 1957 and ran for three years.

The early 60s saw William in the film *This Sporting Life*, which was to lead to the role for which he will be eternally remembered, Doctor Who.

The programme, which first appeared on TV screens in 1963, was expected to run for only six weeks and cast the actor as a long, white-haired Time Lord, journeying from age to age in his Tardis, a beaten-up old police telephone box.

He left the series in 1966, partly because he was suffering from multiple sclerosis but also because he felt the programme was becoming unsuitable for children. *Doctor Who* continued, however, with the Doctor's character having the power to transmute into different human forms, actor Patrick Troughton subsequently becoming the Time Lord.

William, who later appeared on television in *Crime of Passion*, died at the age of 67 after suffering a series of strokes. He was married to former actress and playwright Heather McIntyre, and had one daughter, Anne.

Russell Harty

b. 5 September 1934
d. 8 June 1988

ONE of the most likeable of TV chat-show hosts, Russell Harty's down-to-earth manner, northern twang, nasal vowels and sensitivity made him a hit on both sides of the TV camera.

Born Fredric Russell Harty in Blackburn, Lancashire, son of a fruit and vegetable stallholder on the local market, he was a bright boy, attending the town's Queen Elizabeth Grammar School, before winning a scholarship to Exeter College, Oxford, where he read English.

On leaving university, he became an English and drama teacher in his beloved Giggleswick, North Yorkshire – throughout his life, Russell continued to commute between London and this pretty Yorkshire village, where he had a cottage.

In 1964, he started a year lecturing in English literature at the City University of New York, and finally began his broadcasting career three years later, when he became a radio producer with the BBC Third Programme, working on arts and book programmes.

In 1969 he moved into television, with LWT, when he launched the peak-time arts series *Aquarius*, presented by Humphrey Burton. He went on to win an Emmy award for his programme on the Spanish artist Salvador Dali, *Hello Dali*, and the Golden Harp award for another documentary, *Finnian Games*.

In 1972, Russell's popularity was acknowledged when LWT gave him his own chat-show, *Eleven Plus*, followed by *Russell Harty Plus* and *Russell Harty Plus One*. He also won a Pye award for Most Outstanding New Personality and the Royal Television Society Award for Most Outstanding Newcomer.

It was in these chat-shows that his effective, although sometimes irritating, manner of questioning evolved. His "You have, have you not . . . ?" style became legendary.

Russell also hosted *Saturday Night People*, with Clive James and Janet Street-Porter, a slightly satirical show that was hardly seen on ITV outside the London region.

In 1980, he left ITV to join the BBC, where he presented another chat-show, *Russell Harty, All About Books* and *Harty at the Seaside*, as well as making documentaries.

His chat-show continued as before, guests feeling relaxed with this unassuming Northerner, although some perhaps relaxed a little too much. Who could forget the evening when actress-singer Grace Jones aimed a swipe at Russell because she felt he was ignoring her, or the time when The Who's drummer, Keith Moon, stripped down to his underpants?

In 1987, Russell took over the reins of the TV series *Favourite Things* – devised by *Desert Island Discs* presenter Roy Plomley – where guests were invited to talk about what gave them the most pleasure in life. He even managed to get Margaret Thatcher to reveal her penchant for poached eggs on Bovril-smeared toast.

Russell was an avid *Coronation Street* fan

and, with Poet Laureate Sir John Betjeman, playwright Willis Hall and broadcaster Michael Parkinson, formed the British League for Hilda Ogden.

In addition to his broadcasting skills, he displayed his brilliant wit in his weekly 'Notebook' column in *The Sunday Times*.

Russell, who never married, died after a long battle against hepatitis. His last documentary series, *Mr Harty's Grand Tour*, had him conducting his own tour of Europe, sampling the delights and delicacies of each country. He wrote a book of the same name, published in 1988.

Hans and Lotte Hass

Hans Hass, b. 1919
Lotte Hass, b. 1929

A USTRIAN undersea explorers Hans and Lotte Hass were the adventurous pair who brought the mysteries of the deep to television viewers in the 50s, facing devil-fish and sharks to bring to the screen pictures that the general public had never seen before.

Based in Lichtenstein, where he ran his Institute of Submarine Research, Hans made his name as a pioneer of underwater exploration, writing a book called *Diving to Adventure* and making two cinema documentary films, *Under the Red Sea* and *Under the Caribbean*.

Lotte Berl, with model-girl good looks, started as his secretary and later became his wife and diving partner.

In 1950, they spoke about an adventure under the Caribbean in the BBC radio Light Programme series *Danger is Our Business*, describing how a sea-lion attacked Hans and a giant clam seized Lotte by the foot and held her below the water, with Hans using a spear to kill the animal and save her life.

A 1953 expedition in which they took 8000 photographs of fish and coral formations along 200 miles of the 800-mile Great Barrier Reef – where many people had been killed by sharks – brought the couple further publicity.

The following year, they were diving among whales in the Pacific, photographing their huge jaws and recording their strange, creaking 'roars'. They also returned with film of hammer-head sharks and coral whose brilliant colours had never been seen before.

Hans and Lotte's move into television came in 1956 with the BBC series *Diving to Adventure*. They roamed the Red Sea, the Caribbean and the Indian Ocean for pictures and became the small-screen equivalents of wildlife pair Armand and Michaela Denis.

A subsequent series was titled *The Undersea World of Adventure* and, in 1966, Hans presented a rather different type of programme, studying the sex-play and all-round behaviour of humans throughout the world in *Man*.

Today, Hans and Lotte continue their scientific research, as well as writing books.

Arthur Haynes

b. 1915
d. 19 November 1966

A comedian who exploited his natural droll personality, Arthur Haynes appealed to the anarchist in everyone and became one of television's highest-paid comedians of the 50s and 60s.

Born in London, the son of a baker, Arthur worked as a bus conductor and railwayman on leaving school, but performed as a pub singer in his spare time. When the Second World War came, he became an entertainer of the troops and was picked by Charlie Chester to appear as a bit-part player in his BBC radio show *Stand Easy*.

He made his television debut in *The George and Alfred Black Show* and, in 1956, appeared in a new ITV programme called *Strike a New Note*, made by ATV, the then new ITV company with Lew Grade at the helm. By the second week of its run, he had become its undoubted star and later had his own *Arthur Haynes Show*, written by Johnny Speight, with Nicholas Parsons as his stooge.

In 1960 ATV made him one of the small screen's top comedians, offering him £75 000 over three years.

He created an array of characters who included a bemedalled tramp called Oscar Pennyfeather, turning his back on convention and showing total disrespect for authority, but convincing audiences that his attitudes were normal and that other people were sadly lacking.

Arthur, who will also be remembered for his Crosse & Blackwell soup commercials, won a Variety Club of Great Britain award

and was named Television Personality of the Year, in 1961, and two years later appeared at the London Palladium for the first time, in the hit show *Swing Along*, although he eventually had to leave through illness.

In 1964, he travelled to Hollywood to act alongside Gina Lollobrigida in the big-screen sex comedy *Strange Bedfellows* and he also made a successful television appearance there in *The Ed Sullivan Show*.

A year later, he made one more film, *Doctor in Clover*, and was due to make another television series when, in 1966, after a cabaret season at the Grosvenor Hotel, in London, he died suddenly.

Richard Hearne

b. 30 January 1909
d. 25 August 1979

WHEN versatile Richard Hearne burst on to the small screen as the accident-prone Mr Pastry in 1953, nobody realised that there was a legend in the making.

Born in Norwich to a theatrical family – his father was an acrobat and clown and his grandfather a groom in the famous Sanger's Circus – it was naturally assumed that Richard would follow in the family tradition.

An acrobat himself, he took great pride in his ability to fall in 49 different ways, which

came in extremely handy when he played the clown in Jack Buchanan's *Flying Trapeze* show, in 1935, three years after his London debut, in the pantomime *Dick Whittington*.

In addition to his great gymnastic skills, Richard was also a celebrated comedian, actor, writer and dancer. No one who saw it could forget his solo performance of the Lancers dance.

But it was a role in a Leslie Henson London West End comedy show that changed the course of Richard's life. He was, quite literally, an overnight sensation as an agile old gentleman – a character who was to become the template for subsequent roles. He possessed a white, whiskery walrus moustache, which when teamed with a white tie and flapping coat tails, made him an unforgettable, slightly eccentric character.

The actor, who made his first television appearance in 1939, went on to become an international star at the age of 37 with his acclaimed character. In Britain he was Mr Pastry, a loveable, albeit clumsy, old gentleman in a top hat, created by Richard's friend Fred Emney for a show called *Big Boy*. In France he was Papa Gateau, and in Germany he was Mr Sugar Tart.

As well as his slapstick children's TV programmes, Richard appeared in almost 20 films, making his debut in the 1934 picture *Give Her a Ring* and bringing his most

celebrated creation to the screen in the 1950 short *Mr Pastry Does the Laundry*.

At the end of the 50s, he spent 18 months with Chipperfield's Circus, but in 1970 Richard retired from popular entertainment, claiming it had become too smutty, although he did tread the boards for one last time to act in the pantomime *Cinderella*.

In the same year, he was awarded an OBE for his charity work. He had worked tirelessly to raise thousands of pounds to build swimming pools for spastic children when, after a visit to a special school in Croydon, he realised how much the water meant to them.

Richard, who died of a heart attack in 1979, was married to Yvonne Ortner and had two daughters.

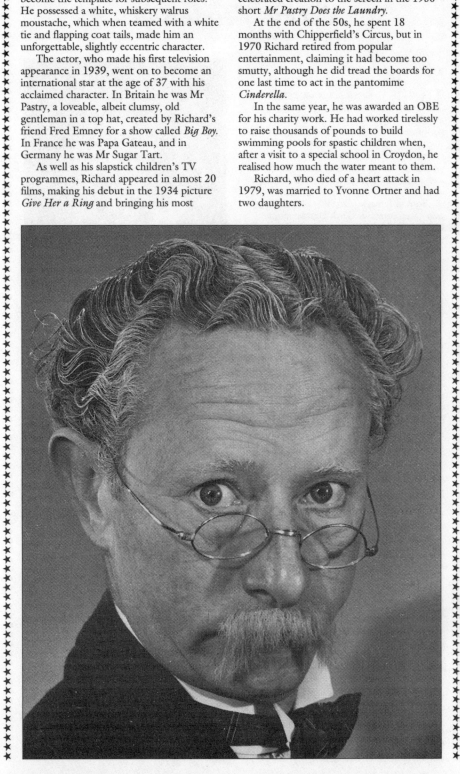

Dickie Henderson

b. 30 October 1922
d. 22 September 1985

DICKIE Henderson was a man who could turn his hands (or feet) to anything – he sang, danced, told jokes and performed the most gravity-defying acrobatic tumbles. In short, he was a professional, all-round entertainer – anything short of perfection was just not good enough for him and he pushed himself to the limit striving to attain it.

Born in London, Dickie was the son of celebrated comedian Dick Henderson, a rondelet Yorkshireman who made the original recording of the popular song 'Tiptoe Through the Tulips', and his sisters Triss and Win were the delightful song-and-dance duo The Henderson Twins.

He was educated in both Hollywood, when his father was touring in vaudeville, and Britain, at St Joseph's College, Beulah Hill, London. But it was while in America, in 1932, that Dickie broke into showbusiness. He was offered a role in the film *Cavalcade*, playing the son of Clive Brook and Diana Wynyard.

He was also in the running for *David Copperfield*, but his father insisted that they decline the part and return to Britain because he felt that Hollywood was no place for a young boy.

Back home, Dickie made his theatre debut, aged 16, in 1938 as an eccentric dancer, appearing with his sisters on a tour of Scotland. He went on to play in serious productions, pantomime and variety, but it was not until 1953 that he made his TV debut, in *Face The Music*, followed by Arthur Askey's show *Before Your Very Eyes*.

He subsequently had his own programme, *The Dickie Henderson Show*, a situation-comedy with Dickie appearing as himself and June Laverick as his wife. The show proved so popular that it ran for 120 episodes over 12 years. His other television shows were *A Present For Dickie*, *I'm Bob*,

He's Dickie, with Bob Monkhouse, and *I'm Dickie – That's Showbusiness*.

The late 50s and early 60s were the definitive Henderson years – he had scaled the dizzy heights of stardom and was a family favourite. During this time, he appeared as an actor in the West End hit *Teahouse of the August Moon*, made several appearances in Royal Variety Performances and had his own shows at the London Palladium.

In addition to performing, Dickie was heavily involved with charity work and he, along with other members of the Variety Club of Great Britain, launched a fund to raise money to provide a bus to take polio victims to the seaside.

He was also involved with organisations that dealt with such problems as cystic fibrosis. In 1977, his hard work was recognised when he was awarded an OBE.

Dickie, who died from cancer of the pancreas, was married twice. First wife Dixie Ross, with whom he had two children, Linda and Matthew, died and he subsequently married Gwynneth.

Ian Hendry

b. 13 January 1931
d. 24 December 1984

STARRING roles in *Police Surgeon* and as a tortured alcoholic in *The Lotus Eaters* put Ian Hendry in the top bracket of TV

fame in the 60s and early 70s, but subsequent years saw his decline through drinking and bankruptcy, followed by his untimely death from a heart attack.

Born in Ipswich, Suffolk, Ian was studying drama part-time when he made his

showbusiness debut as a stooge to Coco the clown in cabaret. After National Service in the Royal Artillery, he trained at the Central School of Speech and Drama and worked in repertory theatre in Hornchurch and Worthing.

Ian was particularly notable on stage in Goldoni's *Servant of Two Masters* at the Edinburgh Festival, but came to wider attention after a performance of *Dinner with the Family* at the Oxford Playhouse, subsequently appearing on the London stage.

His early film appearances were in *Simon and Laura*, in 1956, and in *The Secret Place*. He then appeared in *Room at the Top, Sink the Bismarck!, Live Now – Pay Later, Casino Royale, Get Carter, Tales From the Crypt, Damien – Omen II, The Bitch* and *McVicar*.

He made his mark on television as a polio patient in *Emergency – Ward 10* and was in *Probation Officer*, before starring as Dr David Keel in *Police Surgeon*. When *The Avengers* began, the character was transferred to the new series, swearing vengeance on the drug barons who had gunned down his fiancée in a London street.

Ian was joined by actor Patrick Macnee for *The Avengers*, which started in 1961 and evolved into an entirely different programme after Ian left following a TV actors' strike a year later. He was replaced by 'glamour girl' Honor Blackman.

It was ten years before he found another major success, as hard-drinking Erik Shepherd in *The Lotus Eaters*, a 1972 series about a group of British expatriates living on Crete. His second wife, Janet Munro, was to have played his wife in the programme, but the couple split up and she withdrew from the role shortly before it was due to be made, dying from drink-related problems later that year, at the age of 38.

Ian then surfaced in *Village Hall, The New Avengers* and *Crown Court*, but his own drinking was becoming a cause for concern and, in 1980, he was declared bankrupt. He secured his discharge partly thanks to the money earned from the TV series *For Maddie with Love*, alongside Nyree Dawn Porter.

Later, he did a short stint in the Channel Four serial *Brookside*, as alcoholic, on-the-make father to Petra Taylor, Michelle Jones and Marie Jackson. His character, Davy Jones, was an old seadog who turned up when he heard that Petra had died and left money to her two sisters. He left with Michelle's catalogue money but no more.

Ian, who died at the age of 53, was married three times. He was divorced from his first wife, make-up artist Joanna, in 1962, had two daughters, Sally and Corrie, by his second wife, actress Janet Munro, and another, Emma, by his third wife, former children's nanny Sandy Jones.

Benny Hill

b. 21 January 1925
d. 18 April 1992

THE clown prince of TV, Benny Hill was the small screen's most popular comedian, with his shows selling around the world more than any others. He was the first variety star to be made famous by television and, for more than 30 years, his seaside-postcard humour brought laughs to millions.

As the years went on, the new shows became fewer, but they were watched just as avidly, as were repeats and compilations of the old shows.

At the time of his death, Benny was in the process of making a comeback, after being dropped by commercial television several years earlier, largely as a result of a backlash from the new wave of comedians in the 80s.

However, as his old shows continued to top the list of programmes exported, and praise was heaped on him by fellow artists

and writers who transcended fashion, he was planning a new series that would certainly have had the same blend as the old – comedy sketches, impressions, songs and dances, all rooted in the music-hall tradition that Benny had brought to television.

Born Alfie Hawthorne Hill in Southampton, the son of a surgical appliance fitter who had once worked as a clown, Benny was encouraged to be a comedian by his English teacher, Horace King, who later became Speaker of the House of Commons and Lord Maybray-King. At 14, Benny joined the semi-professional Bobby's Concert Party as a vicar, wearing one of his father's collars back to front. However, on leaving school a year later, he was faced with the reality of finding a job and worked as a stock-room clerk in Woolworths, a weighbridge operator and a milkman, complete with horse and cart.

The Second World War had already

started and the budding star, who had established a Max Miller-style routine, as well as singing and playing drums, was anxious to establish himself as an entertainer before being called up.

So, in 1940, he travelled to London with a cardboard suitcase and slept on Streatham Common until he found a job at the East Ham Palace, as assistant stage manager, and appeared in a few productions there.

Benny – whose elder brother, Leonard, had persuaded him to change his name because it would look better on bill posters – was touring in a revue when military police arrived in Cardiff to take him off for Army service because his call-up papers had not reached him.

He was a driver and mechanic, seeing service in France, before transferring to a *Stars in Battledress* company entertaining the troops.

After the War, theatrical agent Richard Stone – who had been his commanding officer – signed Benny as a straight man to comedian Reg Varney. He won the job against competition from Peter Sellers.

Benny then went solo and, in 1949, after offering comedy sketches to Ronnie Waldman, the BBC's Head of Light Entertainment, he was given the chance to appear on television. Six years later, he was given his own programme, *The Benny Hill Show*, which transferred to ITV in 1969, produced by Thames Television.

He was the first comedian to be made by the medium of television, although he had also appeared on radio, in the 50s series *Educating Archie* and *Archie's the Boy*.

In his early TV days, Benny was also a natural for Ealing comedies and made his debut in their 1955 film *Who Done It?*, as an ice-rink sweeper setting himself up as a private detective and chasing a spy ring.

It was a box-office hit but, with Ealing Studios' days numbered, it turned out to be his only starring role in the cinema, although he gave cameo performances in pictures such as *Light Up the Sky*, *Those Magnificent Men In Their Flying Machines*, *Chitty Chitty Bang Bang* and *The Italian Job*. Clips from his TV show were also released in a 1974 film compilation, *The Best of Benny Hill*.

The television programme brought revue-style comedy to the small screen, combining visual gags with a well informed, sophisticated humour that was often thrown into sketches in passing. However, it was the array of scantily-clad women who trooped across the screen, often with Benny in hot pursuit – and even more often the other way round – that was to bring accusations of sexism, although the star pointed out that the humour was firmly in the McGill English seaside-postcard tradition and he was always

shown to be the loser, something actor Mickey Rooney later called 'the mark of a genius'.

Ironically, the accusations of sexism were to grow after Benny's shows were repackaged in 1979 for foreign markets, concentrating on the visual jokes to overcome language barriers. The programmes quickly became Thames Television's biggest export and made Benny a star in America, although his brilliance with word play was never seen by foreign audiences.

Then, he fell victim to the 'alternative' comedians who broke through into television in the 80s and were not afraid to pillory anyone or anything they did not like. As well as throwing their irreverent and sometimes foul-mouthed insults at politicians and other pillars of the Establishment, they singled out several comedians.

In 1986, 'alternative' comedian Ben Elton criticised Benny for sketches in which he chased women with few clothes on while, at the same time, the incidence of rape was on the increase. With others supporting Elton's view, the Broadcasting Complaints Commission saying it wished to eradicate this sort of comedy and veteran American film-maker Hal Roach – who would have seen only the visual gags – comparing Benny to greats such as Charlie Chaplin and Laurel and Hardy, but adding that he needed to 'clean up' his act, Thames Television dropped *The Benny Hill Show* in 1989, denouncing it as sexist.

It was a blow to the star, who was still brimming with ideas and had, in fact, already done away with Hill's Angels and other buxom, barely dressed females. Thames Television continued to make millions from its Benny Hill compilations sold abroad and Benny was awarded the Charlie Chaplin International Award for Comedy in 1991. The following year, Central Television offered him a new ITV show. With his comeback imminent, the BBC arts series *Omnibus* featured him in an episode titled *Benny Hill – Clown Imperial*, which included other stars and writers giving Benny glowing tributes. Unfortunately, he was to die of a heart attack before he could complete his new series.

Outside his own shows, Benny's appearances were few, but he was acclaimed for his wonderfully funny television role as Bottom in *A Midsummer Night's Dream*, in 1964.

Benny, who in his younger days proposed to two actresses, only to be turned down on both occasions, never married. Although a multi-millionaire, he lived a simple life and found little to spend his money on, apart from foreign holidays, which would often be spent jotting down notes for sketches.

McDonald Hobley

b. 1917
d. 30 July 1987

ONCE one of the most famous faces of the small screen, McDonald Hobley was the first post-war announcer when the BBC's television service reopened.

Dennys Jack Valentine McDonald-Hobley was born in the Falkland Islands, where his father was Naval chaplain at the cathedral in Port Stanley. He was educated at an English prep school, then in South America, before moving on to Brighton College.

Deciding that showbusiness was the life for him, McDonald joined the repertory company at the Theatre Royal, Brighton. Under the name Robert Blanchard, he also appeared in Cambridge and Bath, and toured in J B Priestley's *Time and the Conways*.

At the outbreak of war, he signed up for the Royal Artillery, serving on the staff of Lord Mountbatten, before working for South Eastern Asia Command radio, in Ceylon.

Leaving the Army in 1946, McDonald was selected from 281 applicants to become BBC television's only male continuity announcer. Although the salary was a mere £12 a week, the job was highly prestigious and required him to don a dinner-jacket in front of the cameras. He and fellow-programme announcers Sylvia Peters and Jasmine Bligh – later replaced by Mary Malcolm – became extremely popular with viewers.

One of McDonald's unfortunate 'misannouncements' – of which there were few – told viewers that they were about to

hear "the Rt. Hon Sir Stifford Crapps" in television's first party political broadcast.

In 1954, he was voted TV Personality of the Year and became chairman of the popular radio series *Does the Team Think?*

Two years later, although his salary had nearly doubled in ten years, McDonald left the BBC and joined Associated British Cinemas, an independent TV company which offered him £100 a week as a commentator. There he remained for three years, until his contract expired and then he returned to the theatre, appearing in a diverse range of plays and pantomimes, as well as performing in London's West End in *No Sex, Please – We're British.*

Despite his stage work, he continued to be involved in television and, in 1986, returned to the Falklands for a Channel Four programme.

McDonald had been married three times and all but his third marriage ended in divorce.

Gordon Honeycombe

b. 29 September 1936

NATIONALLY known as a television newscaster, 6ft 4in Gordon Honeycombe has also been an actor and best-selling author, as well as having a fascination in tracing his family tree, which led to his own TV series on the subject.

Born in Karachi, British India, of Scottish parents, Gordon was educated at the Edinburgh Academy and University College, Oxford – gaining an MA in English language and literature – before doing National Service with the Royal Artillery in Hong Kong. It was there that he entered broadcasting, as an announcer for Radio Hong Kong.

On leaving the Forces, he became an actor, performing with the Royal Shakespeare Company and on television. He joined ITN as a scriptwriter and newscaster in 1965, staying for 12 years, in which time he was deluged with thousands of fan letters.

While he was there, Gordon began to find success as a novelist and had already decided to leave when, in 1977, he publicly supported a national firemen's strike. Suspended by ITN, he resigned and planned to become a full-time writer.

A year earlier, he had a critically acclaimed novel called *Red Watch*, which was written after discovering that his great-grandfather, Samuel, had been the founder of the first fire brigade based at Northfleet, in Kent.

It was this interest in genealogy that led to Gordon's 1979 BBC television series *Family History*. Twenty-four years earlier, he had discovered in a local newspaper that an Edinburgh girl once married a man from Jersey called Roy Honeycombe, and this began his work on the subject, tracing his family tree back to 1318. His research took him all over Britain, searching through parish registers, old wills and house deeds.

As well as appearing in other TV programmes and narrating *Arthur C Clarke's Mysterious World*, Gordon has written two

Royal Galas, stage and radio dramatisations and three TV plays, *The Golden Vision, Time and Again* – winner of the silver medal at the 1975 New York Film and TV Festival – and *The Thirteenth Day of Christmas.*

He has also continued to write books, including the best-selling *Royal Wedding* – recounting Prince Charles's marriage to the Princess of Wales, in 1981 – and *The Murders of the Black Museum.*

In 1984, he returned to news presenting as senior newscaster at the original ITV breakfast station, TV-am, where he stayed for five years.

Gordon, who is single and lives in London – as well as having a flat in Perth, Western Australia – has subsequently returned to acting, touring in *Run for Your Wife*, writing and directing his own play, *The Redemption*, performed at the Festival of Perth, and writing the book and lyrics of a new musical, *The Princess and the Goblins.*

Kenneth Horne

b. 26 February 1907
d. 14 February 1969

MUCH loved on radio for *Round the Horne* and on television for his *Horne A' Plenty* show, Kenneth Horne was without doubt one of the wittiest entertainers of his time.

Born in London, the son of the Reverend Silvester Horne, a leading Congregationalist minister and former Liberal MP, Charles Kenneth Horne studied at Magdalene College, Cambridge, before drifting into the world of showbusiness during the War, while serving as a Wing Commander in the RAF.

It was here that he teamed up with Richard Murdoch and the two made their names in radio programmes such as *Ack Ack Beer Beer* and *Much Binding in the Marsh*, a tale based around an airfield. A succession of shows followed, including seven series of *Beyond Our Ken* and three of *Round the Horne*.

Kenneth was a master of *double entendres* and word play. His puns were delivered with undisguised delight and were often as outrageous as they were undeniably witty.

After suffering a stroke in 1958, Kenneth was left partially paralysed and unable to speak. But, determined to concentrate on his showbusiness career, he decided to withdraw from his many business interests, which included the chairmanship of Chad Valley Toys and five other companies, in addition to the directorship of others.

Days spent lying in his bed being nursed back to health by his wife, Marjorie, gave him time to reflect and it was not long before his thoughts reached fruition.

His first radio programme after his stroke was *Beyond Our Ken*, which succeeded in attracting ten million listeners on Sunday afternoons, and he became chairman of *Twenty Questions*, as well as joining several panel game teams.

He had already moved into television with *Down You Go*, in 1953, and his radio hit *Round the Horne* switched to television as *Horne A' Plenty* in the mid-60s but failed to attract the same following as its predecessor.

By the time of his death, at the age of 61, Kenneth had succeeded in rebuilding his career from scratch.

Trevor Howard

b. 29 September 1916
d. 7 January 1988

ONE of Britain's finest home-grown film stars, Trevor Howard also brought his authority to television in programmes such as *Hedda Gabler*, *The Exile of Jonathan Swift* and an adaption of Paul Scott's *Staying On*.

Born in Cliftonville, Kent, of an English father and Canadian mother, he won a scholarship to RADA in 1933 and, the following year, made his professional debut while still a student, after winning a BBC acting competition.

On leaving drama school, he joined the Shakespeare Memorial Theatre company, at Stratford-upon-Avon, before enlisting into the Army in 1940.

Trevor served in the First Airborne Division, taking part in the invasions of Norway and Sicily, until he was invalided out. He returned to civilian life with a Military Cross and first trod the boards again in a revival of *The Recruiting Officer*, at the Arts Theatre, London.

However, it was not long before the young actor was lured away to the bright lights of films to make his debut in a forgettable 1944

Russian production entitled *Volga-Volga*, in which he dubbed an actor's voice.

Eventually, Trevor carved a niche for himself as a quality actor capable of playing either the hero or the villain of the piece. However, it was with the film *Brief Encounter*, in 1946, that he really began to climb to the top. Chosen for the part by Noël Coward and director David Lean, he played a doctor embroiled in a hesitant love affair with a married woman.

His other notable roles included the guilt-ridden police commissioner driven to suicide in Graham Greene's *The Heart of the Matter* and the hard-drinking coal miner father in D H Lawrence's *Sons and Lovers*, which earned him an Oscar nomination.

His 90 films also included *Cockleshell Heroes, Around the World in 80 Days, Mutiny on the Bounty, Von Ryan's Express, The Charge of the Light Brigade, Ryan's Daughter, Superman* and *Ghandi*.

Although Trevor was very much a film actor, he made his mark on television as Lovborg in *Hedda Gabler* and gave an Emmy award-winning performance in the title role of the American production of *The Invincible Mr Disraeli*.

He also appeared with Celia Johnson in *Staying On*, an adaptation of the Paul Scott novel from his *Raj Quartet*, appeared in the TV movie *Inside the Third Reich* and took the title role in *The Exile of Jonathan Swift*, as well as reading Bible passages in the ITV religious show *Stars on Sunday*.

Trevor, who died from influenza and bronchitis, had been married to actress Helen Cherry since 1944.

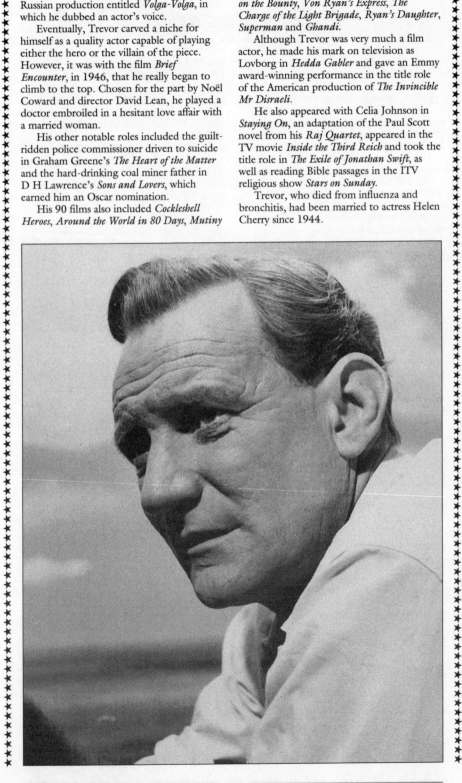

Jack Howarth

b. 19 February 1896
d. 31 March 1984

AS the grumpy, skinflint pensioner 'Uncle Albert' Tatlock in *Coronation Street* from its first episode, Jack Howarth immortalised a generation who had fought through two world wars and wondered at the lack of respect they received from the young for keeping their country free from Fascism.

Born in Rochdale, Lancashire, in the last years of the 19th century, Jack went to school with Gracie Fields. The son of a comedian, he began selling programmes in the auditorium, before starting to act at the age of 12, playing children's roles with Churchill's Minstrels at The Happy Valley, Llandudno.

He served with the Lancashire Fusiliers in France during the First World War and was later with Leslie Henson's company, before working as a stage director for Hamilton Deane on the original British productions of *Dracula* and *Frankenstein*. During the Second World War, Jack ran his own theatre in Colwyn Bay, taking most of the male roles himself because of the lack of men available.

As well as appearing in 18 films – including the role of clogmaker Tubby in Charles Laughton's *Hobson's Choice* – and in 100 TV programmes, Jack was on radio as Mr Maggs in *Mrs Dale's Diary* for 14 years, before joining *Coronation Street* when it began, in December 1960.

His character, Albert Tatlock, famous for his cloth cap and penchant for a drop of rum in the Rovers Return, was uncle of Ken Barlow's first wife, Valerie. He, Ena Sharples, Minnie Caldwell and Martha Longhurst were the serial's older generation, forever talking of the past and only grudgingly coming to terms with changing times.

For all of his 23 years and 1700 episodes of the serial, Jack wore the same suit – a dark grey, three-piece, woollen, single-breasted outfit – which was a feat included in the children's TV programme *First Post*, in a look behind the scenes at Granada. Only on very special occasions did Uncle Albert sport a newer suit.

Jack was made an MBE in 1983 for his charity work – especially for spastics organisations – and died a year later, the last of *Coronation Street*'s original pensioners.

He was married to actress Betty Murgatroyd, had a son, John, and lived in Deganwy, Gwynedd, staying at the four-star Midland Hotel, Manchester, while recording the *Street*. The couple enjoyed opera and cricket, and holidaying in exotic places.

Frankie Howerd

b. 6 March 1917
d. 19 April 1992

ONE of the great comedians of the post-war era, Frankie Howerd was at his most popular on television in his bawdy series *Up Pompeii*, inspired by the American musical *A Funny Thing Happened on the Way to the Forum*, in whose British stage version he had starred. His combination of low comedy and high camp made him a favourite with millions, although his life was a constant battle against nerves.

Born Francis Alex Howard in York, he was brought up in Woolwich, south-east London. His father, who was a sergeant-major in the Army, died when he was three and his mother took cleaning jobs to bring in money for her three children.

Although nervous and suffering a stammer, which he later emphasised and turned into his trademark, Frankie joined a church dramatic society at the age of 13 and made his stage debut in *Tilly of Bloomsbury*, wearing a beard and playing Tilly's father.

Five years later, he auditioned for RADA with hopes of becoming an actor, but was turned down and decided to become a comic. After failing auditions for Carrol Levis talent contests, Frankie found a job as a junior insurance clerk in London. Further rejections came when, while serving with the Royal Artillery during the Second World War, he switched to a forces entertainment unit but failed auditions for both *Stars in Battledress* and ENSA.

Unperturbed, Frankie unleashed his comic patter on troops in canteens and barrack rooms, learning to control his stammer and developing the bumbling manner for which he would later become known.

A year after the War finished, he performed in a troop show at the Stage Door

Canteen, in London, resulting in an agent signing him and getting him a spot in the roadshow *For the Fun of It*, starring Donald Peers. Appearing at the bottom of the bill with Max Bygraves, another showbusiness hopeful, he changed the spelling of his surname from Howard to Howerd, because there were so many Howards around and he hoped that this would help him to get noticed.

He made further stage appearances, but it was radio that catapulted Frankie to fame, and he became a regular in *Variety Bandbox*, with Eric Sykes writing his scripts. He was in the show for four years from 1948, during which he topped the bills at variety theatres, toured as principal comedian in Bernard Delfont's revue *Ta Ra Rah Boom de Ay*, starred with Binnie Hale and Nat Jackley in *Out of This World* at the London Palladium and, in 1950, appeared in the Royal Variety Performance for the first time.

Soon, Frankie's catchphrases were sweeping the nation. "Please yourselves," he would implore, and drew further laughter by pleading with his audiences not to laugh.

During the 50s, as well as playing Idle Jack in *Dick Whittington* at the Palladium and starring in the Folies Bergère revue *Pardon My French* at the Prince of Wales Theatre, and as Lord Fancourt Babberley in *Charley's Aunt* at the Globe, he tried to establish himself as a straight actor, winning acclaim for his performance as Bottom in *A Midsummer Night's Dream* at the Old Vic.

But Frankie's forté was comedy and he went through a bleak period after the music halls closed and he suffered a 1958 stage flop in his first musical, *Mr Venus*.

He made his comeback four years later with an appearance at Peter Cook's Establishment club, in London, with a script by Johnny Speight – who went on to write *Till Death Us Do Part* – and followed it with an appearance on the BBC TV satirical show *That Was the Week That Was*, and the roles of Prologus and Pseudolus in the London stage production of Stephen Sondheim's musical *A Funny Thing Happened on the Way to the Forum*.

The television series *Up Pompeii*, starting in 1969, was loosely based on the musical and had Frankie as Roman slave Lurcio, dressed in a toga and delivering his thoughts to the audience. Full of innuendos, the programme's own star originally regarded the scripts as vulgar, but then put them in the category of music hall.

He made three film spin-offs, *Up Pompeii*, *Up the Chastity Belt* and *Up the Front*, although the cinema had never been an entirely appropriate medium for his talents. He made his big-screen debut in the 1954 picture *The Runaway Bus* and made 20

pictures in all, including cameos in *Further Up the Creek*, *The Fast Lady*, *The Mouse On the Moon*, *The Great St Trinian's Train Robbery*, *Carry On Doctor*, *Carry On Up the Jungle*, the horror spoof *The House in Nightmare Park* and *Sergeant Pepper's Lonely Hearts Club Band*.

Frankie's first television show had been *The Howerd Crowd*, in 1952, and he subsequently starred in *The Frankie Howerd Show*, *Francis Howerd in Concert*, *The Frankie and Bruce Show* – with Bruce Forsyth – *Francis Howerd's Tittertime* and *A Touch of the Casanovas*.

His later television appearances included *The Howerd Confessions*, *Frankie Howerd on Campus* and *Further Up Pompeii*.

Awarded an OBE in 1977, Frankie was also winner of two Variety Club of Great Britain Showbusiness Personality of the Year awards. His biography, *On the Way I Lost It*, was published in 1976, and another book, *Trumps*, came out six years later. Due to appear in the new *Carry On* film, *Carry On Columbus*, Frankie died of a heart attack shortly before it was made.

His final television series, *Frankie Howerd: Then Churchill Said To Me*, recorded for the BBC in 1982 but not shown because of the Falklands War, was screened on the satellite channel UK Gold 11 years later.

Frankie never married but had a long relationship with actress Joan Greenwood, who eventually dropped him for another actor.

Roy Hudd

b. 16 May 1936

IT is old-fashioned music-hall that Roy Hudd has always loved, and some of his most memorable performances have been tributes to stars such as George Formby, Max Miller and Bud Flanagan.

Born in Croydon, Surrey, it was at the town's Empire Theatre that he fell in love with showbusiness, when his mother took him to pantomimes there. She had been a waitress at the giant rotunda restaurant in the 2500-seater Davis Cinema in Croydon. His father was a carpenter and decorator of Eastern European Jewish descent.

It was a shock when Roy's mother committed suicide while his father was serving in the Army in Italy, although he was simply moved in with his grandmother, Alice Bahram, and not told about the tragedy until years later. His interest in theatre was fuelled by further visits to the Croydon Empire to see Max Wall, Bud Flanagan, Sandy Powell, Jimmy James, Hettie King, Max Miller and other top variety acts of the day.

Although he trained in bricklaying, plumbing and carpentry at Croydon Technical School, Roy joined the Sir Phillip Game Boys' Club Concert Party and appeared in many shows.

After National Service in the RAF – as a telephonist at Waterbeach, near Cambridge – and work as a commercial lettering artist, he entered showbusiness in 1957, playing banjo and singing in clubs, then becoming a holiday camp entertainer at Butlin's in Clacton-on-Sea the following year. After his summer season there, he formed a comedy double-act – Hudd and Kay, 'The Peculiar Pair' – with an old boys' club friend, Eddy Cunningham, and appeared in the television programme *Bid for Fame*.

Within a couple of months, Roy had gone solo and was appearing in another TV programme, *Tell It to the Marines*. He was also in *Workers' Playtime* on radio, with Jimmy James.

But his big break came in 1964, when the awkward six-footer with dark-rimmed spectacles was chosen by producer Ned Sherrin to appear in the 1964 satirical BBC series *Not So Much a Programme, More a Way of Life*, sequel to the hugely successful – and daring – *That Was the Week That Was*. Among its most controversial sketches was one about contraceptives in which Roy portrayed a Catholic priest.

The show made him a household name and led to his own series *Hudd*, a TV mime film *The Maladjusted Busker* – which won the Press Prize at the 1966 Montreux Festival – and more series, *The Illustrated Weekly Hudd* and *The Roy Hudd Show*.

He was acclaimed for his portrayal of music-hall legend Dan Leno in BBC television's adaptation of *Dan Leno Book* for *Omnibus*, which he researched and co-produced.

A long-running series of Lyons Quick Brew Tea commercials on TV kept Roy in the public eye. The money he earned from them also enabled him to accept straight acting roles that were not so well paid, playing Pistol in *Henry V* and appearing in several Tom Stoppard plays, such as *Rosencrantz and Guildenstern Are Dead*, at the Young Vic Theatre, in London.

Roy made his London West End stage debut as Jim Busby in *The Giveaway* in 1969, followed it by appearing as principal comedian in Danny La Rue's Show *Danny At the Palace* and has since played Fagin in a revival of *Oliver!* and Bud Flanagan in *Underneath the Arches*, which he co-wrote.

His eight films include *Up Pompeii*, *Up the Chastity Belt*, *The Alf Garnett Saga* – a 1972 spin-off from the TV series *Till Death Us Do Part* – and *Up Marketing*.

As well as many guest appearances on TV, such as in Dennis Potter's 50s musical drama series *Lipstick on Your Collar*, he drew on his variety background to present *The Puppet Man*, *Halls of Fame* and *Hometown*. He is popular on radio for his topical weekly satirical programme *The News Huddlines*.

Roy has a son, Max – named after his idol, Max Miller – from his first marriage, to Ann, who had been his dancing school teacher in Croydon. He and his second wife, Deborah, live in Oxfordshire.

★★★★★★★★★★★★

John Inman

b. 28 June 1935

WITH a hand on his hip and the catchphrase "I'm free!", John Inman made the character of camp Mr Humphries one of the most memorable in the comedy series *Are You Being Served?*

Insisting on taking inside-leg measurements even when customers wanted a shirt was part of the slapstick from an actor who loved appearing in variety shows and pantomimes.

Born in Preston, Lancashire, where his family owned a hairdressing business, John moved to Blackpool when his family closed the business and decided to live by the sea. His mother ran a boarding-house there and the young boy frequently went to local shows, with Northern comedian Frank Randle – who told blue jokes and wore no dentures on stage – his favourite performer.

At the age of 13, John made his stage debut in a play called *Freda*, at the South Pier Pavilion, Blackpool. On leaving school two years later, he was taken on there as a dogsbody and earned money by becoming a trainee window dresser. He later moved to London and secured a similar job at the Austin Reed shop in Regent Street.

Joining Crewe Rep at the age of 21, after an out-of-work actor told him of a job, he found himself playing old men in cloth caps for many years. He was also half of a celebrated 'Ugly Sisters' act, with Barry Howard, in *Cinderella* productions throughout the country.

John made his London West End debut in the musical *Ann Veronica*, at the Cambridge Theatre, and followed it with roles in *Salad Days*, *Let's Get Laid* and *Charley's Aunt*. His other stage appearances include his own show *Fancy Free*, and *Pyjama Tops*, *My Fat Friend* and *Bedside Manners*.

National fame came in 1973, with the role of menswear assistant Mr Humphries in the BBC department-store comedy *Are You Being Served?*, which ran for 11 years. John played his part with blatant homosexual overtones – based, he said, on assistants he had known in his days as a window-dresser –

and was the object of criticism from gay rights groups. Writers Jeremy Lloyd and David Croft also wrote a spin-off film and the TV sequel, *Grace and Favour*, set in a stately home and first broadcast in 1992.

The original series was responsible for John being chosen as a subject of *This is Your Life* and, in 1976, being named both BBC TV Personality of the Year and *TVTimes* readers' Funniest Man on Television. He also starred in a stage show of the programme and an Australian television version.

John also played the part-owner of a Littlehampton rock factory in the 1977 series *Odd Man Out* and, four years later, the secretary to whom Rula Lenska dictated in *Take a Letter Mr. Jones*, as well as appearing in the BBC's *Good Old Days* variety show.

His many pantomime appearances have included regular performances of *Mother Goose*, *Babes in the Wood* at the London Palladium, *Aladdin* and *Jack and the Beanstalk*. A bachelor, John lives in London.

★★★★★★★★★★★★★

Gordon Jackson

b. 19 December 1923
d. 14 January 1990

ON the small screen, Gordon Jackson will always be remembered for his chalk-and-cheese roles, first as Hudson, the pleasantly pompous butler in the hugely popular series *Upstairs, Downstairs*, then as Cowley, the tough anti-terrorist chief in *The Professionals*.

Born Gordon Cameron Jackson in Glasgow, he was the youngest of five children, whose father taught printing in the city.

Educated at Hillhead High School, he left at the age of 15 to train as an engineering draughtsman at Rolls-Royce, until he left to become a full-time actor, having taken time off work to make his film debut as a soldier in Ealing Studios' *The Foreman Went to France*, following it with other wartime films such as *Nine Men* and *Millions Like Us*.

For the next ten years Gordon, who had acted in BBC radio plays while still at school, worked in repertory theatre in Glasgow, Worthing and Perth, before making his London stage début in 1951, in the long-running farce *Seagulls Over Sorrento*.

Four years later, he played Ishmael in Orson Welles's London stage production of *Moby Dick* and performed as Horatio in Tony Richardson's 1969 production of *Hamlet*, at the Round House, which won him the Clarence Derwent Award for Best Supporting Actor.

He subsequently played Tesman in *Hedda Gabler*, the title role in *Noah* at the Chichester Festival Theatre and Malvolio in *Twelfth Night*.

During this time, he continued acting in films. In his early cinema days, Gordon was cast as young soldiers and juvenile leads, in pictures such as *Whisky Galore*, *The Baby and the Battleship* and *Sailor Beware*, before graduating to substantial supporting roles in films such as *The Great Escape*, *The Ipcress File*, *Those Magnificent Men in Their Flying Machines*, *The Prime of Miss Jean Brodie*, *Kidnapped* and *The Shooting Party*.

But it was on television that Gordon found fame and fortune, first as butler Angus Hudson in *Upstairs, Downstairs*, which ran for five years from 1971. His performance, as the genial, if rather stuffy, gentleman from below stairs who knew his place in the household and made sure that everyone else knew theirs, won the actor the Royal Television Society's 1975 Best Actor award.

The role could not have been more different from that of Cowley, head of top-secret anti-terrorist squad CI5, which Gordon played in the violent, action-packed series *The Professionals* from 1977. In this part, he became a tough cookie who stood no nonsense from his crackshot team – Bodie and Doyle – played by Lewis Collins and Martin Shaw.

During his career, Gordon also appeared on television in *Dr Finlay's Casebook*, *The Soldier's Tale* and *Noble House*. He even cropped up in the Australian series *A Town Like Alice*, which starred Bryan Brown, and the family saga *My Brother Tom*.

Awarded an OBE in 1979, Gordon was married to actress Rona Anderson, with whom he had two sons, Graham and Roddy. He died of bone cancer at the age of 66.

Hattie Jacques

b. 7 February 1924
d. 6 October 1980

A deliciously dumpy star, Hattie Jacques kept audiences laughing with her antics in *Carry On* films and as Eric Sykes's sister in the long-running television comedy *Sykes*.

Born Josephina Edwina Jacques in Sandgate, Kent, she trained as a hairdresser and spent two years as a Red Cross nurse and welder during the Second World War, before turning to the world of entertainment and making her professional debut singing Victorian songs at the Players' Theatre, London, at the age of 20. It was there that she first nurtured her famed Christmas Fairy persona, which she used in pantomime for years to come.

Although she went on to tour with the Old Vic as Smeraldina in *The King Stag*, Hattie always remained faithful to the Players' and would come back to perform there whenever she could, appearing in many favourite pantomimes, such as *The Sleeping Beauty* and *Beauty and the Beast*.

But it was in radio that this buxom brunette first found popularity, playing the gluttonous schoolgirl Sophie Tuckshop, to whom eating was a major hobby, in Tommy Handley's show *ITMA* (*It's That Man Again*), and Agatha Danglebody in *Educating Archie*. She also appeared in some of the original radio episodes of *Hancock's Half Hour*.

Hattie once remarked that because of her size she tried to make people laugh *with* her, rather than *at* her – a sad reason, perhaps, but one that was extremely effective. Everyone loved her, and her ample proportions were part of the reason. Who could fail to giggle as Hattie, dressed to kill as the hospital matron in *Carry On Docter* bounced blusteringly down the wards in pursuit of her life's passion – the weedy doctor played by Kenneth Williams, who would scuttle away from her attentions like a frightened rabbit.

During her 16 years and 14 films with the *Carry On* team, Hattie played matrons five times and always appeared in domineering roles, playing every conceivable character from policewoman to church organist.

The *Carry On* adventures proved so popular that they tended to overshadow her earlier, more serious cinema work. She had made her film debut in *Green for Danger*, in 1946, and followed it with pictures such as *Nicholas Nickleby*, *Oliver Twist*, *Scrooge* and *The Pickwick Papers*.

After appearing as an Army medical officer in the first *Carry On* film, *Carry On Sergeant*, in 1958, Hattie continued to act in other pictures, including *The Navy Lark*, *The Punch and Judy Man* – alongside Tony Hancock again – *The Magic Christian* and Eric Sykes's wordless comedies *The Plank* and *Rhubarb*.

Her television career was no less prolific. She had met Eric Sykes when she was in the radio show *Educating Archie*, which he wrote, and for 20 years she enjoyed a television partnership with him in the situation-comedy *Sykes*, which began in 1960 and followed the antics of an accident-prone brother and his put-upon sister as they ran their sweet shop. Hattie continued in the role until her death.

Her other TV appearances included *Our House* – with Hylda Baker – *Paromania* and *Happy Holidays*.

Hattie, who died at the age of 56 from a heart attack, married actor John Le Mesurier in 1949, but their relationship ended in an amicable divorce 16 years later. They had two sons, Robin and Kim, who are both rock musicians.

Sid James

b. 8 May 1913
d. 26 April 1976

THE battered-looking, bloodhound face of Sid James was one of the most popular ever to grace the small screen and, for almost 30 years, he kept audiences entertained with his roles in comedy classics such as *Hancock's Half Hour*, *George and the Dragon* and *Bless This House*.

Sid was born in Johannesburg, South Africa, where his parents played in music-halls, but he was in no hurry to follow them into the world of showbusiness and, until the age of 25, had jobs such as a coal heaver and diamond digger. He also fought in the ring as a boxer, rising from amateur to semi-professional and professional, and this contributed to the punchbag that passed for a face.

During the Second World War, Sid served in an entertainment unit and, subsequently realising that his face was never going to be his fortune, he resigned himself to the fact that he would never be a leading man, but a character actor. With this in mind, he settled down to several years in repertory theatre and made his film debut in *Black Memory*, in 1947, before being given the first of his many cockney roles, in the film *It Always Rains on Sundays*.

His first major screen comedy was *The Lavender Hill Mob*, in which he and Alfie Bass were part of a bullion robbery gang headed by Alec Guinness and Stanley Holloway. He then made two more comedies, *Lady Godiva Rides Again* and *The Galloping Major*, and appeared on the London stage in *Kiss Me Kate*.

In 1954, he teamed up with Tony Hancock for the radio show *Hancock's Half Hour*, with the show transferring to television two years later. Sid's half in the partnership succeeded in establishing him as one of the top comedy stars of the day, as the straight man who poured water on Hancock's relentless optimism about his abilities and social standing at their home, 23 Railway

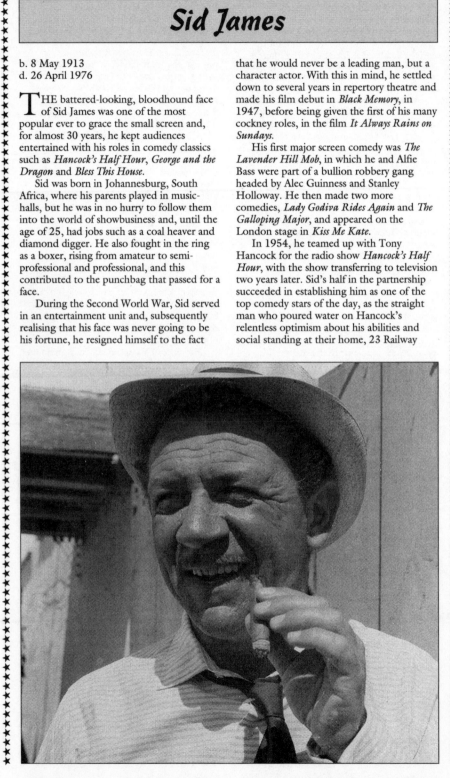

Cuttings, East Cheam. The partnership ended when, in 1960, Hancock dropped his co-star from the show. But, instead of sinking, Sid ricocheted back as king of the *Carry On* films. He made 19 altogether, beginning with *Carry On Constable* in 1960. Perhaps Sid's popularity as part of the *Carry On* gang was that, whatever character he played, it was still him – even under inch-thick grease paint and a huge ginger wig!

Success also followed on television, where Sid appeared in his own comedy series, *Citizen James*, before going on to head the cast in several well-received sitcoms, such as

East End, West End, George and the Dragon – appearing with Peggy Mount as a handyman and housekeeper at a stately home – and *Bless This House*, in which he starred with Diana Coupland as the parents with troublesome teenaged children, played by Sally Geeson and Robin Stewart.

Although he survived a heart attack in 1967, Sid died from a second attack nine years later, at the age of 62.

He had been twice married, first to Meg Williams, with whom he had a daughter, and second to Valerie Ashton, with whom he had a son and a daughter.

David Janssen

b. 27 March 1931
d. 13 February 1980

DURING the 60s, *The Fugitive* gripped viewers around the world and made its star, the gravel-voiced David Janssen, not only very rich, but one of the top actors in American television – the equivalent of Roger Moore and Patrick McGoohan on British TV.

Born David Harold Meyer in Naponee, Nebraska, the actor witnessed the break-up of his parents' marriage while he was still a baby. His mother, a former Ziegfeld girl, subsequently married Eugene Janssen and the family settled in Los Angeles.

David made his film debut in *It's a Pleasure* at the age of 14 and followed it with appearances in pictures such as *King of the Roaring Twenties*, *Hell to Eternity* and *The Green Berets*. Thirty-two of his films were for Universal Studios. But, never fully realising his potential on the big screen, he scored a hit on television in the title role of the detective series *Richard Diamond, Private Eye*, which ran for two years from 1957. Diamond's business was run by secretary 'Sam', never seen on screen apart from her legs (which, in real life, belonged to Mary Tyler Moore).

However, it was his next major TV role, as Dr Richard Kimble in *The Fugitive*, that made David an international star. In the series, which began in 1963, his character was on the run from avenging policeman Lt Philip Gerard after being sentenced to death following the murder of his wife. His attempts to find the real killer – a one-armed man whom he had seen running away from his house – spanned four years and 120 episodes.

There was uproar when the first part of the final, two-part episode was screened in

the middle of a British summer, with many loyal viewers away on holiday. The final part was screened in many countries on the same day, with no advance publicity about the climax, in which Kimble tracked down the one-armed killer, struggled with him and was about to be pushed from a ledge when Lt Gerard arrived and shot dead the murderer, who made a confession just before he died.

After appearances in various films and TV movies, David scored his third hit series in three decades, playing downbeat detective Harry Orwell in *Harry O*, running for two years from 1973.

Shortly before his death from a heart attack, at the age of 48, David appeared in the TV movie *The Golden Gate Murders* – again as a detective – and in the film *Inchon!* He had also started filming a new series, *Father Damien – The Leper Priest*. The actor's first marriage, to Ellie Graham, ended in divorce and he later wed Dani Greco.

Jimmy Jewel

b. 4 December 1909

A tale of two showbusiness careers is that of Jimmy Jewel, who spent more than 30 years as half of the legendary Jewel and Warriss comedy partnership, before switching to acting in TV comedies and drama.

Born James Arthur Thomas Marsh in Sheffield, South Yorkshire, son of James Marsh Sr., who was a comedian under the name of Jimmy Jewel, the youngster made his stage debut in *Robinson Crusoe* at the age of four, in Barnsley, performed with his father from the age of 10 and subsequently became stage manager for the family show.

When young Jimmy started his own act, his father would not let him use the name Jimmy Jewel, so he performed as Maurice Marsh because he was always doing Maurice Chevalier impersonations.

He made his first London stage appearance at the Bedford Music Hall, Camden Town, in 1925, and worked as a solo act until 1934, when he teamed up with his cousin, Ben Warriss, to appear in revue for J D Robertson at the Palace Theatre, Walthamstow.

The pair, who became Britain's leading double-act in variety, were top of the bill in two London Palladium shows – *Gangway* and *High Time* – in the 40s, toured Australia and America, appeared in the 1946 Royal Variety Performance and starred in five pantomimes for Howard and Wyndham at the Opera House, Blackpool.

In 1947, Jewel and Warriss launched a popular radio series, *Up the Pole*, and they later appeared on television in *The Jewel and Warriss Show, Re-Turn It Up, Sunday Night at the London Palladium* and *It's a Living*. They also appeared on *The Ed Sullivan Show* in America and, at their height, were earning £2500 a week.

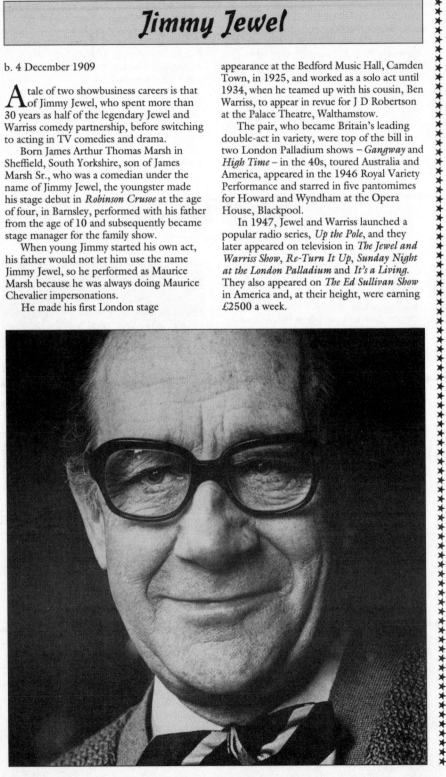

By 1967, when their variety act seemed outdated and the two split, Jimmy had already been working as a carpenter and carpet-layer. He concentrated on his new skills and put his showbusiness days behind him, until Frank Muir offered him a part in a BBC play.

Embarking on a new career as an actor, Jimmy subsequently starred as pickle factory owner Eli Pledge in the 1968 comedy series *Nearest and Dearest*, alongside Hylda Baker, although the two were rumoured to row constantly. He followed it, five years later, with the role of retired railway worker Tommy Butler in *Spring and Autumn*. He also appeared in the comedy series *Thicker Than Water* and in *Worzel Gummidge*.

In 1981, he starred in *Funny Man*, a touching series about a family music-hall act, written by Adele Rose and based on Jimmy's father's company in the 20s and 30s.

He also scored a stage success, in 1976, in the Trevor Griffiths play *Comedians*, first at the Nottingham Playhouse, then at the National Theatre in London.

Although he has more recently been on television in an episode of the comedy series *One Foot in the Grave*, many of his screen appearances have been in straight roles, in programmes such as the one-off drama *Missing Persons*, an episode of *Casualty* and the comedy-drama series *Look at it This Way*. He also played Cannonball Lee in the film *The Krays*.

Jimmy, whose wife Belle Bluett is now dead, has a son, Kelly – who is a comedian and impresario – and an adopted daughter, Piper. He won a Variety Club of Great Britain Special Award in 1985 and lives in West London.

Peter Jones

b. 12 June 1920

WITH his carefully measured and cultivated tones, Peter Jones brought authority to a string of situation-comedies in the 60s and 70s, from *The Rag Trade* to *Beggar My Neighbour* and *Mr Digby Darling*. In later years, he provided cameo roles in comedies and dramas.

Born in Wem, Shropshire, he learned his craft in repertory theatre and revues, and subsequently appeared in 30 London West End plays, including *Pass the Butler*. After making his film debut in *Fanny by Gaslight*, in 1944, Peter appeared in more than 40 pictures, including *The Browning Version*, *Blue Murder at St Trinian's*, *The Bulldog Breed*, *School for Scoundrels*, *Carry On Doctor*, *The Return of the Pink Panther* and *Carry On England*.

Television fame did not come until he was into his 40s, but when it did it was worth waiting for. As Mr Fenner, boss of Fenner Fashions in *The Rag Trade*, Peter created a classic comedy role, with his character taking on the militant shop steward, played by Miriam Karlin, but not averse to dodgy deals himself.

The series, which began in 1961, was revived in the 70s with Peter and Miriam the only survivors from the original cast, but without the same impact.

Peter himself went on to star with Pat Coombs, June Whitfield and Reg Varney – who played his supervisor in *The Rag Trade* – in another comedy, *Beggar My Neighbour*, although he left after the first series, then played the title role in *Mr Digby Darling*, with Sheila Hancock, who was also in the original *Rag Trade* series. It ran for three series and Peter later appeared in Sheila Hancock's own TV show, *But Seriously – It's Sheila Hancock*.

Also a writer, Peter scripted and starred in his own *Comedy Playhouse* and co-scripted and starred in two series of *Mr Big* and, with *Emmerdale* creator Kevin Laffan, a series of *I Thought You'd Gone*, which experimented without using a studio audience's laughs on the soundtrack and proved to be a disaster.

Other comedies Peter has acted in include three series of *Oneupmanship*, as well as *Whoops Apocalypse* – playing crazy British Prime Minister Kevin Pork – and guest appearances in *The Goodies*, *Love Thy Neighbour*, *Here's Harry*, *Wodehouse Playhouse* and *Man About the House*.

In more serious vein, he was in *C.A.T.S. Eyes* and *Rumpole of the Bailey*, before playing a detective in the series *The Mixer* and acting in an American soap, *As the World Turns*.

Peter also narrated the hit radio and television series *The Hitch-Hiker's Guide to the Galaxy*, and has been a regular on TV quizzes and game shows, such as *Cabbages and Kings*, *Blankety Blank*, *Celebrity Squares*, *Give Us a Clue*, *Crosswits*, *Movie Memories* and, as chairman, in *M'Lords, Ladies and Gentlemen*.

Married to American actress-writer Jeri Sauvinet, he has one daughter, actress Selena Carey-Jones, and two sons, TV and radio producer Bill Dare – who made *Spitting Image* – and Charles.

Yootha Joyce

b. 20 August 1927
d. 24 August 1980

SEXUAL frustration and class warfare were the key elements in Mildred Roper's small world, and red-headed actress Yootha Joyce played them to perfection. Her pouting pink lips, fluttering false lashes, wiggling hips and vulgar innuendos sent husband George scuttling behind his newspaper with a headache – and left many viewers helpless with laughter.

Born in Wandsworth, South London, the only child of Hurst Needham and former concert pianist and singer Jessica Revitt, Yootha left school at the age of 15, after being evacuated to Hampshire during the Second World War. She then trained at RADA, to which she used to travel each day with former James Bond star Roger Moore. She subsequently left to join a tour with the Forces entertainment organisation ENSA.

Later, she became a member of Joan Littlewood's Theatre Workshop, in East London, at the recommendation of her future husband, actor Glynn Edwards. It was there that she had her first break, in a production of *Fings 'Ain't Wot They Used T' Be*, staged at the Theatre Royal, Stratford East, then in the West End. Yootha's other theatre work included *Man in the Glass Booth*, and the London Palladium pantomime *Cinderella*.

She also made more than 20 films during her career, making her debut in *Sparrows Can't Sing*, in 1962, and following it with pictures such as *A Man for All Seasons*, *Charlie Bubbles* and TV spin-offs *Nearest and Dearest*, *Never Mind the Quality, Feel the Width* and *Steptoe and Son Ride Again*.

However, it was on television that Yootha really made her name. After appearances in programmes such as *Brothers in Law*, *Me Mammy* and *The Victoria Line*, her man-eating character of Mildred Roper was first let loose on the British public in 1973, when she and Brian Murphy – who played her spineless husband, George – were supporting characters in the situation-comedy *Man About the House*. The programme centred on Richard O'Sullivan as student chef Robin Tripp, who shared a flat with two young women, Paula Wilcox playing Chrissy and Sally Thomsett in the role of Jo. Their

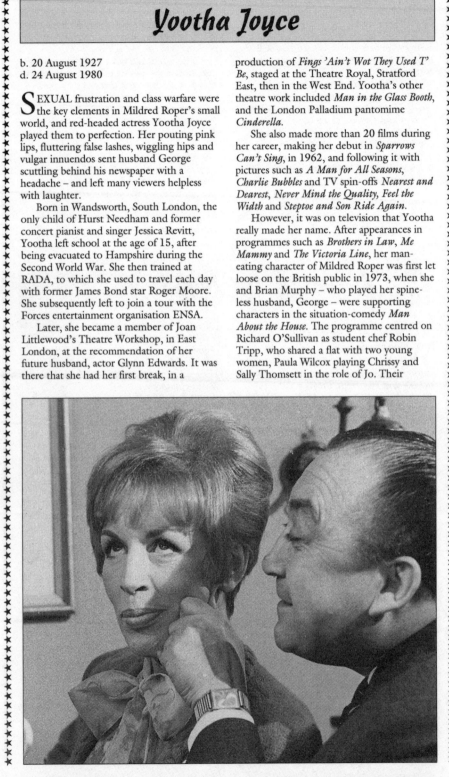

landlords, the Ropers, were so awful that audiences adored them and they often stole the limelight.

Their true popularity was soon acknowledged and, in 1976, they were given their own series, *George and Mildred*, in which the couple moved to a middle-class estate full of young, aspiring executives. George hated it from the start, but Mildred revelled in her imagined new-found status. The banter between the Ropers and their posh next-door neighbours, the Fourmiles, was comedy at its best.

Yootha appeared in film spin-offs of this and their previous hit comedy, *Man About the House*.

The way Yootha portrayed Mildred, with such strong, resilient and dragon-like qualities, concealed the actress's real-life alcohol problem. When she died from cirrhosis of the liver at 53, a chronic alcoholic, it was revealed that for the last ten year's of her life she had downed half a bottle of brandy a day. The pathologist reporting at the inquest of her death said that her liver was twice the normal size and that her heavy drinking had also affected her heart and lungs.

Yootha and her actor husband Glynn Edwards divorced in 1968 and, after that, she lived with two men – firstly, pop manager Cyril Smith and then her own manager, Lee Dickson.

Miriam Karlin

b. 23 June 1925

HER cry was "Everybody out!" and, as militant shop steward Paddy in *The Rag Trade*, Miriam Karlin was one of the first actresses to bring a strong female role to television comedy.

Born Miriam Samuels in Hampstead, North London, she was brought up as an Orthodox Jew, with ancestors who died at the Nazi concentration camp in Auschwitz. Her father, barrister Henry Samuels, wrote books about trade unions.

After training at RADA, Miriam made her stage debut for ENSA – the Forces entertainment organisation – in wartime shows, and subsequently appeared in repertory theatre and cabaret.

Her plays included *The Diary of Anne Frank*, *The Bad Seed*, *The Egg*, *Fiddler on the Roof* and *Bus Stop*, and she made her film debut in the 1952 picture *Down Among the Z Men*, following it with 20 further features, including *Room at the Top*, *Heavens Above!*, *A Clockwork Orange*, *Barry Lyndon* and Ken Russell's *Mahler*.

On television, Miriam made her name as the union leader embroiled in shopfloor rows with manager Peter Jones and foreman Reg Varney at Fenner Fashions in *The Rag Trade*, which began in 1961 and came hot on the heels of the British film comedy *I'm All Right, Jack*, which satirised union-employer relations. The series, written by Ronald Wolfe and Ronald Chesney, was revived in the 70s but failed to have the same impact as the original.

Miriam subsequently appeared on stage for the Royal Shakespeare Company at Stratford-upon-Avon, the Aldwych Theatre and the Barbican Centre, and acted in *Torch*

Song Trilogy and Agatha Christie's *And Then There Were None*, both in London's West End, and a national tour of *84 Charing Cross Road*. She became the first woman to play the central role in Harold Pinter's *The Caretaker*.

Miriam was in the 1989 TV movie *The Strange Case of Dr Jekyll and Mr Hyde* and, three years later, made a surprise return to television as ghost Yetta Feldman, hoping for a reunion with her daughter, in the BBC comedy series *So Haunt Me*.

A lifelong campaigner for Jewish and left-wing causes, she has also been an active member of the actors' union, Equity, and was awarded an OBE for her union and welfare work.

The actress, who has never married, lives in South London.

Barbara Kelly

b. 5 October 1923

IN the 50s and 60s, the panel game *What's My Line?* was one of the hottest shows on television and Barbara Kelly was one of its most charismatic stars.

Born in Vancouver, Canada, she began her showbusiness career in radio at the age of 16, playing the Virgin Mary in *The York Mystery Plays* for the Canadian Broadcasting Corporation. She also played a variety of Shakespearean roles in *The Stage Series*.

In 1942, Barbara married actor Bernard Braden and, seven years later, the couple

moved to Britain. She was offered a part in a BBC radio series and a lead role on stage in *The Male Animal*, alongside Canadian actor Arthur Hill, winning her a Best Actress award.

She joined *What's My Line?* when it began on BBC television in 1951 as the quiz where a panel of celebrities had to guess a member of the public's occupation. It quickly became the most popular programme in Britain, with Barbara as a regular, alongside such memorable panellists as Gilbert Harding and Lady Isobel Barnett. She stayed with the programme, on and off, for all of its 12-year run and, with host Eamonn Andrews, was the sole survivor from the original team when the show was revived by ITV in 1984.

Her other television appearances include those in *Kelly's Eye*, *The Criss Cross Quiz* and *Leave Your Name and Number*. She was in the TV plays *The Concert* and *Carissima*, and starred with Bernard Braden in the comedies *Bedtime with Braden* on radio and *The Bradens* on TV, as well as playing the title role in a 50th anniversary stage production of *Peter Pan*.

Barbara, who with her late husband, who died in 1993, had a son, Christopher, and two daughters, Kelly and actress Kim, runs an international entertainments consultancy called Prime Performers.

She says she would like to be buried in a small town called Nanyuki, at the foot of Mount Kenya, "in the vain hope that, if there is any such thing as reincarnation, I will return as a Bougainvillaea!"

Kenneth Kendall

b. 7 August 1924

AS one of BBC television's first newsreaders, Kenneth Kendall was always a bit poker-faced, ensuring that no reaction to the stories crept in to hint at any bias, which would have flouted the ideals of the Corporation's first Director-General, Lord Reith. Later, as presenter of the game show *Treasure Hunt*, he showed a warmer, more human side.

Born in South India – where his father worked – but brought up in Cornwall, Kenneth studied at Oxford University, served as a captain in the Coldstream Guards during the Second World War and began a career in teaching.

Joining the BBC in 1948, he was chosen, seven years later, as one of its first three television newsreaders seen on screen for the first time, pre-empting the arrival of ITN on the new Independent Television channel. Previously, radio broadcasters such as Richard Baker had read the news, with only their voices heard from behind pictures that illustrated the day's events.

Kenneth soon became known for his elegant dressing and was even voted best-dressed newsreader by *Style International*. He left the BBC in 1961 to freelance, returned eight years later and then retired from his job in 1981.

Immediately, Kenneth was working again, presenting *The South West Week*, a round-up of the week's news for the deaf and hard-of-hearing in the then TSW ITV region, and beginning the hugely successful *Treasure Hunt* series on Channel Four, initially with Anneka Rice as 'skyrunner'. The programme,

which ran throughout the 80s, was a ratings-topper. He has also presented *Songs of Praise* and, in the 60s, made guest appearances in *Doctor Who* and *Adam Adamant Lives!*, a series starring Gerald Harper.

Kenneth, who has never married, lives in London and enjoys reading and going to the theatre.

Roy Kinnear

b. 8 January 1934
d. 20 September 1988

A bald-headed barrel of a man, Roy Kinnear brought laughter into millions of homes as one of the stars of the 60s satirical BBC series *That Was The Week That Was*. The show, which made Roy a household name, attracted a massive following and was the first of its kind to hit the small screen.

Born in Wigan, Lancashire, the son of a rugby international, he was educated at George Herriot School, in Edinburgh, which his father had attended. At the age of 17, he enrolled at RADA but experienced a slight hiccough in his training when he was signed up for National Service during the War.

Roy acted in repertory theatre for the first time in 1955, when he appeared in a show at Newquay, before going on to act in Nottingham, Glasgow, Edinburgh and Perth.

In 1959, he was invited by Joan Littlewood to join her Theatre Workshop, in Stratford, East London, and he appeared in such shows as *Make Me an Offer* and *Sparrers Can't Sing* – both of which went to the West End.

He cropped up regularly in theatre for the rest of his life, later appearing in productions such as *The Travails of Sancho Panza*, playing the title role, and in *The Cherry Orchard*, in 1985.

But it was the television show *That Was The Week That Was* that made Roy famous. This BBC series, first shown in 1962, paved the way for a new permissive and alternative type of programme. Fronted by the then little-known David Frost, with a team of accomplices that included Roy, the show attracted up to ten million viewers. It was highly controversial and made no apologies for it – that was its aim.

Roy later had his own series, *Inside George Webley*, which cast him as a compulsive worrier, before he moved on to play in Keith Waterhouse and Willis Hall's marital comedy *Cowboys*, as the manager of a dishonest building firm.

Roy, a highly polished performer who never seemed to get the praise he deserved, was also an established film actor, having made his debut in the 1962 picture *Tiara Tahiti* and following it with *Heavens Above!*, the Beatles' *Help!*, *A Funny Thing Happened on the Way to the Forum*, *The Bed Sitting Room*, *The Three Musketeers – The Queen's Diamonds*, *The Four Musketeers – The Revenge of Milady*, *The Hound of the Baskervilles* and *Squaring the Circle*. It was while filming *The Return of the Musketeers*, in Spain, that he died after falling from a horse, at the age of 54.

Roy and his wife, Carmel Cryan, had two daughters, Karina and Kirsty, and one son, Rory.

David Kossoff

b. 24 November 1919

LONG before David Jason and company brought the Larkin family stories of H E Bates to the television screen, there was another, completely different Larkin series, with David Kossoff as the hen-pecked husband who, with Peggy Mount, ran a country pub.

Born of Russian-Jewish parents in London's East End, the young Jew won a scholarship to an architectural college but had to take a job as a trainee draughtsman to bring in money for his poor family. He worked first in a furniture designer's workrooms and later in engineering.

Interested in the theatre, David learned mime from a French café cook who had performed as a clown, and took voice lessons from a children's elocution teacher. By 1939, he had decided to become a professional actor but, with the outbreak of war, became a back-room boy at aircraft factories.

In his spare time, David belonged to an amateur theatre group in London, writing, producing and acting in a factory revue that toured shelters. He joined the Unity Theatre, London, in 1942 and three years later was acclaimed for his performance in *Yellow Star*, then joined BBC radio's repertory company.

He played hundreds of parts in radio plays over the next six years and acted the folk hero Lemmie in *Journey into Space*, attracting eight million regular listeners. On stage, David took over the role of the Russian Colonel in Peter Ustinov's play *The Love of Four Colonels*, in 1952, to great acclaim, and made his television debut the same year in *Make Me an Offer*, before more stage success in London's West End in *The Shrike* and a Wolf Mankowitz double-bill, *The Bespoke Overcoat* and *The Boychik*.

In 1957, he took his own one-man show, *One Eyebrow Up*, to South Africa, beating the colour bar in theatres there by performing in front of mainly blacks two nights running in a hall in an outlying district. His subsequent one-man shows have been titled *Kossoff, A Funny Kind of Evening* and *As According To Kossoff*.

After making his first film appearance in the 1953 picture *The Good Beginning*, David followed it with *The Young Lovers* – playing an Iron Curtain diplomat – *Svengali, A Kid for Two Farthings, The Mouse That Roared, The Two Faces of Dr Jekyll, The Mouse on the Moon* and *Summer Holiday*, as well as a short of his stage hit *The Bespoke Overcoat*.

In 1958, he teamed up with Peggy

Mount as Alf and Ada in *The Larkins*, which immediately became a TV success, running for three series and earning a 1960 spin-off film, *Inn for Trouble*.

David revived *The Bespoke Overcoat* for television, repeating his performance as Morrie, one of the greatest portrayals of a Jew ever seen on screen. His own experience as a draughtsman also made him perfect for the part of the father teaching screen son Francis Matthews the ins and outs of the furniture business in a 1964 series, *A Little Big Business*.

He later had his own programme, *Kossoff and Company*, and became known for his Bible readings on television, in programmes such as *Storytime*.

But tragedy struck in 1976 when his younger son, Paul – lead guitarist in the rock group Free – died of drug-induced heart failure. The 25-year-old had a history of drug abuse and David has since campaigned against such dangers. He performed his own one-man show, *Late Great Paul*, at the Queen Elizabeth Hall and on a tour of universities and public schools.

The actor has also written eight books, including *Bible Stories Retold By David Kossoff, The Book of Witnesses, The Voices of Masada* and *Sweet Nutcracker*, as well as the play *Big Night for Shylock*.

David and his wife Jennie have another son, Simon, and live in Hatfield, Hertfordshire.

Sam Kydd

b. 15 February 1915
d. 26 March 1982

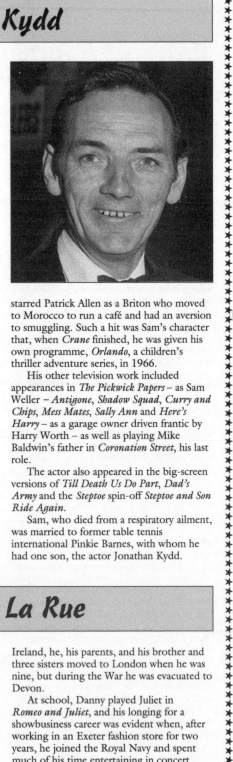

BOTH youngsters and their parents delighted in actor Sam Kydd's most famous role, as smuggler Orlando O'Connor, first seen in the adult drama series *Crane*, then in the children's spin-off *Orlando*.

An Army officer's son, Sam was born in Belfast but moved to England with his family while still a child. On leaving school, the youngster was determined to follow a career in showbusiness, which was initially limited mainly to working as MC with the Oscar Rabin Orchestra.

But it was during the Second World War, when he was taken prisoner in Calais in 1940, that Sam really became involved with acting.

He was interned in a Polish prisoner-of-war camp where, for the next five years, he took command of the camp's theatrical activities – devising and staging plays. He felt so strongly about his work there that, when he was offered repatriation after three years, he turned it down to continue with his theatrical duties. In recognition of his valuable services during these years, he was awarded a pair of drama masks made by the Red Cross from barbed wire.

Returning to Britain after the War, Sam resumed a budding film career, which had started back in 1940 with *They Came By Night*. He went on to make a further 200 films, including such memorable pictures as *The Blue Lamp*, *Father Brown*, *Reach for the Sky*, *The Thirty Nine Steps* and *I'm All Right, Jack*, often playing resilient cockneys.

Sam's television career was no less successful and, for many years, he was seen in a variety of roles, the most famous being as the loveable smuggler Orlando O'Connor, first seen in the 1963 series *Crane*, which

starred Patrick Allen as a Briton who moved to Morocco to run a café and had an aversion to smuggling. Such a hit was Sam's character that, when *Crane* finished, he was given his own programme, *Orlando*, a children's thriller adventure series, in 1966.

His other television work included appearances in *The Pickwick Papers* – as Sam Weller – *Antigone*, *Shadow Squad*, *Curry and Chips*, *Mess Mates*, *Sally Ann* and *Here's Harry* – as a garage owner driven frantic by Harry Worth – as well as playing Mike Baldwin's father in *Coronation Street*, his last role.

The actor also appeared in the big-screen versions of *Till Death Us Do Part*, *Dad's Army* and the *Steptoe* spin-off *Steptoe and Son Ride Again*.

Sam, who died from a respiratory ailment, was married to former table tennis international Pinkie Barnes, with whom he had one son, the actor Jonathan Kydd.

Danny La Rue

b. 26 July 1927

AS a female impersonator, there has never been anyone to touch Danny La Rue. His act, steeped in the traditions of British variety and music-hall, has been seen around the globe, and Bob Hope once called him 'the most glamorous woman in the world'.

Born Daniel Patrick Carroll in Cork,

Ireland, he, his parents, and his brother and three sisters moved to London when he was nine, but during the War he was evacuated to Devon.

At school, Danny played Juliet in *Romeo and Juliet*, and his longing for a showbusiness career was evident when, after working in an Exeter fashion store for two years, he joined the Royal Navy and spent much of his time entertaining in concert parties while on board Lord Mountbatten's invasion task force bound for Singapore.

After a spell working in an Oxford Street department store, he turned professional as an entertainer, touring as a chorus boy in revue and appearing in pantomimes and drag shows such as *Forces in Petticoats*.

Still performing under his real name of Danny Carroll, he made his London debut in a revue at the Irving Theatre, just off Leicester Square, turning up to find himself billed as Danny La Rue. "In your costumes," the show's organiser explained, "you look very glamorous. You're tall and lean, and remind me of a French street." Charles Landau spotted him there and booked him to appear in cabaret at the fashionable Churchill's Club, in Bond Street. He moved on from there to Winston's, becoming producer and star of his own show, then opened his own club in Hanover Square in 1964. It ran for eight years, its clientele including royalty and Hollywood stars, until property redevelopment caused its closure.

Danny made his West End debut in *Come Spy with Me*, taking it on a national tour before it opened at the Whitehall Theatre in 1966, running to packed houses for 18 months. He followed it with *Queen Passionella and the Sleeping Beauty*, teaming up with his long-time ugly sister Alan Haynes again, in what proved to be one of the longest-running pantomimes on the London stage.

Then came *Danny La Rue at the Palace*, running for two years at the Palace Theatre,

the pantomime *Queen of Hearts*, in Manchester, *The Danny La Rue Show* – which took a record £1 million at the Prince of Wales Theatre box-office – *The Exciting Adventures of Queen Danniella*, at the then London Casino, *Aladdin* at the London Palladium, with Danny starring as Widow Twankey, and *Hello, Dolly!* at the Prince of Wales Theatre, in the lead role of Dolly Levi.

He has also performed in the 1969, 1972 and 1978 Royal Variety Performances, and starred in the 1972 film *Our Miss Fred*, as an actor fleeing Nazi-occupied France during the Second World War by dressing in women's clothes.

Several of Danny's stage shows have been broadcast on TV, including *Come Spy with Me*, *Danny La Rue at the Palace* and *Queen of Hearts*. He also appeared in *The Good Old Days* many times and has starred in an original television production of *Charley's Aunt*, as well as his own specials, such as *A Night Out with Danny La Rue*, *Tonight with Danny La Rue* and *The Ladies I Love*, and as the subject of a special, hour-long *This Is Your Life*, in 1984.

In 1968, he made a record, *On Mother Kelly's Doorstep*, which reached number 33 in the singles chart. As well as touring Britain, he frequently takes his variety show to Australia and New Zealand.

Bachelor Danny was named the Variety Club of Great Britain's Showbusiness Personality of the Year in 1969. His autobiography, *From Drags to Riches*, was published in 1987.

Ronald Lacey

b. 28 September 1935
d. 15 May 1991

ONE of television's classic bad guys and the definitive Dylan Thomas, throughout his career Ronald Lacey played the leering hard case, in programmes ranging from *The Secret Agent* to *Ladykillers*.

Born in Harrow, Middlesex, he trained at LAMDA after doing his National Service, before going on to make his name at the Royal Court Theatre in 1962 as Smiler in *Chips with Everything*. The role required him to wear a fixed smile, which became his trademark in later years.

Ronald's theatrical career, however, was cut short by the ill health that seemed to dog him for most of his life. In his 20s, an abdominal operation where most of his intestines were removed left him lacking in energy, making arduous stage productions extremely difficult. So he decided to opt for the relatively less taxing demands of television and film, rarely returning to the stage.

The most memorable time when he actually *did* return was to play all four villains in *Private Dick*, at the Lyric Theatre, Hammersmith.

His television roles, although frequent, were often as a member of the supporting cast, although his face was one that viewers knew but could not quite place. He appeared as the villain of the piece in many series, including *The New Avengers*, *The Sweeney*, *Scarecrow & Mrs King* and *Unnatural Causes* but, despite his apparent penchant for playing baddies, Ronald was keen to escape typecasting and eagerly took other roles.

Perhaps his two most memorable pieces of television were as the reformer Charles James Fox in *Fight Against Slavery*, in 1975, and as Dylan Thomas in *Dylan*. Ronald had a great affinity with the poet and even toured for several months in his own stage show, *Dylan and Liz*.

He also demonstrated a talent for comedy and gave fine performances in *Whatever Happened to the Likely Lads?*, the long-running *Porridge*, *Last of the Summer Wine* and *Haggard*. His other TV appearances included those in *The Nightmare Years*, *Connie*, *Boon* and *Bergerac*.

Many cinema-goers will remember Ronald for his spine-chilling Nazi in Steven Spielberg's *Raiders of the Lost Ark*, in 1981, and it was this sinister quality that the actor showed in his many other films, such as *Zulu Dawn*, *Red Sonia*, *Gunbus*, *Stalingrad* and *Landslide*.

Ronald, who died from a heart attack at the age of 55, was twice married. He had a daughter, Rebecca, and a son, David, from his first marriage, to actress Mela White, which ended in divorce, and a son, Matthew, from his second marriage, to Joanne Baker, who died before him.

Michael Landon

b. 31 October 1936
d. 1 July 1991

ONE of the small screen's truly likeable stars, Michael Landon reigned supreme in three hugely successful television series, *Bonanza*, *Little House on the Prairie* and *Highway to Heaven*.

Born Eugene Maurice Orowitz in Forest Hills, New York, he was a talented javelin thrower and won a sports scholarship to the University of Southern California. Unfortunately, he lost his scholarship after pulling a ligament and ended up working as a petrol-pump attendant, where he was discovered by a Warner Brothers executive, who invited him to join the film studio's acting school. Michael didn't need asking twice and it wasn't long before he made his film debut in *I Was a Teenage Werewolf*, in 1957, followed by *God's Little Acre* and *The Legend of Tom Dooley*.

But it was in television that he really became a household name and his first series, a Western called *Restless Gun*, launched him into better things. As a result of appearing in it, he was chosen for the Western series *Bonanza*, in 1959. Michael appeared as Little Joe, the youngest of the Cartwright brothers, for 14 years and, by the mid-60s, the programme had become the most popular on American television.

While most actors are lucky to have starred in one popular series, Michael was fortunate enough to have three. The second was the children's saga *Little House on the Prairie*, which he not only acted in, but adapted for television from Laura Ingalls

Wilder's famous books, as well as producing and writing many of the episodes.

As Charles Ingalls, he was the dependable and loving 'Pa' to three doting girls, Mary, Laura and Carrie. The series was fresh, simple, based on traditional values and lingered on the Ingalls family in their log home in Plum Creek, Minnesota, as they struggled to etch out a living in the bare and often cruel prairies. Audiences loved the programme, which ran for nine years from 1974.

Michael's third hit series, shown between 1984 and 1989, was the fantasy drama *Highway to Heaven*, which saw him as a probationary angel who had returned to heaven to do good things. Sentimental and mushy, it was guaranteed to leave viewers weepy-eyed.

Before Michael found out he was suffering from inoperable pancreatic cancer, from which he eventually died, he had signed with the American television network CBS to produce and star in a new weekly series called *Us*. In it, he was cast as a man released from prison and returning home to his family after wrongly being locked up for 18 years.

Unfortunately, Michael's illness took its toll and production on the programme was brought to a halt.

Michael's first two marriages, to Dodie Fraser and Lynn Noe, ended in divorce. In 1983, he wed Cindy Clerico. Altogether, he had nine children – two adopted sons from his first marriage, two sons, two daughters and one stepdaughter from his second, and one son and one daughter from his third marriage.

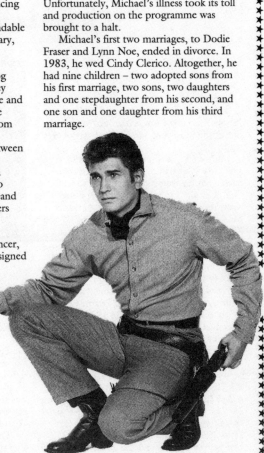

Philip Latham

b. 17 January 1929

AFTER playing the gentle financial whiz-kid in both *Mogul* and *The Troubleshooters* in the 60s, Philip Latham followed the role up with that of a snob in *The Pallisers*, one of the BBC's 70s costume dramas.

Born in Leigh-on-Sea, Essex, he trained at RADA after doing his National Service and gained experience in repertory theatre in Farnham, Salisbury and Northampton, before appearing in the London West End production of *The Gazebo* and tours of *Missing Persons* – starring opposite Anna Neagle – *The Letter* and *The Winslow Boy*, in the role of Arthur Winslow.

His films include *The Dam Busters*, *Dracula – Prince of Darkness* and *Force 10*

from Navarone, but it was on television that he found fame, first between 1965 and 1971 as Willy Izzard in *Mogul* and then its long-running sequel, *The Troubleshooters*, his character contrasting sharply with the young go-getters played by Robert Hardy and Ray Barrett in stories that brought TV viewers drama from the boardroom to the bedroom.

Then, in 1975, Philip starred as Plantagenet Palliser in the BBC's adaptation of *The Pallisers*, based on Anthony Trollope's novels, and later played the father of a rich family in the pre-war family serial *The Cedar Tree*, as well as appearing in *The Professionals*, *Nanny*, *No. 10* – as Wellington – *Doctor Who*, *Man from the Pru* and the TV movie *From a Far Country: Pope John Paul II*.

Philip and his wife Eve have a daughter, Amanda, and a son, Andrew.

John Laurie

b. 25 March 1897
d. 23 June 1980

A distinguished Scottish actor, John Laurie was best known to TV viewers as Private Frazer, the undertaker in *Dad's Army*, one of the most successful comedy series ever made.

Although it was on television that he really made his name, Dumfries-born John's talents reached out into theatre, radio and film. Basically a classical actor, he appeared many times at the Old Vic, playing Hamlet, Macbeth, Touchstone, Feste, Richard III and King Lear, after making his debut there as Pistol in *The Merry Wives of Windsor*, in 1922. He had originally planned to become an architect but, after serving with the Hon. Artillery Company during the First World War, switched to acting and trained at the Central School of Speech and Drama.

John's film career began in 1930 with *Juno and the Paycock* but, again, it is the classics for which he is best remembered on the big screen.

He was outstanding in Olivier's productions of *Henry V*, *Hamlet* and *Richard III*. His other pictures included *Old Mother Riley's Ghosts*, *Old Mother Riley Cleans Up*, *The Life and Death of Colonel Blimp*, *Fanny by Gaslight*, *Caesar and Cleopatra*, *Bonnie Prince Charlie*, *Kidnapped*, *One of Our Dinosaurs is Missing* and *The Prisoner of Zenda*.

Many of his early cinema roles had him cast as either fanatical or eccentric characters, but, for John, widespread popularity came at a late age when, in 1968, viewers laughed at the antics of the wild-eyed Scotsman Private Frazer in the hit TV comedy series *Dad's Army*.

The programme charted the madcap adventures of the calamitous platoon of fighting men who made up the Home Guard, a gallant group of old soldiers whose task it was to guard Britain's coastlines against possible enemy invasion during the Second World War.

The series ran for nine years and the cast also appeared in a 1971 film spin-off, which was considerably better than many big-screen versions of TV hits. John, who died in 1980 at the age of 83, was married twice. His first wife, who tragically died in 1926, was Florence Saunders, whom he met at the Old Vic in his early acting days. He later married Oonah V Todd-Naylor, with whom he had a daughter.

John Le Mesurier

b. 5 April 1912
d. 15 November 1983

STAR of the hugely successful comedy show *Dad's Army*, John Le Mesurier entertained audiences for almost 50 years.

Born John Elton Halliley in Bedford, but brought up in Bury St Edmunds, Suffolk, he suppressed his ambition to become an actor on leaving school and began work as an articled clerk for a firm of solicitors in the town. However, before long, the lure of the bright lights proved too strong and he went to the Fay Compton School of Dramatic Art to train as an actor.

Taking his mother's maiden name as his stage name, John made his professional debut at the Palladium Theatre, Edinburgh, and toured in shows until the outbreak of the Second World War, when he served as a captain in the Royal Armoured Corps, both at home and in India.

Demobbed in 1946, he was back acting in repertory theatre in Birmingham and also frequently broadcasting for the BBC Midland region.

John's distinctive flapping gestures and worried, dead-pan expression made him an ideal support player in many British comedy films. Throughout his career, he made more than 100 films, starting with *Death in the Hand*, in 1948, which was followed by pictures such as *Private's Progress, Brothers in Law, The Admirable Crichton, Ben-Hur, I'm All Right, Jack, The Pure Hell of St Trinian's, The Rebel* and *The Punch and Judy Man* – both with Tony Hancock – *The Pink Panther, Those Magnificent Men in Their Flying Machines, Doctor In Trouble* and *The Fiendish Plot of Dr Fu Manchu*.

John had already appeared on television with Tony Hancock, in *Hancock's Half Hour* and *Hancock*, when he was cast in the 1966 comedy series *George and the Dragon*, alongside Peggy Mount and Sid James, who played the housekeeper and the handyman of a large stately home.

But it was in the long-running *Dad's Army*, beginning two years later, that he really became a household name. His portrayal of Sergeant Arthur Wilson in the Home Guard was superb, and his character provided the perfect foil to Arthur Lowe, who played the pompous, blustering platoon leader, Captain Mainwaring. The pair's relationship was pure perfection, as Lowe's character – although superior in rank to Le Mesurier's, but of inferior class – struggled to hide the chip on his shoulder.

After his success in *Dad's Army*, which ran for nine years and earned a 1971 film spin-off, John also appeared in *The Goodies, Doctor at Large, Anywhere But England, A Class by Himself, The Dick Emery Show* and *Worzel Gummidge*. His was also the voice that informed viewers that 'graded grains make finer flour' in commercials for Homepride flour.

Although his niche was definitely in comedy, John was also a talented straight actor, winning a Society of Film and Television Arts Best Television Actor award for his memorable performance as a character based on the spy Kim Philby in Dennis Potter's TV play *Traitor*, in 1971.

His serious television roles included those in *Brideshead Revisited, A Christmas Carol* and the lead in David Mercer's play *Flint*.

On radio, John played the part of Bilbo Baggins in a production of *Lord of the Rings*.

His last TV appearance, in 1983, was in an adaptation of Piers Paul Read's novel *A Married Man*, but his final work was in the BBC Radio 2 show *It Sticks Out Half a Mile*, a spin-off from *Dad's Army*, with John reviving his old character of Sergeant Wilson.

Only three days later, he died from an abdominal illness. John had been a heavy drinker for many years and suffered with cirrhosis of the liver.

The actor was married three times. He was divorced from his first wife, actress June Melville, after the War and he subsequently married celebrated comedy actress Hattie Jacques, with whom he had two sons, Robin and Kim. They divorced in 1965 and, one year later, John wed Joan Malin, the former wife of actor Mark Eden.

John's best-selling autobiography, *A Jobbing Actor*, was published posthumously in 1984.

★★★★★★★★★★★★

Liberace

b. 16 May 1919
d. 4 February 1987

A more glamorous entertainer than Liberace there could never be. He had it all – rhinestones, rings, bouffant hairdo and a permanent grin.

You either loved or loathed him, but to the millions of fans who followed every move of his diamond-decked fingers he was Mr Showmanship.

Born Wladiziu Valentino Liberace in West Allis, Milwaukee, son of a penniless Italian immigrant, he learned the piano from the age of four and won a scholarship to music college, where at the age of nine he made his professional debut playing with the Chicago Symphony Orchestra.

During the 30s America was all but brought to its knees by the Depression and finding work to supplement his scholarship was not easy for the young musician. Although he deeply resented doing so, Liberace earned extra money by playing to small gatherings at supper clubs and ladies' groups.

Changing his name to Walter Busterkeys, he made the move to Las Vegas, where he was just another small fish in a big pond. The real success he so craved seemed to elude him, until he reverted to his old name and landed his own television programme, *The Liberace Show*.

This unique performer soon became one of the 50's most popular small-screen acts. His show, screened around the world, literally dripped with glitz and glamour. Candelabras surrounded his piano, while – dressed in glittering costumes with velvet bow-ties – Liberace teased his hair into a wispy bouffant and flashed his huge rhinestone rocks at the TV cameras.

He loved to entertain and appeared in the 1978 Royal Variety Performance in a replica of George V's coronation robes.

In addition to his concerts and shows, he also appeared in a handful of film roles, as a pianist in *East of Java*, in 1949, and as an undertaker in *The Loved One*, in 1965.

Despite his fame and fortune, Liberace was often surrounded by sexual scandals. In 1959, he found himself the centre of a legal wrangle when he sued Cassandra (William O'Connor) of the *Daily Mirror* for malice when the columnist wrote a piece questioning Liberace's sexuality. The court ruled in the star's favour and awarded him £8000, which he donated to a cancer charity. Then, in 1982, he settled out of court in a case brought by his former chauffeur.

Liberace was a jackdaw – he loved anything that sparkled. His passions were antiques and motor cars, which he collected with profusion, and, in 1979, he opened his own museum in Las Vegas. Among the many fascinating items on show were a lock of Liszt's hair and a tea set presented to him by the Queen.

Margaret Lockwood

b. 15 September 1916
d. 15 July 1990

A glittering film star of the 40s, Margaret Lockwood brought her charm and acting ability to the small screen when she played legal eagle Harriet Peterson in ITV's *Justice* series.

Born Margaret Mary Lockwood, in the then Indian city of Karachi, she was the daughter of an English administrator of the Indian railway and a Scottish mother.

At the age of three, Margaret returned to Britain with her mother and brother Lyn and later became a dance student in London, where she made her acting debut at the age of 15, as a fairy in *A Midsummer Night's Dream*, at the Holborn Empire.

But Margaret's excitement at becoming an actress suffered a hiccough in 1931, when her domineering mother made her leave her role in Noël Coward's play *Calvacade*, after hearing that one of the chorus boys had sworn in front of her daughter.

Two years later, Margaret was back and training at RADA – but not for long. Her talent was recognised even in such shining company, when top London agent Herbert de Leon took her off for a screen test after spotting her in the play *Hannele*.

She passed the audition with flying colours and won herself the second-lead in director Basil Dean's 1934 film *Lorna Doone*. Several run-of-the-mill pictures followed until, two years later, she appeared alongside Maurice Chevalier in *The Beloved Vagabond*, the tale of a jilted French artist who becomes a vagabond and falls in love with an orphan girl.

Margaret won enormous success and professional recognition when she appeared in the Carol Reed film *Bank Holiday*, in 1937. A year later, her next film, the thriller *The Lady Vanishes*, brought her international stardom. With the film world at her feet, she left for Hollywood, where she made *Susannah of the Mounties*, with Shirley Temple, and *Rulers of the Sea*, with Douglas Fairbanks Jr.

She had not enjoyed her stay in Tinseltown and returned to Britain, where she continued to make films. She is best remembered for *The Wicked Lady*, starring opposite James Mason as the man-eating Lady Skelton, with her trademark beauty spot painted high on her left cheek and revealing the most daring expanse of naked flesh as her ample cleavage threatened to break free from her tightened bodice. She was the ultimate villainess, a highway woman, reeking of sensuality, but with distinct overtones of evil and darkness.

Margaret's 42-year film career finished in 1976, when she made *The Slipper and the Rose*. It had already begun to wane by the mid-50s, when she returned to her first love,

the stage, acting in plays such as *Pygmalion* and *Private Lives*, before turning to television to appear in a string of programmes that included *Last of Mrs Cheyne*, *Murder Mistaken*, *Call It a Day*, *The Great Adventure*, *The Royalty*, *Palace of Strangers* and *The Flying Swan*, in which her daughter Julia also appeared.

But it was the courtroom series *Justice*, which started in 1971, that established her in a major role on the small screen, as determined barrister Harriet Peterson. It was very much her show, although Anthony Valentine joined her 'chambers' for the second series.

Julia was Margaret's only child, the daughter of Rupert Leon, from whom she was divorced in 1950. Although Margaret was awarded custody of her daughter, her own mother sided with Leon to claim that she was an unfit mother. After her divorce, Margaret never saw her mother again.

Although the actress, who was plagued with middle-ear disease for most of her life, never married again, she lived with actor John Stone, who left her after 17 years to marry a theatre wardrobe mistress.

Margaret was made a CBE in 1980 and spent her last years as a recluse in Surrey, before her death at the age of 73.

Jack Lord

b. 30 December 1922

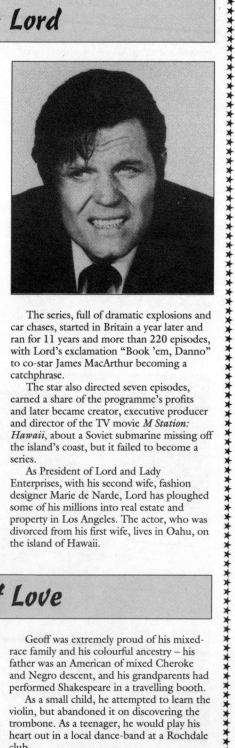

STEVE McGarrett, in his blue business suit, was a TV detective who tracked down ruthless murderers on the beat around the sun-drenched Honolulu beaches in *Hawaii Five-O* – and actor Jack Lord's financial stake in the programme made him a millionaire.

Born John Ryan in New York City, he was third mate in the Merchant Navy, once spending 16 hours in a lifeboat when his ship was torpedoed off East Africa in 1944. He also studied fine art at New York University and organised his own art school in Greenwich Village.

Some of his works have been exhibited in such institutions as the Metropolitan Museum of Art, the Museum of Modern Art, the Brooklyn Museum – all in New York – and the Bibliotheque National, Paris, and British Museum.

After studying at the Neighborhood Playhood and the Actors' Studio, Jack got his acting break in the American TV series *Man Against Crime* and was still using his real name when he made his film debut in *The Red Menace*, a 1949 picture full of McCarthyite propaganda.

With a new stage name, he subsequently appeared in films such as *The Vagabond King*, *The Hangman* and *Dr No*, the first James Bond feature. On television, he turned up in episodes of many legendary series, including *The Untouchables*, *Naked City*, *Rawhide*, *Bonanza*, *Route 66*, *Gunsmoke*, *Dr Kildare*, *Laredo*, *The FBI*, *The Invaders*, *The Fugitive*, *The Virginian*, *The Man From U.N.C.L.E.*, *The High Chaparral* and *A Man Called Ironside*, before becoming the humourless star of *Hawaii Five-O*, in 1968.

The series, full of dramatic explosions and car chases, started in Britain a year later and ran for 11 years and more than 220 episodes, with Lord's exclamation "Book 'em, Danno" to co-star James MacArthur becoming a catchphrase.

The star also directed seven episodes, earned a share of the programme's profits and later became creator, executive producer and director of the TV movie *M Station: Hawaii*, about a Soviet submarine missing off the island's coast, but it failed to become a series.

As President of Lord and Lady Enterprises, with his second wife, fashion designer Marie de Narde, Lord has ploughed some of his millions into real estate and property in Los Angeles. The actor, who was divorced from his first wife, lives in Oahu, on the island of Hawaii.

Geoff Love

b. 4 September 1917
d. 8 July 1991

ONE of the small screen's most famous music men, Geoff Love will be remembered by many as the stooge to Max Bygraves's jokes on his many TV shows.

Born in the industrial West Yorkshire town of Todmorden, his father was a guitarist and champion dancer and his mother was a former actress.

Geoff was extremely proud of his mixed-race family and his colourful ancestry – his father was an American of mixed Cheroke and Negro descent, and his grandparents had performed Shakespeare in a travelling booth.

As a small child, he attempted to learn the violin, but abandoned it on discovering the trombone. As a teenager, he would play his heart out in a local dance-band at a Rochdale club.

It was there that Geoff was spotted by

bandleader Jan Ralfini, who invited him to play with his band. He spent three years with him, growing in confidence and experience, and laying down the foundation for a solo career.

However, the outbreak of the Second World War put his career on a back-burner for a few years, while he served as a bandsman in the King's Royal Rifles.

After being demobbed, Geoff joined bandleader Harry Gold, with whom he remained for several years, until he tired of touring and began work as an arranger in London's Tin Pan Alley.

Under the guise of Manuel and His Music of the Mountains, he also had hit singles with 'Theme From Honeymoon', 'Never On Sunday', 'Somewhere My Love' and, most famous of all, 'Rodrigo's Guitar Concerto de Aranjuez'. He had hit albums of film themes under his own name and three

top 20 LPs as Manuel. He also produced, arranged and accompanied many stars, such as Marlene Dietrich, Connie Francis and Shirley Bassey, during their studio performances.

But it was as bandleader on Max Bygraves's shows that Geoff became known the length and breadth of Britain. Working alongside pianist Bob Dixon, he was the butt of many light-hearted jokes, taking them in the spirit in which they were meant. Audiences loved it and so did the high-profile bandleader.

For 12 years Geoff arranged all the music on Bygraves's TV shows, which included *Max Bygraves*, *Max*, *Singalongamax*, *Max Rolls On*, and the *Max Bygraves – Side By Side With* series.

Geoff, who died in 1991 at the age of 73, was married to Joy and had two sons, Adrian and Nigel.

Arthur Lowe

b. 22 September 1915
d. 15 April 1982

A S the blusteringly pompous Captain Mainwaring in the classic television comedy series *Dad's Army*, Arthur Lowe was lifted from the ranks to enjoy celebrity status.

Born in Hayfield, Derbyshire, the only son of a railway worker, he was raised in Manchester and, on leaving school, his ambition was to join the Merchant Navy. Poor eyesight thwarted his plans, however, so Arthur went to work in an aeroplane factory. He had no interest in acting until he tried his hand at amateur dramatics while serving in the forces during the Second World War. As a Sergeant Major serving in Gaza, he decided that a few impromptu shows might brighten things up for the troops.

After the War, Arthur returned to Manchester, where he made his professional debut at the age of 30 with a local repertory company.

His first London West End appearance came in 1950 at the Duke of York's Theatre and he went on to appear in several London musicals, including *Call Me Madam* and *The Pyjama Game*.

Arthur later joined the National Theatre company for Somerset Maugham's *Home and Beauty*, before appearing in *The Tempest* at the Old Vic, in 1974.

But it was with television that Arthur really became popular. Although his face had occasionally appeared on the small screen from 1953, it was not until the next decade, when he joined *Coronation Street*, as Gamma Garments fashion shop manager Leonard Swindley, that he became a star.

The role saw Arthur develop in the character of an irascible, rather crusty gentleman who was jilted at the altar by Emily Nugent. The part of Swindley was such a success that he was given his own series, *Pardon the Expression*, in 1965.

Then, three years later, the actor found even greater success with *Dad's Army* – a comic look at the gallant band of the Walmington-on-Sea Home Guard, defending the country's coastline against possible enemy invasion.

Cast as the bank manager and platoon captain, the banter between him and his public school deputy, played by John Le Mesurier, was skilfully acted. The show was a comedy classic and is loved just as much now as when it first ran in 1968. There was also a film spin-off, in 1971.

Arthur's later television roles included Mr Micawber in the Dickens classic *David Copperfield*, Irish priest Father Duddleswell in the comedy series *Bless Me Father*, and the title role of a headmaster in *A J Wentworth, BA*, a gentle comedy that suited the actor's droll style. He was also in the TV movies *The Strange Case of the End of Civilization as We Know It*, *The Lion, the Witch and the Wardrobe* and *Wagner*.

In films, Arthur showed himself to be a competent supporting actor, making his debut in *London Belongs to Me*, in 1948, and following it with pictures such as *The Green Man*, *This Sporting Life*, *If . . .*, *The Bed Sitting Room*, *Adolf Hitler – My Part In His Downfall*, *No Sex, Please – We're British*, *The Bawdy Adventures of Tom Jones*, *The Lady Vanishes* and *Britannia Hospital*.

Arthur, who died at the age of 66 after suffering a stroke in his dressing-room at the Alexandra Theatre, Birmingham, where he was appearing in the play *Home at Seven*, was married to the actress Joan Cooper, with whom he had a son, Stephen, and a stepson, David.

Cyril Luckham

b. 25 July 1907
d. 7 February 1989

DISCIPLINED and dependable, Cyril Luckham was one of those character actors who brought integrity to television in popular series such as *The Forsyte Saga*, *The Cedar Tree* and *To Serve Them All My Days*, his talent coming from a solid grounding in the theatre.

Born in Salisbury, Wiltshire, he planned a career in the Royal Navy and reached the rank of lieutenant, but was invalided out in 1931. Switching to acting, he trained with the Arthur Brough Players attached to Folkestone.

His stage debut was as a footman in *The Admirable Crichton*, in Folkestone, and he followed it with repertory work there, then seasons in Manchester, Bristol, Liverpool, Coventry and Southport.

Cyril's first London stage appearance, in 1948, was as Gayev in a Liverpool Playhouse production of *The Cherry Orchard*, at St James's Theatre, which was presenting the works of various repertory companies from around the country. A string of West End plays followed, including roles in Peter Ustinov's *The Moment of Truth* and *The Love of Four Colonels*, and as Gerald Piper in T S Eliot's *The Family Reunion*.

From 1957, he acted with the Royal Shakespeare Company for three seasons, alongside contemporaries such as Michael Redgrave, Charles Laughton and Edith Evans. Cyril excelled in the title roles of *Gonzalo* and *Polonius*, and as Parolles in Tyrone Guthrie's production of *All's Well That Ends Well*.

His many films included *Anne of the Thousand Days*, *A Man for all Seasons* – in which he gave a particularly memorable performance as Archbishop Thomas Cranmer – *The Pumpkin Eater* and *The Naked Runner*.

After his TV debut in the 50s, Cyril was in dozens of television programmes, such as *Vote Vote Vote for Nigel Barton* and *Hadleigh*, before joining *The Forsyte Saga*. He played the baronet Sir Lawrence Mont – known as 'Bart' – who was father to Susan Hampshire's Fleur, then preparing to get married.

His part in *Doctor Who* as a White Guardian – a 'goodie' – brought Cyril a lot of fan-mail, even though he appeared in only half-a-dozen episodes.

Later, he played the grandfather in the daytime serial *The Cedar Tree*, about three generations of an upper-class family in the years leading up to the Second World War, and chairman of the board of governors in the school drama *To Serve Them All My Days*.

Cyril also appeared on television in programmes such as *Public Eye*, *Jennie, Lady Randolph Churchill*, *Wodehouse Playhouse*, *The Omega Factor*, *My Son, My Son*, *Tales of the Unexpected* and *The Barchester Chronicles*. He was a storyteller for *Jackanory* and his last two TV appearances were reading his own choice of poems in episodes of *Five To Eleven*.

The actor, who died at the age of 81, met his actress wife Violet Lamb while they were working in rep together, at the Little Theatre, Bristol. They had a son, Robert, who is a bass baritone with the English National Opera.

Cyril's last stage appearance was as the lawyer Finch MComas, alongside Sir Ralph Richardson, in George Bernard Shaw's *You Never Can Tell*.

The actor, whose family had for generations lived in the Dorset village of Studland, was proud of his heritage, loved the poetry and novels of Thomas Hardy and often, with his wife, gave recitals about the county. His ashes were buried alongside his ancestors in the Anglo-Saxon churchyard in Studland.

Ray McAnally

b. 30 March 1926
d. 15 June 1989

A major theatrical talent for all his adult life, it took half-a-dozen films and his role as Labour Prime Minister Harry Perkins in *A Very British Coup*, in his twilight years, to establish Ray McAnally as a star of the screen.

Born in Buncrana, County Donegal, the son of a bank manager, Ray wrote, produced and staged a musical called *Madame Screwball* for his school at the age of 16.

However, he studied for the priesthood before deciding that acting was the career for him, joining the Abbey Theatre Company, Dublin, in 1947 and playing all the major Irish stage parts there over the next 14 years.

Moving into film and television work, Ray occasionally returned to the Abbey Theatre and, in later years, directed and taught there. He also performed on stage with the Royal Shakespeare Company and had London West End success with plays such as *Who's Afraid of Virginia Woolf?* and *The Best of Friends*.

His screen performances – in films such as *Shake Hands with the Devil*, and more than 150 TV programmes – usually eclipsed the quality of the productions themselves.

It was not until later years that Ray found the right vehicles for his talent. Television roles as Peter Egan's rogue of a father in *A Perfect Spy* and Harry Perkins in *A Very British Coup* won him the BAFTA Best Actor award two years running.

He also achieved film acclaim as the Protestant boss in *Cal*, a former Irish terrorist in *No Surrender* and the Cardinal in *The Mission*, which won him a BAFTA award as Best Supporting Actor and the London *Evening Standard* Drama Awards Best Actor honour.

When the right scripts finally came his way, it was Ray's ability to underplay roles and make moments of silence 'talk' that won him universal respect.

Married to Ronnie Masterton – by whom he had two sons and two daughters – Ray continued to live in Ireland even after finding fame far beyond his homeland. He had only just moved into top gear on screen at the time of his death, at the age of 63.

Patrick McGoohan

b. 19 March 1928

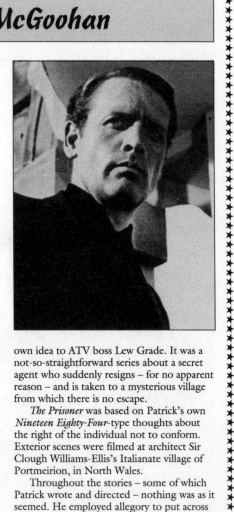

ONE of the biggest stars of the 60s, Patrick McGoohan made his mark as a secret agent in *Danger Man* and followed it by infuriating much of the nation in the cult series *The Prisoner*.

Born in Long Island, New York, Patrick's Irish-American parents decided to return to the family farm in County Leitrim when he was six months old. They later moved to Sheffield, South Yorkshire, where he joined the British Rope Company's wire mills on leaving school. After jobs as a bank manager, chicken farmer and in offices, he joined Sheffield Rep as an assistant stage manager. One of his contemporaries there was Paul Eddington, later James Hacker, MP, of *Yes Minister*, and he married fellow-actress Joan Drummond.

After four years, Patrick left to gain wider experience with the Midland Repertory Company, the Bristol Old Vic, the Windsor and the Q, before making his London West End debut in *Serious Charge*, at the Garrick Theatre in 1953.

The following year, he made his first film appearance, in *The Dam Busters*, and acted in Orson Welles's stage version of *Moby Dick*. After several more films, he signed a studio contract with the Rank Organisation, taking lead roles in productions such as *Hell Drivers* and *The Gypsy and the Gentleman*.

Dissatisfied with the parts he was being given, Patrick switched back to the theatre, gaining notable success in Ibsen's *Brand*, for which he won the 1959 Best British Theatre Actor Award, later performing on television the role of the priest who destroys himself and everyone around him in the name of God's will.

After acting in various television plays, Patrick was chosen to take the lead role of John Drake in *Danger Man*, which began on ITV in 1960 and ran for six years. The series was seen on American television under the title *Secret Agent* and the star directed three of the 72 episodes. He became the highest-paid star on British TV and reportedly turned down an offer to play Simon Templar in *The Saint*, objecting to the scripts pairing the character off with a different woman every week. Roger Moore took the role and became his arch-rival on the small screen.

Between series of *Danger Man*, Patrick starred in films such as *The Quare Fellow* and the Disney pictures *Dr Syn – Alias The Scarecrow* and *The Three Lives of Thomasina*. Looking for a new TV vehicle, he took his own idea to ATV boss Lew Grade. It was a not-so-straightforward series about a secret agent who suddenly resigns – for no apparent reason – and is taken to a mysterious village from which there is no escape.

The Prisoner was based on Patrick's own *Nineteen Eighty-Four*-type thoughts about the right of the individual not to conform. Exterior scenes were filmed at architect Sir Clough Williams-Ellis's Italianate village of Portmeirion, in North Wales.

Throughout the stories – some of which Patrick wrote and directed – nothing was as it seemed. He employed allegory to put across the themes, and viewers jammed ITV companies' switchboards with complaints.

The star who had been given it all was forced to bring the story to an early end, after 17 episodes. Not fully appreciated at the time, the series has since become a cult, twice repeated in its entirety on Channel Four.

Shortly after making *The Prisoner*, Patrick moved to California and has since appeared in films such as *The Moonshine War*, *Escape From Alcatraz* – as the menacing prison governor – and *Kings and Desperate Men*. He was also in the TV movies *The Man in the Iron Mask*, *Jamaica Inn* and *Three Sovereigns for Sarah*, and in the title role of a low-key American TV series, *Rafferty*, in 1977.

As a director, he has made the film *Catch My Soul* – a rock musical version of Shakespeare's *Othello* – and various episodes of the TV detective series *Columbo*, in which he also appeared.

Fulton Mackay

b. 12 August 1922
d. 6 June 1987

FEW of the great stars of television can be as talented in all spheres of acting as Fulton Mackay, the totally 'unstarry' Scotsman best known as the ferocious prison warder in the comedy series *Porridge*.

Born in Paisley, Renfrewshire, in the 20s, Fulton was brought up in Clydebank by a widowed aunt after the death of his mother. His father was in the NAAFI.

On leaving school, he trained as a quantity surveyor, then volunteered for the RAF in 1941. A perforated ear drum kept him out and, during the Second World War,

he served in the Black Watch instead, staying in the Army for five years, including three spent in India.

After being demobbed, Fulton decided on a career in acting and trained at RADA. His first work was with the Citizens' Theatre, Glasgow, clocking up nine seasons there between 1949 and 1958.

He also worked at the Royal Lyceum Theatre, Edinburgh, before making his mark at the Arts Theatre Club, London, where – in 1960 – he played Oscar in *Naked Island*, a play about POWs in Singapore.

Two years later, at the same theatre, he appeared in Russian playwright Maxim Gorki's classic *The Lower Depths* for the Royal Shakespeare Company. He then acted with the Old Vic company and the National Theatre, performing in such productions as *Peer Gynt* and *The Alchemist*.

Other roles for the Royal Shakespeare Company included Squeers in *Nicholas Nickleby* and the drunken jailer in *Die Fledermaus*.

Fulton was a director of the Scottish Actors' Company and, in 1981, he co-founded the Scottish Theatre Company, with whom he acted.

He appeared in surprisingly few films. After his screen debut in the 1952 feature *I'm a Stranger*, his most notable roles were those in *Gumshoe, Britannia Hospital, Local*

Hero – as the wise, old Scottish fisherman – and *Defence of the Realm*.

On television, Fulton stayed true to his Scottish roots, acting in productions such as *Clay, Smeddum and Greenden, Three Tales of Orkney* and *The Master of Ballantrae*. He reached a wider audience in series such as *Special Branch* – playing Derren Nesbitt's boss, Chief Supt. Inman – and *The Foundation*, and played an RAF psychiatrist in an episode of *Some Mothers Do 'Ave 'Em*.

But it was his role in *Porridge*, as Chief Warden Mackay, that made him a household name. He also appeared in the film version of the series. The ensemble playing of Mackay, Ronnie Barker, Richard Beckinsale and Brian Wilde made scriptwriters Dick Clement and Ian La Frenais's stories one of the most successful comedy series ever.

As well as making guest appearances in the TV sequel, *Going Straight*, Fulton also appeared as Colonel Norriss in Eric Sykes's TV film *If You Go Down in the Woods Today*, in 1981, was the Captain in Jim Henson's *Fraggle Rock* and, under the pseudonym Aeneas MacBride, he wrote plays for BBC television and radio.

Married to Irish actress Sheila Manahan, Fulton – who died at the age of 64 – did much work for the Glasgow children's charity Child and Family Trust, was awarded an OBE in 1984 and enjoyed oil-painting.

Robert McKenzie

b. 11 September 1917
d. 12 October 1981

WITH his 'Swingometer', Robert McKenzie made General Elections interesting entertainment for the small-screen viewer.

Born and educated in Vancouver, Canada, he subsequently studied at the University of British Colombia, where he later worked as a lecturer. In 1943, he joined the Canadian Army and a year later, with the rank of captain, was sent to London, where he remained for the rest of his working life.

Leaving the services three years later, Robert joined the London School of Economics to work for a doctorate. In 1949, he was given a sociology lectureship there and was promoted to chairman in 1964.

He wrote many academic books and papers during his extensive career, including *British Political Parties* and *Angels in Marble*, but it was through television and radio that he was to make his name.

His broadcasting career began when he

was invited by the BBC to give occasional talks on the Overseas Service, before becoming involved in domestic radio and TV.

It was with the TV coverage of General Elections that Robert really made his mark, taking part in every one since 1955. He was charming, eloquent, flamboyant and enthusiastic. When results started to filter in, the larger-than-life Canadian would jump around explaining excitedly the relationship between votes and seats as the 'Swingometer' went into action.

Robert was also an extremely talented interviewer. Who could forget him penetrating Lord Hailsham's defences during the Profumo scandal, or coaxing Harold Macmillan into uttering more than just a few words?

Despite his success on television, he remained chiefly an academic, delighting in the history of politics.

Robert, who died from cancer, never married. He lived in a house on a Thames island where he entertained his many friends.

Fred MacMurray

b. 30 August 1908
d. 5 November 1991

MAINLY recognised for his vast array of big-screen roles, and at one time Hollywood's highest-paid actor, Fred MacMurray found small-screen fame in the long-running American television situation-comedy *My Three Sons*.

Born Frederick Martin MacMurray in Kankakee, Illinois, he started out in the entertainment world as a musician, working his way through college as a saxophonist and singer in a local band.

From there, he moved to a more established group, with whom he performed on Broadway in a little-known revue and then in the Jerome Kern musical *Roberta*, in which he was spotted by a Paramount film studio talent scout and put under contract.

Fred made his film debut in *Girls Gone Wild*, in 1929. Although he played dramatic, passionate characters in a few of his pictures, he was usually cast as the affable, homely best buddy or fatherly type. Typical of this were his roles in *The Princess Comes Across*, *Sing, You Sinners*, *Take a Letter, Darling* and *Follow Me, Boys!*

His other films included *Hands Across the Table*, with Carole Lombard, and *The Apartment*, with Shirley MacLaine and Jack Lemmon, with Fred giving a brilliant portrayal of a cynical, womanising businessman.

He retired from the cinema in 1978, after making his last film, the disaster tale *The Swarm*, about an out-of-control swarm of killer bees.

Although his TV appearances had been few, Fred became hot property as the beleaguered father in *My Three Sons* during the 50s and early 60s. The series, based in the heart of suburbia, demonstrated a brand of bland, rather homogenised middle-class American life. His other small-screen appearances included the TV movies *False Witness*, *The Chadwick Family* and *Beyond the Bermuda Triangle*.

Fred's first wife died in 1953 and he married actress June Haver a year later.

no double indemnity !!

Patrick Macnee

b. 6 February 1922

THE suave, typically English John Steed, complete with bowler hat, rolled umbrella and elegant suits, made Patrick Macnee a worldwide star in *The Avengers*. But success was a long time coming for the apparently confident actor.

Born in London, a cousin of actor David Niven and the son of a racehorse trainer, Patrick rode with champion jockey Gordon Richards as a boy and intended to become a jockey himself, until he grew too tall.

He attended Eton College – where his contemporaries included Michael Bentine and Humphrey Lyttelton – but was expelled and decided on a future in acting, starting in repertory theatre in Bradford at the age of 18. He found more repertory work, in Letchworth, and made his London stage debut in *Little Women*, after touring in the production.

Patrick's first film was *Sailors Three*, in 1940, and he followed it with *Major Barbara* and *The Life and Death of Colonel Blimp*, before the War intervened and he joined the Royal Navy, commanding a motor-torpedo boat in the North Sea.

Afterwards, he picked up the threads of his acting career, although jobs were infrequent and he moved between Britain, the USA and Canada in search of work. Between acting jobs, he even earned money as a barman in a strip club.

In the early days of Canadian TV, Patrick appeared in *The Moonstone*, a series that ran from 1952, and in the USA he played a sheriff in the popular Western series *Rawhide*.

He acted in the Old Vic's American tour of *A Midsummer Night's Dream*, in 1954, and his three dozen films include *Scrooge, Les Girls* and *The Sea Wolves*. He often appeared as cowboys in Hollywood Westerns, but it was the role of John Steed in *The Avengers* that finally brought Patrick fame and fortune.

The programme started with Patrick and Ian Hendry – star of *Police Surgeon*, the series on which *The Avengers* was based – as the leading characters. But, when Ian left after the first series, he was succeeded by a series of beautiful female sidekicks – Honor Blackman, Diana Rigg and Linda Thorson.

The Avengers, capturing the mood of the 'Swinging 60s' and with James Bond-style gadgetry, ran for five series and 83 episodes, from 1961 to 1969.

When French television producers wanted to revive it, the programme returned as *The New Avengers*, in 1976, although Patrick's role was not as prominent as it had been.

He was well into middle-age and Gareth Hunt stepped in as the more youthful Gambit, with Joanna Lumley providing the glamour as Purdey. The revamped programme ran for two series.

Since then, Patrick has appeared in the TV movies *The Return of the Man From U.N.C.L.E.* and *The Return of Sam McCloud*, and in TV series such as *Magnum, Murder, She Wrote* and in his own show, *Patrick Macnee Presents Sherlock Holmes*.

He has been married and divorced twice – to actress Barbara Douglas and to Catherine Woodville – and he has a daughter, *cordon bleu* cook Jennie, and a son, TV documentary producer-director Rupert, both from his first marriage. His autobiography, *Blind in One Ear*, was published in 1988.

Ronald Magill

b. 21 April 1920

FOR almost 20 years, Ronald Magill formed one of the most enduring double-acts in TV soap history as Amos Brearly, alongside Arthur Pentelow's Henry Wilks, running The Woolpack pub in *Emmerdale*.

Landlord Amos was the dour one with bushy sideburns, although neither characteristic formed a part of Ronald. However, like his screen alter-ego, the quietly spoken actor has always been something of a loner.

Born in Hull, East Yorkshire, he was brought up in a Birmingham orphanage from the age of nine, after his schoolteacher father died, and would visit his mother during holidays. On leaving school, he worked in a brass foundry, then a tyre company.

Ronald had already been caught by the acting bug when he joined the Royal Corps of Signals during the Second World War and toured with the *Stars in Battledress* concert party, acting alongside other then 'unknowns' such as Terry-Thomas, Michael Denison and Charlie Chester.

He returned to being a tyre salesman after the War but was determined to break into acting professionally. A year later, he joined the Arena travelling theatre company, which performed around the country in a circus tent. He spent three years with Arena before moving on to other repertory theatre work and has since appeared on most provincial stages outside London.

A great lover of the classics, Ronald joined the new Nottingham Playhouse in 1963 and stayed for nine years, as actor and artistic director, combining productions of Shakespeare with those of modern playwrights who were making their names with 'socially aware' theatre in the early 60s. He worked with legendary director Tyrone Guthrie on *Coriolanus* and stars such as Leo McKern and John Neville, as well as up-and-coming actors who included Ian McKellen and Michael Crawford. He also starred at the Bristol Old Vic as Willy Loman in Arthur Miller's *Death of a Salesman* and as Crocker Harris in *The Browning Version*, as well as adapting two plays by Goldoni – *Mine Hostess* and *The Servant of Two Masters* – and Molière's *The Miser* and *Treasure Island*. Ronald also wrote the book of a musical version of *A Christmas Carol*.

In 1970, he appeared in the film *Julius Caesar*, alongside a star-studded line-up that included Charlton Heston and John Gielgud. He had also broken into television, with roles in programmes such as *Special Branch* and *Parkin's Patch*, by the time he auditioned for the forthcoming serial *Emmerdale Farm* in 1972.

Coming straight from an appearance in an Edwardian play, he turned up with bushy sideburns and expected to shave them off if he landed the role of licensee Amos Brearly, but he was told they were perfect for the part – and so was he.

Ronald, who lives in South London and has never married, finally ended the screen partnership with Arthur Pentelow when he left the programme at the end of 1989 to concentrate on theatre work. However, he has since reappeared as Amos on brief visits to whisk Annie Sugden off for long holidays in Spain.

Karl Malden

b. 22 March 1914

TOUGH cop Mike Stone of *The Streets of San Francisco* was one of the endless stream of policemen who patrolled TV screens in the 70s, but Karl Malden of the bulbous nose was more memorable than most.

Born Karl Mladen Sekulovich of Yugoslav parents in Gary, Indiana, he was a good athlete at school and won an athletics scholarship to the Arkansas State Teachers' College but, without enough money to continue, he left after a year.

Karl returned to the steel mills of Gary, then attended the Goodman Theater's drama school at the Chicago Art Institute, earning money by playing professional basketball. Then, he changed his name to Malden and set off for New York, appearing in the Group Theater's production of *Golden Boy* and training at the Actors' Studio, where he met Richard Widmark, Elia Kazan and Marlon Brando.

Elia became a director on Broadway and gave Karl various roles. Karl and Marlon's big break came when they appeared on stage in *A Streetcar Named Desire*, a play by another then unknown, writer Tennessee Williams. It was turned into a film by Elia, with both actors playing the same roles, and Karl won the 1951 Best Supporting Actor Oscar for his part as an ageing bachelor courting Blanche Dubois, played on screen by Vivien Leigh.

Then, Elia directed Karl on Broadway in *All My Sons* and *Quiet City*, and the films *Boomerang!*, *On the Waterfront* – which won Karl an Oscar nomination – and *Baby Doll*.

When Marlon Brando turned to directing, Karl was the first actor he cast in *One-Eyed Jacks*, as the sheriff and former friend on whom outlaw Brando sought revenge. The favours were completed when, in 1957, Karl directed Richard Widmark in the courtroom drama *Time Limit* but did not appear in it himself.

Karl's subsequent film appearances included those in *Birdman of Alcatraz*, *How the West Was Won*, *Cheyenne Autumn*, *The Cincinatti Kid*, *Beyond the Poseidon Adventure* and *The Sting II*. From 1966, he spent a month each year teaching acting at various universities.

He is best known to television viewers as Detective Lieutenant Mike Stone in *The Streets of San Francisco*, which began in 1972. The character, a native San Franciscan, was depicted as always having wanted to be a policeman and working his way through the ranks after a period in the Marines.

Karl's heart-throb sidekick was Michael Douglas – son of actor Kirk – as Inspector Steve Keller, and the series ran for five years.

In 1979, the star made another series, *Skag*, which won acclaim for his performance but little else, ending after just eight episodes. His subsequent TV movies have included *My Father, My Son* and *Absolute Strangers*.

Karl is married to former actress Mona Graham, by whom he has two daughters, Mila and Carla, and lives in Brentwood.

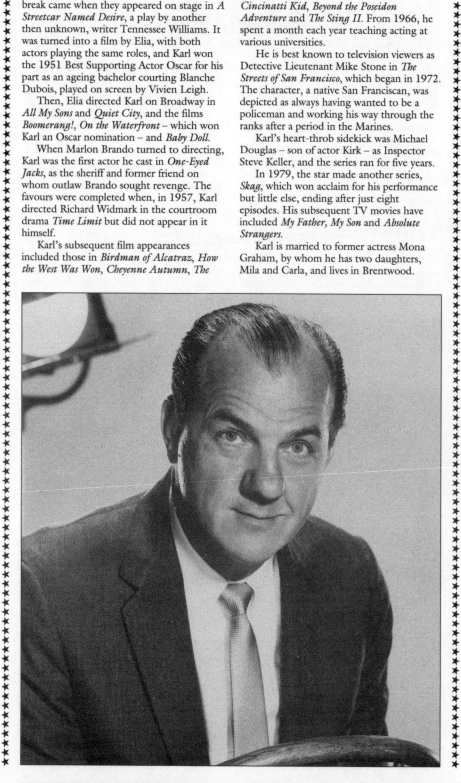

E G Marshall

b. 18 June 1910

PERHAPS second only to screen lawyer Perry Mason in the popularity stakes, veteran actor E G Marshall made Lawrence Preston a favourite with television viewers in the 60s series *The Defenders* and followed it with the role of a doctor in *The Bold Ones*, before several notable TV cameos.

Born in Owatonna, Minnesota, of Norwegian parents, Everett Marshall – the name under which he acted for two decades – was educated at Charleton College and the University of Minnesota and harboured thoughts of becoming a minister, before deciding on a career in showbusiness.

He began by singing and playing guitar on radio in St Paul, Minnesota, in 1932, and made his stage debut with the Oxford Players a year later, performing Shakespeare. The company subsequently moved to Chicago, where it became the nucleus of the Federal Theater's classical wing.

Broadway beckoned and Marshall first appeared there in *Jason*, in 1942, following it with Eugene O'Neill's *The Iceman Cometh* – first as the alcoholic law student, then in the leading role of Hickey – *Waiting for Godot*, a revival of *The Little Foxes* and *The Gin Game*.

Marshall made his first film appearance in *The House on 92nd Street*, in 1945, and followed it with roles in 40 pictures, including featuring as one of the original *Twelve Angry Men* in director Sidney Lumet's first film, a long-suffering husband in Woody Allen's *Interiors*, an American president in *Superman II* and a senator in *Power*. On television, he has appeared in more than 500 programmes, including starring roles in 50s productions of *The Little Foxes* and *Mary*

Poppins. But it was for *The Defenders*, which began in 1961, that he won two Emmy awards and achieved small-screen stardom.

The series, featuring Marshall and Robert Reed as father-and-son lawyers Lawrence and Kenneth Preston, was based on a story by Reginald Rose, who had written the star's film *Twelve Angry Men*. Dealing with issues such as abortion and euthanasia, the programme was highly respected for its realism in portraying the legal system.

Marshall followed its five-year run with the starring role of Dr David Craig in *The Bold Ones*, playing a renowned general surgeon and director of the David Craig Institute of New Medicine, and he hosted a revived *CBS Radio Mystery Theater*.

His subsequent television roles have included those as the American Ambassador to Vietnam in the British TV movie *Saigon - Year of the Cat* and Joe Kennedy, father of the famous brothers, in the *Kennedy* mini-series. He was also the first American actor to appear at the new National Theatre, in London, when – in 1977 – he starred in Bill Bryden's *Old Movies*.

Marshall, who is National Spokesman and a fundraiser for the American Judicature Society, is married with two daughters, Jill and Degan, and lives just outside New York.

Millicent Martin

b. 8 June 1934

MILLIE'S the name, song-and-dance is her game – and the 5ft 2in redhead took British television by storm after finding fame in the 60s satirical series *That Was the Week That Was*.

Born in Romford, Essex, the daughter of a master-builder, Millicent Martin was in her early teens when she took part in the children's chorus of *The Magic Flute* at the Royal Opera House, Covent Garden, in 1948. Two years later, she became an £8-a-week chorus girl in in *Blue for a Boy*.

At the age of 20, the vivacious performer began a three-year tour of America as Nancy in *The Boy Friend*. Back in Britain, she attracted attention on the London stage in *Expresso Bongo*, in 1958. Her other theatre work included roles in *Our Man Crichton*, *Peter Pan* and *Absurd Person Singular*.

Millicent became a star of the small screen with her jazz-style singing in *That Was the Week That Was*, the first TV programme that dared to lampoon the Establishment, on the BBC from 1962. Each show would begin with her singing the theme song, which changed with every episode to incorporate the week's news.

Once fame had arrived, Millicent got her own TV series – *Millie*, *Mainly Millicent*, *The Millicent Martin Show* and *From a Bird's Eye View*.

Having already made her film debut in *The Horsemasters* in 1961 – originally screened as a two-part programme in the *Disneyland* TV show in America – and having appeared in *The Girl on the Boat*, with Norman Wisdom, the spirited performer's new-found fame landed her starring roles in *Nothing But the Best*, *Alfie* and *Stop the World, I Want To Get Off*.

She has also made guest appearances on television in *The Morecambe and Wise Show*, *LA Law*, *Max Headroom*, *Newhart*, *Julia and Company* – with Julia McKenzie – and the *Song By Song* series. She also had her own series with Michael Nouri, called *Downtown*.

In recent years, Millicent has appeared on stage in *Side By Side By Sondheim* – opening at the Mermaid Theatre, London, and transferring to Wyndham's Theatre and Broadway – *King of Hearts*, *Move Over Mrs Markham*, *Noises Off*, *Two Into One*, *Follies* and in New York and Los Angeles productions of *42nd Street*.

Her first two marriages, to singer Ronnie Carroll and actor Norman Eshley, ended in divorce. She married her third husband, American Marc Alexander, while starring in *Side By Side By Sondheim* in New York.

Raymond Massey

b. 30 August 1896
d. 29 July 1983

As the paternal Dr Gillespie keeping a watchful eye on naïve, young Richard Chamberlain in the 60s series *Doctor Kildare*, Raymond Massey brought to bear a lifetime of experience from the American and British stage and cinema screen.

Born into a wealthy Toronto family at the end of the 19th century, Raymond's family could trace its ancestry back to the American Revolutionary War. His father owned the giant Massey-Harris Agricultural Implement Co.

During the First World War, Raymond was a lieutenant in the Canadian Field Artillery but was wounded in France and was then sent to America. He surfaced again in a Canadian expeditionary force in Siberia, where he caught the acting bug while putting on entertainment for the troops.

After the War, he sold farm implements for his father, while acting as an amateur in his spare time. Actor John Drew encouraged him to go to London, where he made his professional debut with a small role in Eugene O'Neill's *In the Zone*, in 1922. He followed it with other plays, including the world premiere of Shaw's *Saint Joan*.

Turning to production and management, Raymond went on to join the Everyman Theatre, in London, which gave a chance to new plays and playwrights. He produced 13 plays and acted in 12 roles in 1931.

In the same year, he made his New York debut, receiving disparaging reviews in the title role of Norman Bel Geddes's production of *Hamlet*, but he returned with his own production of *The Shining Hour*, in 1934.

Raymond made his first films in Britain, his debut being in the 1929 silent *The Crooked Billet*, also known as *International Spy*, and, two years later, he played a rather eccentric Sherlock Holmes in *The Speckled Band*.

He also acted in Hollywood pictures and was nominated for an Oscar for his performance as Abraham Lincoln in the 1940 American film *Abe Lincoln in Illinois*, retitled *Spirit of the People* in Britain. He had played the role in the original stage production, specially written for him by Robert E. Sherwood.

During the Second World War, Raymond re-enlisted in the Canadian Army but was invalided out after eight months. He became an American citizen in 1944 and the following year he returned to Broadway as Henry Higgins, opposite Gertrude Lawrence, in *Pygmalion*.

His post-War films included *East of Eden*, as James Dean's father, and a 30-second appearance as Abraham Lincoln in *How the West Was Won*. He also played Lincoln in a 50s television drama, *The Day Lincoln Was Shot*, but it was with the role of Dr Leonard Gillespie in the medical series *Doctor Kildare*, which ran for five years from 1961, that Raymond achieved major stardom on the small screen.

The actor, who made 60 films and wrote two autobiographies, *When I Was Young* and *A Hundred Different Lives*, died from pneumonia on the same day as the death of his great friend David Niven. Shortly before his own death, he completed an autobiographical television show for Canadian TV. Politically a Republican, he had backed Senator Barry Goldwater's 1964 run for president and helped with the campaign film.

His first two marriages, to Peggy Freemantle and actress Adrianne Allen, ended in divorce and he subsequently married Dorothy Ludington Whitney, whose death preceded his by a year. From his marriage to Adrianne Allen, Raymond had two sons, Daniel and Geoffrey, and a daughter, actress Anna. He also had a stepdaughter, Dorothy Witney.

William Mervyn

b. 3 January 1912
d. 6 August 1976

AS the bishop in *All Gas and Gaiters* and Chief Inspector Rose in three different series of the 60s, William Mervyn demonstrated his great versatility as an actor.

Born William Mervyn Pickwoad in Nairobi, Kenya, but educated in Britain before embarking on a stage career, spending five years in provincial repertory theatre, he made his London debut in *The Guinea Pig*, at the Criterion Theatre, in 1946, before parts in plays such as the comedy *Ring Round the Moon*, *The Mortimer Touch*, Oscar Wilde's *A Woman of No Importance* at the Savoy Theatre, in 1953, and Sir John Gielgud's revival of *Charley's Aunt* a year later.

William's later stage roles included those of Lucius O'Trigger in *The Rival*, Lord Grenham in the comedy *Aren't We All?* and Sir Patrick Cullen in *The Doctor's Dilemma*.

Although he was admired in the theatre, it was with television that he became really well known. One of his first major small-screen roles was that of Sir Hector in the 1962 series *Saki*.

Four years later, he played the Bishop of St Ogg's in the comedy series *All Gas and Gaiters*. It was the first break with tradition, allowing a laugh at the expense of the Church.

William also enjoyed enormous success in the role of Chief Inspector Charles Rose in the weird crime series *The Odd Man*. It was under this persona that he attracted equal popularity in subsequent series, *It's Dark Outside* and *Mr Rose*.

The actor, whose 60s fame put him in demand for voice-overs in TV commercials – for products ranging from cameras to sponge cakes – was married to Anne Margaret Payne Cooke and had two sons.

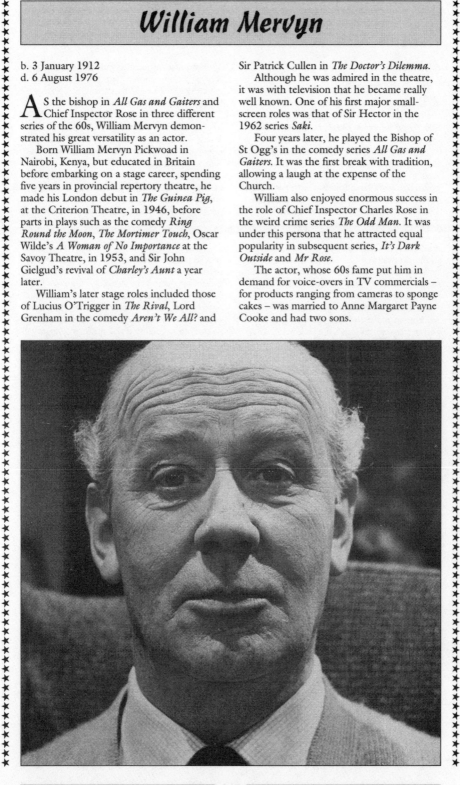

Cliff Michelmore

b. 11 December 1919

AS presenter of the news magazine *Tonight*, Cliff Michelmore was one of the best-known television personalities of the 50s. "And the next *Tonight* is tomorrow night," was his signing-off catchphrase.

Born Arthur Clifford Michelmore in Cowes, on the Isle of Wight, shortly after the First World War, he served in the RAF, before entering broadcasting with the British Forces Network in Hamburg, Germany, in 1947. He became presenter of *Family Favourites*, the radio show that linked families in Britain with their relatives in Germany, with Jean Metcalfe hosting the London end of the programme. The two did not meet until six months after the programme had begun and, after Cliff's return to Britain, they married in 1950.

At the same time, he joined the BBC, working in radio and as a producer, director and writer for children's television programmes, and he also did sports commentaries from 1951. One of the children's programmes Cliff produced was the talent show *All Your Own*, which launched guitarist John Williams on the road to stardom.

In 1955, Cliff was presenter of the interview programme *Highlight*, an early-evening TV show intended to combat the challenge from the new ITV channel, but he became a household name as presenter of the early-evening programme *Tonight*, launched by the BBC in 1957 when the traditional 6–7pm television closedown – intended so that mothers could get their children to bed – was abandoned. A year later, he won a Society of Film and Television Arts award for his work.

Broadcasters such as Fyfe Robertson and Alan Whicker reported for *Tonight*, which gave the news a light touch and a reputation for seeking out the bizarre and eccentric.

When in 1965, after 1800 editions, the programme was replaced by *24 Hours*, Cliff continued as presenter of the programme, alongside other hosts who included Ludovic Kennedy and Kenneth Allsop.

He also reported for *Panorama*, but left current affairs in 1969 to launch the long-running *Holiday* series on BBC1. He also presented the ITV religious show *Stars On Sunday* for a while, as well as *Home On Sunday*.

During the 50s and 60s, Cliff had hosted special programmes on the American space missions, including the first live pictures from the moon during the Apollo-8 flight in 1968, the first live pictures of man walking in space a year later, and the first live colour pictures of the moon's surface in 1969. His other programmes included the motoring series *Wheelbase* and he also worked for Southern Television, the original holder of the ITV franchise for the South and South East of England. He occasionally stepped in as presenter of the news magazine *Day By Day* and hosted *Opinions Unlimited*, a programme in the *Question Time* mould.

Since leaving the *Holiday* programme at the end of the 80s, Cliff has limited his television appearances mainly to the series *Lifeline*, which gives news of voluntary work and charities.

Cliff Michelmore and Jean Metcalfe's autobiography, *Two-Way Story*, was published in 1986. Their son, Guy, is a BBC television reporter and the couple, who have homes in Reigate, Surrey, and on the Isle of Wight, also have a daughter, actress Jenny.

Michael Miles

b. 1919
d. 17 February 1971

AS one of the public's favourite television quizmasters, Michael Miles was seldom off the small screen when his hugely popular show *Take Your Pick* topped the programme ratings for 14 years.

Born in New Zealand, Michael left school to become a broadcaster after pestering his local station for a job every day for six weeks.

He then travelled to Australia, before moving on to Singapore as a newsreader, leaving only days before the island was invaded by the Japanese Army during the Second World War.

Although he produced radio shows during the war years, it was with the transfer of his quiz show *Take Your Pick* to television that he made his name. The programme, which had already been heard on Radio Luxembourg for three years, was one of the

first game shows on ITV when the channel started, in September 1955.

The other quiz show of the time was Hughie Green's *Double Your Money* and the two hosts were seen as bitter rivals.

However, with the exception of *Coronation Street*, it was *Take Your Pick* that appeared in the top ten list of viewers' most popular programmes more than any other.

Masterminded by Michael, who earned the then phenomenal sum of £20 000 a year, it relied on audience participation. When the poor unfortunates were selected from the audience, they were hauled up on stage and put through a barrage of questions to which they had to avoid answering "yes" or "no". If they managed this successfully, they were eligible to select a locked, numbered box or take a wad of money. Each of the boxes

contained either an item that the contestant would be pleased to win or a booby prize. While the participant dithered over the decision, the audience would be whipped into an almost hysterical frenzy.

The show was axed in 1968 when producers Associated Rediffusion were forced into a shotgun marriage with ABC to become Thames Television in the ITV franchise reshuffle, but the show was revived in the 90s with Des O'Connor in the hot seat once occupied by Michael.

However, Michael – an epileptic – returned to TV screens a year after the show's demise with a new quiz show, *The Wheel of Fortune*, which ran until his death, at the age of 51, while on business in Spain.

He was married with a son and a daughter.

Spike Milligan

b. 16 April 1918

SINCE establishing himself in *The Goon Show* on radio, Spike Milligan has fought to find the right TV and film roles for his unique, zany brand of humour. It was the huge success of the show that marked him out as a genius with a talent for anarchic, intellectual comedy.

Born Terence Alan Milligan in Ahmaddnagar, India, he was the son of a gunner in the British Army, who moved to Burma and Ceylon, before being made redundant and returning to Britain and depressed South London in 1933.

He became a jazz singer and trumpet player with the Harlem Club Band, and later played guitar, but his big break came during the Second World War when, as Lance-Bombadier Milligan, he met Harry Secombe in Tunisia and the two performed in Army shows.

In 1949, Spike made his radio debut in the talent show *Opportunity Knocks*. Two years later, when Harry – then on radio in *Educating Archie* – introduced him to Peter Sellers and Michael Bentine, the quartet decided to team up for a new show, written mostly by Spike.

The show started as *Junior Crazy Gang*, before changing its name to *Those Crazy People, The Goons* and then *The Goon Show*. Spike provided the voices for a host of characters, including Bluebottle, Major Denis Bloodnok, Captain Hercules Grytpype-Thinne and Henry Crun.

As in all the top radio shows of the day, catchphrases abounded: "You can't get the wood, you know," "You silly, twisted boy," "Damn clever, those Chinese," and "It's all in the mind, you know," were just some of many.

After The Goons split up, in 1958, Spike concentrated more on the new medium of television. He had made his small-screen debut in *Paging You*, as early as 1947, and followed it with programmes such as *Idiot*

Weekly, Price 2d, A Show Called Fred and Son of Fred, before a string of his own series, including Milligan at Large, Milligan's Wake, Muses with Milligan, The World of Beachcomber, Q, The Other Spike and Milligan for All Seasons.

The humour of Spike Milligan and The Goons inspired later comedians such as the Monty Python team, although Curry and Chips – a 1969 comedy series written by Till Death Us Do Part creator Johnny Speight and starring Spike and Eric Sykes – was dropped after just one series. Viewers complained that the programme, in which Spike was blacked up to play a Pakistani, was racist.

The comedian has made 40 films, the most successful being The Running Jumping and Standing Still Film, The Bed Sitting Room, The Magic Christian, Digby – The Biggest Dog in the World, The Three Musketeers, Monty Python's Life of Brian, History of the World Part I and Yellowbeard.

Spike's own wartime experiences, recounted in his first autobiography, were adapted into a film of the same name, Adolf Hitler: My Part in his Downfall, and his voice is heard in the 1972 animated feature Dot and the Kangaroo, which has enjoyed re-runs on satellite television recently.

His subsequent volumes of autobiography are 'Rommel?', 'Gunner who?', Monty: His Part in My Victory, Mussolini: His Part in my Downfall and Where Have All the Bullets Gone? He has also written many works of fiction, drama, poetry and prose, as well as books of humour – such as A Dustbin Milligan, The Bedside Milligan and The Q Annual – and children's stories.

Spike records have been released almost every year since 1959, some of them excerpts from The Goon Show, others examples of his own style of comedy and, away from the comedy factory that he has created, he has campaigned against the culling of seals and the slaughter of whales for profit, and is a supporter of Greenpeace and Friends of the Earth.

His marriage to first wife June Marlowe was dissolved and he subsequently wed singer Patricia ('Paddy') Ridgway, who died of cancer in 1978, then Shelagh Sinclair, his former secretary. He has two daughters, Laura and Silé, and a son, Sean, from his first marriage, and another daughter Jane, from his second.

A 1986 Channel Four documentary, Spike – Getting to Know a Goon, charted his career. A manic depressive, Spike is patron of the Manic Depression Fellowship and lives in Rye, East Sussex.

Annette Mills

b. 1894
d. 10 January 1955

IN the late 40s and early 50s a generation of children were thrilled by the antics and merriment of Annette Mills and Muffin the Mule on television.

Born in Chelsea, London, the elder sister of actor John Mills, Annette had originally intended to become a concert pianist and organist, before becoming a dancer, subsequently finding fame as an international exhibition dancer.

However, fate struck her a cruel blow when she was forced to retire from professional dancing after breaking a leg. Her career over, she turned her hand to songwriting and penned the two popular tunes 'Boomps-a-Daisy' and 'Home, Sweet Home Again', amongst many others.

Some time later, Annette returned to the stage to take part in cabaret and revues, and it was while she was on her way to entertain the troops during the Second World War that she was involved in a horrific car accident, which left her hospitalised for the next three years.

Annette, however, was unsuppressible.

She fought hard to regain her strength and was rewarded with incredible success on television.

She made her TV debut in June 1946, when she appeared with Muffin the Mule, and really made her mark. Muffin, a puppet worked by Ann Hogarth, used to clip-clop around on top of the piano which Annette played. Annette also wrote several Muffin songbooks and an adventure tale about him, as well as making records.

Later, Annette and Muffin were joined in the BBC's For the Children spot by Prudence the kitten, Mr Peregrine the penguin, Sally the sea lion and Louise the lamb.

Although all the puppets captured the hearts of millions of young viewers, it was Muffin the Mule who stole the show. He really was the first television character to fire children's imaginations and paved the way for others of his kind, such as Sooty and Sweep.

Muffin's last TV appearance was on 2 January 1955, with Annette dying eight days later, at the age of 61, after an operation.

She had been married twice, with a daughter by her first husband and her second marriage, to Robert Sielle, ending in divorce.

Leslie Mitchell

b. 4 October 1905
d. 23 November 1985

WHEN the BBC launched its regular television service in 1936, announcer Leslie Mitchell's voice was the first to be heard. Dubbed 'TV Adonis' by one newspaper, he was later involved with the start of ITV as well – bridging the two with his famous commentaries for *British Movietone News* during the Second World War.

Born Leslie Scott Falconer Mitchell in Edinburgh during the early years of this century, his parents separated while he was still a child and he was brought up by the novelist W J Locke and his wife after his own mother went to America during the early years of the First World War and was unable to return.

Educated at King's School, Canterbury, Leslie was destined for the Navy but failed to get in because of ill health and completed his education at Chillon College, on Lake Geneva, in Switzerland.

After a brief spell as a trainee stockbroker, he secured small roles in stage productions, with no dramatic training but with the assets of good looks and a rich voice. He toured Britain with the Arts League for two years, from 1923, and subsequently appeared in London West End productions.

However, just as Edgar Wallace's *Flying Squad*, in which he had appeared on tour, was about to move into the West End, Leslie suffered multiple injuries in a motorcycle accident and was unable to work for more than a year.

He returned to the West End stage, complete with plastic surgery to his face and a rebuilt jaw, and was just beaten to the part of Captain Stanhope in *Journey's End* by Laurence Olivier. However, he subsequently played the role on a tour of South Africa.

In 1932, Leslie did his first radio work for the BBC, as a commentator for dance bands and, two years later, he became a general announcer, also producing variety programmes.

When the BBC launched its regular television service in 1936, the first in the world, it was Leslie who was chosen from 600 applicants to be its male announcer. Jasmine Bligh and Elizabeth Cowell were the others selected to front the service, but it was Leslie who spoke the first words and became a firm favourite with the limited numbers of people who had television sets. He also conducted interviews for the magazine programme *Picture Page*.

The BBC closed down during the Second World War, but he had left by then and was chief commentator for the newsreels seen in cinemas, always beginning with the introduction, "This is *British Movietone News*, Leslie Mitchell reporting."

Leslie also worked for the Allied Expeditionary Forces Radio, with broadcasts such as *March of the Movies* and *Brains Trust*, and enlisted in the Home Guard.

After the War, he studied publicity methods in America and returned to Britain to become publicity director to film-maker Sir Alexander Korda, but soon returned to freelance commentating and producing.

Leslie was a commentator for the BBC television coverage of then Princess Elizabeth's wedding to Philip and, in 1951, he interviewed Anthony Eden in a General Election programme.

When ITV began, in London in 1955, and in the Midlands a year later, Leslie was there as a 'good omen' for the stations. At Associated-Rediffusion in London, he was head of talks and chaired many discussion programmes, but he returned to freelancing in 1958 and, three years later, narrated with Richard Dimbleby a celebration of BBC television's 25 years. He later hosted a 40th-anniversary documentary, as well as presenting *Those Wonderful TV Times* for Tyne Tees Television, the ITV company in the North East.

Leslie, whose biography *Leslie Mitchell Reporting . . .* was published in 1981, married twice. In 1965, his first wife, Phyllis, daughter of London impresario Firth Shephard, died and, a year later, Leslie wed Inge Jørgensen. He died at the age of 80 after years of ill health.

★★★★★★★★★★★★★

Warren Mitchell

b. 14 January 1926

LOUDMOUTH Alf Garnett, bigoted, patriotic and a Conservative Party supporter, took 60s TV by storm in the classic Johnny Speight comedy series *Till Death Us Do Part*, making Warren Mitchell's character a small-screen legend. But – in real life – Garnett was a million miles away from the actor, who loves playing classical roles on stage.

Born Warren Misell in Stoke Newington, London, in 1926, the son of a Jewish china and glass merchant, he started singing and dancing lessons at the age of seven, at Gladys Gordon's Academy of Dramatic Arts. Warren went on to Oxford University to study physical chemistry in 1944, but left after six months to join the RAF, training as a navigator in Canada.

He travelled to Canada with Richard Burton, whom he had met at Oxford, and he soon longed for a life in the theatre. On leaving the RAF, he trained at RADA, but lack of work afterwards meant that he had to make ends meet by working as a porter at Euston station and a labourer at Walls' ice-cream factory, although he did perform on stage at the Unity Theatre, London.

When success came, it was in the classic TV series *Hancock's Half Hour*, alongside the one and only Tony Hancock. Warren had already made his film debut in the 1954 picture *The Passing Stranger* and followed it with such features as *Tommy the Toreador*, *Two Way Stretch*, *Carry On Cleo*, the Morecambe and Wise picture *The Intelligence Men*, *The Spy Who Came in from the Cold* and the Beatles film *Help!*

In 1965, he played the role of Alf Ramsey in what was intended to be a one-off show, as part of an experimental BBC *Comedy Playhouse* series, but the Johnny Speight-scripted *Till Death Us Do Part* became a series the following year, with the Ramseys becoming the Garnetts, and ran until the mid-70s – although clean-up campaigner Mary Whitehouse was an early critic, particularly objecting to the bad language.

Alf was a docker and West Ham United supporter whose views on everyone and everything were heard loud and clear every week. Blacks, permissiveness and his feminist daughter, long-suffering wife, Else, and long-haired, 'Scouse git' son-in-law all bore the brunt of his verbal tirades.

Warren also played Alf on stage at Chequers Night Club, in Sydney, and in a film version of the programme, in 1969, and another big-screen spin-off, *The Alf Garnett Saga*, three years later. In the same year, the cast of the show performed a sketch at the Royal Variety Performance.

An American version of *Till Death Us Do Part*, titled *All In the Family* – with American actors – started in the 70s.

Warren returned to TV in a sequel, *In Sickness and In Health*, which began in 1985 and ran for six series, although this never matched the spark of the original.

Throughout his years as Alf, the actor has also played many other TV roles. He was in *The Merchant of Venice*, *The Caretaker* and *Tickets for the Titanic*, before finding another starring role in a comedy series, as Ivan Fox in *So You Think You've Got Troubles*.

Warren has made over 50 films, including *Moon Zero Two*, *Jaberwocky*, *Stand Up Virgin Soldiers*, *Knights and Emeralds* and *Foreign Body*, although he has never found as much big-screen success as in theatre and television.

On stage, he has performed at the National Theatre in *Death of a Salesman* and *The Caretaker*, and was in a national tour of Harold Pinter's *The Homecoming*, followed by a five-month run at The Comedy Theatre, London. A frequent performer on the Australian stage, Warren played Harold in *Orphans*, at the Opera House Drama Theatre, Sydney, and again acted in Harold Pinter's *The Homecoming*, this time with the Sydney Theatre Company, and *Uncle Vanya*, at the Sydney Opera House.

Married to actress Constance Wake, Warren has two daughters, Rebecca and Anna, one son, Daniel, and lives in London.

Clayton Moore

b. 14 September 1914

ESSENTIALLY an actor in Westerns, it was as the Lone Ranger on television that Clayton Moore made his name. "Hi-yo, Silver away!" was his famous battlecry.

He revived the character on TV in 1949, 16 years after writer Fran Striker's creation had ridden the early West for radio. This followed the small-screen success of *Hop a long Cassidy* and teamed Clayton with Mohawk Indian Jay Silverheels, a former national lacrosse champion from Canada, as his faithful friend, Tonto.

Clayton, complete with black mask and white hat, starred in *The Lone Ranger* for eight years and 169 episodes, on and off, with Rossini's *William Tell Overture* heralding his arrival on the screen – although actor John Hart had played the character briefly at the start of the show's run.

At the height of *The Lone Ranger*'s run, in 1956, Clayton also starred in a film of the same name and, two years later, followed it with *The Lone Ranger and the Lost City of Gold*.

His other work includes the films *Kit Carson*, *The Son of Monte Cristo*, *Riders of the Whistling Pines*, and the serials *Jesse James Rides Again* and *The Black Dakotas*.

Clayton lives in San Fernando Valley, California, with his wife, Sally.

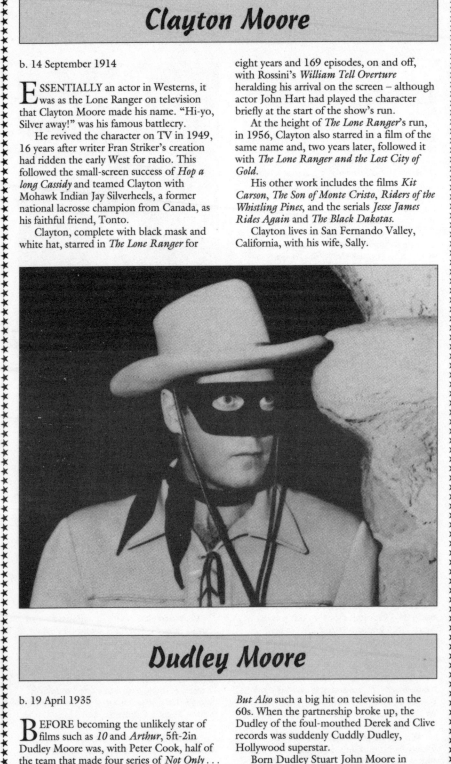

Dudley Moore

b. 19 April 1935

BEFORE becoming the unlikely star of films such as *10* and *Arthur*, 5ft-2in Dudley Moore was, with Peter Cook, half of the team that made four series of *Not Only . . .*

But Also such a big hit on television in the 60s. When the partnership broke up, the Dudley of the foul-mouthed Derek and Clive records was suddenly Cuddly Dudley, Hollywood superstar.

Born Dudley Stuart John Moore in

Dagenham, Essex, with a club foot that left one of his legs slightly shorter than the other, he was a shy child who found an outlet for his energy in music, learning the piano from the age of eight, the violin four years later, then the organ.

After studying at the Guildhall School of Music, he won an organ scholarship to Magdalen College, Oxford, gaining bachelor of arts and bachelor of music degrees, before touring America with the Vic Lewis Band and, on his return, writing incidental music for Royal Court Theatre plays and playing with the Johnny Dankworth Band.

In 1960, he teamed up with fellow-Oxford graduate Alan Bennett and Cambridge graduates Peter Cook and Jonathan Miller to star in the *Beyond the Fringe* revue at the 1960 Edinburgh Festival. A year later, they performed the show in London's West End.

After being spotted by the BBC playing with his jazz trio at Cook's new London club, The Establishment, Dudley was given his own TV show, a one-off special called *Strictly for the Birds*.

He asked Peter Cook to write a couple of sketches, and these included the first Dud and Pete sketch – with the cloth-capped pair philosophising on life – and the show was such a success that they were given their own series, *Not Only . . . But Also*, in 1965. It was in the vein of the satirical programme *That Was the Week That Was* and its successors, and ran for four series.

Peter and Dudley then branched out into films, appearing together in *The Wrong Box*, *Bedazzled* and *Monte Carlo or Bust*, and teamed up on American TV in *The Two of Us*. Dudley also had his own TV series, *Not to Mention Dudley Moore*.

He had made his film debut as the narrator of a short called *The Hat*, in 1964, and as well as acting in more than 30 subsequent pictures was called on to narrate several times. One such film was the documentary *To Russia with Elton*, an account of the first tour of Russia by a Western rock star, Elton John.

Dudley teamed up with Peter Cook again in 1981 for *Derek and Clive Get the Horn*, a big-screen extension of the pair's Derek and Clive characters, renowned for their filthy language.

By then, Dudley had found the key to superstardom, following his decision to split with Peter after the duo's disappointing 1977 film, a Sherlock Holmes spoof called *The Hound of the Baskervilles*.

A year later, he starred with Goldie Hawn in *Foul Play*, as a bachelor trying to lure women with his array of adult toys, paving the way for his 1979 breakthrough in *10*, as a lovesick composer who falls for Bo Derek.

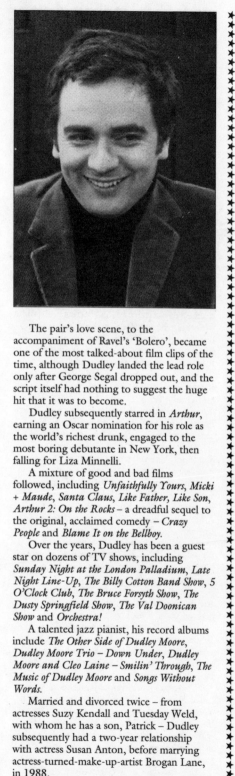

The pair's love scene, to the accompaniment of Ravel's 'Bolero', became one of the most talked-about film clips of the time, although Dudley landed the lead role only after George Segal dropped out, and the script itself had nothing to suggest the huge hit that it was to become.

Dudley subsequently starred in *Arthur*, earning an Oscar nomination for his role as the world's richest drunk, engaged to the most boring debutante in New York, then falling for Liza Minnelli.

A mixture of good and bad films followed, including *Unfaithfully Yours*, *Micki + Maude*, *Santa Claus*, *Like Father, Like Son*, *Arthur 2: On the Rocks* – a dreadful sequel to the original, acclaimed comedy – *Crazy People* and *Blame It on the Bellboy*.

Over the years, Dudley has been a guest star on dozens of TV shows, including *Sunday Night at the London Palladium*, *Late Night Line-Up*, *The Billy Cotton Band Show*, *5 O'Clock Club*, *The Bruce Forsyth Show*, *The Dusty Springfield Show*, *The Val Doonican Show* and *Orchestra!*

A talented jazz pianist, his record albums include *The Other Side of Dudley Moore*, *Dudley Moore Trio – Down Under*, *Dudley Moore and Cleo Laine – Smilin' Through*, *The Music of Dudley Moore* and *Songs Without Words*.

Married and divorced twice – from actresses Suzy Kendall and Tuesday Weld, with whom he has a son, Patrick – Dudley subsequently had a two-year relationship with actress Susan Anton, before marrying actress-turned-make-up-artist Brogan Lane, in 1988.

Patrick Moore

b. 4 March 1923

FROM the time the 'Space Age' started, monocled Patrick Moore was on screen explaining to viewers the significance of every rocket and space mission – and, if they wanted to know more about the universe, his long-running *Sky at Night* programme answered their questions.

Born Patrick Caldwell-Moore in Pinner, Middlesex, he was only six months old when his family moved to Sussex, where he grew up and has lived ever since. He missed much of his schooling because of ill health, although he passed the common entrance exam for public school but never went.

With private tuition, he passed his exams and intended to go to university, but war broke out. Despite heart problems and already wearing a monocle on his right eye because of defective vision, Patrick realised he would not be accepted by the Army or Navy but thought that flying was a possibility. Rigging the medical, he was accepted by the RAF as a navigator, flying mainly in bombers.

While across the Atlantic learning to fly, Patrick went on leave to New York, where he met Orville Wright – who had designed and flown in the first powered aircraft – and Albert Einstein. He even accompanied Einstein, a superb violinist, on the piano at a reception.

After the War, Patrick pursued his childhood love of astronomy, having been a member of the British Astronomical Association from the age of 11. He gave a lecture at Cambridge University that was reported in a New York newspaper and an American publisher then commissioned him to write a book about the Moon.

He followed *Guide to the Moon* with *Guide to the Planets*, and astronomy became his career, leaving him no time to go to university, as he had planned.

As well as setting up his own observatory and writing books on astronomy, Patrick penned boys' novels.

When BBC television producer Paul Johnstone, an archaeologist interested in science programmes, had the idea of making a monthly series about astronomy, he asked Patrick to present it.

The series was originally intended to be called *Star Map*, but the title was changed to *The Sky at Night* before it went on screen for the first time, on 26 April 1957, complete with Sibelius's 'At the Castle Gate', from the suite *Pelleas and Mélisande*, as the theme music.

In those days of live television, Patrick was once called on to play the theme on a harpsichord, when the programme was broadcast from a 17th-century astronomer's home and no one had remembered to take the record. Although he had never played the harpsichord before, he has subsequently given public renditions on the xylophone – and even performed his self-penned 'Hurricane' as a solo at the 1982 Royal Variety Performance.

His other 'entertainment' spots include guest appearances on programmes such as *The Morecambe and Wise Show*, *Face the Music* and *It's a Celebrity Knockout*. More seriously, he was the studio expert throughout the BBC's space coverage. He was actually on air as Neil Armstrong and 'Buzz' Aldrin stepped on to the Moon's surface after the 1969 Apollo-11 landing.

During his early years presenting *The Sky at Night*, the Russians had asked Patrick for his maps of the Moon's 'edge', as seen from Earth, and they used them to plan their 1959 Luna 3 unmanned probe round the Moon. He was subsequently made an honorary member of the Russian Astronomical Society. Later, in the mid-60s, he helped to found a new planetarium in Northern Ireland.

The Sky at Night has become the BBC's longest-running programme. Patrick also presented *One Pair of Eyes*, a series about so-called cranks, whom he preferred to regard as 'independent thinkers'. It featured astrologers, flying-saucer enthusiasts, Atlantis devotees and others who explained their particular beliefs.

Patrick has taken part in the Channel

Four video and computer games programme *The Gamesmaster*, which began in 1992, seen in hazy video form giving tips to young contestants.

As an author, he has achieved best-sellers with *Moon Flight Atlas* and *Atlas of the Universe* and he has also written *The Guinness Book of Astronomy*. With a great dislike for red tape, he also wrote the books *Bureaucrats:*

How to Annoy Them and *The Twitmarsh File*, both under the pseudonym R T Fishall.

Patrick, who was made a CBE in 1989, became President of the British Astronomical Association 50 years after he had been elected a member as a child. The only woman he ever planned to marry was killed during the War and he lives by himself, in a cottage in Sussex.

Roger Moore

b. 14 October 1927

A raised eyebrow and a wry smile are the trademarks of Roger Moore, the suave and debonair actor with a unique brand of sex appeal, who became a TV legend as Simon Templar in the popular 60s series *The Saint*. He has played 'gentlemanly' roles ever since.

Born in London, the son of a policeman, Roger was a film cartoonist and model at the age of 16, before turning to acting in repertory theatre and training at RADA. He made his film debut in the 1945 British extravaganza *Caesar and Cleopatra*, but his career was interrupted by National Service. He made his first Hollywood film appearance, alongside Elizabeth Taylor in *The Last Time I Saw Paris*, in 1954.

Two years later, the small screen beckoned and he played the title role in *Ivanhoe*, a children's TV adventure series in which he performed his own stunts, earning him more than a few bruises. Roles followed in *The Alaskans* and, as Beau Maverick, in the American Western series *Maverick*.

In 1962 came his starring role in *The Saint*, which became the most successful TV series to that date. Based on Leslie Charteris's books and short stories, the character had already been played by nine different actors on radio and in films. Roger became the first – and definitive – TV Simon Templar, an upper-class knight in shining armour, with a halo and sports car. In six years, he made 114 episodes, which were seen by 400 million viewers in 106 countries. A cleverly negotiated contract ensured he made a small fortune from the worldwide programme sales.

As English playboy Lord Brett Sinclair, the actor then teamed up with Hollywood star Tony Curtis in 1971 to make *The Persuaders*, a new series about two wealthy adventurers fighting corruption around the world. Although a hit in many countries, the series failed to win viewers in America and Roger refused to make any further episodes.

His reputation was rescued when he took over as James Bond, after George Lazenby failed to make his mark in the role made popular in the cinema by Sean Connery. From the moment he uttered those immortal words, "Bond – James Bond" in the 1973 film *Live and Let Die*, Roger became a runaway success and went on to appear in a further six Bond films.

During his spell as special agent 007, he continued to make other films, including *The Wild Geese* and *The Sea Wolves*, but since packing away his pistol after his seventh Bond outing, in *A View To a Kill*, he has made only occasional film appearances, preferring to spend more time at his Swiss home with his Italian-born third wife, Luisa Mattioli.

Roger's previous two marriages, to Doorn van Steyn and singer Dorothy Squires, both ended in divorce. He has two sons, Geoffrey and Christian, and one daughter, Deborah, from his third marriage.

Kenneth More

b. 20 September 1914
d. 12 July 1982

ALTHOUGH a film star whose most memorable performance was as Douglas Bader in *Reach for the Sky*, Kenneth More brought his warmth and expression of 'Englishness' to television to portray two characters of literature, Jolyon Forsyte in the BBC's version of *The Forsyte Saga* and the title role in ITV's *Father Brown* adaptation.

Born in Gerrard's Cross, Buckinghamshire, Kenneth spent part of his childhood in the Channel Islands, where his father was general manager of Jersey Eastern Railways. On leaving school, he followed the family tradition by training as a civil engineer but gave it up, worked in Sainsbury's and even went to Canada for a while, before heading for London, where the owner of the famous Windmill Theatre, Vivian Van Damm – a friend of his father – took him on as assistant stage manager.

It was there that he began to stooge for the stand-up comics, but the biggest laughs came when he said his lines the wrong way round. After two years, Kenneth gained acting experience by joining Newcastle Rep, performing in plays such as *Burke and Hare* and *Dracula's Daughter*, for £5 a week. He then worked in repertory theatre in Wolverhampton, until the Second World War broke out and he became a lieutenant in the RNVR (Royal Naval Volunteer Reserve).

In 1946, Kenneth appeared in the first play to be televised after the War, *Silence of the Sea*, and began to get small stage parts in London's West End. His lucky break came when he was spotted by Noël Coward, who cast him in his play *Peace in Our Time*. He was subsequently acclaimed for his 1951 West End role as Freddie, an RAF pilot having an affair with a judge's wife, in Terence Rattigan's *The Deep Blue Sea*.

Shortly afterwards, Kenneth took one of the lead roles in the Rank film comedy *Genevieve*, which brought him stardom, although he had made his big-screen debut as far back as 1935, in *Look Up and Laugh*, and had played Evans in *Scott of the Antarctic* 13 years later.

For the rest of the 50s, he was a leading light in British films, scoring his biggest successes in *Doctor in the House*, *The Admirable Crichton*, *The 39 Steps* and *Sink the Bismarck!*, as well as repeating his stage role of Freddie in the film of *The Deep Blue Sea* and winning his greatest acclaim as disabled flying hero Douglas Bader in *Reach for the Sky*.

As the British film industry began to change in the 60s, his big-screen popularity started to wane and his films became fewer, although he made cameo appearances as the Kaiser in *Oh! What a Lovely War*, the Ghost of Christmas Past in *Scrooge* and Lord Chamberlain in *The Slipper and the Rose*. However, his part in the 1966 film *The Collector*, based on John Fowles's novel, was taken out of the final, edited version seen in cinemas.

When the offer of playing Jolyon Forsyte in BBC2's adaptation of John Galsworthy's novel *The Forsyte Saga* came along the following year, Kenneth was desperate for work and glad of the challenge it presented, having to be seen to age from 37 to 75 during the 26-part serial.

The programme was an instant success, repeated on BBC1 a year later and enjoying two more repeat runs, as well as screenings around the world.

The actor's other television appearances included his role as a wartime Resistance hero in *The White Rabbit* and as the clerical sleuth in a dramatisation of G K Chesterton's *Father Brown* books.

Returning to the West End stage, he scored hits in the William Douglas-Home comedy *The Secretary Bird*, as the defence counsel in a revival of *The Winslow Boy* and as a Labour MP in Alan Bennett's *Getting On*.

Kenneth, who wrote the autobiographies

Happy Go Lucky (1959) and *More or Less* (1978), as well as a book of reminiscences, *Kindly Leave the Stage*, was married three times. His first two marriages, to actress Beryl Johnstone and Mabel Barkby, each produced a daughter, but ended in divorce. He met his third wife, Irish actress Angela Douglas, while making the 1961 film *The Greengage Summer*. He died 21 years later from Parkinson's disease.

Morecambe and Wise

Eric Morecambe, b. 14 May 1926,
d. 28 May 1984
Ernie Wise, b. 27 November 1925

THE greatest comedy double-act in the history of British television was, undoubtedly, Morecambe and Wise, whose 40-year partnership was ended only by Eric Morecambe's premature death. Stars queued up to appear on screen with the pair, often only to be sent up, and their Christmas shows were consistently ratings-toppers, attracting audiences of as many as 28 million.

John Eric Bartholomew, who later used his middle name and adopted the name of his Lancashire birthplace, made his debut as a comic in variety at the Empire, Nottingham, and met Leeds-born Ernest Wiseman when he was auditioning for talent-spotter Bryan Michie's 'discovery' stage show *Youth Takes a Bow*.

Ernie, who from the age of seven performed in the double-act Carson and Kid in working men's clubs with his railway-porter father, had been in the 1939 stage production of the radio programme *Band Waggon* and was already in Michie's show.

Eric and Ernie formed their own double-act in the touring show and subsequently appeared together in *Garrison Theatre* and the George Black revue *Strike a New Note*, at the Prince of Wales Theatre, London.

Then, both went their separate ways to do their National Service, with Ernie joining the Merchant Navy and Eric becoming a Bevin boy down the coal mines, although he was discharged after 11 months with a weak heart.

In 1947, the two met again by chance, when Eric joined *Lord George Sanger's Variety Circus* as feed to the resident comic, who turned out to be Ernie. They teamed up again, this time as Morecambe and Wise, and were soon performing in variety engagements, including nude roadshows in which they provided comic relief. They modelled their cross-talk act on film giants Abbott and Costello but their brilliant timing later caused critics to liken them to Laurel and Hardy. Wise was the straight man, the butt of Eric's buffoonery and insults about "short, fat, hairy legs".

After guest spots on radio, in shows such as *Workers' Playtime*, Eric and Ernie landed their own series, *You're Only Young Once*, in the BBC's Northern region, and in April 1954 the duo began their first television series, *Running Wild*, but the BBC programme proved a disaster and took them several years to live down.

During that time, they continued their act on radio and in summer shows, and returned to television in 1961 with *The Morecambe and Wise Show*, on ITV, following a *Sunday Night at the London Palladium* appearance the previous year.

Running for seven years, the show established them as major stars, although their venture into feature films with three comedy thrillers – starting in 1965 with *The Intelligence Men*, followed by *That Riviera Touch* and *The Magnificent Two* in each of the following years – was less successful.

The duo also appeared in a 1970 short, *Simon, Simon*, and in *Night Train To Murder*, which was such a turkey that it was never shown in the cinema and went straight to TV after Eric's death. Eric also provided a voice in the 1980 short *Late Flowering Love*.

The pair's ITV show finished in 1968, when Eric suffered a heart attack, but he recovered steadily and *The Morecambe and Wise Show* switched channels, with Eddie Braben replacing Dick Hills and Sid Green as scriptwriter.

Eric and Ernie's ten years at the BBC proved to be their most popular era, with Ernie bragging of "a play wot I wrote" and Eric asking, "What do you think of the show so far? Rubbish!" Among the many stars who appeared in the shows and Christmas specials were Glenda Jackson as Cleopatra, newsreader Angela Rippon dancing deftly across the stage, showing off her long legs, and even the Prime Minister Harold Wilson.

The mixture of cross-talk and visual gags, with Eric wearing his glasses on the side of his head and slapping Ernie across the face, was a guaranteed audience-puller, so it was a blow to the BBC when the pair returned to ITV with their own show, in 1978. They were lured back with the promise of more money and a chance to appear in films but, with another change of scriptwriter, *The*

Morecambe and Wise Show never reached the same dizzy heights as it had previously done. The BBC cashed in by repeating their old programmes under the title *Morecambe and Wise at the BBC*.

Sadly, in 1984, Eric died of a heart attack after appearing in a stage show at the Roses Theatre, Tewkesbury, in Gloucestershire. Five years earlier, he had suffered a heart attack and had undergone open-heart surgery. His death, at the age of 58, signalled the end of British television's best-loved comedy duo, who had appeared in five Royal Variety Performances. They had both been awarded the OBE in 1976.

The duo's autobiography, *Eric and Ernie*, was published in 1973 and there were several other books based on their TV shows, *The Best of Morecambe and Wise*, *Morecambe and Wise Special* and *There's No Answer to That*.

Eric wrote four other books, the novel *Mr. Lonely*, the children's stories *The Reluctant Vampire* and *The Vampire's Revenge*, and *Eric Morecambe On Fishing*, which was published posthumously. He was married to former dancer Joan Bartlett and had three children.

After Eric's death, Ernie appeared in cabaret in Australia, starred in the London West End hits *The Mystery of Edwin Drood* and *Run for Your Wife*, and appeared on television as a regular panellist on *What's My Line?* and in three Telethons in New Zealand and one in Australia, as well as starring in the American comedy series *Too Close for Comfort*. In 1991, he was the subject of *This Is Your Life*.

Ernie, who lives with his wife, Doreen, in Berkshire, had his autobiography, *Still On My Way to Hollywood*, published in 1990.

Johnny Morris

b. 20 June 1916

"NEVER work with children and animals" is an old showbusiness adage, but Johnny Morris refused to heed it and brought pleasure to many youngsters with his programmes featuring all sorts of creatures, from the animated ones in *Tales of the Riverbank* to the real-life ones in *Animal Magic*. Putting words into their mouths was his business.

Born in Newport, Gwent, Johnny learned to play the violin as a child and toured the Valleys of South Wales, performing with his cello-playing father. His first job was in a solicitor's office, earning ten shillings a week, then he moved to London and worked as a clerk, before managing a 2000-acre farm in Wiltshire.

He then successfully auditioned for the BBC, using a piece he had written himself, and continued to farm until 1951, when his series *Johnny's Jaunts* began. His book *Around the World in 25 Years*, based on the programme, was published in 1983. During the 50s, Johnny also spent eight years on radio as *The Hot Chestnut Man*, telling stories by his stove.

In 1960, he was heard on television as narrator of *Tales of the Riverbank*, an animated series filmed in Canada that featured such characters as Hammy Hamster and Roderick the Rat. It ran for 11 years.

Then, from 1962, he presented his own BBC television series, *Animal Magic*. Any creature that dared to open its mouth had its thoughts put into words by Johnny. The programme proved very popular and continued until 1983.

Another series, *A Gringo's Holiday*, on BBC2 in 1970, featured the presenter on a jaunt through South America, which included flying into a revolution in Santiago.

Johnny, who was awarded the OBE in 1984, is married to Eileen and lives in a farmhouse in Hungerford. He is still in demand for voice-overs in TV commercials and occasionally works as a story narrator with orchestras. His autobiography, *There's Lovely*, was published in 1989.

Peggy Mount

b. 2 May 1918

A string of situation comedies over three decades made larger-than-life Peggy Mount a star of the small screen – and typecast her as a domineering but homely woman.

Born in Southend-on-Sea, Essex, Peggy worked as a secretary on leaving school but took drama lessons in her spare time, under the tuition of Phyllis Reader.

During the Second World War, she acted in concert parties and, in 1944, played her first straight part, in *Hindle Wakes*, at the Hippodrome, Keighley, before joining the Harry Hanson Court Players for three years, then working in repertory theatre in Colchester, Preston, Dundee, Wolverhampton and Liverpool.

Her big break came in 1955 with the role of Mrs Hornett in *Sailor Beware!* on the London West End stage, playing the fearsome character in more than a thousand performances and repeating the role in a film the following year – her second film, following her debut in the 1954 picture *The Embezzler*.

Peggy then took the role of battleaxe wife Ada in *The Larkins*, a comedy series featuring David Kossoff and herself as a couple running a country pub, on ITV, in 1958. It was a huge success, spawning a film spin-off, *Inn for Trouble*, two years later, and two further series.

She followed it in 1966 with another successful situation comedy, *George and the Dragon*, teaming up with Sid James as the housekeeper and handyman of a stately home. Her subsequent TV hits have included *Lollipop Loves Mr. Mole* and the old people's home comedy *You're Only Young Twice* – both with Pat Coombs.

Since then, Peggy has tended to play straight parts on television, in programmes

such as *The Trial of Klaus Barbie*, *Punishment Without Crime*, *Doctor Who*, *Inspector Morse* – in which she appeared as a ferocious sister of mercy – and *Casualty*.

Her other film work includes the Brian Rix company's farce *Dry Rot*, *Hotel Paradiso*, *Oliver!* and the 1976 serial *The Chiffy Kids*. She also provided one of the voices in *The Princess and the Goblin*, in 1991.

On the West End stage, Peggy has played the Nurse in *Romeo and Juliet*, Mrs. Hardcastle in *She Stoops to Conquer*, Mrs. Malaprop in *The Rivals* and Lady Catherine in *The Circle*. For the National Theatre, she has appeared in *Il Campiello*, *Plunder* and *Larkrise To Candleford*.

The actress, who lives in London and has never married, was with the Royal Shakespeare Company at Stratford-upon-Avon and the Barbican for two years from 1983, acting in *The Dillon*, *Measure for Measure*, *Mary*, *After the Queen* and *The Happiest Days of Your Life*.

Malcolm Muggeridge

b. 24 March 1903
d. 14 November 1990

A celebrated journalist whose work ranged from being *The Manchester Guardian*'s Moscow correspondent to Deputy Editor of *The Daily Telegraph*, the sometimes irreverent and always provocative Malcolm Muggeridge

brought his brilliant mind to television in his political interviewing for *Panorama* and a series of documentaries, most notably *Something Beautiful for God*, on the life of Mother Teresa of Calcutta.

Born in Croydon, Surrey, the son of a lawyer's clerk who became Labour MP for Romford, Malcolm shared his father's crusading socialism, studied at Selwyn College, Cambridge, and subsequently taught in Alwaye, South India, where he became disillusioned with organised religion and flirted with anarchism.

In 1930, after teaching in Britain and Egypt, he joined *The Manchester Guardian* and, two years later, became its Moscow correspondent. Following Ramsay MacDonald's betrayal of the Labour Party, he saw the Soviet Union as offering the only alternative society, but his nine months there – seeing Stalin's oppression of his people and terrible famine – changed the journalist's mind.

After writing for *The Statesman* in India and *The London Evening Standard*'s diary page, he gave up daily journalism, concentrating on books instead.

With the coming of the Second World War, Malcolm enlisted in the Intelligence Corps and later worked for MI6 as an agent. In 1944, he befriended P G Wodehouse in liberated Paris, after his release from internment in Germany.

After the War, Malcolm joined *The Daily Telegraph* as a leader writer, then became its Washington correspondent, before being appointed Deputy Editor. Later, he became the Editor of *Punch*, turning it into a satirical magazine that reflected the times.

During this time, he entered broadcasting with appearances on the BBC radio show *Any Questions?* and as a political interviewer for *Panorama*, which began on television in 1953. When he wrote an article criticising the monarchy, in *The Saturday Evening Post*, the BBC dropped him for a while, but he was soon back on TV with an increasingly high profile.

During the 60s, Malcolm made many celebrated television films, including a return visit to India in *Twilight of Empire*, all the laughs from an American lecture tour in *Ladies and Gentlemen, It is My Pleasure*, and a look at Mother Teresa's life and work in *Something Beautiful for God*.

Making this last documentary had a profound effect on him and he subsequently became a vegetarian and gave up drinking, smoking and watching television. He was also a convert to the Roman Catholic Church.

During his last years, Malcolm made very few television appearances and most of his writing was on religion, publishing a book titled *Conversion* in 1988. His collected journalism, *Tread Softly for You Tread on My Jokes*, had come out in 1966 and he wrote two volumes of autobiography – *Chronicles of Wasted Time: The Green Stick*, in 1972, followed the next year by *The Infernal Grove* – and his diaries, *Like It Was*, in 1981.

Malcolm, who died at the age of 87, was married to Kitty (Katherine) Dobbs, a niece of social reformer Beatrice Webb, and had two sons and one daughter.

Barbara Mullen

b. 9 June 1914
d. 9 March 1979

AS housekeeper Janet in the popular BBC series *Dr Finlay's Casebook*, Barbara Mullen found a role that brought her fame in her later years, although she had already made her mark in the theatre.

Barbara's parents, Pat and Bridget, were from a fishing family on the Isle of Aran, but the family had emigrated to Boston, Massachusetts, where Barbara was born. She made her stage debut there as a dancer at the age of three. When her father returned to Aran, becoming famous as the 'Man of Aran' in Robert Flaherty's classic documentary film of that name, Barbara's mother was left in Boston to bring up ten children.

Barbara sang and danced in various theatres all over America, before crossing the Atlantic in 1934 and training at the Webber Douglas Academy.

At the early age of 24, she wrote her autobiography, *Life is My Adventure*, and a year later made her London stage debut. She became an overnight star, acting the title role in the London West End production of *Jeannie*, a comedy about a Scottish girl

taking a European holiday after coming into money.

She later succeeded Celia Johnson as Mrs de Winter in *Rebecca*, and played Maggie in a revival of J M Barrie's *What Every Woman Knows* and Miss Marple in Agatha Christie's *Murder at the Vicarage*.

Barbara repeated the role of Jeannie on television and in the 1941 British film, which was her cinema debut, alongside Michael Redgrave, and she followed this with appearances in 20 further films, including *A Place of One's Own*, *Corridor of Mirrors* and *Innocent Sinners*.

She appeared on television in Britain and America, in such programmes as *Juno and the Paycock* and *The Danny Thomas Show*, before landing the role of Janet in *Dr Finlay's Casebook*, which began on the BBC in 1962. Janet was the efficient housekeeper to Doctors Finlay and Cameron at Arden House, in the fictional Scottish village of Tannochbrae.

When the series finished on television nine years later, it moved to radio, running until 1978.

Barbara, who died of a heart attack at the age of 64, was married to film producer John Taylor and had two daughters, Briged and Susannah.

Arthur Negus

b. 29 March 1903
d. 5 April 1985

THE man who got everyone rummaging in their attic and bringing out the family heirlooms, silver-haired Arthur Negus thrilled and fascinated many with his popular small-screen antiques fairs, *Going for a Song* and *Antiques Roadshow*.

Arthur George Negus was born in Reading, Berkshire, the son of a cabinet-maker. At the age of 17 he took over his father's shop, following his father's death, becoming an antiques dealer for the next 20 years.

When the shop was bombed during the Second World War, during which Arthur was serving as a War Reserve Policeman, it left him without a job. So, in 1946, he joined a Gloucester firm of fine-art auctioneers, Bruton, Knowles & Co., after answering their advert for an appraiser.

Arthur remained with the firm and became a partner in 1972. Thanks to his skill in valuing house contents, he was chosen to appear as the resident expert in the new BBC television programme *Going for a Song*, with Max Robertson as chairman.

The show ran for ten years from 1965 and made Arthur an instant celebrity – and a natural choice as presenter of *Antiques Roadshow*, which began in 1979. He toured the country with a resident team of experts, inviting people to bring along their treasures for valuation.

Part of the show's popularity was down to the viewers themselves, who would queue up to have their family heirlooms examined, before blushing and stammering that, just as a matter of interest, they would like to know how much the dusty old things were worth.

Arthur unearthed some real gems in the

process, including a £100 000 Victorian painting dumped in a garden shed and a Ming-dynasty temple-bell worth £30 000.

He retired from the programme in 1983 and, the following year, made another series involving his passion for antiques, *Arthur Negus Enjoys*.

Arthur, who wrote the book *Going for a Song: English Furniture* and an autobiography, *A Life Among Antiques*, published in 1982, was awarded an OBE in the same year. He died in 1985, leaving his wife, Amy Hollett, and two daughters.

Dandy Nichols

b. 1907
d. 6 February 1986

AS Alf Garnett's 'silly old moo' in *Till Death Us Do Part*, Dandy Nichols enjoyed fame late in her career, but she showed the programme's millions of fans her skills of voice nuance, facial expression and perfect timing that made her the perfect foil to Warren Mitchell's foul-mouthed anti-hero.

Born Daisy Nichols in Hammersmith, West London, she started her working life as a secretary in a London factory. Twelve years later, after drama, diction and fencing classes, she was spotted in a charity show by a producer and offered an acting job with his repertory theatre company, in Cambridge.

During her early career on stage, she acted under the name Barbara Nichols, but she later changed it to Dandy, which had been a childhood nickname.

During the Second World War, she returned to office work for two years but undertook a six-week tour with the entertainment organisation ENSA. When peace came, she went back into the theatre and then broke into film comedies, becoming typecast as maids and chars.

Dandy made her big-screen debut in *Hue and Cry*, in 1947, and became much in demand, following it with performances in *Nicholas Nickleby*, *The Winslow Boy*, *The History of Mr Polly*, *Scott of the Antarctic*, *Mother Riley Meets the Vampire* and *The Pickwick Papers*.

Her 50-plus films also included *Carry On Sergeant* and *Carry on Doctor*, the Beatles picture *Help!*, *The Knack . . . and how to get it*, *The Birthday Party*, *Doctor in Clover*, *The Bed Sitting Room*, *Confessions of a Window Cleaner* and *Britannia Hospital*. She also supplied one of the voices in the cinema version of the Richard Adams book *The Plague Dogs*.

On television, Dandy was also in great demand, appearing in series such as *Emergency – Ward 10*, *Dixon of Dock Green*, *Mrs Thursday*, *No Hiding Place* and the Harry Worth show *Here's Harry*.

The part of Alf Garnett's long-suffering wife Else in television's *Till Death Us Do Part* came in 1966. Gretchen Franklin, later to play Ethel Skinner in *EastEnders*, had taken the role in a pilot episode included in a BBC *Comedy Playhouse* series the previous year, when the Garnetts were known as the Ramseys, but Dandy took over for the series.

An immediate hit, the programme ran for a further ten years, although Dandy left in 1973, saying she could no longer work with screen husband Warren Mitchell. By then, she had already appeared in the two film spin-offs, *Till Death Us Do Part* and *The Alf Garnett Saga*, as well as in a Garnett family sketch in the 1972 Royal Variety Performance.

However, Dandy returned as Else when the programme's sequel, *In Sickness and In Health*, began in 1985, although by then she was in poor health and confined to a wheelchair.

After first finding fame as Else, Dandy was given other opportunities to prove her worth on television, most notably playing opposite Alastair Sim in the William Trevor play *The Generals Day*. She also made appearances in *Flint*, *The Tea Ladies* and *Bergerac*.

On the West End stage she starred in *The Clandestine Marriage* and the Ben Travers comedy *Plunder*, as well as playing alongside Ralph Richardson and John Gielgud in David Storey's *Home*, in London and on Broadway.

Dandy, whose only marriage had ended in divorce, died at the age of 78.

David Nixon

b. 29 December 1919
d. 1 December 1978

AN all-round entertainer, David Nixon belonged to that golden age when performers could keep an audience enthralled for hours with their highly polished routines.

Born in London, David had fallen in love with conjuring as a young boy, when he used to practise his tricks on family and friends and, while serving in the Second World War, he was able to demonstrate them on stage during regular service shows.

After the War, he performed his conjuring act in variety shows and, in Scarborough during the summer of 1948, he was joined on stage by Norman Wisdom, who wreaked havoc with his act. The partnership was a roaring success and the two subsequently appeared at the London Casino.

Over the next few years, David developed his style and, by 1953, when he leaped to fame in the BBC television panel game *What's My Line?*, he was positively soaked in charm. In the same year, he was also enjoying success in the children's TV show *Sugar and Spice*.

During the 60s, his popularity was at its peak. Families loved him for his wholesome entertainment and his tricks continued to thrill. So successful was he that David was given his own, early-evening television programmes, *The David Nixon Show* and *David Nixon's Magic Box*.

He kept mums, dads and children transfixed with his amazing range of magical tricks, as well as presenting guests. Basil Brush first found fame after making his debut on *The David Nixon Show* in 1968, before being given his own programme, and in 1974 David turned the tables on Eamonn Andrews, surprising him with the big, red book and making him a 'victim' of *This Is Your Life*.

With his rich, mellow voice, he remained in demand throughout his career as a compere and narrator, and he also worked in pantomimes, which he dearly loved. His earmarked role in panto was that of Buttons in *Cinderella*. With his portly frame and mischievous grin, he often stole the show; one of his most memorable Christmas performances was as the narrator in the show *Emile and the Detectives*, at the Mermaid Theatre.

David died from massive internal haemorrhaging only two years after announcing he had beaten cancer. The entertainer had been married three times. After his first marriage, to actress Margaret Burton, ended in divorce, he wed actress Paula Marshall, who was killed in a car crash at the age of 29. He later married Vivienne Nicholls, with whom he had a son and daughter.

John Noakes

b. 6 March 1934

AS *Blue Peter*'s resident daredevil, John Noakes messed around in racing cars, on bikes and steamrollers, stepped out of an aeroplane at 25 000 feet, climbed Nelson's Column and nearly came a cropper on a two-man bobsleigh in St Moritz.

Born in Halifax, West Yorkshire, he joined the RAF as a turbine mechanic on leaving school and rose to become a junior technician. Failing to make the rank of corporal, John joined the British Overseas Airways Corporation, then decided on a complete change of direction and aimed to become an actor.

He trained at the Guildhall School of Music and Drama, and made his stage debut as a dog and a clown in a Cyril Fletcher pantomime. This led to work as a 'feed' to Cyril in the comedian's summer show, but John soon decided he had to develop himself as an actor and joined the Welsh Children's Theatre Company. Then, he worked in repertory theatre in Harrogate, Bournemouth, York, Manchester, Sheffield, Leatherhead and Worthing, before performing in *Chips with Everything* on Broadway.

In 1966, after various acting roles on television, John joined the BBC children's programme *Blue Peter*. While other presenters were probably best known for demonstrating how to make things in the relatively safe confines of the TV studio, he would be out testing the limits of human endurance.

When John *did* venture into the studio, it was usually with his beloved dog, Shep, although another animal proved to be as hazardous as any of his stunts. During the days of live television, a Sri Lankan elephant was brought along from Chessington Zoo and proceeded to 'disgrace himself', dragging his keeper through the pile for an encore. As the programme came to an end, a relieved John bade farewell to the viewers and promptly stepped back into the excrement!

He stayed with *Blue Peter* for 13 years, and launched *Go with Noakes*, a showcase for his stunts, in 1974. He later presented *Country Calendar* for Yorkshire Television and hosted *The Saturday Show* for the ITV breakfast service TV-am for a period in 1983, when he also presented BBC radio schools programmes.

Throughout the 80s, John appeared in pantomime all over Britain, as well as producing and acting in *Once in a Lifetime*, in Blackpool. He was also heard in commercials for products such as Papermate pens and Everest double-glazing.

During these years, he indulged his love of sailing, setting out on a world cruise in 1982. However, it came to an abrupt end when he was shipwrecked off the coast of Spain. He has since set sail again and now lives on a boat in Majorca with his wife, Victoria, with whom he has a son, Mark.

John has written two books, *The Flight of the Magic Clog* and *Noakes at Large*.

Laurence Olivier

b. 22 May 1907
d. 15 July 1989

CONSIDERED by many to be the
greatest actor of his generation, and
perhaps of all time, Laurence Olivier was
most famous for the classical roles that he
played to perfection on stages around the
world.

He was also a prolific performer in
films, although they tended to be either
exceptionally good or particularly bad, but
his limited number of television performances
were almost always classics, with especially
memorable roles in *Brideshead Revisited*, *A
Voyage Round My Father*, *The Ebony Tower*
and *King Lear*.

Born in Dorking, Surrey, the son of the
Rev. Gerald Olivier, an assistant priest at St
Martin's Church, the young Laurence made
his mark as Brutus in a school production of
Julius Caesar at the age of ten, when the
distinguished actress Ellen Terry saw his
performance and remarked that he was
already a great actor.

Five years later, he appeared at the
Shakespeare Memorial Theatre, in Stratford-
upon-Avon, as Kate in the All Saints Choir
School's performance of *The Taming of the
Shrew*, watched by Sybil Thorndike and
Lewis Casson. He followed this with his
professional debut in Alice Law's *Byron*, in
1924.

Laurence's mother had died when he was
12 and his clergyman father insisted that he
should make a career in the theatre – a
scholarship earned him a place at Elsie
Fogerty's Central School of Speech Training
and Dramatic Art.

In 1926, Laurence joined the
Birmingham Repertory Company,
performing with it for two years, but it was
not until the 30s that he began to make an
impression, joining John Gielgud's company
and playing Boswell in *Queen of Scots* and
Romeo in *Romeo and Juliet*.

In the decades that followed, he would
play all the great heroes of the classics, but
during the early years of the Second World
War Hollywood would claim his matinée-idol
looks and keep him away from the theatre.

He had made his first films, *Too Many
Crooks* and *The Temporary Widow*, in 1930,
and appeared in more than a dozen pictures
before being cast as Heathcliff in the
stunning American production of *Wuthering
Heights*, in 1939.

Although returning to Britain to join the
Fleet Air Arm and the RNVR (Royal Naval

Volunteer Reserve) during the War, he was
given time off to take similar romantic
leading roles in the films *Rebecca* and *Pride
and Prejudice*, before returning to the classics
to direct and star in his remarkable film
version of *Henry V*, in 1944.

After providing commentaries for several
pictures intended as propaganda at a time of
war, the film was also aimed at boosting
morale, but its cinematic brilliance
overshadowed this aim and won the actor a
Special Oscar.

In 1948, Laurence followed this by
winning an Oscar for Best Actor for his
screen version of *Hamlet*, which he had also
produced and directed, and which won the
Best Film Oscar. Seven years later, he
completed his big-screen Shakespearean trio
with *Richard III*.

By then, he had once again made his
mark in the theatre. From 1943, he spent five
years as Co-director, with Ralph Richardson
and John Burrell, of the Old Vic Company at
the New Theatre, with acclaimed productions
of *Richard III* and *King Lear*. However,
despite providing the Old Vic with the best
theatre it had ever seen, the board of
governors chose not to renew the Directors'
contracts.

Laurence then staged a mixture of
classical and modern plays at the St James's
Theatre, before moving to the Royal Court,
where he starred as fallen comedian Archie
Rice in John Osborne's *The Entertainer*. He
loved the role, rating it his second favourite
to Macbeth, and he repeated it in a 1960 film
version.

After a period spent directing at the
Chichester Festival Theatre, he made one of
his lasting contributions to the acting
profession, as founder-Director of the
National Theatre, in 1963.

Artistic director for its first ten years, he
made it a showcase for the world's best
drama, starting with a production of *Hamlet*
that starred Peter O'Toole, and following it
with the works of all the great playwrights,
from Chekhov and Ibsen to Feydeau and
Coward.

In his later years, Laurence brought his
mighty talent to television in some of its most
acclaimed productions. He had made his
small-screen debut in the 1958 play *John
Gabriel Borkman* and was first choice as
narrator for *The Valiant Years*, based on
Churchill's Second World War memoirs,
although Richard Burton was eventually
given the job because he was more
affordable.

However, Laurence *was* a narrator of a tribute to Sir Winston Churchill during the BBC's funeral coverage, in 1965, as well as ITV's epic documentary series *The World at War*, eight years later.

He appeared in the classic *Jesus of Nazareth*, in 1977, was in the TV movie *Love Among the Ruins* and produced a *Laurence Olivier Presents . . .* series featuring plays such as *The Collection* and *Cat on a Hot Tin Roof.*

However, it was in the 80s that he gave his greatest performances on television. Starting in 1982, he was in productions for three successive years: as Lord Marchmain returning home to die in *Brideshead Revisited*, in the title role of *King Lear* and as the elderly painter, with playthings Toyah Willcox and Greta Scacchi, in John Fowles's *The Ebony Tower.*

The great actor also appeared in John Mortimer's *A Voyage Round My Father* and in his last TV appearance, as has-been comedian Harry Burrard in *Lost Empires*, he relived the role of entertainer Archie Rice.

During his final years, Laurence fought courageously against cancer of the prostate, pneumonia, pleurisy, appendicitis, thrombosis, a rare wasting disease, a kidney operation and a hip replacement. He died, at the age of 82, at his home in Steyning, West Sussex.

Knighted in 1947 and created a baronet in 1970, he had written two autobiographies, *Confessions of an Actor* and *On Acting*, published in 1982 and 1986. His first two marriages, to actresses Jill Esmond and Vivien Leigh, both ended in divorce. He had a son from his second marriage and a son and two daughters by his third wife, acclaimed actress Joan Plowright.

Nicholas Parsons

b. 10 October 1928

FOREVER destined to be remembered as genial host of the ITV 70s quiz show *Sale of the Century*, and straight man to comedians such as Arthur Haynes and Benny Hill, Nicholas Parsons actually enjoyed a successful acting career in British film comedies before finding fame on television.

Born in Grantham, Lincolnshire, the son of a doctor, Nicholas was 15 when he finally beat the stutter that had hindered him throughout childhood. With a script in front of him, he could speak with confidence, so he

took to the stage, making his debut with the Stock Exchange Players at the Cripplegate Theatre, near Liverpool Street, London, after his family moved to the city.

On leaving school, he started an engineering apprenticeship on Clydebank, before studying at Glasgow University. Working in his spare time as an impersonator and comedian in concert parties, he was spotted by Carroll Levis and given his first radio broadcast, *The Radio Deceiver*.

Nicholas moved into repertory theatre and made his film debut at the age of 19 in *Master of Bankdam*, before gaining more stage experience in cabaret and revues in London, including six months as resident comedian at the Windmill Theatre. Then, in the 50s, he joined BBC radio's drama repertory company.

His 16 films, over a period of almost 30 years, included *Carleton-Browne of the FO*, *Doctor in Love*, *Carry On Regardless* – as a lecherous wine-taster – and *The Best of Benny*

Hill. He acted on stage in productions such as *Boeing-Boeing* and the Brian Rix company's farce *Uproar in the House*.

Nicholas first found fame on television as the straight man in *The Eric Barker Half-Hour* and *The Arthur Haynes Show* in the 50s. He later played straight man to Benny Hill and was chairman of the radio show *Just a Minute* for 13 years, before finding TV fame in his own right with *Sale of the Century*, which started in 1971.

Critics were sometimes unkind to him, but he had the last laugh when, in the late 80s, he sent himself up as a quizmaster in *The Alphabet Quiz*, in ITV's *Night Network* programme. He later presented *Laughlines* on the short-lived satellite channel BSB.

Nicholas, who wrote and produced a short film called *Mad Dogs and Cricketers*, met his actress wife, Denise Bryer, while they were working together in BBC radio's drama repertory company. They have a daughter, Suzy, and a son, Justin.

Jack Payne

b. 22 August 1899
d. 4 December 1969

BANDLEADER Jack Payne was a star of BBC radio who made a significant contribution to British dance music with his easy-going, cheerful style, and was a familiar face when television became the dominant medium, with his series *Words and Music* and appearances in the pop show *Juke Box Jury*.

John Wesley Vivian Payne was born in Leamington, Warwickshire, the only son of a music warehouse manager. He played the piano in amateur dance-bands while serving in the Royal Flying Corps and, after being demobbed, formed his own band at the Hotel Cecil, in the Strand, London, in 1925.

The BBC broadcast some of the band's music on radio and, in 1928, appointed Jack its director of dance music. During his four years with the Corporation, he directed the BBC Dance Orchestra, making daily broadcasts from Station 2LO (later the National Programme), as well as records.

His signature tune was Irving Berlin's 'Say It with Music' and, as well as announcing the numbers, he performed the vocals himself. The 16-strong BBC Dance Orchestra, under Jack, played at the London Palladium in 1930 and 1931.

During that second performance, Jack produced one of his most popular pieces of showmanship, simulating a massive engine running out of the stage backdrop into the

stalls while members of the band sat on various parts of the engine playing the popular contemporary hit 'Choo Choo'.

In 1932, he left the BBC to take his band on nationwide tours and make a film, *Say It with Music*, followed three years later by another, *Sunshine Ahead*, but he spent less time touring in the late 30s, so that he could concentrate on running a theatrical agency.

As a composer, Jack had three successful waltzes, *Blue Pacific Moonlight*, *Underneath the Spanish Stars* and *Pagan Serenade*, which were published at the beginning of the 30s.

With the outbreak of war, his band entertained servicemen, but – in 1946 – he put down his baton and became a disc-jockey. Thirteen years later, however, he returned to the dance-music scene to present his own television show, *Words and Music*, which ran for three series. He also appeared on TV as a panellist reviewing new pop records in *Juke Box Jury* and was in *It's a Square World* – Michael Bentine's madcap series – and *A Pair of Jacks*.

Jack, who during his final years ran a hotel in Tonbridge, Kent, which proved to be a less than successful financial venture, was married twice. His first wife died after 16 years of marriage, and he later wed second wife Peggy, with whom he had an adopted daughter.

He wrote two autobiographies, *This is Jack Payne*, in 1932, and *Signature Tune*, 15 years later.

Arthur Pentelow

b. 14 February 1924
d. 6 August 1991

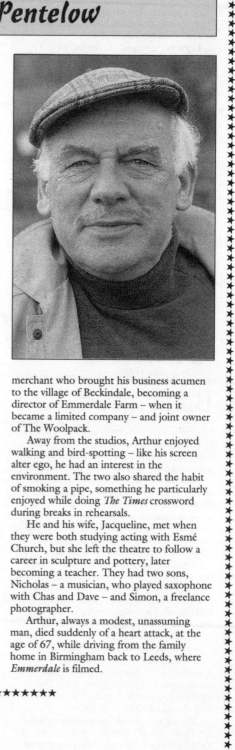

As the reflective, pipe-smoking businessman Henry Wilks, who ran The Woolpack pub in *Emmerdale*, Arthur Pentelow enjoyed the respect and friendship of all around him, both on screen and off. It was his double-act with Ronald Magill, who played landlord Amos Brearly, that added a humorous dimension to the ITV soap for almost 20 years.

Born in Rochdale, Lancashire, Arthur fell in love with drama while studying Shakespeare at grammar school, but he started his career as a cadet clerk in the local police force. During the Second World War, he served in the Royal Navy and did radar work in Normandy.

When peace came, he became a student teacher and acted as an amateur with the Curtain Theatre Company, in Rochdale, before joining the new Bradford Civic Playhouse Theatre School, under the tuition of Esmé Church, where other aspiring actors included Bernard Hepton, Bill Gaskill and Robert Stephens.

Between jobs selling ice-cream and sliced bread, and taking people's washing to the laundry, Arthur worked in repertory theatre at the Bristol Old Vic, Guildford and Northampton, before joining the company at Birmingham, where his contemporaries included Derek Jacobi, Ian Richardson, Albert Finney, Rosemary Leach and Julie Christie. He also appeared on stage in Orson Welles's celebrated 1951 London West End production of *Othello*.

The actor appeared in the films *Charlie Bubbles*, *Privilege* and *The Peace Game*, and was seen on television in *Z-Cars*, *Emergency – Ward 10*, *Budgie*, *Armchair Theatre*, *The Troubleshooters*, *Hadleigh* and *Play for Today*.

Before he joined *Emmerdale Farm*, when it began in 1972, he had already appeared in two other serials – as the football supporters' club chairman in *United!* and as park-keeper George Greenwood, an old friend of Hilda Ogden who gave Emily Bishop driving lessons, in *Coronation Street*.

The character of widower Henry Wilks in the rural soap was a retired Bradford wool merchant who brought his business acumen to the village of Beckindale, becoming a director of Emmerdale Farm – when it became a limited company – and joint owner of The Woolpack.

Away from the studios, Arthur enjoyed walking and bird-spotting – like his screen alter ego, he had an interest in the environment. The two also shared the habit of smoking a pipe, something he particularly enjoyed while doing *The Times* crossword during breaks in rehearsals.

He and his wife, Jacqueline, met when they were both studying acting with Esmé Church, but she left the theatre to follow a career in sculpture and pottery, later becoming a teacher. They had two sons, Nicholas – a musician, who played saxophone with Chas and Dave – and Simon, a freelance photographer.

Arthur, always a modest, unassuming man, died suddenly of a heart attack, at the age of 67, while driving from the family home in Birmingham back to Leeds, where *Emmerdale* is filmed.

★★★★★★★★★★★★

Jon Pertwee

b. 7 July 1919

TWO of television's most distinctive and popular characters, Doctor Who and walking, talking scarecrow Worzel Gummidge, were brought to the small screen by Jon Pertwee – the Man of a Thousand Voices – who had already been one of the stalwarts of radio comedy in Britain.

Born John Pertwee in London, the son of playwright Roland, theatre was in the family blood. His brother Michael also became a playwright and his cousin Bill went into acting, becoming best known as ARP Warden Hodges in *Dad's Army*.

Jon decided on acting as a career but was expelled from RADA after being considered incompetent. Joining the Arts League of Service Travelling Theatre, with director Donald Wolfit, he performed in a different town every night. He went on to work in a circus and even appeared on ice, before gaining repertory experience in Brighton, York, Liverpool and Jersey.

During the Second World War, the actor served in the Royal Navy. Meeting radio star Eric Barker led him into comedy in 1944, performing in *HMS Waterlogged*, part of the Forces show *Merry-Go-Round*. Two years later, it continued in its own right as *Waterlogged Spa*. Jon followed it with the Jimmy Jewel–Ben Warriss show *Up the Pole*, then the longest-running radio comedy ever, *The Navy Lark*, in which he was the chief petty officer – although he was not in the film version.

He had made his film debut as far back as 1937, in *A Yank at Oxford*, the first major Anglo-American feature, of which his father was one of the writers. He went on to appear in more than 40 films, including *Carry On Cleo*, *Carry On Cowboy*, *Carry On Screaming*, *A Funny Thing Happened on the Way to the Forum*, *The House That Dripped Blood* and *One of Our Dinosaurs is Missing*. He even stood in for Danny Kaye in the London scenes of *Knock on Wood*, in 1954, and gave his voice to the children's films *Wombling Free* and *The Water Babies*.

But the big screen never provided Jon with a star vehicle. Instead, it was as the third Doctor Who on television, following William Hartnell and Patrick Troughton, that he became a major star.

His previous television appearances had been few, popping up in the BBC pop show *6.5 Special* and as a compere of *Sunday Night at the London Palladium*. *Doctor Who*, in which he appeared for five years from 1970, made him a children's favourite and gave him the chance to indulge his love of gadgetry. He later returned to the role for the series' 20th-anniversary special, *The Five Doctors*, in 1983.

Looking for another character to play on television, Jon recalled the *Worzel Gummidge* books written by Barbara Euphan Todd, which he had read as a child. Southern Television agreed to produce a series, Keith Waterhouse and Willis Hall wrote the scripts, and James Hill – a celebrated maker of children's films, as well as the Oscar-winning *Guiseppina* and TV series such as *The Avengers* – directed it.

Together, they made 30 episodes, in four hugely popular ITV series, starting in 1979, and *Worzel's Christmas Special*, subtitled *A Cup o' Tea an' a Slice o' Cake*, two years later.

The beautifully made programmes, full of warmth, humour and pathos, attracted more adult viewers than children – and featured cameo appearances from such stars as Barbara Windsor, Billy Connolly, Bill Maynard, Connie Booth and John Le Mesurier.

Unfortunately, Southern Television lost its ITV franchise and no more programmes were made until the series was resurrected by a producer in New Zealand. Two series of *Worzel Gummidge Down Under* were made, screened in Britain on Channel Four, starting in 1987. Jon also played the character on stage and recorded an album, *Worzel Gummidge Sings*, and a Christmas single.

His other TV appearances include three series as presenter of the ITV crime quiz *Whodunnit?*, storytelling in *Jackanory*, a guest part in *The Goodies* and the role of a psychiatrist consulted by Father Christmas in *The Curious Case of Santa Claus*.

Jon, whose London stage shows include *A Funny Thing Happened on the Way to the Forum*, *There's a Girl in My Soup*, *Oh Clarence* and *Irene*, was divorced from his first wife, *Upstairs, Downstairs* actress and creator Jean Marsh, whom he had married at the age of 35. In 1960, he wed novelist Ingeborg Rhosea and the couple have two children, daughter Dariel and actor son Sean.

★★★★★★★★★★★★

Conrad Phillips

b. 13 April 1925

SWASHBUCKLING series thrived on ITV during its early years and *William Tell*, starring Conrad Phillips as the Swiss hero, was one of the most popular.

Born Conrad Philip Havord, in London, he joined the Royal Navy at the age of 17 by lying about his age, seeing active service in the Atlantic, North Sea and Mediterranean. However, he was invalided out in 1945, after surviving the mining of a landing craft.

Deciding on acting as a career, Conrad trained at RADA and made his stage debut in *Vice Versa* at the Theatre Royal, Stratford, East London, before appearing at the Lyric, Hammersmith, in the premiere of Sean O'Casey's *Oak Leaves and Lavender*.

He made his first London West End appearance in *The Vigil*, at the Prince of Wales Theatre, before landing the lead role in the 1948 film *The Gentlemen Go By*.

He followed this with repertory theatre work in Worthing, Bromley, Richmond-upon-Thames, Amersham and Oxford, and more than 30 films, including *Sons and Lovers, Impact* – of which he was the star and writer – and *Heavens Above!*, as well as many second features.

After the beginning of ITV, in 1955, Conrad became sought after for roles in film series such as *The Count of Monte Cristo, Charlie Chan* and *On Special Service*. Three years later, he landed the title role in *William Tell* – the first time the story had been filmed – and became a household name. The series, which ran until 1966, was also sold around the world.

Afterwards, he concentrated on film and theatre work, including a starring role in the West End stage hit *Tomorrow With Pictures*, three separate productions of James Joyce's only play, *Exiles*, and tours of *Private Lives* and *Jane Eyre*, in which he played Rochester.

Performing with the English National Opera at the Coliseum, Conrad played Pasha Selim in Mozart's *Seraglio* and narrated Stravinsky's *Oedipus*.

In 1972, he bought a hill farm in south-west Scotland and ran it for six years, at the same time appearing in TV series such as *Sutherland's Law, Heidi, Cribb* and *Fawlty Towers*. However, with two young children to bring up, Conrad decided to leave the isolation of Scotland and move to Chippenham, in Wiltshire.

On television, he has played Robert Malcolm in *The Newcomers*, NY Estates managing director Christopher Meadows in *Emmerdale Farm*, and Chief Supt. Keen in *Silent Evidence*, as well as appearing in *The Gaffer, The Dick Emery Show, The Morecambe and Wise Show, Into the Labyrinth, Sorry, Never the Twain, Room Service, Farrington of the FO, Dark Angel, The Adventures of Sherlock Holmes, Howards' Way*, the mini-series *The Master of Ballantrae* and the TV movie *Arch of Triumph*.

After working on a late-80s Anglo-French-American remake of *William Tell*, called *Crossbow*, this time playing Tell's elderly mentor, Stefan, on and off over three series, he bought a barn in Normandy and converted it into a house, where he now lives with his second wife Jennifer Slatter, a film casting director, with whom he has two daughters, Kate and Sarah.

Conrad was previously married to actress Jean Moir, whom he met while training at RADA, but the two divorced and she later died. Their son, Patrick, was tragically killed in a drowning accident.

Pat Phoenix

b. 26 November 1923
d. 18 September 1986

FOR more than 20 years, Pat Phoenix was the nearest that British soap came to having a Hollywood-style star. On screen, she was the brash, tempestuous, man-chasing Elsie Tanner in *Coronation Street*. Away from the studios, she lived life to the full, wearing mink coats and diamond necklaces, and marrying three times. In the mid-60s, the then Chancellor of the Exchequer, James Callaghan, called her "the sexiest thing on television".

Born in Manchester, Pat faced the stigma of being labelled illegitimate when her father, Tom Mansfield, was revealed to be a bigamist. Her mother, Anna Maria Josephine Noonan, left him and later married painter and decorator Richard Pilkington, whom the aspiring actress hated.

He scoffed at her ambition to go on the stage, which was fuelled by trips to the Palace Theatre, Manchester, to see Laurence Olivier, Sybil Thorndike and Ralph Richardson. But Pat had the last laugh, landing a role in a radio play and following it with regular work on *Children's Hour* at the age of 11, after submitting a monologue.

Leaving school, she worked by day as a filing clerk for Manchester Corporation's gas department and acted by night with the Manchester Arts Group and Shakespearian Society. She later joined the Arts Theatre, Manchester, and other Northern repertory companies.

More work gradually came her way – she played comedian Sandy Powell's wife in the 1948 film *Cup Tie Honeymoon* and did a summer season in Thora Hird's Blackpool show *Happy Days*.

She acted with Joan Littlewood's Theatre Workshop, in Stratford, East London, during the 50s and, in 1958, had parts in the horror films *Blood of the Vampire* and *Jack the Ripper*, as well being auditioned for the role of Alice Aisgill in the film *Room at the Top*, which eventually went to French actress Simone Signoret. Pat also drew on her early *Children's Hour* scriptwriting experience to write for ventriloquist Terry Hall and his puppet, Lenny the Lion, and for comedian Harry Worth.

It was during these years that she met her first husband, Peter Marsh, an actor whom she married in Bradford Cathedral. The marriage lasted just a year and the couple were later divorced. He went on to become an advertising executive.

After the break-up, Pat's career went downhill. It was at such a low ebb by the summer of 1960 that she returned to Manchester, ready to give up acting. Then, she auditioned at Granada Television for the role of Elsie Tanner in *Coronation Street*, a new serial about a Northern backstreet, thinking she had no chance of getting it.

The programme's producer, Stuart Latham, asked Pat to take off her coat so that he could see what she looked like, but she refused, saying, "You'll just have to bloody well guess, won't you?" The fiery temperament and ample bosom perfectly fitted the part of Elsie and the part was hers.

The character began as a divorcée with two grown-up children. Two more marriages – to Steve Tanner and Alan Howard – and a string of affairs followed but, instead of growing old and undesirable, Elsie seemed to improve with age.

By the time of her *Street* success, the actress had changed her name from Pilkington to Phoenix, after the mythological bird that rose from the ashes, and Pat, who made a cameo appearance as a cockney prostitute in the classic 1963 British film *The L-Shaped Room* while still in the serial, was one of British soap opera's first true legends, enjoying a glamorous lifestyle and newspaper headlines that charted her every move.

It made a good story when, in 1972, she married screen husband Alan Browning and both later left the *Street* to return to theatre work. But, after little more than two years away, Pat returned to the programme – alone. She and Browning were still living together, but a separation followed, before his tragic death from alcoholism.

When she decided to leave *Coronation Street* for good, in 1984, Elsie was despatched to Portugal and old flame Bill Gregory. Looking for new horizons, Pat became an agony aunt for TV-am and starred in her own comedy series, *Constant Hot Water*, as Blackpool landlady Phyllis Nugent.

She was set to play a high-powered, glamorous businesswoman in *The Legacy*, a planned new soap opera with American backing, but her last screen role was as a bed-ridden former actress in an ITV play called *Hidden Talents*, in the *Unnatural Causes* series.

Shortly afterwards, in September 1986, Pat herself was lying in a Cheshire hospital, dying of lung cancer. Wearing blue satin pyjamas and diamonds, she sat up in bed, took a sip of champagne and married actor Tony Booth.

They had first met almost 30 years earlier, while working in rep together, but it was only after she had found success as Elsie Tanner, and he had become known as Alf Garnett's 'Scouse git' son-in-law in *Till Death Us Do Part*, that they became lovers.

After the hospital ceremony, Pat ventured outside in a wheelchair and gave her adoring fans a wave, with the words, "Thank you very much, loves, and ta-ra!" A few days later, she was dead and, at her funeral, a Dixieland jazz band played 'When the Saints Go Marching In'. It was her wish that everyone left the service feeling good.

Pat wrote two autobiographies, *All My Burning Bridges*, published in 1974, and *Love, Curiosity, Freckles and Doubt* nine years later.

Wilfred Pickles

b. 13 October 1904
d. 27 March 1978

ALTHOUGH a star of radio, Wilfred Pickles found small-screen fame in his later years as a lovestruck pensioner in the popular TV series *For the Love of Ada*, alongside veteran comedienne Irene Handl.

Born in Halifax, West Yorkshire, he worked in the family building firm during his early years. However, it collapsed during the Depression, leaving massive debts that he vowed to pay off and, over the next 20 years, he did so.

Wilfred's road to stardom began in amateur dramatics and, after appearing in the BBC's *Children's Hour* in 1927, he became a radio actor, then a newsreader for the BBC's North Region, before being transferred to the BBC's National Programme, in 1941. His Yorkshire accent caused great controversy among listeners, who had previously heard the news read only in standard English.

A year later, he was made producer of radio features and drama, but he left in 1946 to make his London West End stage debut, in *The Gay Dog*, at the Piccadilly Theatre. Six years later, he was to make his film debut in the screen version of this comedy. His later pictures included *Billy Liar* and *The Family Way*.

After completing the run of his first West End show, Wilfred returned to broadcasting to take up his own programme, *Have a Go!*, with his wife, Mabel, who played the piano in the celebrated radio series.

He made his first television appearance in a variety show broadcast from Radiolympia. Other TV work followed, including *Ask Pickles* in 1954, again presented by Wilfred and Mabel. The show concentrated on making the man in the street's dreams come true – its speciality appeared to be reuniting long-lost family members.

Tears were shed by the bucketful as Wilfred, who positively revelled in sentimentality, egged them on. So successful was the show that it topped the ratings for two years.

He also acted in *Dr Finlay's Casebook*, but his most famous television role was in the comedy *For the Love of Ada*, in which he and Irene Handl played a couple of lovelorn pensioners.

Beginning in 1970 and running for three years, the series told the quaint, rather funny, romantic tale of frustrated love in the pair's twilight years. It proved so popular that a spin-off film was made, in 1972, although it did not enjoy the same success as the TV programme.

Wilfred wrote various books, including an autobiography entitled *Between You and Me* (1949), two poetry anthologies – *Personal Choice* and *For Your Delight – Sometime Never, Ne'er Forget the People* and *My North Countrie*.

Awarded an OBE in 1950, he and Mabel had one son, who died of polio in infancy.

Donald Pleasence

b. 5 October 1919

BEST known as a star of the cinema screen, Donald Pleasence has also brought his sinister looks and abundant talent to television in a variety of productions, from a 1954 version of *1984* to appearances in *Centennial* and *Scoop*.

Born in Worksop, Nottinghamshire, Donald became a railway clerk at Swinton, in South Yorkshire, on leaving school, while looking for a break as an actor. When it came, with Jersey Rep in 1939, he made his debut as Hareton in *Wuthering Heights*. His first London stage appearance was as Valentine in *Twelfth Night*, three years later.

Shortly afterwards, he joined the RAF for war service and, after being shot down, was a prisoner-of-war from 1944 until 1946, when he returned to the theatre as Mavriky in Alec Guinness's adaptation of *The Brothers Karamazov*, at the Lyric Theatre, Hammersmith.

Repertory work followed in Birmingham and Bristol, and Donald made his New York debut when Sir Laurence Olivier's company performed *Antony and Cleopatra* and *Caesar and Cleopatra* at the Ziegfeld Theater, in 1951.

A year later, he played Huish in his own play, *Ebb Tide*, at the Edinburgh Festival, which subsequently transferred to the Royal Court Theater, London. Then, he performed with the Shakespeare Memorial Theatre, Stratford-upon-Avon, as Lepidus in *Antony and Cleopatra*, the production later moving to the Prince's Theatre, London.

His theatre work continued regularly, in London and New York, with the actor gaining particular acclaim for his roles in Harold Pinter plays, such as *The Caretaker*. By then, Donald had become an established film actor, making his first big-screen appearance in a leading role in the 1954 picture *The Beachcomber*.

He followed it with more than 100 films, most notably *A Tale of Two Cities*, *Look Back in Anger*, *Sons and Lovers*, *Dr Crippen* – which established him as a brilliant player of evil roles – *The Greatest Story Ever Told*, the James Bond feature *You Only Live Twice*, *The Eagle Has Landed*, the *Halloween* series and Woody Allen's *Shadows and Fog*.

Although his television appearances have been infrequent, they are many and have usually made their mark. One of his earliest was in *1984*, a 1954 BBC adaptation of George Orwell's 'Big Brother' warning.

Donald has also acted in *Columbo*, *Orson Welles' Great Mysteries*, *Shades of Greene*, *The Rivals of Sherlock Holmes*, *Centennial*, *Barchester Towers*, *Miss Marple: A Caribbean Mystery*, the mini-series *The Great Escape: The Final Chapter* and the TV movies *Arch of Triumph*, *The Corsican Brothers* and *Scoop*.

The actor won an Emmy award for his

performance in *The Defection of Simas Kudirka* on American television and was particularly memorable for his solo performance in *The Private Thoughts of Julius Caesar.*

His first two marriages – to actress Miriam Raymond and actress-singer Josephine Crombie – both ended in divorce

and he is now married to singer Meira Shore.

Donald has five daughters, actress Angela Pleasence and Jean from his first marriage, Lucy and Polly from the second, and Miranda from the third. He has written two books, *Scouse the Mouse*, published in 1977, and *Scouse in New York*, which came out a year later.

Eric Porter

b. 8 April 1928

WHEN television producers were casting demons and po-faced characters in the 60s and 70s, Eric Porter seemed to be on all their shortlists, becoming a star as Soames Forsyte in *The Forsyte Saga*, after more than 20 years in acting.

Born in London, the son of a bus conductor, his parents wanted him to qualify as an electrical engineer, so he went to technical college but switched to a stage career at the age of 16.

Eric had acted in school plays and a schools drama organiser obtained an interview for him with Robert Atkins, director at Stratford-upon-Avon, which later became the Royal Shakespeare Company. He was signed up and made his stage debut carrying a spear, for £3 a week.

He then joined Lewis Casson's theatre company in a revival of *Saint Joan*, making his London debut in 1946 at the Kings Theatre, Hammersmith (now the Lyric), as Dunois's page, a part played by Jack Hawkins in the original production.

After National Service in the RAF, Eric toured with Sir Donald Wolfit, acted in repertory theatre in Birmingham, Bristol and at the London Old Vic, and appeared in John Gielgud's Hammersmith season and in London's West End.

He made his first Broadway appearance as the Burgomaster in *The Visit* at the opening of the Lunt-Fontanne Theatre and, back in Britain, played Rosmer in *Rosmersholm* at the Royal Court Theatre, winning him a *London Evening Standard* Drama Award for Best Actor.

Rejoining the Stratford company, by now the RSC, Eric appeared there and at the Aldwych, in London, in such parts as Ulysses in *Troilus and Cressida* and the title roles in *Becket*, *King Lear* and *Doctor Faustus*. More recently, he was in *Cat On a Hot Tin Roof* at the National Theatre.

His first film was the 1956 murder-mystery *Town on Trial*, and he followed it with pictures such as *The Fall of the Roman Empire*, *The Pumpkin Eater*, *The Heroes of Telemark*, the Hammer productions *The Lost Continent* and *Hands of the Ripper*, *Antony and Cleopatra*, *Nicholas and Alexandra*, *Day of the Jackal*, *Hitler: The Last Ten Days*, *The Belstone Fox*, *The Thirty-Nine Steps* and the big-screen spin-off from the TV thriller *Callan.*

Eric's television career began with *The Physicist* and he later appeared in *The Wars of the Roses*, before fame finally came with the part of brutal Soames Forsyte, in 1967.

The Forsyte Saga was an instant hit, featuring the actor as a tyrant who was incredibly cruel to his screen wife Irene, played by Nyree Dawn Porter (no relation), and became adored by female viewers throughout the world. However, the scene where Soames raped Irene shocked everyone.

His role in the 26-part series, screened initially on BBC2 but repeated on BBC1 the following year and enjoying another two repeat runs, won him Best Actor awards from BAFTA and the Guild of Television Producers and Directors.

Having made his name, Eric took the title roles in the TV plays *Cyrano de Bergerac* and *Macbeth*, appeared in *The Winslow Boy*, *Man and Superman* – opposite Maggie Smith – *Julius Caesar* and *Separate Tables*. He and Nyree Dawn Porter played husband and wife again in an episode of *Love Story* titled *Spilt Champagne.*

Ten years after *The Forsyte Saga* made waves, the actor reprised his viciousness in a BBC adaptation of *Anna Karenina*, in 1977, throwing his pregnant screen wife, played by Nicola Pagett, across the bedroom into a chair.

His subsequent TV roles have included Neville Chamberlain in *Winston Churchill: The Wilderness Years*, a po-faced deputy governor in *The Crucible*, Moriarty in *The Adventures of Sherlock Holmes* and Fagin in *Oliver Twist*. He was also in the blockbuster series *The Jewel in the Crown* and narrated the BBC TV film *Tutankhamun.*

A bachelor, Eric has homes in London and Stratford-upon-Avon.

Nyree Dawn Porter

b. 1936

A S Irene in *The Forsyte Saga*, Nyree Dawn Porter was described by one critic as "the first romantic sex symbol of the telly age".

Born in New Zealand, her first professional work was touring with the New Zealand Players Trust. She was acclaimed for roles such as Jessica in *The Merchant of Venice* and Juliet in *Romanoff and Juliet*. She also performed in revues and musicals including *Love from Judy* and *The Solid Gold Cadillac*.

Nyree moved to Britain in 1958 after winning a Miss Cinema talent competition for young actresses organised by Rank, with the prize of a round-the-world trip and a film test in London.

Although the film test was little more than a publicity stunt, she decided to stay and was soon acting in the theatre. Her first West End appearance was in the revue *Look Who's Here*, at the Fortune Theatre, Drury Lane.

She followed it with the role of Connie in Neil Simon's first West End play, *Come Blow Your Horn*, and a string of other appearances including those in *The Duel*, *The Dragon Variation*, *Murder in Mind*, *Anastasia* and *Deadly Nightcap*.

Nyree also had two roles in Stephen Sondheim's *Sunday in the Park with George*, at the National Theatre in 1990, and played Olivia in *Twelfth Night* at the Shaw Theatre, London, and Rosalind in *As You Like It* at the Ludlow Festival, as well as touring Australia in Jeffrey Archer's *Beyond Reasonable Doubt* and, later, in *The King and I*.

Her film appearances, which have been

few and far between, include those in *The Cracksman*, *Two Left Feet*, *Live Now – Pay Later*, *Jane Eyre*, *To Die, To Sleep, Perchance to Dream* and *The Martian Chronicles*.

It was in television that Nyree really made her name. She had already appeared in *Madame Bovary* and *Judy Paris* when, in 1967, she was cast as Irene in BBC2's 26-part serial *The Forsyte Saga*. The story of wicked Soames Forsyte's marriage – including the rape of Irene – gripped viewers in Britain and around the world, and it was soon repeated on BBC1.

Nyree was an overnight star as the Victorian woman trapped in a loveless marriage and won a BAFTA award and, in 1970, the OBE for her performance. Later, she did a stage tour of *The Forsyte Sage*.

Riding high on her success, she starred in the 1968 comedy series *Never a Cross Word* and, three years later, alongside Robert Vaughn in puppet master Gerry Anderson's

'live-action' series *The Protectors*. She also appeared in *Doctor In Charge*, *Anne of Green Gables* and the BBC serial *David Copperfield*, as the mother of David's best friend, James Steerforth.

Nyree then played the title role in the 26-part daytime serial *For Maddie with Love*, as a woman with only a few months to live. Ian Hendry was her screen husband – they had previously worked together in the film *Live Now – Pay Later* – and the programme ran for two series, in 1980 and 1981. She also appeared as a dotty games mistress in a *Dick Emery Show* sketch and was the subject of *This Is Your Life*.

Nyree's first husband, Bryon O'Leary, died in 1970 after an accidental drugs overdose. During their 13-year marriage, she miscarried three times. In 1975, the actress married actor Robin Halstead, 11 years her junior, after giving birth to a daughter, Tassy (Natalia), but the couple divorced in 1987.

Magnus Pyke

b. 29 December 1908
d. 19 October 1992

A human windmill, Magnus Pyke entertained millions of viewers when, arms flailing and eyes popping, he would explain some scientific phenomenon with relish in the TV show *Don't Ask Me*.

Born into a wealthy family in West London, he gained a degree at McGill University, in Montreal, Canada, after emigrating and working as a labourer during the summer and studying during the winter months.

It was there that Magnus nurtured a deep interest in nutrition and, when he graduated in 1933, he became a research scientist.

When war broke out, he was summoned to the Ministry of Food, where he became one of the scientists responsible for introducing rosehip syrup, which is rich in vitamin C, as a substitute for orange juice.

After the war, he took up a post at the Distillers company in Scotland, until 1973, when he became secretary and chairman of the British Association for the Advancement of Science.

While many others would have been glad to take things easy during their retirement, Magnus was thrilled when he was invited to be the scientific authority in Yorkshire Television's two science programmes, *Don't Ask Me* and *Don't Just Sit There*, both seen nationally on ITV.

Don't Ask Me also featured Dr Miriam

Stoppard and botanist David Bellamy, presenting scientific issues at a level that ordinary men and women could understand. Launched in 1974, the programme posed such questions as "Why do jellies wobble?" and "Do crocodiles really shed tears?"

While his co-presenters answered in a fairly subdued manner, Magnus could not contain himself, and his obvious enthusiasm went into overdrive as he explained, with great relish, some of life's curious little queries, including why toast falls butter side down and why the sun's rays are yellow.

The follow-up series, *Don't Just Sit There*, was in the same vein and, in 1975, Magnus won the Pye Colour Television Award for Most Promising Male Newcomer. His other broadcasts included the radio shows *Any Questions?*, on which he was a panellist, and *Desert Island Discs* – as a castaway – as well as the TV programme *Enough Food on Our Plate*.

Awarded an OBE in 1978, he wrote many books, including *Manual of Nutrition* and his 1981 autobiography *Six Lives of Pyke*.

In addition to his degree from McGill University, he held a philosophy doctorate, was a member of the Fellowship of the Royal Institute of Chemistry, the Institute of Biology and the Royal Society of Edinburgh, and a Fellow of the Institute of Food and Technology.

Magnus was married to chartered accountant Dorothea Vaughan, who died in 1986. They had a son and a daughter.

Anthony Quayle

b. 7 September 1913
d. 20 October 1989

ONE of the stage's great classical actors, who also found a niche in war films such as *The Guns of Navarone*, Anthony Quayle brought to television the qualities that had rocketed him to fame in both of those mediums, with the biblical epic *Moses the Lawgiver*, the historical drama *The Last Days of Pompeii* and an Emmy award-winning performance as the lawyer defending an author accused of libel in the 1974 mini-series *QB VII*.

Born in Ainsdale, Lancashire, Anthony was educated at Rugby School and trained at RADA, before making his professional debut at the Q Theatre as Richard Coeur de Lion and Will Scarlett in *Robin Hood*, in 1931.

He was noticed three years later in the role of Guildenstern in John Gielgud's production of *Hamlet*, and began appearing in classical parts for the Old Vic.

During the Second World War, he served with the Royal Artillery, fighting behind enemy lines with Albanian partisans and reaching the rank of major.

On being demobbed, in 1945, he returned to the stage, starring as Jack Absolute with Edith Evans in *The Rivals* at the Criterion Theatre, a role he had previously played at the Old Vic.

A year later, he directed his first London West End play, *Crime and Punishment*, for John Gielgud and, after a celebrated

performance as Enobabus in *Antony and Cleopatra*, entered the most satisfying chapter of his career, at the Shakespeare Memorial Theatre, in Stratford-upon-Avon, where – after roles as Iago, Petruchio and Claudius – he was appointed the company's director, in 1948.

Over the next eight years, he played Henry VIII, Falstaff, Othello and Bottom, but the greatest critical acclaim was reserved for his 1955 performance as Aaron in Peter Brook's production of *Titus Andronicus*, in London, New York and across Europe, with Laurence Olivier as Titus.

Anthony's subsequent theatrical career included well-received performances in *Long Day's Journey into Night*, *The Right Honourable Gentleman*, *Galileo*, *Sleuth* and *Old World*, for the Royal Shakespeare Company, and his tour-de-force, *King Lear*, at the Old Vic.

In 1983, he formed his own theatre company, Compass, which toured the provinces, and he played Prospero in *The Tempest* and Couchon in *Saint Joan*, before repeating his *King Lear*.

A film career that began with *Moscow Nights*, in 1935, was irregular until the turn of the 50s, although he had by then appeared in *Pygmalion* and Laurence Olivier's *Hamlet*, but it was films such as *The Guns of Navarone*, *HMS Defiant*, *Lawrence of Arabia*, *The Fall of the Roman Empire* and *Anne of the 1000 Days* that finally established Anthony as a major star of the big screen. Other film appearances included the Woody Allen comedy *Everything You Always Wanted to Know About Sex But Were Afraid To Ask*, *The Eagle Has Landed* and *Buster*.

He had already played a string of roles on television when he was cast as criminologist Adam Strange in *The Strange Report* series, in 1968. Two years later, he narrated the celebrated BBC series *The Six Wives of Henry VIII* and, in 1974, he won an Emmy award for his performance in the mini-series *QB VII*. He also appeared in *Moses the Lawgiver* – which was released in the cinema, as *Moses* – and in the TV movies *Great Expectations*, *Murder by Decree*, *Masada*, *Dial M for Murder*, *The Manions of America*, *The Last Days of Pompeii* and *The Bourne Alternative*.

Made a CBE in 1952 and knighted in 1985, Anthony was married twice. After his first marriage, to Hermione Hannen, ended in divorce, he wed actress Dorothy Hyson, with whom he had two daughters, Rosanna and Jenny. He died of cancer at the age of 76.

Ted Ray

b. 21 November 1905
d. 8 November 1977

WHEN the music-hall tradition died, comedian Ted Ray arrived on radio and television, bringing with him a charming manner that was in danger of being forgotten. With his own small-screen programme, *The Ted Ray Show*, he brought the golden age of entertainment into homes and won himself a place in the hearts of millions of viewers.

Born Charlie Olden in Wigan, Lancashire, the son of a comedian of the same name, on leaving school he worked as a clerk, ship's steward and a dance-band violinist, before bringing his talents ashore.

Using a routine packed with tomfoolery and wisecracks, he became a top music-hall attraction during the 30s, with his act billed as "fiddling and fooling". Changing his name to Ted Ray – which belonged to a golfing hero of the day – he made his stage debut at the Palace Theatre, Prescot, Lancashire, in 1927 and appeared in London for the first time three years later, at the London Music Hall, Shoreditch. For the next 30 years, he continued on stage, including three South African tours and four Royal Variety Performances.

Ted made his radio debut in 1939 and, ten years later, landed his own series, *Ray's a Laugh*, launched by the BBC as a successor to *ITMA* (*It's That Man Again*), following the death of its much-loved star, Tommy Handley. The show, an instant success, was based on his fictional marriage and included the voices of Peter Sellers, Kenneth Connor and Charles Hawtrey.

In 1950, he became MC on the BBC show *Calling All Forces*, as well as a long-term member of the *Does the Team Think?* quiz.

But it was in 1955 that Ted first came to TV screens with his own programme, *The Ted Ray Show* – the ideal showcase for his brand of humour. Ted always went down well with viewers because he had the ability to make them feel like part of his show, as if they were really there with him and not watching at home on the television.

During his TV career, he also appeared in *Jokers Wild*, in which he and a group of his fellow-comedians would stand up and joke away, and as a regular panellist on the 70s talent show *New Faces*.

He had already appeared in the 1930 picture *Elstree Calling* and *Radio Parade of 1935*, four years later, when, during the Fifties, he acted in seven films, *A Ray of Sunshine*, *Meet Me Tonight*, *My Wife's Family*, *The Crowning Touch*, *Please Turn Over* and, most notably, as the respected headmaster in *Carry On Teacher*. The comedian also wrote two autobiographies, *Raising the Laughs* and *My Turn Next*, and a book about his hobby, *Golf – My Slice of Life*.

Ted, who died from a heart attack at the age of 72 – two years after being seriously injured in a car accident – was married to Dorothy Sybil Stevens, with whom he had two sons, Andrew and Robin.

Arnold Ridley

b. 7 January 1896
d. 12 March 1984

MANY will remember actor Arnold Ridley as the weak-kneed Private Godfrey in television's popular, long-running comedy series *Dad's Army*, but he was also a playwright who first found fame as the creator of the stage thriller *The Ghost Train*.

Born in Bath, Avon, he studied at Bristol University, before embarking on a career in the theatre. After making his debut in *Prunella*, at the Theatre Royal, Bristol, in 1914, he joined the Army, from which he was discharged three years later, after being wounded in the First World War.

In 1918, he joined Birmingham Repertory Theatre, staying for two years and playing 40 parts, before moving on to Plymouth, where he eventually had to take a break from the stage when his old war injuries began to trouble him.

His luck changed when he wrote the legendary theatre hit *The Ghost Train*, in 1925. It was the tale of passengers stranded at a haunted railway station in Cornwall, one of them an undercover detective trying to catch smugglers. Without warning, the show became an overnight success, enjoying 665 performances in London's West End and two revivals. There were even two film versions, a silent one in 1927 and one of the first sound pictures, four years later. As a dramatist, Arnold was riding the crest of a wave and his subsequent play, *The Wrecker*, in 1927, also received great acclaim.

He continued writing plays and directing until he joined the Army for the Second World War, serving with the British Expeditionary Force in France. The War over, he returned to the theatre, began writing once again and was in several radio shows, including *The Archers*.

However, it was with two television parts that Arnold became widely known, first as the vicar in the ITV soap *Crossroads*, then as Private Godfrey in *Dad's Army*.

By the time he appeared in *Dad's Army*, which began in 1968, the actor – a real-life veteran of two world wars – was in his 70s. He played one of the gallant but bungling bunch of men in the Home Guard, entrusted with keeping Britain's coastline defended against German invasion. Doddering Private Godfrey suffered from weak knees and an even weaker bladder, blending in perfectly with the other old-timers, led by pompous Captain Mainwaring and his deputy, Sergeant Wilson. The series ran for nine years and the cast also appeared in a 1971 film spin-off.

Arnold, who died at the age of 88, was awarded an OBE in 1982.

Michael Robbins

b. 14 November 1930
d. 11 December 1992

GRAVEL-voiced 'Arfur' in the hit 70s comedy *On the Buses* is the role for which Michael Robbins will be best remembered, forming a double-act with Anna Karen as his screen wife, Olive, who bore the brunt of his hurled insults and cruel temperament.

Born in Lewisham, South London, Michael began his working life as a bank clerk, before turning to acting in repertory theatre for six years, at the Library Theatre, Manchester, and Birmingham Rep.

Much later, he experienced stage successes as the lecherous brother-in-law in Alan Ayckbourn's *Time and Time Again*, opposite Tom Courtenay at the Comedy Theatre, in the musicals *Liza of Lambeth* and *The Ratepayers' Iolanthe*, and with a tour of Bob Larbey's comedy *A Month of Sundays*.

The actor's many films included *The Whisperers*, *The Looking Glass War*, *All the Way Up*, *Zeppelin*, *Villain*, *Victor Victoria* and *The Pink Panther Strikes Again*, in which he memorably played a nightclub drag queen, with Julie Andrews's voice dubbed over his singing performance.

He showed great versatility on television, making his debut as the cockney soldier in *Roll-On Bloomin' Death* and following it as a ruffian who bargained for his soul in Shaw's *Major Barbara* and a flight sergeant in *Ross*, as well as appearances in *The Hunting of Lionel Crane*, *The Dirt on Lucy Lane* and *Danton*.

Then came the role of Reg Varney's morose screen brother-in-law Arthur in *On the Buses*, which started in 1969, ran for six years and more than 70 episodes, and spawned three film spin-offs, *On the Buses*,

Mutiny On the Buses and *Holiday On the Buses*.

The comedy was boisterous and often below-the-belt, but Michael and Anna Karen – as Arthur and Olive – provided a compelling secondary storyline to that of Varney's capers at the bus depot. They squabbled continually, with gravel-voiced Arthur always putting down long-suffering Olive, most often seen in face cream and curlers, and the part gained Michael a nomination as the Variety Club of Great Britain's 1970 Personality of the Year.

In 1988, the cast toured Australia in a stage version of the comedy. By then,

Michael had clocked up many more roles, including a television version of his stage hit *Time and Time Again*.

During his career, he had been a stooge to comedians such as Tommy Cooper and Dick Emery, and was a great favourite as King Rat in pantomime.

His last TV appearances were in *El C.I.D.*, *The New Statesman*, *Adam Bede* and *A Little Bit of Heaven*, in which he spoke of his Catholic faith.

Michael, who received a Papal Award for his services in the Catholic Stage Guild, died of cancer at the age of 62. He and his actress wife, Hal Dyer, had a son and a daughter.

Fyfe Robertson

b. 1902
d. 4 February 1987

ONE of television's most eccentric broadcasters, Fyfe Robertson – with his bristling beard and deerstalker hat – was best loved for his reports in the legendary *Tonight* programme during the 50s and 60s.

Born in Edinburgh, he spent many years working as a journalist on newspapers, including *The Glasgow Herald*, *The Sunday Express* and *The Daily Express*. He joined the great *Picture Post* magazine in 1943, remaining until its demise 13 years later. He was then a natural for the BBC television early-evening magazine programme *Tonight*, which started in 1957 and mixed serious and light current affairs items.

At first, it attracted only a million viewers, but by the end of its first year the programme was pulling in audiences of more than five million. It made stars of Cliff Michelmore, the presenter, and reporters such as Fyfe and Alan Whicker. Although the programme was revived in a late-night slot in 1975, *Tonight* really ended in 1965, after 1800 editions, and was succeeded by *24 Hours*, for which Fyfe also reported, eventually clocking up 750 reports for both programmes. His other documentaries included *The Trade in Animals*, in 1968, and *Why Zoos?*, a year later.

Fyfe made a series of reminiscences called *Robbie*, in 1978, and his final documentary, *The Peat Programme*, was broadcast in 1981.

Despite being a heavy smoker, he remained in good health and in his late 60s took part in two exhausting televised expeditions, across the Scottish Highlands on horseback and paddling down the Severn in a canoe.

Fyfe, who died at the age of 84, had been married twice. First wife Betty, with whom he had two daughters, died in 1973 and he went on to marry an old family friend, widow Vera Ford, five years later.

Cardew Robinson

b. 14 August 1917
d. 27 December 1992

IMMORTALISED as 'Cardew the Cad', the gangling, overgrown schoolboy, with cap, long scarf and short trousers, Cardew Robinson created a comic character whose roots were firmly planted in the British humour of the mid-20th century.

Born Douglas Robinson in Goodmayes, Essex, he enjoyed acting in school productions and loved the books of Frank Richards, featuring Billy Bunter of Greyfriars, and the weekly magazine *The Gem*, with the adventures of Ralph Reckless Cardew of St Jim's.

On leaving school, he took a job with a local newspaper, but it closed down and he joined Joe Boganny's touring Crazy College Boys, opening at the Lyric Theatre, Hammersmith, in 1934.

However, deciding he wanted a more traditional training, Cardew went into repertory theatre, where one of his roles was as the monster in *Frankenstein*.

It was while serving in the RAF during the Second World War that he created his famous 'Cardew the Cad of the School' character, having written one verse and four choruses for a performance with one of Ralph Reader's Gang Shows.

Promoted to flight-sergeant and put in charge of a show, Cardew toured France, Belgium and Holland with it and, after the War, appeared with the commercial production of the Gang Show in variety theatres.

Developing 'Cardew the Cad' as a schoolboy at St Fanny's, whose headmaster was Dr Jankers, Cardew soon took the stories to the BBC radio series *Variety Bandbox*, where he became resident comedian. "Here is the news from St Fanny's and this is Cardew the Cad reading it!" he would intone.

The character was even featured, from 1949, in the children's comic *Radio Fun*, which inspired the feature film *Fun at St Fanny's*, in 1955, a year after the actor formally changed his professional name to Cardew.

As a young man he had appeared in films as early as 1938, starting in a short in the series *Ghost Tales Retold* and following it ten years later with *A Piece of Cake*, starring Cyril Fletcher, but his famous character provided him with his only starring role on the big screen, supported by Fred Emney, Stanley Unwin, Peter Butterworth, Gerald Campion (TV's Billy Bunter) and Ronnie Corbett. Later film roles included supports in pictures such as *Sink the Bismarck!*, *Reach for the Sky*, *Alfie* and *Shirley Valentine*, as well as the slightly blue *What's up Nurse?* and *Come Play with Me*.

Cardew's TV work included the 1964 series *Fire Crackers*, featuring the mishaps of the Cropper's End Fire Brigade, *The Small World of Samuel Tweet*, Spike Milligan's *Q6* and *Last of the Summer Wine*, as well as guest appearances in shows such as *Whodunnit?*, *Celebrity Squares*, *Call My Bluff* and *Quick on the Draw*.

On stage, the actor appeared as Sir Petronel Flash in Ben Jonson's *Eastwood Ho!*, at the Mermaid Theatre in 1962, and as King Pellinore in all 650 performances of *Camelot*, at the Theatre Royal, Drury Lane, two years later. He wrote scripts for Peter Sellers, Dick Emery and other comedians, and was deviser of the radio game show *You've Got To Be Joking* and writer of the book *How to Be a Failure*.

Cardew, who was divorced by the time he died at the age of 75, had two daughters, Leanne and Lindy.

Jane Rossington

b. 5 March 1943

FROM speaking the first words in the ITV soap *Crossroads*, blonde Jane Rossington was the only member of the cast to last the 23-year course – and many critics regarded it as strewn with obstacles.

Born in Derby during the Second World War, the daughter of a bank manager, Jane and her family moved to Sutton Coldfield when she was four.

After acting as an amateur, she trained at the Rose Bruford College of Speech and Drama, before landing the role of Monica Downs in the long-running radio serial *The Archers*. She subsequently acted in repertory theatre in Sheffield and York, in touring productions and on television, as probationer nurse Kate Ford, in *Emergency – Ward 10*.

While appearing in *Alfie* on stage in York, Jane rushed to ATV's Birmingham studios for an audition for the role of Jill Richardson, daughter of motel owner Meg, in *Crossroads*, a new, five-days-a-week serial based in the fictional Midlands village of King's Oak.

She won the part and, on 2 November 1964, spoke the first words of the first scene: "Crossroads Motel. Can I help you?"

Through more than two decades, Jill survived a bigamous marriage, two legal ones, two children by different fathers, two miscarriages and many other calamities in what was launched as a programme set around a family-run business.

In real life, Jane married a *Crossroads* director, Tim Jones, in the 60s, but they later divorced and she wed chartered surveyor David Dunger, by whom she has a daughter, Sorrel, and a son, Harry.

When she was expecting her first baby, the pregnancy was written into the serial's script, but Jane suffered a miscarriage. She subsequently became pregnant again, with

Sorrel, and the pregnancy continued on screen for 11 months, although, by that time *Crossroads* viewers had grown to expect such stretching of reality. Sorrel appeared in the serial as Jill's baby, Sarah Jane, and in that role she was bridesmaid at Jill's wedding to her second husband, Adam Chance.

When Central Television took over the Midlands ITV franchise from ATV in 1981, it reduced the programme's number of episodes to four a week, tried to revamp it twice and and finally axed it altogether, with the last episode seen on Easter Monday, 1988. Fittingly, Jane spoke the last words: "I always thought Crossroads was an awfully good name."

Since then, she has appeared on television only once, in an episode of the children's series *Dramarama*, and, for a while, she had her own show on Beacon Radio, her local station, then on its sister station WABC, and she toured in the stage plays *Murder in Mind* and *Don't Rock the Boat*.

Jane lives in a Queen Anne manor house near Lichfield, Staffordshire.

Leonard Rossiter

b. 21 October 1926
d. 5 October 1984

THE leering grin of lecherous landlord Rigsby in *Rising Damp*, and the efforts of a business executive to escape the mundane routine of suburbia in *The Fall and Rise of Reginald Perrin*, were both brought to the television screen by the genial, beaky-faced Leonard Rossiter, a classical actor who always clung to his stage roots.

Born in Liverpool, he lived over the barber shop owned by his father, who was killed in an air raid during the Second World War, thwarting Leonard's ambitions to study languages at university.

Leaving school early, he worked in an insurance office and acted as an amateur, until turning professional at the age of 27 and making his stage debut in *The Gay Dog*, in Preston.

He spent many years in repertory theatre, culminating at the Bristol Old Vic and, later, he scored a hit with his role as the demonic, Hitler-like gangster in Brecht's *The Resistible Rise of Arturo Ui*, his first London West End part, in 1969.

He followed it with Harold Pinter's *The Caretaker*, an Old Vic production of *Frontiers of Farce* and the title role in *Tartuffe*, as well as *Semi-Detached*, *Make and Break* and *Rules of the Game*.

Leonard branched out into films at a time when socially-aware dramas were being shown in the cinema, making his debut in *A Kind of Loving*, in 1962, and following it with a string of character roles, such as the undertaker in *Billy Liar* and Mr Sowerberry in *Oliver!*, plus appearances in *The Witches*, *2001: A Space Odyssey*, *Barry Lyndon*, *The Pink Panther Strikes Again* and *Britannia Hospital*.

However, he never showed as much presence in films as on stage and television. On the small screen, he had already acted in *Z-Cars* – as Detective Inspector Bamber, in

the 60s – *Thick As Thieves* and *The Magistrate* when he landed the role of Rigsby in Eric Chappell's stage farce *The Banana Box*, the basis for the hit comedy *Rising Damp*, which began on television in 1974.

The series cast him as the embittered, lip-curling landlord keeping more than a benign eye on his tenants. He would burst in on Alan and Philip (Richard Beckinsale and Don Warrington), hoping to find something amiss in their flat, and would play the sympathetic landlord to spinster Miss Jones (Frances de la Tour), on whom he doted.

Leonard repeated the role in a 1980 film spin-off, by which time he had already added another popular TV comedy character to his repertoire, acting the title role in *The Fall and Rise of Reginald Perrin*.

For four years, from 1976, he played the suburban business executive who, on the verge of a nervous breakdown, faked his death and came back as a new man with a new empire.

Unusually, the David Nobbs-scripted comedy was a serial, with elements of the story continuing from one week to another.

Unfortunately, the actor's 80s TV roles, in the wrestling comedy *The Loser* and as a harassed supermarket manager in *Tripper's Day*, were not so successful – although Bruce Forsyth took over the part in a second stab at the latter series when Leonard died of a heart attack during the interval of Joe Orton's stage play *Loot*, at the Lyric Theatre. He had been playing Inspector Truscott.

His starring role in *King John*, shown posthumously in the BBC's *Shakespeare* series, was a reminder that Leonard had never let his theatre work die even at the height of his television stardom. He will also be remembered for his classic TV commercials for Cinzano, with Joan Collins.

Leonard's marriage to actress Josephine Tewson ended in divorce and he later married actress Gillian Raine and had a daughter, Camilla.

Rowan and Martin

Dan Rowan, b. 2 July 1922,
d. 22 September 1987
Dick Martin, b. 1923

STANDING in for Dean Martin on his television show during the summer of

1966 gave American comedy duo Dan Rowan and Dick Martin the chance they had been looking for in almost 15 years of performing together.

They were offered their own show, *Rowan & Martin's Laugh-In*, which became

Dan Rowan

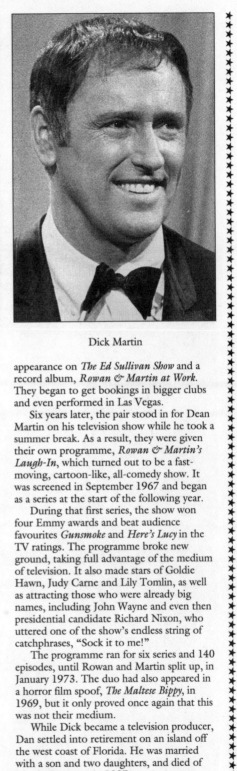

Dick Martin

an immediate hit, winning four Emmy awards in its first year and running for 140 episodes and a further five years, with all the top stars of the day queuing up to appear amid the quickfire gags.

Born in Beggs, Oklahoma, Dan Hale Rowan was the only child of carnival workers and was orphaned while young. Although he excelled in sports at school, his first job was with the film giant Paramount, in Hollywood, first in the post-room, then as a junior writer, although his talents were stemmed with America's involvement in the Second World War and he served as a fighter pilot with the Fifth Air Force, based in New Guinea.

After the War, Dan attended UCLA (the University of California, Los Angeles) and the University of Southern California, where he studied acting, as well as jointly owning a dealership in foreign cars.

Comedian Tommy Noonan introduced him to Dick Martin – who was born in Detroit, Michigan – an aspiring comedy writer working as a barman. They formed a double-act, with Dick playing the idiot and Dan the suave, suntanned straight-man, toured nightclubs and even appeared in a film, the unacclaimed 1958 Western spoof *Once Upon a Horse*.

But they failed to take over the mantle of Dean Martin and Jerry Lewis, who had split up in the mid-50s, although they had been tipped to do so.

Their big break came in 1960 with an appearance on *The Ed Sullivan Show* and a record album, *Rowan & Martin at Work*. They began to get bookings in bigger clubs and even performed in Las Vegas.

Six years later, the pair stood in for Dean Martin on his television show while he took a summer break. As a result, they were given their own programme, *Rowan & Martin's Laugh-In*, which turned out to be a fast-moving, cartoon-like, all-comedy show. It was screened in September 1967 and began as a series at the start of the following year.

During that first series, the show won four Emmy awards and beat audience favourites *Gunsmoke* and *Here's Lucy* in the TV ratings. The programme broke new ground, taking full advantage of the medium of television. It also made stars of Goldie Hawn, Judy Carne and Lily Tomlin, as well as attracting those who were already big names, including John Wayne and even then presidential candidate Richard Nixon, who uttered one of the show's endless string of catchphrases, "Sock it to me!"

The programme ran for six series and 140 episodes, until Rowan and Martin split up, in January 1973. The duo had also appeared in a horror film spoof, *The Maltese Bippy*, in 1969, but it only proved once again that this was not their medium.

While Dick became a television producer, Dan settled into retirement on an island off the west coast of Florida. He was married with a son and two daughters, and died of lymphatic cancer in 1987.

Leonard Sachs

b. 26 September 1909
d. 15 June 1990

THE grand old days of music-hall were kept alive on television for 30 years with *The Good Old Days*, and the programme's chairman, Leonard Sachs, kept his audience awake by giving the acts such magnificent introductions, teeming with alliterative and even nonsensical adjectives, so that he himself was as watchable as the famous and not-so-famous artists.

Born in the South African town of Roodepoort, in the Transvaal, he made his stage debut as Jim Hawkins in a Johannesburg production of *Treasure Island*,

in 1926, and travelled to Britain three years later, gaining experience in repertory theatre and making his London debut as the poet in *The Circle of Chalk*.

With fellow-actor Peter Ridgeway, he founded the Players' Theatre underneath the railway arches at Charing Cross, in London, in 1936, but Peter died and Leonard found himself running the theatre single-handed.

Among the acts he booked were Peter Ustinov, Hattie Jacques and Bernard Miles. He was also master of ceremonies in what became a venue for music-hall artists, and he stayed there – apart from army service during the Second World War – as director and producer until 1947.

With the death-knell sounding for music-hall, Leonard returned to the legitimate theatre, with roles in plays such as *Anna Christie* and *The Three Sisters*. However, when BBC television producer Barney Colehan started *The Good Old Days* in 1953, Leonard – with his experience at the Players' Theatre – was his first choice as chairman and the actor obliged with a false moustache and sideboards, a gavel that he banged to bring order, and a big build-up for every act, from the seasoned music-hall entertainers to those looking for their first break.

The show, with 'Down at the Old Bull and Bush' as its theme song, came from one of the great homes of music-hall, the City Varieties Theatre, in Leeds, and the hundreds of artists who appeared included Arthur Askey, Danny La Rue, Ken Dodd, Hylda Baker and Morecambe and Wise.

The Good Old Days, which ran for 250 episodes, finally ended with a Christmas special in 1983, long after music-hall had died in Britain's theatres, although the programme had been screened worldwide.

Throughout the show's run, Leonard had continued his acting career, giving character performances on television in *A Family at War*, *The Man from Haven* and *Crown Court*, as well as the roles of warehouse owner Sir Julius Berlin in *Coronation Street* and as Tom Conti's father in *The Glittering Prizes*.

He recorded his last TV play, *Lost for Words*, shortly before his death, and his last London West End stage appearance was as Weismann in the Stephen Sondheim musical *Follies*, at the Shaftesbury Theatre.

Leonard, who had a small part in the original 1936 film version of *1984*, gave his year of birth as 1909, but might actually have been two years older. He was married to actress-comedienne Eleanor Summerfield – whom he auditioned for the Players' Theatre in 1947 – and had two sons, actor Robin and Toby.

Joan Sanderson

b. 24 November 1912
d. 24 May 1992

PLAYING a series of battleaxes, from teacher Miss Ewell in *Please Sir!* to Prunella Scales's mother in *After Henry* and the elderly, deaf guest giving John Cleese a hard time in *Fawlty Towers*, Joan Sanderson brought terror and an impeccable style of comedy acting to television.

Born in Bristol, Avon, she trained at RADA and made her debut at the Shakespeare Memorial Theatre, Stratford-upon-Avon, before acting in repertory theatre.

After the Second World War, she appeared in London's West End for the first time, in *See How They Run*, at the Whitehall Theatre, later performing there in the Brian Rix company's farce *Simple Spymen*. On stage, she was also in *When We Are Married*, at the National Theatre, and West End productions of Alan Bennett's *Habeas Corpus* – as Lady Rumpus – and the satirical comedy about Margaret and Denis Thatcher, *Anyone for Denis?*, as the custodian of Chequers.

Joan had already appeared in the 60s TV comedy series *All Gas and Gaiters*, starring William Mervyn, when she landed the role of Miss Ewell in the classroom comedy *Please Sir!*, in which she chastised young teacher John Alderton for his soft approach to the kids of form 5C at Fenn Street Secondary Modern School, in the East End of London.

She repeated the part in a 1971 film spin-off of the series and her other pictures included *The Muppet Movie* and Alan Bennett's story of playwright Joe Orton, *Prick Up Your Ears*, which required her, as a shorthand expert, to transcribe and read out a particularly filthy passage from the tragic subject's diary.

Other actresses had turned down the part because of this, but "in Joan's characteristically disinfectant tones it became funny and ironic", recalled Bennett, who lamented that her big-screen appearances had been few and suggested that she would have been a regular performer in the Ealing comedies if they had continued.

On television, Joan appeared in *Upstairs, Downstairs*, the children's series *The Ghosts of Motley Hall*, and the comedies *Rising Damp* and *Ripping Yarns*, before her memorable performance as the deaf woman who caused John Cleese great irritation in *Fawlty Towers*. She was also in *The Other 'Arf*, a *Play for Today* entitled *Intensive Care*, the small-screen version of *Anyone for Denis?*, Michael Palin's TV film *East of Ipswich*, *Full House* and *Land of Hope and Gloria*.

She was a regular in four series of *Me & My Girl*, as the snooty grandmother, and fulfilled much the same role in *After Henry*, which began on BBC radio in 1985 and was later adapted for television. Joan, who was married to actor Gregory Moseley, died at the age of 79, shortly after finishing a fifth series of the comedy.

Terry Scott

b. 4 May 1927

DIVIDING his time between the big and small screens, Terry Scott has become one of Britain's longest-running comedy actors, with parts in film comedies such as the *Carry On* adventures and his own starring role, alongside June Whitfield, in *Happy Ever After* and *Terry and June*.

Born in Watford, Hertfordshire, the son of a postman who retired to run a corner shop, he studied accountancy and served in the Royal Navy during the Second World War, before deciding on an acting career, working with seaside repertory companies in Grange-over-Sands, Cumbria, and other resorts.

Switching to comedy, Terry auditioned for the BBC and performed on radio with Bob Monkhouse, but not entirely successfully. He then learned his craft in pubs, clubs, summer shows and pantomimes, before teaming up with Bill Maynard on stage.

The two actors then landed a TV situation-comedy, *Great Scott, It's Maynard*, in which their characters shared a flat, but Bill wanted to do more straight acting and the pair split up.

Terry was a success on radio second time around, alongside performers such as Charlie Chester and Frankie Howerd, and he appeared in the first *Carry On* film, *Carry On Sergeant* – following it with six others, over a period of 15 years – and returned to television in 1962, with Hugh Lloyd, in *Hugh and I*.

It ran for seven series and the duo also appeared in *Sunday Night at the London Palladium*, before Terry teamed up with his third screen partner, June Whitfield, in 1969 for the series *Scott On . . .*, in which they performed domestic sketches together.

Five years later, they were cast in the first of their two domestic situation-comedies, *Happy Ever After*, as husband and wife Terry and June Fletcher, living the middle-class life in suburbia after their children had left home.

After five series, the same characters were featured in *Terry and June*, following a copyright row over the original title. The new series, written by Eric Merriman and Christopher Bond, ran until 1988, by which time Terry had overcome a string of health problems, including brain surgery, cancer of the bladder and a nervous breakdown.

On the small screen, he is also particularly remembered dressed as a schoolboy for a string of commercials for Curly Wurly chocolate bars in the early 70s.

Apart from the *Carry On* series, his 28 films include *Blue Murder at St. Trinian's* – his big-screen debut, in 1957 – *Too Many Crooks, I'm All Right, Jack, The Night We Got the Bird, The Great St. Trinian's Train Robbery*, and *Bless This House*.

On stage, Terry performed in farces with Brian Rix's Whitehall Theatre company in the 60s and has subsequently appeared in *The Mating Game, A Bedful of Foreigners* and *Run for Your Wife*.

After his first marriage was dissolved, he married ballet-dancer-turned-choreographer Margaret Pollen, by whom he has four daughters, Sarah, Nicola, Lindsay and Alexandra. The couple live in Surrey.

Peter Sellers

b. 8 September 1925
d. 24 July 1980

ZANY television programmes such as *Idiot Weekly, Price 2d, A Show Called Fred* and *Son of Fred* bridged the transition of Peter Sellers from radio fame with *The Goons* to film superstardom in the comedies *I'm All Right, Jack, Heavens Above!* and the legendary *Pink Panther* series.

His greatest ability was as an actor, but his inventive comic genius and mastery of disguise and funny voices were the icing on the cake that made his a unique talent.

Born Peter Richard Henry Sellers in Southsea, Hampshire, a descendant of the Portuguese-Jewish prize-fighter Daniel Mendoza, his parents owned a seaside theatre in the town and he started his working life sweeping it.

During the Second World War, he performed with the entertainment organisation ENSA and subsequently appeared as a stand-up comic at the famous Windmill Theatre, in London, doing impressions of film stars. It was there, in 1948, that he was spotted by a radio scout and given a spot in *Show Time*.

A year later, Peter made the first of four appearances at the London Palladium and joined Ted Ray's radio series *Ray's a Laugh*, developing his array of comic characters, before teaming up with Spike Milligan, Harry Secombe and Michael Bentine in 1951 to found The Goons. Their first series was called *Junior Crazy Gang*, before a change of name to *Those Crazy People, The Goons* and, finally, *The Goon Show*.

Their anarchic humour revolutionised British broadcasting and The Goons – minus Michael Bentine, who had by then left – brought their musings to television in *Idiot Weekly, Price 2d*, which was followed by *A Show Called Fred* and *Son of Fred*, all in 1956.

In the same year, Peter provided the voices for the first Brooke Bond PG Tips chimps commercials. His only subsequent television appearances were as a guest star in *Not Only . . . But Also*, with Peter Cook and Dudley Moore in 1965, and *The Muppet Show*, 11 years later.

It was in films that he made his greatest impact, following his 1951 debut in *Penny Points to Paradise* with more than a dozen pictures that made use of his talent for mimicry, including the roles of one of the gang of weird murderers in *The Ladykillers* and an elderly cinema projectionist in *The Smallest Show on Earth*.

But the first film to win Peter acclaim as a major star, in which he played militant shop steward Fred Kite, was *I'm All Right, Jack*, the Boulting Brothers' classic comic look at trade unions, and it won him a British Film Academy award.

His 70 other film roles included three parts in both *The Mouse That Roared* and *Dr Strangelove* (subtitled *Or: How I Learned To Stop Worrying and Love the Bomb*), the way-out clergyman in *Heavens Above!*, an appearance in the James Bond spoof *Casino Royale* and the eccentric millionaire in *The Magic Christian*.

However, all those were eclipsed by his unforgettable characterisation of bungling French detective Inspector Clouseau in the *Pink Panther* films, starting in 1963 with *The Pink Panther* and followed by *A Shot in the Dark, The Return of the Pink Panther, The Pink Panther Strikes Again* and *Revenge of the Pink Panther*.

The last of Peter's films to be screened in cinemas before his death cast him in a very different role, as Chancy, the simple-minded gardener, in *Being There*, a part to which he brought great pathos.

His final film, *The Fiendish Plot of Dr Fu Manchu*, was screened posthumously and the planned *Romance of the Pink Panther* was never made, although *Trail of the Pink Panther*, a disappointing attempt to link old Sellers footage with newly shot pieces, came

out in 1982 and director Blake Edwards cast Ted Wass in the starring role for a new film, *Curse of the Pink Panther*, the following year.

As well as two double-A-sided Goons singles, 'I'm Walking Backwards for Christmas'/'Bluebottle Blues,' and 'Bloodnok's Rock 'n' Roll'/'Ying Tong Song', Peter had solo hits with 'Any Old Iron' and 'A Hard Day's Night' as well as two with Sophia Loren, 'Goodness Gracious Me' and 'Bangers and Mash'.

The actor, who died following a massive heart attack – his fifth in 16 years – at the age of 54, was made a CBE in 1966 and was married four times.

Divorced from his first three wives, Australian actress Anne Howe, Swedish film star Britt Ekland and Miranda Quarry, step-daughter of Cunard chairman Lord Mancroft, Peter wed actress Lynne Frederick in 1977. She filed for divorce two years later, but the couple were reunited shortly before his death.

He had three children, son Michael and daughter Sarah from his first marriage, and daughter Victoria from his second.

Phil Silvers

b. 11 May 1912
d. 1 November 1985

AS loveable rogue Sgt. Bilko, Phil Silvers became one of the most famous faces of the small screen in the 50s, with re-runs making his comic character a hit with several future generations.

Born Philip Silversmith in Brooklyn, New York, he was the youngest of eight children, his father a poor Russian immigrant Jew who worked on the early New York skyscrapers.

Phil started entertaining at the age of 11, when he would sing in cinemas, filling in when the projector broke down. He left school two years later to sing as a tenor in professional revues, before appearing in vaudeville as a stooge, when his voice eventually broke.

In 1934, he decided to go solo, becoming a bespectacled, bottom-of-the-bill comic at small theatres, but five years later he had got out of the gutter and risen to the dizzy heights of Broadway in a show called *Yokel Boy*.

From there, he moved into films, making his screen debut in the 1941 picture *Hit Parade*, but it was not until the RKO feature film *Tom, Dick and Harry* – in which he played an ice-cream seller – that he won any notable parts.

Phil continued to act in supporting roles in a never-ending string of musicals and light comedies, the more memorable being *Cover*

Girl, Summer Stock – in which he appeared alongside Gene Kelly and Judy Garland – and *Top Banana*, a screen adaptation of a Broadway show which won him a 1951 Tony award.

In films, he was always the leading man's buddy but never the hero. However, all that was to change when Sgt. Ernie Bilko marched on to TV screens in 1955 in *You'll Never Get Rich*, subsequently entitled *The Phil Silvers Show* and syndicated as *Bilko*. Phil was made for the role. He could identify with it, taking as his inspiration the stuffed-shirt officers of the Korean War in the best-selling novel of the day, *From Here to Eternity*, James Jones's realistic version of war, revealing the Army's class system.

He used Jones's contempt for the bumbling officers to create the satirical version of Sgt. Bilko, who ruled the roost at his army base, Fort Kansas. Rather than actually working, Bilko would hustle, gamble and generally outmanoeuvre his superiors. The confrontations between him and his long-suffering adversary, Colonel Hall, were pure genius.

Bilko became a folk hero, with millions of GIs following his antics during the show's four-year run, winning Phil three Emmy awards and the Television Showman award.

Bilko can still be seen on television screens around the world today – the show is repeated constantly. There is no doubt that the programme was the pinnacle of the actor's career and nothing that he did afterwards ever quite matched it, although he did try another TV series in 1964, in which he played a factory foreman, but the old Bilko magic was just not there.

Phil went on to appear in several light comedy films, as well as guesting on many TV programmes. He even came to Britain to star in *Follow That Camel* with the *Carry On* team (it was later re-released as *Carry On – Follow That Camel*), when they were looking to get into the American market.

He was also one of the team involved in the hilarious screen version of *A Funny Thing Happened on the Way to the Forum* and later starred in a revival of the stage hit, winning a 1972 Tony award.

For the last five years of his life, he was in poor health following a stroke, but he continued to work, taking cameo roles in various films. Twice married and divorced – to Jo Carroll Dennison and TV hostess Evelyn Patrick – he had five daughters, Tracey, Nancy, Laurey and twins Cathy and Candy. He died at the age of 73.

Bill Simpson

b. 11 September 1931
d. 21 December 1986

AS television's original Dr Finlay, watched over by old-fashioned Dr Cameron, in the hugely successful series *Dr Finlay's Casebook*, Bill Simpson became a national celebrity.

Born in the Scottish fishing village of Dunure, in Ayrshire, he studied drama in Glasgow, before making his professional debut with the Gateway Theatre, in Edinburgh.

After two years as an announcer for Scottish Television, in Glasgow, he went on to become a household name throughout the land in the title role of *Dr Finlay's Casebook*, based on the stories of A J Cronin.

The series, which started in 1962 and ran on BBC television for nine years, was set in the 20s, in the quaint fictional Scottish village of Tannochbrae, where the young, impetuous Dr John Finlay and his crusty, old partner, Dr Cameron, ran their small surgery from Arden House, with housekeeper Janet keeping them in line.

Bill played the part for 206 TV episodes and, when the programme was axed from the small screen, it continued for a further seven years on radio.

In 1993, the series was revived on ITV as *Doctor Finlay*, with David Rintoul in the part made famous by Bill, seen returning from the Second World War after serving in the Army as a major.

Bill's subsequent television appearances included the roles of a vet in *The McKinnons* and a secret agent in the thriller series *Scotch on the Rocks*. He also acted in the London West End musical *Romance*, but the show proved a massive flop and closed after only five days.

His later theatre roles included two years as the Open University professor in a touring production of Willy Russell's smash hit *Educating Rita*.

Bill, who died at the age of 55, was twice married and divorced, to actresses Mary Miller and Tracy Reed, with two daughters from the second marriage.

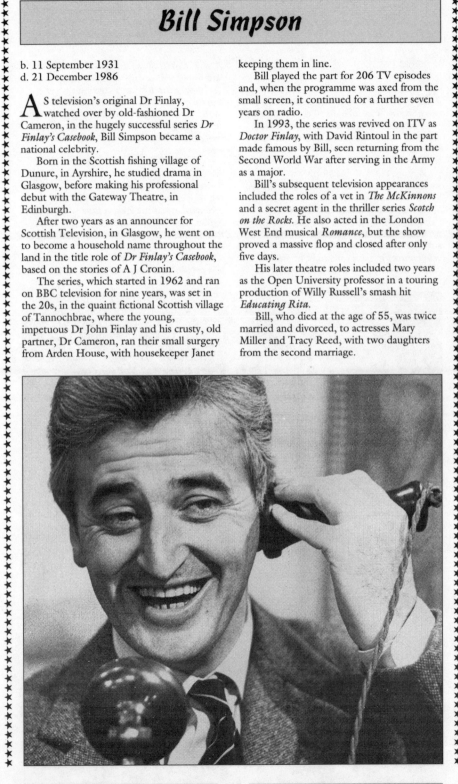

Valerie Singleton

b. 9 April 1937

AS one of *Blue Peter*'s presenters during the 60s and early 70s, Valerie Singleton was a big sister to millions of children who were brought up on the wholesome BBC children's programme that showed them how to make all sorts of useful objects and told them about the world.

Born in Hitchin, Hertfordshire, she started her career as an actress after training at the Arts Educational School and RADA. She performed with Bromley Repertory Company for a year, before doing voice-overs for commercials and appearing in several advertising magazines, which were programmes in their own right broadcast during the early days of ITV. In one, *The*

Arnold Doodle Show, she appeared on Sunday afternoons with a cartoon character.

Joining the BBC as a continuity announcer in 1962, Valerie soon became one of the presenters of *Blue Peter* and gave up announcing two years later, when the weekly programme started being transmitted twice a week.

As well as being involved in the famous Sri Lankan elephant incident (it messed on the studio floor, resulting in chaos), one of the highlights of her ten years with the programme was the special *Blue Peter Royal Safari*, in which she followed the Princess Royal on her first visit abroad as president of the Save the Children Fund.

In 1972, Valerie – who in the mid-60s had extolled the virtues of Flash cleaner in a

TV commercial – switched to grown-ups' television as part of *Nationwide*'s consumer unit, before becoming a main presenter of the early-evening current affairs programme four years later. Throughout this time, she also made four series of *Blue Peter Special Assignment*, which took her all over the world.

Valerie was still an occasional guest presenter on *Blue Peter* and made three series of *Val Meets the VIPs*, interviewing various personalities ranging from Margaret Thatcher to Morecambe and Wise.

In 1978, she became presenter of the current affairs programme *Tonight*, revived as a late-night show but never re-creating the magic it had in the 50s and 60s when Cliff Michelmore, Alan Whicker and Fyfe Robertson were among its mainstays.

More *Blue Peter Special Assignments* followed, as well as two BBC2 documentaries, *Migrant Workers in Europe* and *Echoes of Germany*, before she became a presenter of *The Money Programme*, on the same channel, in 1980.

She ended her run on the programme in 1988 but continued to host *PM*, the BBC Radio 4 early-evening current affairs show, which she had joined seven years earlier. She also narrated a radio documentary, *Maxwell – The Last Days*, and, in 1993, became a presenter of the TV holiday programme *Travel UK*.

Valerie, who lives in London and once appeared as herself in the BBC TV comedy series *Citizen Smith*, has never married, although she was once engaged to actor-turned-disc jockey Pete Murray.

Ray Smith

b. 1 May 1936
d. 15 December 1991

ONE of television's great character actors, Ray Smith was notable for his roles as bluff Northern miner George Barraclough in the ITV series *Sam* and the tough Chief Supt. Gordon Spikings in *Dempsey and Makepeace*.

Born in the Rhondda village of Trealaw, in Mid Glamorgan, Ray fell in love with acting while at school and was determined not to become a miner, like his father, who was killed in a pit accident when he was only three.

On leaving school, he became a builder's labourer and, after national service in the Army, broke into acting at the Prince of Wales Theatre, Cardiff, then joined the Grand Theatre, Swansea, as an assistant stage manager.

Moving to London, Ray spent a year on the dole before landing a part in a play about the Hungarian uprising. More roles followed thick and fast, but it was in television that time and again he brought to parts a gritty integrity that elevated them from run-of-the-mill performances.

After making his TV debut in *Shadows of Heroes*, in 1959, and appearances in series such as *Z-Cars*, *Softly, Softly*, *Gideon's Way*, *Callan* and *A Family at War*, he played Det. Insp. Percy Firbank – alongside Alfred Burke – in *Public Eye*, which started in 1971.

Two years later came one of his most memorable roles, as George Barraclough in *Sam*, one of Granada Television's down-to-earth Northern drama series of the 70s,

featuring Mark McManus as the grown-up Sam and Ray as his collier uncle.

Ray was killed off after two series and turned down other parts as miners for fear of becoming typecast. He later gave a wonderful portrayal of punch-drunk old boxer Dai Bando in *How Green Was My Valley*, BBC2's serialisation of Richard Llewellyn's novel, before playing Michael Brandon and Glynis Barber's no-nonsense boss, Det. Supt. Gordon Spikings, in the popular ITV police action series of the 80s *Dempsey and Makepeace*.

His last TV role was as Charlie, the stately, mild alcoholic, in *The Old Devils*, a three-part BBC2 adaptation of Kinglsey Amis's novel. His revelatory performance proved to be a fitting epitaph, for he died of meningitis shortly after making the programme, which was broadcast after his death.

Ray's films included *Exodus*, *Tomorrow at Ten*, *Under Milk Wood* – as Mr. Waldo – *Operation Daybreak* and *Masada*, and he was in the TV movies *Rogue Male* and *The Sailor's Return*. He also won a 1986 Sony Award for his performance in the Radio 3 play *A Kind of Hallowe'en*.

A Welsh nationalist all his life, Ray was South Wales organiser for Plaid Cymru during the 60s and tried to establish a Welsh National Theatre by founding Theatre Wales, which lasted only a few years.

His first marriage, to actress Gale Richardson, ended in divorce and Ray was survived by his second wife, singer Siân Hopkins. He had a son and a daughter both from his first marriage.

Doris Speed

b. 3 February 1899

THE airs and graces of Annie Walker, landlady of the Rovers Return pub in *Coronation Street* for almost a quarter of a century, could hardly be more removed from the down-to-earth traits of actress Doris Speed, who has been a lifelong socialist and has never forgotten the hardship she endured as a child.

Born in Manchester to struggling music-hall artists George Speed and Ada Worsley, Doris spent her childhood on tour with them, moving to different schools almost every week.

She made her stage debut at the age of three, toddling on to the stage in her nightdress, carrying a candle and singing a song about a golliwog. Two years later, she made her acting debut, as the velvet-suited infant Prince of Rome in a Victorian melodrama called *The Royal Divorce*.

At the age of 14, Doris took a shorthand and typing course so that she could earn money to pay the rent and bills as her parents found themselves less in demand in the theatre. She joined the Guinness brewery seven years later, on the great Trafford Park industrial estate, in Manchester, starting as a clerk and working her way up to be personal secretary to the regional manager. She stayed with the company for 41 years – until she left to take the role of Annie Walker in *Coronation Street*.

During that time, she worked as an actress in amateur and semi-professional theatre – with the Unnamed Society, in Manchester, Chorlton Rep and other companies – and on BBC radio.

On stage, Doris performed many Shakespearean roles, as well as leading the chorus of women in *Murder in the Cathedral* and playing the mother in *The Lady's Not for Burning*, and Mrs Sullen in *The Beaux' Stratagem*. In *Amphitryon 38*, by French dramatist Jean Giraudoux, she was the Greek beauty Leda, to whom the god Zeus in the shape of a swan made love.

After the Second World War, Doris acted in hundreds of radio plays, before moving into television. She was a regular in two Granada Television series on ITV, *Shadow Squad* in 1958 and *Skyport* a year later – in which she was the trolley-pushing tea lady. She also appeared in two television plays, *The Myth Makers* and *Vital Statistics*, as well as in the 1959 film *Hell is a City*, a Hammer production about the search by Manchester police for an escaped jewel thief, starring

Stanley Baker, Donald Pleasence and Billie Whitelaw.

Then, in 1960, while acting in the BBC radio serial *The Tenant of Wildfell Hall* – based on Anne Brontë's novel – and on stage in Bristol, Doris was asked to audition for the role of Annie Walker in the new ITV serial *Coronation Street*. She turned down the opportunity twice but was eventually persuaded to rush back to Manchester, where 24 actresses had already been passed over.

In fact, series creator Tony Warren had written the part specially for Doris, recalling her acting in a *Children's Hour* play on BBC radio in which he had also performed. The part was hers and she left her full-time job with Guinness shortly before she was due to retire. She couldn't believe her luck when the *Street* turned into TV's biggest success, earning her enough money to take holidays abroad after a lifetime of thrift.

Doris revelled in the role of Annie, a snob who looked down on most of her regulars and lauded it over them when she became Mayoress of Weatherfield for a year.

In 1983, the actress – already partially deaf – was suddenly taken ill, suffering from an abdominal complaint. She has not appeared in the soap since, but made a comeback for a special, ten-minute *ITV Telethon* edition five years later.

Doris, who was made an MBE in the Queen's 1977 Silver Jubilee Honours List, lived for many years in the Manchester suburb of Chorlton and, until her illness, enjoyed travelling to the theatre in Stratford-upon-Avon, and the festivals at Chichester and Pitlochry. She now has a luxury flat at a private nursing home in Bury, Lancashire, and is an avid reader of books about the theatre.

Robert Stack

b. 13 January 1919

BODIES usually ended up littering the streets when crime-fighter Eliot Ness of *The Untouchables* tackled violence in the Chicago of the 30s Prohibition era, and it was actor Robert Stack who portrayed the fearless FBI agent.

Born Robert Modini, into a theatrical family in Los Angeles, he travelled Europe with his mother during childhood, then studied at the University of Southern California, before training as an actor at the Henry Duffy School of Theatre, where a Universal Studios talent scout spotted him.

He signed a contract with Universal and made his debut in *First Love*, opposite Deanna Durbin, in 1939, appearing in another nine films before he joined the US Navy during the Second World War.

Robert resumed his film career in 1948 and he has since been in almost 40 pictures, including *Written on the Wind* – in which his role won him an Oscar nomination – *The Tarnished Angels* and *Airplane!*

He was offered the role of Eliot Ness in *The Untouchables* after Van Heflin and Van Johnson turned it down. The TV series, beginning in 1959, ran for five years and 114 episodes, and gained a reputation as 'the weekly bloodbath' and the most violent programme on American television.

During the whole of its run, it was top of the critics' hit-list of blood-and-gore programmes, but Robert won an Emmy for his performances as Ness, based on a real-life federal agent leading a US Treasury Department which took on bootlegging gangsters during Prohibition in Chicago.

He followed it with two, less successful series, *The Name of the Game* and *Most Wanted*, and has appeared in many TV movies, including *Perry Mason: The Case of the Sinister Spirit*, and the mini-series *Hollywood Wives*.

Robert, who wrote an autobiography called *Straight Shooting*, is married to former actress Rosemarie Bowie. They have a daughter, Elizabeth, a son, Charles, and live in California.

Nigel Stock

b. 21 September 1919
d. 23 June 1986

FOR an actor who through childhood yearned to be a doctor, Nigel Stock made his dream come true only on screen, with perhaps his most famous television part as Dr Watson in two 60s *Sherlock Holmes* series, as well as the title role in *Owen MD* and a part in *The Doctors*.

Born in Malta, the son of an Army captain, Nigel was educated at St Paul's School, in London, and trained at RADA – where he won the Principal's Medal – deciding on a career in acting after trying to match his sister's party pieces as a child.

That career had begun on stage at the age of 12, with juvenile parts in London's West End and at the Old Vic, but he made his professional debut in *Tobacco Road* in 1937, the same year in which he made his first film, *Lancashire Luck*.

During the Second World War, he served first with the London Irish Rifles and then with the Assam Regiment of the Indian Army in Burma and China, rising to the rank of major and twice being mentioned in despatches.

After the War, Nigel returned to acting and, in 1949, after acting in the school farce *The Happiest Days of Your Life* and making his New York debut in Shaw's *You Never Can Tell*, he became a member of the Old Vic company.

The following year, he found a lengthy West End role in another farce, *Seagulls Over Sorrento*, which ran at the Apollo Theatre for more than three years. His subsequent theatre roles included Winston Churchill in a touring production of *A Man and His Wife*, and his 40 films included *Goodbye Mr Chips!*, *Brighton Rock*, *The Dam Busters*, *The Great Escape*, *The Night of the Generals*, *The Lion in Winter*, *Cromwell*, *Yellowbeard* and *The*

Young Sherlock Holmes, in the role of Waxflatter.

On television, the actor played Dr Watson in the 1965 series *Sherlock Holmes* with Douglas Wilmer and, three years later, in *The Cases of Sherlock Holmes*, alongside Peter Cushing, who had already played the sleuth on the big screen.

Nigel acted the part of a medical student in *And No Birds Sing* and, in the early 70s, played another doctor, Dr Thomas Owen, in the medical series *Owen MD*, which was set in the Cotswolds. His other TV appearances included those in *Churchill's People*, *Van Der Valk*, *Tinker, Tailor, Soldier, Spy*, *A Tale of Two Cities*, *Yes Minister*, *The Pickwick Papers* and *The Barretts of Wimpole Street*.

Nigel's first marriage, to Sonia Williams – with whom he had two daughters, Penny and Polly, and one son, Robin – ended in divorce. He subsequently wed actress Richenda Carey, a cousin of Rex Harrison, and died at the age of 66.

Elaine Stritch

b. 2 February 1926

DURING ten years in Britain, American actress Elaine Stritch enjoyed two successful situation-comedies, *Two's Company* and *Nobody's Perfect*, lived at the Savoy Hotel and shopped at Fortnums.

Born in Detroit, Michigan, a staunch Catholic and relative of Cardinal Stritch of Chicago, she studied for the stage under Erwin Pisactor at the Dramatic Workshop of the New School, New York. While there, she dated Marlon Brando, who was one of her classmates.

Elaine made her stage debut in 1944 and first appeared on Broadway in *Loco*, following it with shows such as *Made in Heaven, Angel in the Wings, Call Me Madam* and *Pal Joey.*

She made her first dramatic appearance in New York in *Bus Stop*, which led to her performance as Helen Ferguson in the 1957 film *A Farewell to Arms*. She had already appeared in one film – *The Scarlet Hour*, two years earlier – and followed it with big-screen performances in *The Perfect Furlough, Who Killed Teddy Bear?, Sidelong Glances of a Pigeon Kicker, The Spiral Staircase, Providence, September* and, much later, *Cocoon: The Return*, and Woody Allen's *September.*

In America, the actress dined with the Kennedys and turned down offers of marriage from Ben Gazzara and Gig Young because she was a Catholic and they had both been divorced.

In 1962, Elaine travelled to Britain to appear in her friend Noël Coward's musical *Sail Away.*

She had already made her TV debut in America, in the series *Growing Pains*, in 1949, appeared in another series, *My Sister Eileen*, and was a regular panellist in *Pantomime Quiz.*

After moving between Britain and her home country during the 60s, Elaine and her husband, John Bay, settled into a two-room apartment at the Savoy Hotel overlooking the Thames.

She had starring roles on the London stage in Neil Simon's *The Gingerbread Lady* and Tennessee Williams's *Small Craft Warnings*, before becoming a household name in the ITV comedy series *Two's Company*, with Donald Sinden playing the English butler to her American lady.

Elaine followed it with another situation-comedy, *Nobody's Perfect*, featuring Richard Griffiths as her GP husband. It ran for two years from 1980, and she also appeared on British television in *Shades of Greene, Tales of the Unexpected, Quartet* and *Providence*, alongside Dirk Bogarde and John Gielgud.

Since returning to America in 1982, buying a 110-year-old house in South Nyack, on the Hudson river, Elaine has been in *The Cosby Show*, the pilot for *Steel Magnolias*, played Victoria Principal's mother in *Sparks*, and appeared in *Archie's Wife* – alongside Michael Tucker and Jill Eikenberry – and *An Inconvenient Woman*, for which she received an Emmy nomination.

On stage, she has triumphed in *Love Letters*, with Jason Robards, and as star of a revue at Rainbows and Stars, in New York.

Eric Sykes

b. 4 May 1923

FROM his early days as a comedy scriptwriter on radio to TV success in his own long-running situation-comedy, Eric Sykes has gained the respect of all around him in showbusiness. Films never projected him as well, but he could be relied on to turn up with his distinctive tributes to the old silents, with wordless comedies such as *The Plank* and *Rhubarb*.

Born in Oldham, Lancashire, the son of a cotton-mill worker, Eric followed his father into the mill but was sacked while singing 'In the Blue of the Night' Bing Crosby-style and later worked in a sawmill and a grocery shop, at the same time gaining experience of performing in front of the public as a drummer in a dance-band.

When the Second World War came, Eric served in the RAF, and met other aspiring comedians such as Peter Sellers, Tony Hancock, Spike Milligan and Harry Secombe.

Afterwards, he wrote scripts for the *Stars in Battledress* concert party and for Bill Fraser, whom he had known during the War. He also joined Oldham Rep as an actor but was sacked because he asked for a pay rise from £3 to £4 weekly.

While touring music-halls, comedian Frankie Howerd advised Eric to concentrate on scriptwriting and he subsequently wrote for the radio show *Variety Bandbox* as well as scripts for other comedians.

Eventually, he became the writer of the legendary *Educating Archie*, featuring Peter Brough and his ventriloquist's dummy Archie, with appearances by Benny Hill and Hattie Jacques during its four-year run.

When it finished, in 1954, Eric returned to performing by making his film debut as a lowly soldier in *Orders Are Orders*, alongside Tony Hancock, Peter Sellers and Sid James.

He followed it with 25 further films, including *Tommy the Toreador*, *Heavens Above!*, *Those Magnificent Men in Their Flying Machines*, *The Alf Garnett Saga* – the second spin-off from the TV series *Till Death Us Do Part* – and *Absolute Beginners*.

Eric also wrote and directed *The Plank*, a 1967 silent short that he later remade for television, and a 1970 sequel, *Rhubarb*, as well as writing and starring in the TV movie *Mr. H Is Late* and supplying scripts for stars such as Frankie Howerd.

By then, he had already had success with his own situation-comedy series, *Sykes*, which ran on the BBC from 1960 and teamed him with Hattie Jacques, as his sister, and, later, Deryck Guyler, as neighbourhood policeman Corky. The first script, *Sykes and the*

Telephone, was written by Johnny Speight and had Hattie as Sykes's wife, but the star decided that the couple's relationship should be as siblings and he took over as scriptwriter.

The series ran until Hattie Jacques's death, in 1980, although they took a seven-year break from it in the middle years, and Eric made programmes such as *Sykes Versus ITV* and the 1969 Johnny Speight comedy series *Curry and Chips*, in which he starred with a blacked-up Spike Milligan.

He revived *Sykes* in 1973 after receiving a large tax bill and, during its run, also managed to make other programmes, including *The Eric Sykes Spectacular*, *Charley's Aunt*, his small-screen remake of *The Plank* – which won the Press Award at the Montreux Festival – and *If You Go Down in The Woods Today*, a 1981 TV film that he directed.

After *Sykes* ended, a collection of the best episodes were put together under the title *Sykes of Sebastopol Terrace*, but its star has failed to find another vehicle for his talents –

It's Your Move and a 1989 series, *The 19th Hole*, not gaining the same affection from viewers.

On stage, Eric has toured the world in his own show, *A Hatful of Sykes*, and with Jimmy Edwards in *Big Bad Mouse*, which was originally a London West End hit for them, complete with Edwards' ad-libs, which sometimes reduced the plot to nonsense.

The partnership ended on Edwards's death, in 1988. By then, Eric had also appeared in the West End and toured Canada in the farce *Run for Your Wife*.

Hearing problems have dogged him since a mastoid operation in 1952, which affected just his right ear but subsequently spread to both ears and caused him to pull out of a Royal Variety Performance in the 60s.

Author of a novel called *The Great Crime of Grapplemick*, published in 1985, and a recipient of the OBE a year later, Eric is married to Edith and has three daughters, Katherine, Susan and Julie, and one son, David.

Jimmy Tarbuck

b. 6 February 1940

FROM his early days as host of *Sunday Night at the London Palladium* to his time as quizmaster of *Winner Takes All* and *Tarby's Frame Game*, Jimmy Tarbuck is one of a half-a-dozen comedians who enjoyed television fame over several decades alongside their stage careers.

Born in Liverpool, the son of a bookmaker, during the Second World War, Jimmy numbered future Beatles John Lennon and George Harrison among his classmates at school and his ambition was to play football for Liverpool. He went as far as two trials but failed to make the grade.

Starting work at 15 as a garage mechanic, he was later sacked from that and other jobs – which included being a milkman – for fooling around.

Aged 18, he joined a touring rock 'n' roll show as compere, before becoming a Redcoat at Butlin's in North Wales, working in Liverpool and Manchester clubs, and making his television debut in *Comedy Bandbox*, in 1963.

He was on *Sunday Night At the London Palladium* during the same year, made several more appearances and then became its resident compere from September 1965.

In 1981, Jimmy enjoyed a resurgence in popularity after appearing in *The Bob Hope Classic Cabaret* and that year's Royal Variety Performance. His own TV series have

included *It's Tarbuck*, *Tarbuck's Back* and *Tarbuck and Friends*. He also presented *A National Salute to the Falklands Task Force*, live from the London Coliseum, in 1982, and the following year returned to the mine-host role in the variety series *Live from Her Majesty's*, following it with *Live from the Palladium* and *Live from the Piccadilly*.

In 1975, Jimmy had become quizmaster in the ITV series *Winner Takes All*, which ran with him as quizmaster for 12 years, after which he launched *Tarby's Frame Game*.

Shortly afterwards, he found himself no longer wanted by ITV, which was anxious to project a new image and leave comedians such as Jimmy in the television past. Since then, he has concentrated on his stage act, in summer seasons and cabaret.

Jimmy, who was the subject of an hour-long *This Is Your Life* special in 1983 and won the Variety Club of Great Britain's Showbusiness Personality of the Year award three years later, has written two books, *Tarbuck on Golf* and *Tarbuck on Showbusiness*.

He and his wife have two daughters, Cheryl and actress Liza – one of the stars of the comedy series *Watching* – and one son, James. The couple split their time between Surrey and Spain, both homes conveniently close to golf courses so that Jimmy can indulge his hobby. He also plays in pro-am tournaments, stages his own World Classic each year in Spain or Portugal, and takes part in the 4 Stars charity golf tournament.

Terry-Thomas

b. 14 July 1911
d. 8 January 1990

WITH his cheesy, gap-toothed grin, Terry-Thomas made a brilliant career out of playing cads and con men in many hilarious film comedies, but he also took television by storm in its early days, with his own show in Britain and appearances in top-flight entertainment specials in America.

Thomas Terry Hoar-Stevens was born into an upper-class London family and was educated at Ardingly College. The second cousin of fellow-actor Richard Briers, he began his working life in a grocery firm before sticking a foot firmly in the door of showbusiness by taking part in amateur theatricals and working as a film extra.

Although latterly known for his work in films, Terry-Thomas made his name on television during the late 40s and 50s, when he appeared in his own programme, *To Town With Terry*, followed by the popular series *How Do You View?* – which was also one of his famous catchphrases – and *Strictly Terry-Thomas*.

He also starred in many successful American television shows, appearing with stars such as Danny Kaye and Judy Garland, but he never succeeded in gaining equal small-screen popularity in Britain. When he returned from America, in 1968, his BBC series *The Old Campaigner* received a lukewarm reception.

Although Terry-Thomas made his film debut in *This'll Make You Whistle*, in 1936, he had to wait another 19 years for a starring role in the cinema, in *Private's Progress*, uttering those immortal words, "You're an absolute shower", in his wonderful upper-class-twit voice.

His ability to assume any number of rakish expressions made him an ideal comic villain and was instrumental in establishing him as one of Britain's finest comedy actors.

His most credit-worthy films included *The Green Man*, *Brothers in Law*, *Blue Murder at St. Trinian's*, *Lucky Jim*, *I'm All Right, Jack*, *It's a Mad, Mad, Mad, Mad World*, and *Those Magnificent Men in Their Flying Machines*.

When Terry-Thomas's career began to dwindle, as the public's passion for films of this genre began to cool, he found work in America, where he first appeared in the 1962 film *Bachelor Flat*, followed four years later

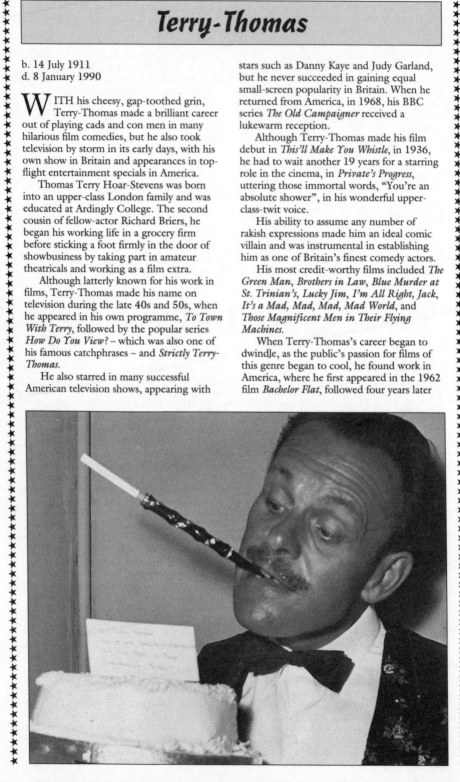

with the role of Jack Lemmon's valet in *How to Murder Your Wife*, although he still appeared in British films.

By the end of the 70s, however, he had learned that he was suffering from Parkinson's disease and was unable to continue with his work. His last screen performance was in the film *The Hound of the Baskervilles*, with Peter Cook and Dudley Moore.

The actor, who had indulged in all the trappings of stardom, such as Rolls-Royces, was found to be living in a south-west London flat, provided by a church charity, not long before his death – with the earnings from a lifetime in entertainment eaten up by expensive medical bills.

When his unfortunate plight became public knowledge, his showbusiness friends staged a benefit night for him at the Theatre Royal, Drury Lane, although he was too ill to appear himself.

After his divorce from dancer Ida Patlanski, Terry-Thomas married second wife Belinda, by whom he had two sons, Tiger and Cushan.

Linda Thorson

b. 18 June 1947

CANADIAN actress Linda Thorson shot to fame as Diana Rigg's successor in *The Avengers* at the end of the 60s, but has hardly been seen on TV since.

Born Linda Robinson in Toronto, Canada, Linda took a secretarial course, before working in her father's confectionery business.

Moving to Britain in 1965, she trained at RADA and left two years later with an honours diploma and a prize for the best student at voice production.

Athletic, 5ft 9in-tall Linda went straight into *The Avengers* at the age of 20, chosen from 200 actresses to play Tara King, in 1968.

The character was the first of Steed's female sidekicks to enjoy a hinted-at relationship, but in her 33 episodes Linda never made the impact of her predecessors, Honor Blackman and Diana Rigg, and the tongue-in-cheek spy series ended a year later, after a run of eight years.

In the last episode, it was Linda's character who accidentally pressed the lift-off button on a rocket and she soared into space with Steed and his boss, 'Mother'.

In 1971, she starred with Michael Crawford and Anthony Valentine in the London West End stage hit *No Sex, Please – We're British* and later played Titania in *A Midsummer Night's Dream* at the Open Air Theatre, Regent's Park, and Diana in *Ring Round the Moon* at the Chichester Festival Theatre and on tour. She has also acted on stage in America and Canada, winning the Theatre World Award for her performance in *Steaming* and the Drama Desk Award for *Noises Off*, both on Broadway. She played Marie in Berg's opera *Wozzeck* in Toronto and Fiona in *How the Other Half Loves* in Edmonton.

Linda's films include *Valentino*, *The Greek Tycoon*, *Sweet Liberty* and *Olympus Force*. She has been on television in *The Caucasian Chalk Circle*, *The Oresteia* and *Ladykillers* in Britain, *A Month in the Country* – with Susannah York – the 24-part series *Marblehead Manor* and episodes of *Moonlighting*, *Dynasty* and *St. Elsewhere* in America, and *Sidestreet*, *King of Kensington* and *The Great Detective* in Canada.

She now lives in America and has been married three times, first to Canadian TV cameraman Barry Bergthorson – taking part of his name for her own professional name – in Canada when she was 16.

After their divorce, she married wealthy Texan widower Cyril Smith, whom she subsequently divorced, before marrying American TV reporter Bill Boggs. The couple separated soon after the birth of their son, Trevor.

Bob Todd

b. 15 December 1921
d. 21 October 1992

ONE of the great stooges of television comedy, Bob Todd was a foil to such stars as Sid James, Dick Emery, Marty Feldman, Mike and Bernie Winters, Michael Bentine and Des O'Connor, but he will be best remembered as sidekick to Benny Hill, of the seaside-postcard humour.

Born in Faversham, Kent, Bob trained to be a dentist, before wartime service as an RAF navigator. He was then a manager at London Airport and a fruit-picker, but hoped to earn money from cattle-breeding when he decided to make a life as a farmer.

The business failed, however, and almost made him bankrupt, so he found himself looking for a new career at the age of 42. Meeting scriptwriters Ray Galton and Alan Simpson in a pub, he bluffed them into believing that he was an actor and landed the part of the policeman in the Sid James comedy series *Citizen James*, in 1963. He subsequently stooged in *The Dick Emery Show*, *Marty* and *The Mike and Bernie Winters Show*, before joining *The Benny Hill Show*, in 1979, and staying with the programme – which consistently topped the TV ratings – until Thames Television axed it ten years later.

Bob's only starring role was in his own 1972 ITV series *In for a Penny*, although he appeared in the Jimmy Jewel series *Funny Man* and in Eric Sykes's 1970 film *Rhubarb*, as well as making guest appearances on Jim Davidson and Allan Stewart's shows, *What's On Next?*, *The Generation Game*, *The Steam Video Show* and Spike Milligan's *Q9*. He was seen in the cinema in films such as *Carry on again Doctor* and *The Return of the Musketeers*.

Bob and his wife, Monica, had one daughter, Anne, and two sons, John and Patrick. He died at the age of 70.

Richard Todd

b. 11 June 1919

A celebrated British film actor of the 50s, Richard Todd found his screen popularity waning during the following decade and turned more towards theatre and television work, bringing his experience to the small screen with guest roles in programmes such as *Doctor Who*, *Jenny's War* and *Murder, She Wrote*.

Richard Andrew Palethorpe Todd was born in Dublin, Ireland. He went to school in Shrewsbury and had ambitions to follow a literary career, perhaps as a playwright. However, on training at the Italia Conti Stage Academy, mainly to learn about the theatre, he switched to the idea of acting and made his professional debut in *Twelfth Night*, at the Open Air Theatre, Regent's Park, in 1936.

Three years later, after repertory work and a season with the Ben Green Company, Richard was a founder-member of the Dundee Repertory Company, but he volunteered for Army service the day after the Second World War broke out and received a commission in the King's Own Yorkshire Light Infantry. Later, he was seconded to the Parachute Regiment and took part in D-Day, the Battle of the Bulge and the Holland Rhine crossing.

He rejoined Dundee Rep after the War, before making his 1948 film debut as the star of *For Them That Trespass*, playing a man seeking to prove himself innocent of a crime for which he had served 15 years in jail.

As a Scot dying of a kidney wound in his third film, the 1949 picture *The Hasty Heart* – which featured Ronald Reagan – Richard received international acclaim, as well as an Oscar nomination, The Hollywood Golden Globe, the British National Film Award and several others.

A top box-office attraction, he made more than 20 films during the 50s, including *The Sword and the Rose*, *The Dam Busters*, *Yangtse Incident* and *Saint Joan*.

In 1962, he was star and executive producer of *Don't Bother to Knock*, which was made by his own production company, Haileywood Films, but Richard's appeal was already beginning to fade and, by the end of the decade, he was treading the boards of British theatres again.

In 1970, he formed Triumph Theatre Productions, with Duncan C Weldon and Paul Elliott, presenting plays in London, America, Canada and Australia, as well as many touring productions throughout Britain. Richard starred in some of the plays himself, including *Roar Like a Dove*, *A Christmas Carol* – in which he played Scrooge – and *The Winslow Boy*.

He was subsequently on the Royal Shakespeare Company's tour of the United States and Canada with *The Hollow Crown* and *Pleasure and Repentance*, in Peter Schaffer's production of *Equus* for the Australian National Theatre Company and other plays in South Africa and Hong Kong. He toured with Margaret Lockwood in *Quadrille* and, for seven years, he played the lead of Mr Stone in *The Business of Murder*, which opened at the Mayfair Theatre in 1981.

Richard's first television role was as Heathcliff in *Wuthering Heights* and he followed it with a Hollywood production of *The Last Hunter*, with Olivia de Havilland. Back in Britain, he played Bulman in the popular children's drama series *Boy Dominic* – whose producer, Jess Yates, also persuaded him to give Bible readings in *Stars On Sunday* and to narrate *The Glories of Christmas* – and guest-starred in *Doctor Who*, the mini-series *Jenny's War*, *Murder, She Wrote* and, as H G Wells, in *Beautiful Lies*.

The actor's marriage to Catherine Grant-Bogle, with whom he had a son, Peter, and a daughter, Fiona, ended in divorce. He later married actress Virginia Mailer and they have two sons, Andrew and Seumas.

Richard was awarded an OBE in the 1993 New Year's Honours List.

Roger Tonge

b. 30 January 1946
d. 26 February 1981

FOR more than 15 years, Roger Tonge played disabled Sandy Richardson in the much maligned ITV soap *Crossroads*, but it was the actor's own fight against an incurable cancer that resulted in his departure from the programme before the axe fell on it.

Born Anthony Roger Tonge in Birmingham, he was working as an £8-a-week post office clerk and performing in amateur dramatics in the evenings when he landed the role of motel owner's son Sandy in *Crossroads*, his first professional job.

It was 1964, and the serial was about to begin production. Roger dropped in at ATV during his lunch break to enquire about acting parts and a cleaner, presuming he had an audition for *Crossroads*, sent him to a production meeting. He arrived just as production manager Margaret French was leaving. She gave him a script and invited him to return for an audition.

Producer Reg Watson had already auditioned hundreds of youngsters for the role of 14-year-old Sandy, without success. Eventually, when Roger and one other actor were shortlisted for the part, both were asked to react to their pet dog being run over. Roger obliged with the requisite emotional response and the part was his.

As the programme became loved by millions of TV viewers, there were just as many who hated it – and newspaper critics gave it a hard time for every one of its 23 years on screen. Roger was often the butt of criticism for his style of acting, but he laughed it off with a T-shirt exclaiming "I'm Allergic To Criticism!"

When the character of Sandy later broke his back in a car accident and was paralysed for life, Roger had to play his scenes in a wheelchair. The decision to make Sandy disabled came after Roger had a car crash in real life, breaking his arm and needing 80 stitches in his face.

Producer Reg Watson originally intended the character to start walking again after six months, but the injuries inflicted on him by the scriptwriters were so severe that they put paid to that idea, although Sandy was later allowed to walk with calipers.

Roger was frequently asked to meet and give talks to the handicapped and often stunned the serial's avid fans when they saw him in public – walking. The publicity generated by the programme's storyline led to the Crossroads Care Attendant Scheme being launched in 1974, allowing carers to have occasional breaks while fully trained attendants looked after the disabled. The scheme spread all over the country and has since become an official EC charity.

Although he was a regular in the soap, Roger found time to appear on TV in *Z-Cars*, *Nearest and Dearest* and *Detective* in the 60s, and on stage at the Library Theatre, Manchester, and Belgrade Theatre, Coventry. He was also in the film *Catch Me Going Back*.

In 1981, after a long fight against Hodgkin's disease – a cancer of the lymph glands – Roger died at the age of 35. He had caught chickenpox and died of heart failure, his system unable to cope with the infection.

A constant companion at the star's bedside during his final days was his actress girlfriend Sonia Fox, who played Sheila Harvey in *Crossroads*. She had already left the serial and the couple had kept their romance secret from the Press.

Noele Gordon, who played Roger's screen mother, paid tribute to him as the son she had never had in real life.

Toke Townley

b. 6 November 1912
d. 27 September 1984

PROLIFIC film character actor Toke Townley brought to *Emmerdale Farm* an integrity and warmth that helped to establish the serial on the ITV network in its early years.

Born in Margaret Roding, Essex, he was a vicar's son and was christened John, but the family then decided they must not lose the surname of one of their ancestors and had the forename on his birth certificate changed to Toke.

On leaving school, he became a factory clerk, acting in his spare time. It was not until the age of 32 that he turned professional with Birmingham Rep, before appearing in many BBC television programmes during the early, pioneering days at Alexandra Palace.

Between 1951 and 1970, in the heyday of the British studios, Toke appeared in almost 30 films, including *Lady Godiva Rides Again*, *Doctor at Sea*, *The Quatermass Experiment*, *The Admirable Crichton*, *Carry On Admiral*, *Look Back in Anger*, *HMS Defiant*, *Doctor in Distress* and *The Scars of Dracula*.

Many of his roles were as country bumpkins, so it was an appropriate move when Toke joined *Emmerdale Farm* as Annie Sugden's father, Sam Pearson, complete with cloth cap and collarless shirt, when the serial began, in 1972. 'Grandad' to Annie's sons, Jack and Joe, the country-loving, pipe-smoking character was obstinate, but with a wry humour. Retired from farming, he still made sure his views were heard.

Although much loved by the rest of the cast, Toke was a private person, living alone at a Leeds hotel, to which he returned after working on the serial, and allowing himself none of the so-called comforts of modern life, such as a car or television, but he did eat out every evening.

Another of his pleasures was playing the flute, and he would occasionally give performances on screen, usually accompanying children dancing.

In 1984, Toke suddenly died of a heart attack at the age of 71, after appearing in more than 800 episodes of *Emmerdale Farm*, marking the end of an era for the serial.

Tommy Trinder

b. 24 March 1909
d. 10 July 1989

A sharp-witted, working-class comic, Tommy Trinder brought his special brand of music-hall magic to both the big and small screens, where his famous catchphrase, "You lucky people", became known to millions.

Born in Streatham, South London, the son of a tram driver, he made his professional debut on a South African theatre tour at the age of 12. The following year, he made his London debut as a vocalist at Collins Music Hall, Islington, London, and continued to tour Britain on variety bills for many years – promoted for a while as Red Nirt, his name spelled backwards – until he found international success in 1937, when he appeared in the revues *Tune In* and *In Town To-Night*.

Two years later, he was brought in to help the sinking *Band Waggon* show at the London Palladium, based on the radio series featuring Arthur Askey and Richard Murdoch. This was to be the first of many appearances at the venue, which became his second home.

Over the next five years, Tommy appeared almost constantly at the Palladium, in such shows as *Best Bib and Tucker* and *Happy and Glorious*, which made history by running for two years at the theatre.

The 40s saw him on the big screen, after making his film debut in the 1938 picture *Almost a Honeymoon*. He became the star of pictures such as *Sailors Three*, *The Bells Go Down* and *Champagne Charlie*, in which he portrayed George Laybourne.

A favourite of the royals, Tommy would often perform for them at Buckingham Palace, and he participated in many Royal Variety Performances.

By the mid-50s, he was making an increasing number of television programmes,

his most famous role being as compere of *Sunday Night at the London Palladium*, when it began on ITV in 1955, the year the channel started.

He presented the first show, which included Gracie Fields, and the programme became an institution on the new commercial station, opening with the high-kicking Tiller Girls and including the Beat the Clock game in the middle, with Tommy challenging contestants to perform comic tasks within a time limit.

Never one to be idle, he maintained a punishing work schedule until his mid-70s, making regular appearances in one-man shows, summer seasons and pantomime.

Away from the razzle-dazzle and greasepaint, Tommy – who was made a CBE in 1975 – was an immensely likeable man with a passion for football. In fact, he was chairman of Fulham football club for many years. He was married with a daughter.

Patrick Troughton

b. 25 March 1920
d. 28 March 1987

ONE of the most flamboyant and exciting Doctor Whos, Patrick Troughton kept families on the edge of their seats when, as the fearless Time Lord, he

battled with the baddies on the nation's television screens.

Born Patrick George Troughton, in London, he trained at the Embassy School of Acting, before winning a scholarship to Leighton Rollin's Studio for Actors, in Long Island, New York.

After serving in the Royal Navy during the Second World War, where he had attained the rank of commander, Patrick joined the Bristol Old Vic, in 1946, concentrating on their Shakespearean productions.

One of his most memorable stage performances was in 1950, when he played Hitler in *Eva Braun*, at the Gateway Theatre, Edinburgh.

Although he made his television debut in 1948, his real success came in 1966 with the title role in *Doctor Who*.

The series, which was created by Terry Nation and had begun three years earlier, has seen a colourful parade of actors in the coveted role of the Doctor, a wise and gallant Time Lord who always comes out on top, no matter who the adversary. He certainly had enemies, ranging from the quavery-voiced Daleks to silver Cybermen and parrot-faced Sea Devils.

Patrick, who played the part for three years, took over after the original star, William Hartnell, left, suffering from multiple sclerosis and tired of rows with the BBC, feeling that the programme was no longer suitable for children. Prior to finding fame as Doctor Who, Patrick had played George Barton, father of union organiser Peggy Barton, in *Coronation Street*. His other TV work included *Dr. Finlay's Casebook*, *A Family at War*, *The Six Wives of Henry VIII*, *Colditz* and *Churchill's People*.

The actor made many films after his big-screen debut in Laurence Olivier's celebrated *Hamlet*, in 1948. They included *Treasure Island*, *Richard III*, *The Curse of Frankenstein*, *The Phantom of the Opera*, *Scars of Dracula*, *Frankenstein and the Monster from Hell*, *The Omen* and *Sinbad and the Eye of the Tiger*.

Patrick, who collapsed and died at the age of 67 while attending a *Doctor Who* convention in Georgia, USA, had been married three times. His last marriage was to Shelagh and he had two daughters, Joanna and Jane, one step-daughter, Jill, four sons – actors David and Michael, and Peter and Mark – and a step-son, Graham.

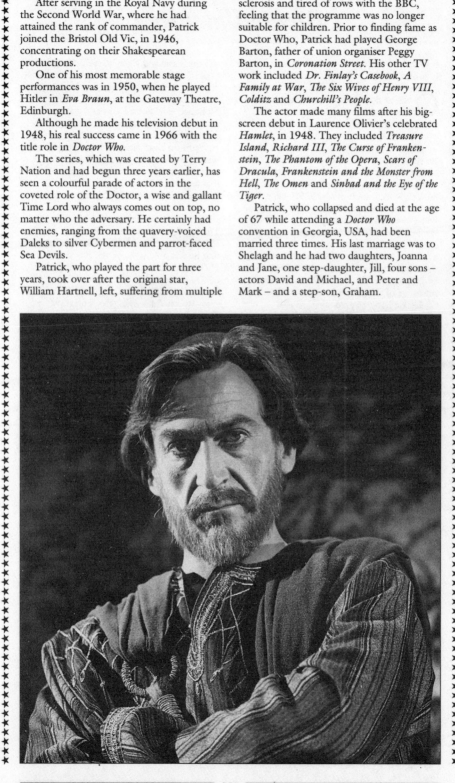

Dickie Valentine

b 1930
d. 6 May 1971

ONE of the most popular singers of the 50s, an entire generation mourned when Dickie Valentine was tragically killed in a road accident.

The son of a lorry driver, Dickie made his stage debut at the Palace Theatre, Manchester, at the age of 14, before becoming a pageboy at the London Palladium when his father's work took him south. However, bosses at the Palladium soon sacked him for being cheeky and the chirpy lad moved on to the Haymarket Theatre as a call-boy, running errands for the stars.

When he became a celebrity himself, in the 50s, he got his revenge on the Palladium by topping the bill there as one of the first solo stars of the pre-rock era.

Dickie had been launched to this prominent position by the Ted Heath Orchestra and it was while performing in a show with the band on Valentine's Day, 1949, that he decided to change his professional name.

During the 50s, he had top ten hits with 'All the Time and Everywhere', 'In a Golden Coach', 'Mr Sandman', 'A Blossom Fell,' 'I Wonder', 'Christmas Island' and two number ones, 'Finger of Suspicion' and 'Christmas Alphabet'. His good looks and golden tones made him a heart-throb for millions of teenaged girls.

With his chart success, Dickie presented a serious challenge to the previously untouchable American charts – so much so that he was invited to appear on the Ed Sullivan and Eddie Fisher shows over there.

The high spot of his stage routine was a string of impersonations, including Al Jolson, The Ink Spots and Johnny Ray, and – by 1957 – he had amassed such a large following that he was able to book the Royal Albert Hall for his fan club's annual get-together.

Dickie appeared in the first televised Royal Variety Performance, in 1960, and six years later had his own television show, on ITV.

The singer, who died in a road crash at the age of 41, was married twice. He first wed ice-skater Elizabeth Flynn, with whom he had two children, and he later married actress Wendy Wayne.

Dick Van Dyke

b. 18 December 1925

IN the 60s, Dick Van Dyke had the world at his feet, with the top-rated *Dick Van Dyke Show* screened on TV around the globe and a string of films, including *Mary Poppins* and *Chitty Chitty Bang Bang*, that projected his all-singing, all-dancing talent. Unfortunately, he found that such fame could not compensate for bad material in later years.

Born in West Plains, Missouri, Dick served in the United States Air Force during the Second World War, then opened an advertising agency in Illinois, but it folded within a year. He began his showbusiness career touring in a double act, Eric and Van, The Merry Mutes, who mimed to records.

He gained experience in broadcasting as a disc jockey and, in 1953, hosted TV shows in Atlanta and Orleans, before presenting a peak-time cartoon programme in New York.

One of his biggest breaks was appearing in *The Phil Silvers Show* and, by 1961, his reputation was such that he landed his own programme, a family situation-comedy called *The Dick Van Dyke Show*, with Mary Tyler Moore playing his wife. The series was a male version of *The Lucy Show*, although the bright-and-breezy air that Dick brought to the programme once caused him to describe himself as "the male Julie Andrews".

It offered more than the usual, one-dimensional content of such family programmes, with Dick – as Rob Petrie, chief scriptwriter for a TV comedian – frequently seen in his office exchanging the sort of jokes that would be expected more in a nightclub.

For three consecutive years from 1964, he won Emmy awards, two for Best Actor in a Series and the third for Best Actor in a Comedy Series.

The Dick Van Dyke Show ran for five years and 158 episodes, with the star deciding to finish it while it was still topping the ratings. He intended to concentrate on films, having made his debut in the 1963 picture *Bye Bye Birdie* and finding a massive hit the following year with *Mary Poppins*, alongside Julie Andrews.

His decision proved to be disastrous. He subsequently starred in the successful *Chitty Chitty Bang Bang* but found no other hits with cinema audiences, even though he gave a touching performance as the Stan Laurel-style silent comedian in *The Comic*.

In 1971, he returned to television as chat-show host Dick Preston in *The New Dick Van Dyke Show*, which lasted three series, but it never achieved the same success as the original and it was at this time that the star made public the alcohol problem that he and his wife had faced and beaten as he grappled with a sinking career.

In 1974, Dick portrayed that struggle in a TV movie, *The Morning After*, which he co-scripted. Three years later, he was back in *Van Dyke and Company*, concentrating on his mime skills. The show was axed after just three months, but it still won an Emmy award for Best Comedy-Variety Series.

A further television show, *The Wrong Way Kid*, won him another Emmy, for 1984's Best Performer in a Children's Programme.

Sadly, other films and TV movies failed to make an impression, although Dick did appear in the 1990 Madonna–Warren Beatty picture *Dick Tracy* and, two years later, his voice was heard in *Freddie Goes to Washington*.

Reg Varney

b. 11 July 1922

THE role of Stan Butler in *On the Buses* made 5ft 5in former variety artist Reg Varney a major star at the turn of the 60s. "I 'ate you, Butler," his boss Blakey would intone, in the successful comedy that resulted in three spin-off films.

Born in London's East End, the son of a tyre factory worker, Reg started performing as a child, dressed as a Russian gypsy and playing 'Tiger Rag' on the piano. He was a singer, pianist and accordion player in working men's clubs at the age of 14 and, a year later, sang with big bands.

He also played piano at the Windmill Theatre's girlie revues, before serving with the Royal Electrical and Mechanical Engineers as a sheet-metal worker during the Second World War, also performing in the *Stars In Battledress* concert party during a tour of the Far East.

After the War, Reg developed his act in music-hall and summer shows, with Benny Hill as his stooge. Benny went on to become a star in his own right, but Varney had to wait longer for fame.

In 1961, he landed the TV role of foreman Reg in *The Rag Trade*, helping his boss (Peter Jones) to keep shop steward Miriam Karlin in check, but he usually found himself stuck in dilemmas between the shop floor and management. Reg's comedy timing was one of the programme's attractions and it was an instant hit, running for three series on BBC television.

He followed it with two series of the children's programme *The Valiant Varneys*, in which he played his supposed ancestors, and three series of another situation-comedy, *Beggar My Neighbour*, which also featured Peter Jones, Pat Coombs and June Whitfield.

Then, in 1969, came *On the Buses*. Like *The Rag Trade*, it was written by Ronald Wolfe and Ronald Chesney, and featured situations in the workplace. But this time Reg's character – bus driver Stan Butler – was also seen at home, sparring with his sister, played by Anna Karen, brother-in-law (Michael Robbins) and mother (Cicely Courtneidge, later Doris Hare) just as keenly as with his inspector, played by Stephen Lewis, at the bus depot. His only ally was bus conductor Bob Grant.

The comedy was raucous – and popular, running for more than six years. Reg and his co-stars made three spin-off films, *On the*

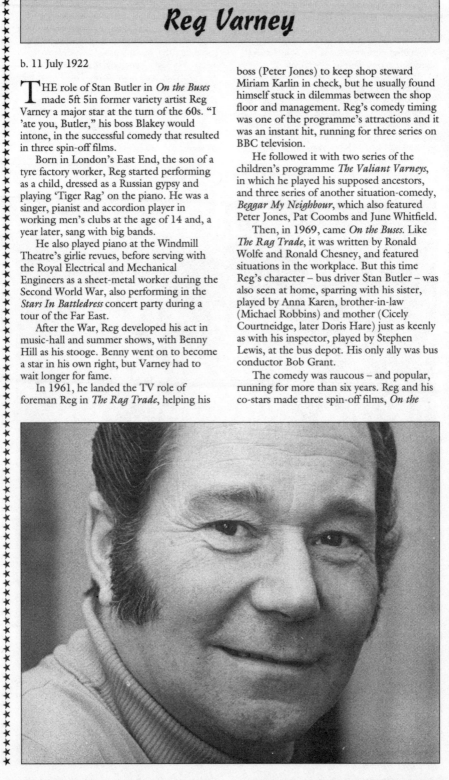

Buses, Mutiny On the Buses and Holiday On the Buses. His previous big-screen appearances included those in Miss Robin Hood – his 1952 big-screen debut – Joey Boy and The Great St. Trinian's Train Robbery.

New-found stardom brought more film roles to Reg, in Go for a Take and as an ageing holiday camp drag artist in The Best Pair of Legs in the Business.

He played a Billingsgate Market fish porter in another, almost forgotten TV situation comedy, Down the Gate, then left television behind to take his cabaret act to Australia, New Zealand and Canada. He also toured Australia in a stage production of On the Buses, in 1988.

Seven years earlier, he had suffered a heart attack and, as a result, has done little acting since, although his new-found talent for painting landscapes in oils – which he started during his convalescence – is a hobby that keeps him busy. He has even had exhibitions of his work.

Reg and his wife, Lily, have one daughter, Jeanne.

Norman Vaughan

b. 10 April 1927

ONE of ITV's biggest hits of the 50s and 60s was Sunday Night at the London Palladium, which at its height attracted almost half the nation's population, and Norman Vaughan's three-year run as its compere made him a star. It also led to his making a commercial for chocolates with the slogan "Roses grow on you".

Born in Liverpool, Norman left school at the age of 14 and made his stage debut in a revue with the Eton Boys Choir, singing 'D'ye Ken John Peel'. A year later, he formed a dance trio called the Dancing Aces and toured with it, until he was called up to join the Army in 1945.

Serving as a sergeant in Italy and the Middle East, he performed in troop shows alongside Harry Secombe and Spike Milligan, who were later to form The Goons. In 1951, he starred with Secombe again, when they performed on the same bill in variety.

After two years in a variety show in Australia, Norman returned to Britain to appear in summer seasons of a show called Twinkle and, by the end of the decade, he was the compere of a show starring Cliff Richard.

Norman was making a name for himself as an entertainer and his big break came when he stepped into Bruce Forsyth's shoes to host Sunday Night at the London Palladium, in 1962. By then, the programme – which was broadcast live – was already a national institution, with 20 million regular viewers, and he overcame his first-night nerves to become an instant star.

For three years and more than 100 programmes, he introduced the country's top stars and his comic patter held the show together, with the words 'swinging' or 'dodgy' accompanied by the appropriate thumbs-up or thumbs-down gestures.

In 1972, Norman returned to television

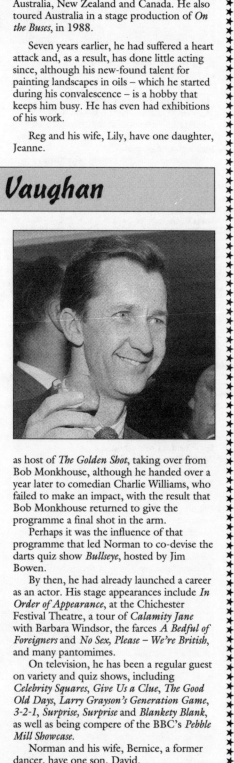

as host of The Golden Shot, taking over from Bob Monkhouse, although he handed over a year later to comedian Charlie Williams, who failed to make an impact, with the result that Bob Monkhouse returned to give the programme a final shot in the arm.

Perhaps it was the influence of that programme that led Norman to co-devise the darts quiz show Bullseye, hosted by Jim Bowen.

By then, he had already launched a career as an actor. His stage appearances include In Order of Appearance, at the Chichester Festival Theatre, a tour of Calamity Jane with Barbara Windsor, the farces A Bedful of Foreigners and No Sex, Please – We're British, and many pantomimes.

On television, he has been a regular guest on variety and quiz shows, including Celebrity Squares, Give Us a Clue, The Good Old Days, Larry Grayson's Generation Game, 3-2-1, Surprise, Surprise and Blankety Blank, as well as being compere of the BBC's Pebble Mill Showcase.

Norman and his wife, Bernice, a former dancer, have one son, David.

Max Wall

b. 12 March 1908
d. 22 May 1990

DRESSED in black tights, wig, white socks and enormous boots, Max Wall entertained audiences as the champion of the funny walk, with a brand of comedy that was firmly rooted in music-hall.

Maxwell George Lorimer was born in Brixton, South London, and his first professional job was as a member of a pantomime cast touring the West Country in 1922, although he had first appeared on the stage at the age of two.

He made his London debut in 1925, in a revue at the Lyceum Theatre, where he performed mainly as a dancer and was affectionately known as "the boy with obedient feet".

Max's first work as a comedian was in the Broadway show *Vanities* and, from then on, there was no looking back. He subsequently appeared as a comic in London West End shows such as *Black and Blue* and *Make It a Date*.

During the Second World War, he served in the RAF for three years, before eventually being invalided out, in 1943.

Once back in civvy street, Max appeared in the musical *Panama Hattie*, with Bebe Daniels, at the Piccadilly Theatre and on a national tour, before returning to London's West End, at the Adelphi.

He also went into radio and it was through programmes such as *Hoop-La*, with Robb Wilton, in 1944, his own show, *Our Shed*, and *Petticoat Lane*, with Elsie and Doris Waters, that he was set on course to become a star.

His other radio work included guest spots on *Workers' Playtime* and *Mid-day Music Hall*, as well as being resident comedian in *Variety Bandbox*. Then, in the early 50s, he became one of the first comedians to be given his own television show.

Back on stage, he enjoyed rapturous success in the West End with the American musical *The Pajama Game*, which opened in 1955 and ran for 18 months but, while he positively revelled in his professional triumph, Max's personal life was to bring him grief both privately and publicly.

His 15-year marriage to dancer Marian Pola, with whom he had five children, broke up and he was branded by the tabloid press as a heartless scoundrel who had abandoned his wife and family for a young beauty queen, Jennifer Chimes, who subsequently became his second wife. That marriage later failed, as did the next.

His career was decimated by the publicity and he was reduced to working the Northern club circuit, until he was offered his first straight role, in the surreal play *Ubu Roi*, at the Royal Court Theatre.

Stage work continued, including roles in productions such as *The Old Ones* and *Cockie*, which saw his return to the West End. Max later performed at the Greenwich Theatre, where he spent three happy years in plays such as *The Last Entertainer*, *Krapp's Last Tape* and *The Caretaker*.

He performed his one-man show, *Aspects of Max Wall*, at the Garrick Theatre, in 1975, and it proved so successful that it enjoyed an extended season at the Shaw Theatre and won the Variety Club of Great Britain's Special Award for that year. Audiences witnessed Max in his most famous guise, that of pianist Professor Wallofsky, the hilariously attired character who strutted ostrich-style around the stage.

In straight roles on television, he played Walter Soper, cousin of Arthur Brownlow in *Crossroads*, and Elsie Tanner's friend Harry Payne in *Coronation Street*.

Max, who died at the age of 82, wrote an autobiography entitled *The Fool on the Hill*.

Jack Warner

b. 24 October 1895
d. 24 May 1981

AS the old-fashioned bobby Dixon of Dock Green, first seen in a 40s film and then in a long-running television series, Jack Warner became one of the small screen's best-loved policemen.

Born Horace John Waters in Bromley, Kent, the brother of variety comediennes Elsie and Doris Waters – better known as Gert and Daisy – he studied automobile engineering after leaving school and, a year later, set off for Paris to work as a mechanic.

During the First World War, he served in France as a driver with the Royal Flying

Corps and was awarded the Meritorious Service Medal in 1918.

Afterwards, he returned to Britain and a life as an entertainer. Rising through the ranks of Sutton Amateur Dramatics Club to become a full-time cabaret performer, he made his London West End debut in 1935, as half of the double-act Warner and Darnell.

It was then that he decided to change his name from Waters to Warner so that people would not think him guilty of trading on his sisters' famous name.

Seven years later, Jack made his first film, *The Dummy Talks*, but it was his sixth picture, *Holiday Camp*, that first showed him as a homely, father figure. He played Joe Huggett, head of a cockney family, struggling with his wife to bring up three children. The Huggetts proved such a sensation that they appeared in three more films, as well as in a radio show – *Meet the Huggetts* – that ran from 1953 to 1962.

His other films included *The Quatermass Experiment*, *The Ladykillers* and *Carve Her Name with Pride*.

Although Jack had never considered himself to be one of the finest actors, he resented the typecasting into which he had inadvertently slipped and was therefore delighted to perform more serious roles. Examples of these can be witnessed in *It Always Rains on Sunday* and *The Final Test*.

But it was with television that he became a household name, as PC George Dixon in *Dixon of Dock Green*, the popular police series that ran for 21 years.

The character of Dixon had been seen previously on the big screen, in the 1949 film *The Blue Lamp*, but he was shot dead after only a few minutes. However, Dixon was brought back to life six years later to star in the television programme created by Ted Willis.

In the first TV series ever to be based on a film, Jack started each episode with the words "Evenin' all!", speaking directly to the camera and introducing the story that followed, after the catchy theme tune, 'Ordinary Copper', had faded out.

Dixon began as a police constable, before being promoted to sergeant, with Jack reigning supreme until the programme's popularity dwindled, with the advent of more modern police series, such as *Z-Cars*.

After he retired as Dixon, in 1976, he continued to work in cabaret until he suffered a stroke, in 1980. A year later, the actor, who had been awarded an OBE in 1965, died from pneumonia after suffering a further stroke.

Jack, who was married to Muriel Winifred ('Molly'), had no children. His autobiography, *Jack of All Trades*, was published in 1975.

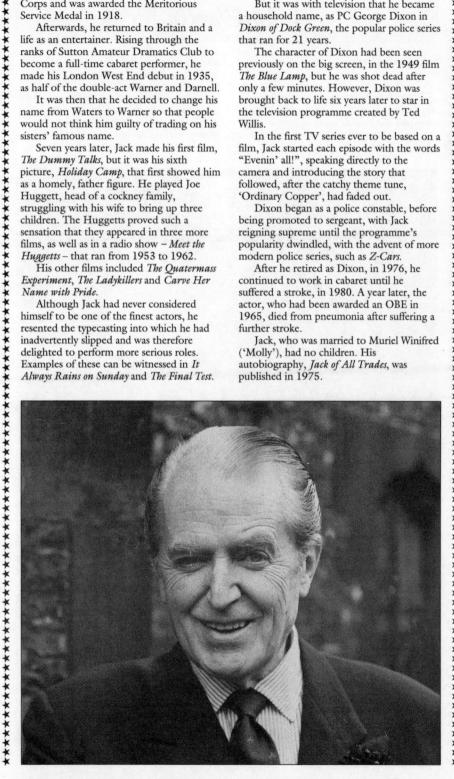

Jack Watling

b. 13 January 1923

A S all-time loser Don Henderson in the 60s, Jack Watling was a star of the aircraft factory drama *The Plane Makers* and its sequel, *The Power Game*.

Born in Chingford, Essex, he trained at the Italia Conti Stage Academy as a child and made his stage debut in *Where the Rainbow Ends*, at the Holborn Empire, in 1936. He made his first film, *Sixty Glorious Years*, two years later and followed it with appearances in *The Housemaster* and *Goodbye Mr Chips!*

The Second World War only partially interrupted Jack's career – he joined the RAF in 1944 and served for three years – and he

appeared in eight films during the War, acting servicemen in pictures such as *Ships with Wings* and *We Dive at Dawn*.

On being demobbed, he continued in films and began to find himself cast as rather shady characters, often with trilby hats. He was in *The Winslow Boy, Meet Mr. Lucifer, Reach for the Sky, The Admirable Crichton, Sink the Bismarck!* and dozens more.

On television, he had already appeared in episodes of *No Hiding Place, Hancock's Half Hour, Ghost Squad* and *Boyd QC* when he landed the role of Don Henderson in *The Plane Makers*, in 1963. Two years later, the story was taken out of the noisy aircraft factory and into the boardroom when the series changed its name and became *The Power Game*.

Jack's other TV appearances have included those in *Dixon of Dock Green, Emergency – Ward 10, Doctor Who, Softly, Softly, Love Story* and the daytime period soap *The Cedar Tree*. He was also in the film of the TV comedy hit *Father, Dear Father* and the small-screen sequel, *The Many Wives of Patrick*.

The actor is married to former actress Patricia Hicks, has a stepdaughter, actress Dilys Watling, two other daughters, actress Deborah and Nicola, and a son, Giles. Jack's first son, Adam, born in 1951, was killed a year later in a fall of snow.

Jack Webb

b. 2 April 1920
d. 23 December 1982

A S creator and star of the American television police series *Dragnet* in the 50s, Jack Webb became a household name, with his laconic style and catchphrase "Just the facts, ma'am."

Born in Santa Monica, California, he first worked as a radio announcer in San Francisco, in 1945, before playing supporting roles in almost 20 films, beginning with *He Walked by Night*, in 1948, followed by pictures such as *Sunset Boulevard, Appointment with Danger* and *The Last Time I Saw Archie*.

Moving into television in 1951, Jack could not have had any idea of the impact that the police series *Dragnet* would have on viewers. The programme, which he himself created, wrote, produced and starred in, soon became a small-screen classic. Audiences found it realistic, and this was Jack's main concern, presenting it in a documentary style, often using amateurs and occasionally the real-life people involved in the crime on which a particular episode was based.

He played Sergeant Joe Friday, a member of the Los Angeles police department, and the programme ran successfully for eight years. There was also a 1954 film spin-off and he returned for another three-year run of *Dragnet*, from 1967, after a period as Head of Warner TV proved unsuccessful. A TV movie of the same title appeared in 1969.

The actor, who died from a heart attack at the age of 62, was married and divorced three times, first to actress and singer Julie London, with whom he had two daughters, then to Dorothy Towne and former Miss USA Jackie Loughery.

Alan Wheatley

b. 14 April 1907
d. 30 August 1991

AS the Sheriff of Nottingham in the 50s series *The Adventures of Robin Hood*, Alan Wheatley played the malevolent adversary to Richard Greene's squeaky-clean hero in Lincoln green.

During the Second World War, Alan left his job as an industrial psychologist to spend five years as a BBC radio announcer, before starting an acting career. The suave, debonair actor with the golden voice made his film debut in the 1936 picture *Conquest of the Air*, which was not released until four years later, but his 30 subsequent films included *Caesar and Cleopatra*, *The Rake's Progress*, *Brighton Rock*, *Calling Paul Temple*, *The Pickwick Papers*, *Simon and Laura* and *Inn for Trouble*, a big-screen spin-off from the popular TV comedy series *The Larkins*.

Stage performances were dominant in his career and he could be seen rising above his material in Clifford Bax's *The House of Borgia*, in 1935, as well as taking the lead role in *This Way To the Tomb* – performed in London and Paris – and playing Harry, a tormented soul, in *The Family Reunion*.

It was on television, as the BBC's first Sherlock Holmes in a series, then as Sheriff of Nottingham in *The Adventures of Robin Hood*, starring alongside 50s heart-throb Richard Greene, that Alan made his name.

The programme, which began in 1955, was one of ITV's first adventure series, made with a view to getting a screening in America. It lasted for four years and 143 episodes, with Alan so convincing in his role that he became one of those television characters whom viewers just loved to hate. As well as receiving sacks of hate-mail, he would often find his car scratched.

The well-respected actor died in 1991, at the age of 84.

Carol White

b. 1 April 1942
d. 16 September 1991

THE stark 60s television play *Cathy Come Home* succeeded in launching Carol White on to the road to Hollywood, as well as providing inspiration for the foundation of Shelter, the charity for the homeless.

Born Carole White in Hammersmith, West London, she made her film debut as a child, in *The Belles of St. Trinian's*, in 1954, and a string of other pictures followed, including *Doctor in the House*, *Doctor at Sea*, *Moby Dick*, *Around the World in 80 Days*, *Blue Murder at St Trinian's* and *Carry On Teacher*.

She trained at the Corona Stage School and, while there, played the girlfriend of Peter Sellers in *Never Let Go*, and later appeared in the Beatles' *Help!*

Carol also made her mark in the BBC's controversial *Wednesday Play* series in 1965, as the Daddy's girl who crosses the Thames to live a life of discos and orgies in *Up the Junction*.

A year later, she was catapulted to stardom in *Cathy Come Home*. The Jeremy Sandford play, directed by Ken Loach, centred on a young London couple played by Carol and Ray Brooks, whose children were taken into care when they became homeless.

The heartbreaking realism touched the hearts of millions, with Carol portraying Cathy as a picture of vibrance and youthful naïvety, whose spirit had become totally crushed by poverty and helplessness.

The actress subsequently starred as a promiscuous young mother in Ken Loach's 1967 film *Poor Cow* and, in the same year, was cast in Michael Winner's picture *I'll Never Forget What's 'Is Name*, a comedy based on the world of advertising. Carol then received acclaim for her performance in *The Fixer*, alongside Alan Bates and Dirk Bogarde, but a string of less distinguished films followed.

Unfortunately, her real life was almost as trouble-strewn as her film roles. She experienced drug abuse and alcoholism, had a shoplifting conviction and made more than one suicide attempt.

Her autobiography, *Carol Comes Home*, published in 1982, logged all her personal disasters and included claims of affairs with many of Hollywood's leading men.

Carol was married and divorced three times, first to singer Michael King, with whom she had two sons, then to Stuart Lerner and, finally, to Michael Arnold, who left her for an Italian heiress. She died at the age of 49.

Kenneth Williams

b. 22 February 1926
d. 15 April 1988

THE uncrowned king of the *double entendre*, Kenneth Williams was a true star with his *Carry On* film capers, his adenoidal whine and bug-eyed expressions becoming legendary, but he also brought his humour to the small screen in his own show.

Born in London, he lived as a child in a flat above a hairdresser's shop, his father a strict Methodist who worked as a van driver with the London, Midland and Scottish Railways.

A practical, down-to-earth man, he wanted his son to learn a trade, so the young Kenneth left school at the age of 14 to become an apprentice cartographer. Four years later, with the outbreak of the Second World War, he joined the Army, making maps for the Royal Engineers.

It was during his service days that he realised his talent for comedy and he was later posted to Combined Services Entertainment, touring Burma and Malaya, where he and Stanley Baxter performed a double act.

After being demobbed, Kenneth looked set to spend the rest of his life as a draughtsman, until his old Army colleague Stanley persuaded him to try for the stage.

Several unsuccessful attempts later, Kenneth was finally accepted by a repertory theatre company in Newquay, Cornwall.

After four years gaining experience and confidence, he left and headed for London, where he gave a badly received performance in *Peter Pan*, before playing in *Saint Joan* at the Old Vic and taking the lead in the West End show *Share My Lettuce*. It gradually became obvious that drama was not Kenneth's niche – he was a man with the rare gift of making people laugh, using his extensive repertoire of funny voices. This talent was wonderfully exhibited when he appeared on the radio shows *Beyond Our Ken*, *Hancock's Half Hour* and, later, *Round the Horne* and *Just a Minute*.

A year after *Hancock's Half Hour* first hit the airwaves, in 1954, Kenneth had stolen the limelight with his insufferable pest 'voices' shrieking, "Stop messing about!" Audiences loved him, but Hancock loathed what he classed as the actor's "cartoon characters" and dropped him from the show.

Kenneth had already made less than auspicious appearances in films – starting with *Trent's Last Case*, in 1952 – when he returned to the big screen in *Carry On Sergeant*, as a snooty recruit. This was the first of the *Carry On* sagas, which began in 1958 and ran for 20 years, with Kenneth featuring in all but four of them.

During his *Carry On* days, he played a wide variety of characters, from the pompous egghead of a doctor in *Carry On Matron* to the power-crazed Khazi of Kalibar in *Carry*

On Up the Khyber, his versatile features and screen eccentricities lending themselves so completely to the films.

Although mainly a film actor, he had several television successes, including his own programmes, *The Kenneth Williams Show* and *Stop Messing About*, as well as appearing in children's programmes such as *Jackanory* and as the voice in various cartoons, the most famous being *Willo the Wisp*.

His two most prized attributes of voice and dazzling wit made him a valuable commodity on chat-shows and much in demand for TV commercials – his vocal performance in the Brobat Bloo Loo advert made compulsive viewing.

Kenneth vigilantly kept a diary, the contents of which were partly revealed in his autobiography, *Just William*. He also wrote several other anecdotal books. A homosexual, the actor never married and, at the age of 62, was found dead from an overdose of sleeping pills, only weeks before he was due to go into hospital for an operation.

Mike and Bernie Winters

Mike Winters
b. 1930
Bernie Winters
b. 6 September 1932, d. 4 May 1991

FOR almost 30 years, Mike and Bernie Winters were one of British television's top comedy duos with a boisterous form of knockabout humour and music-hall cross-talk, but they split up amid the acrimony that affects many double-acts, with Bernie going on to carve out a new solo career for himself.

Born Michael and Bernie Weinstein, into a Russian Jewish family in Islington, North London, Bernie was the first to enter showbusiness full-time after working as a salesman – appearing as a stand-up comic in dance halls by night – and serving in the Merchant Navy.

He failed to find success until teaming up with his brother Mike, who had studied at the Royal Academy of Music and was playing clarinet with a quartet at the Stage Door Canteen, the services entertainment centre.

Bernie joined on drums and the brothers subsequently formed a threesome with comedian Jack Farr in an act called Three Loose Screws, which included impressions of Lionel Barrymore and Ronald Colman. They performed in variety halls and as musicians and stooges in a Canadian Army show unit for a while.

Branching out on their own, the brothers worked the clubs and were in radio shows such as *Variety Parade*. Further breaks came with their appearance on the same bill as Tommy Steele, in 1956 – gaining the pair a reputation with young audiences – and their residency as comics on the BBC pop show *6.5 Special*, which began the following year.

Ups and downs followed, and the duo even considered emigrating to Australia, but their career was revived by their appearances as hosts of the TV variety show *Big Night Out*, in 1965. Over the next nine years, they appeared in *The Mike and Bernie Show* and *Mike and Bernie's Music Hall*, although two attempts at going into situation-comedy failed. Their comedy had its roots in music-hall, with an unsubtle humour that relied little on verbal wit, Mike playing the straight man to Bernie's gormless idiot.

Throughout their days as a television double-act, Mike and Bernie were in the shadow of Morecambe and Wise, never quite scaling the same dizzy heights.

In 1978, they finally parted. They had made the decision five years earlier but delayed the break-up until after the death of their father, who had encouraged them so much during their early years.

While Mike crossed the Atlantic, and settled in Florida, where he became a businessman, Bernie launched himself as a solo comedian, first taking his toothy leer and outsize clothes into his own show, *Bernie*, in the year of their split. In television, he went on to host *Make Me Laugh*, the quiz show *Whose Baby?* – with a celebrity panel trying to guess the identity of children's famous parents – and *Scribble*, as well as becoming a frequent guest in programmes such as *Punchlines*, *Give Us a Clue* and *Blankety Blank*.

Bernie also turned to acting, playing Bud Flanagan in the TV musical *Bud 'n' Ches*, in 1981, with Leslie Crowther playing Chesney Allen. Two years later, the pair repeated their roles in a stage show, *Underneath the Arches*.

But Bernie's permanent 'partner' during his solo career was his 11st St Bernard, Schnorbitz, and together they enjoyed a consistent popularity that had always eluded Mike and Bernie as a double-act. The two feuding brothers made up their differences in 1985, but never performed together again.

Bernie, who died of stomach cancer at the age of 58, was married to former dancer Sigfrid (Siggi) Heine and had a son, Ray.

Norman Wisdom

b. 4 February 1915

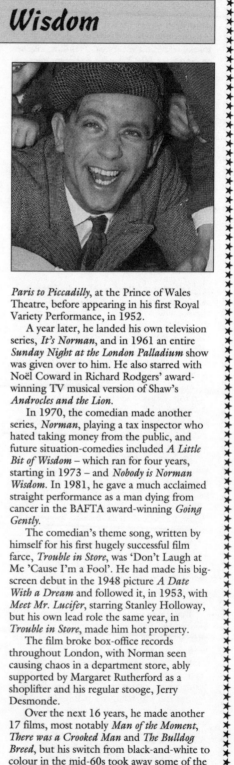

ONE of television's earliest phenomenons, madcap comedian Norman Wisdom went on to become one of the British cinema's most popular funnymen, complete with tight-fitting 'gump' suit and tweed cap with turned-up peak.

Born in Paddington, North London, Norman was nine when he and his brother were left to be brought up by their drunken father after their mother walked out.

Leaving school at the age of 13, he became an errand boy in a grocer's and a trainee waiter, before walking from London to Cardiff to seek work in a coalmine. Instead, he became a cabin-boy on a ship that was sailing from the city's docks to Argentina.

On his return, Norman joined the Army as a band boy in the 10th Hussars, learning the clarinet, piano, xylophone, saxophone, violin and trumpet. By the time war broke out, he had moved to the Royal Corps of Signals.

It was in the Army that he first became an entertainer, appearing with a concert party and developing a comedy act, which included falls and acrobatics that he taught himself.

On leaving the Army, the comic – who stood at barely 5ft tall – made his professional debut in variety at Collins Music Hall, in December 1945. After appearances in variety, pantomime and revues, he made his West End debut at the London Casino, in 1948, followed it by topping the bill at the Golders Green Hippodrome and spent the summer of that year in *Out of the Blue*, at the Spa Theatre, Scarborough.

It was there that he introduced the gormless character Norman, for which he would later become known worldwide, as well as performing his own, 12-minute speciality act.

Coming out of the audience as a 'volunteer', he would wreck conjuror David Nixon's magic act, and so successful was the partnership that the pair followed it with a run at the London Casino.

In the same year, Norman went on to make his TV debut, in *Wit and Wisdom*, and continued to work in variety theatres around the country, as well as appearing in the revue *Sauce Piquante*, at the Cambridge Theatre, London.

He was later in band-leader Henry Hall's show *Buttons and Bows*, with Donald Peers, four consecutive pantomime seasons, a tour of America and the Folies Bergère production

Paris to Piccadilly, at the Prince of Wales Theatre, before appearing in his first Royal Variety Performance, in 1952.

A year later, he landed his own television series, *It's Norman*, and in 1961 an entire *Sunday Night at the London Palladium* show was given over to him. He also starred with Noël Coward in Richard Rodgers' award-winning TV musical version of Shaw's *Androcles and the Lion*.

In 1970, the comedian made another series, *Norman*, playing a tax inspector who hated taking money from the public, and future situation-comedies included *A Little Bit of Wisdom* – which ran for four years, starting in 1973 – and *Nobody is Norman Wisdom*. In 1981, he gave a much acclaimed straight performance as a man dying from cancer in the BAFTA award-winning *Going Gently*.

The comedian's theme song, written by himself for his first hugely successful film farce, *Trouble in Store*, was 'Don't Laugh at Me 'Cause I'm a Fool'. He had made his big-screen debut in the 1948 picture *A Date With a Dream* and followed it, in 1953, with *Meet Mr. Lucifer*, starring Stanley Holloway, but his own lead role the same year, in *Trouble in Store*, made him hot property.

The film broke box-office records throughout London, with Norman seen causing chaos in a department store, ably supported by Margaret Rutherford as a shoplifter and his regular stooge, Jerry Desmonde.

Over the next 16 years, he made another 17 films, most notably *Man of the Moment*, *There was a Crooked Man* and *The Bulldog Breed*, but his switch from black-and-white to colour in the mid-60s took away some of the simplicity of his slapstick comedy and, by the end of the decade, his film career was over – although he was nominated for a Best Supporting Actor Oscar for his role in the 1968 picture *The Night They Raided Minsky's*.

Norman returned to television and the stage, where he had already had success on Broadway with *Walking Happy*, a 1966 musical version of *Hobson's Choice*. He also starred in the New York show *Not Now Darling*.

Since his film and TV days, the zany comedian's appearances have been mainly in summer seasons and pantomimes.

Norman was twice the subject of *This Is Your Life*, in 1957 and 1987, and wrote his autobiography, *Don't Laugh at Me*, with William Hall, in 1992.

Googie Withers

b. 12 March 1917

WELL-groomed prison governor Faye Boswell was a hit with viewers in the 70s, when *Within These Walls* was on TV screens. Veteran film actress Googie Withers played the part for two years, returning from exile in Australia to star in her first television series.

Born Georgette Lizette Withers of British parents in what was then the Indian city of Karachi, she trained as a dancer under Italia Conti, Helena Lehmiski and Buddy Bradley, and made her stage debut with her dancing school in 1929, at the age of 12, in *The Windmill Man* at the Victoria Palace.

Her first film, five years later, was *The Girl in the Crowd* and, after having her brunette hair dyed blonde, she was soon typecast in roles that required dumb humour and stooging for comics such as George Formby.

All that changed in the 40s, however, and she went on to become one of the glamorous stars of the British cinema, particularly in straight 'bad-girl' roles. Her 50 films include *The Lady Vanishes*, *Jeannie*, *One of Our Aircraft is Missing*, *Dead of Night*, *Pink String and Sealing Wax*, *Miranda*, *The Magic Box* and *Devil on Horseback*.

Googie met actor John McCallum while they were both filming *The Loves of Joanna Godden*, in 1947, and they married the following year.

She was lost to the British cinema when, in 1958, the couple moved to his native Australia, where he was to give up acting and take up a managerial appointment with a leading theatre company.

He then moved into television, responsible for series such as *Skippy* and *The Great Barrier Reef*, as well as the revitalised Australian cinema, directing Googie and their daughter, Joanna, in *The Nickel Queen*, in 1970.

Four years later, Googie was back in Britain, starring as Faye Boswell, governor of Stone Park women's prison, in *Within These Walls*. Up to 16 million viewers tuned in to the programme, but she pulled out after two series and actress Katharine Blake stepped in as a new governor.

Googie's few previous TV appearances included the 1958 BBC production of the Jean Giraudoux play *Amphitryon 38*, *The Deep Blue Sea* and *Court Circular*.

Although she returned to Australia, she has since been on the small screen in the TV movies *Time After Time*, *Hôtel du Lac* and *Northanger Abbey*.

As well as Joanna, Googie and her husband have another daughter, Amanda, and a son, Nicholas.

Barbara Woodhouse

b. 9 May 1910
d. 8 July 1988

FAMOUS for her "Walkies!" catchphrase, Barbara Woodhouse was television's number one authority on dog training. Millions of viewers tuned in to watch the elderly woman in a tartan kilt and sensible shoes striding along next to her canine charge, yanking its choke-chain and booming out commands. Neither the dogs nor their owners would dare disobey her.

Born in Rathfarnham, Co. Dublin, one of five children, Barbara's father was a schoolmaster who died when she was just nine years old, leaving her to be brought up by her mother and various nannies.

A keen horsewoman, she began training horses in her teens and continued to do so after leaving school and moving to the Harper Adams Agricultural College. She then opened her own riding school in Oxford, before travelling to Argentina, where she hoped the experience would broaden her views on farming. It was during her three-and-a-half years there that an old Indian taught Barbara her later much-publicised trick of blowing up a horse's nostrils as a form of greeting.

On returning to Britain, she began to write about her unusual methods of training and farming, and her first book, *Talking to Animals*, was published in 1955. In the same year, she appeared in her first dog-training film, *Love Me, Love My Dog*.

But it was not until 1980 that Barbara really became a celebrity, appearing in her own television show, *Training Dogs the Woodhouse Way*, although she had first appeared on the small screen as a subject in *What's My Line?*

This unlikely television star – who won the TV Personality of the Year award from both Pye and the Writers' Guild of Great Britain – seemed to court controversy with her unique style of training and was much-criticised as well as being adored by many viewers.

The RSPCA branded the choke chains used by Barbara as cruel and other trainers said she was simply barking up the wrong tree. She, however, was relentless in her conviction. When asked by chat-show host Michael Parkinson what should be done if a dog is seen fouling in a public place, she answered, "Take the nearest heavy object, like a book or a rolled-up newspaper, and give the culprit a hefty smack on the head." Parkinson raised his eyebrows in surprise and queried, "Hit the dog?" "No, you silly boy –

the owner," she replied, crossly.

As well as *Training Dogs the Woodhouse Way*, Barbara presented *The Woodhouse World of Animals*, *The World of Horses and Ponies*, *Barbara Woodhouse Goes to Beverly Hills* and *Barbara Woodhouse's Problem Dogs*. Many documentaries, a best-selling record and 17 books later, she seemed well established as a TV celebrity, although the success did not go to her head. Instead of hogging the limelight, which she could so easily have done, she preferred to relax on her farm with her animals.

Barbara, who died at the age of 78, was married to Dr Michael Woodhouse and had two daughters, Pamela and Judith, and one son, Patrick. Training 17000 dogs earned her a place in *The Guinness Book of Records* and she wrote an autobiography, *Talking to Animals*.

Harry Worth

b. 20 November 1917
d. 20 July 1989

ONE of the small screen's greatest funnymen, Harry Worth entertained millions with his bungling routines and shows.

Born Harry Burlon Illingsworth in Tankersley, near Barnsley, West Yorkshire, one of 11 children, he was the son of a miner who was killed in a pit accident when Harry was only five months old. At the age of 14, he followed in the family tradition and went to work down the mine.

During the Second World War, he served in the RAF as a mechanic and fitter but enjoyed his off-duty time entertaining his fellow servicemen with a ventriloquism act.

It was during the war years that he gained entertainment experience in Gang Shows, before appearing at the famous Windmill Theatre, London, once back in civvy street.

Harry eventually abandoned his two ventriloquist's dummies, Fotheringay and Clarence, on the advice of Stan Laurel, with whom he had toured for two years, and he made his debut as a stand-up comic at the Newcastle Empire, discovering his clumsy, bungling routine quite by chance, when his nerves got the better of him.

His career seemed on the right track and in 1962, after several years of playing at the London Palladium and in London's West End, summer shows and pantomimes, he was given his own television programme, *Here's Harry*.

In this series, he established the routine that was to become his trademark, standing in the corner of a shop window and raising one arm and leg, using the reflection to make it appear as if he was doing the splits in mid-air.

The show was a delight to watch, a gentle comedy based around suburban chaos, with Harry ensconced in 52 Acacia Avenue, prattling on about his cat, Tiddles, and his dear, old auntie. It ran for more than 100 episodes.

His other TV series were *My Name is Harry Worth* and the situation-comedy *How's Your Father*, in 1979, in which he played a single parent struggling to cope with a teenaged son and daughter. A year later, he appeared in *O Happy Band*, another comedy series, based around a village brass band, and he also acted in the ITV spoof version of Evelyn Waugh's *Scoop*.

A year before he died, after a long battle against cancer, Harry – although wheelchair-bound – had his own radio show, *Thirty Minutes Worth*, and had been planning a new series at the time of his death.

Married to former singer Kay, he had one daughter, Jobina.

Patrick Wymark

b. 11 July 1926
d. 20 October 1970

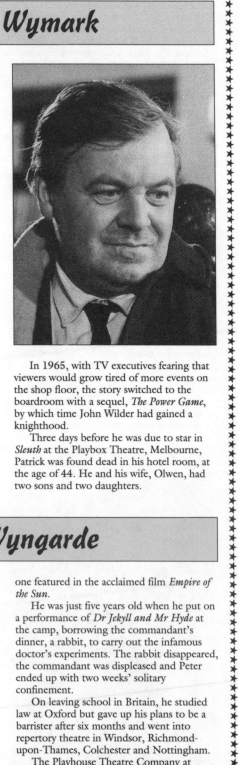

AS powerful tycoon John Wilder, Patrick Wymark became a household name in two of the 60s' most popular series, *The Plane Makers* and *The Power Game*.

Born Patrick Cheeseman in Cleethorpes, Lincolnshire, he attended University College, London, before training at the Old Vic Theatre School and making his first stage appearance in a walk-on part in *Othello* with the Old Vic company, in 1951. He toured South Africa the following year.

Moving to the Shakespeare Memorial Theatre, Stratford-upon-Avon, Patrick played a wide range of roles, from Dogberry in *Much Ado About Nothing* and Stephano in *The Tempest* to Marullus in *Julius Caesar* and Bottom in *A Midsummer Night's Dream*.

Other stage parts included the title role in *Danton's Death* and, with the Royal Shakespeare Company, Bosola in *The Duchess of Malfi* and Epihodov in *The Cherry Orchard*. Later, he played King John in John Arden's *Left-Handed Liberty*. He also appeared in films such as *The Criminal*, *Dr Syn – Alias the Scarecrow*, *Operation Crossbow* and, as Strafford, in *Cromwell*.

On television, Patrick made his name as the ruthless, power-hungry managing director John Wilder in the 1963 series *The Plane Makers*, featuring the management-and-union wrangles in an aircraft factory. It earned him the TV Actor of the Year award and ran for two series.

In 1965, with TV executives fearing that viewers would grow tired of more events on the shop floor, the story switched to the boardroom with a sequel, *The Power Game*, by which time John Wilder had gained a knighthood.

Three days before he was due to star in *Sleuth* at the Playbox Theatre, Melbourne, Patrick was found dead in his hotel room, at the age of 44. He and his wife, Owlen, had two sons and two daughters.

Peter Wyngarde

b. 1928

IN the early 70s, best-selling novelist-turned-private investigator Jason King was the most popular TV hero in the world – after Robin Hood and the Saint – and Peter Wyngarde of the flamboyant wardrobe carried him through two hugely successful series.

Born Cyril Louis Goldbert in Marseilles, of Anglo-French parents, his father was a diplomat who was in the Far East when the Second World War broke out. When he was sent elsewhere, Peter stayed with family friends in Lung Hua, in China, then was sent to the Japanese internment camp there – the

one featured in the acclaimed film *Empire of the Sun*.

He was just five years old when he put on a performance of *Dr Jekyll and Mr Hyde* at the camp, borrowing the commandant's dinner, a rabbit, to carry out the infamous doctor's experiments. The rabbit disappeared, the commandant was displeased and Peter ended up with two weeks' solitary confinement.

On leaving school in Britain, he studied law at Oxford but gave up his plans to be a barrister after six months and went into repertory theatre in Windsor, Richmond-upon-Thames, Colchester and Nottingham. The Playhouse Theatre Company at

Nottingham were invited to perform in London, where Peter acted Cassio in *Othello* and Gerald in *When We are Married*.

He followed this with a season at the Arts Theatre, in *Saint Joan*, *Intermezzo* and *Histoire de Rire*, and was spotted by director Robert Rossen, who thought him perfect for the title role of his next film, *Alexander the Great*. However, the producers thought differently and Richard Burton took the part. Peter was offered a smaller role.

After joining Alec Guinness's company at the New Theatre, where he played Osric to Guinness's Hamlet, he moved into television, playing Granillo in *Rope*, Sydney Carton in *A Tale of Two Cities* and the title role in *Will Shakespeare*. He starred as Richard the deserter, opposite Dame Edith Evans, in Christopher Fry's *The Dark Is Light Enough*, Oberon in *A Midsummer Night's Dream* – in which Benny Hill played Bottom – and was acclaimed for his performance as De Levis in John Galsworthy's *Loyalties*.

Back on stage, Peter joined the Royal Court Theatre, playing opposite Dame Peggy Ashcroft in *The Good Woman of Szechuan*, and was consequently asked by Sir Laurence Olivier to star opposite Vivien Leigh as Marcellus in *Duels of Angels*, which ran for nine months at the Apollo Theatre and for another six on Broadway.

As a result, Paramount signed him to a film contract, although nothing materialised. More successfully, he appeared in the British films *The Siege of Sidney Street*, *The Innocents* and *Night of the Eagle*.

Moving back into theatre once again, Peter joined the Bristol Old Vic, directing *Long Day's Journey into Night*, playing the title role in *Cyrano de Bergerac* and Petruchio in *The Taming of the Shrew* – which was televised – and acting in the world première of Tennessee Williams's *The Two Character Play*.

International fame came in 1970 with the role of dapper Jason King in the TV series *Department S*, about a fictional offshoot of Interpol that tackled international crimes. King was the novelist-turned-sleuth who led the department. Peter launched a trendsetting hairstyle and the zapata moustache, and went on to his own series, *Jason King*.

He played the character in 52 episodes, over four years, but his career crashed in 1975, when he was found guilty and fined £75 for committing an indecent act with another man in a public toilet, although he denied in court that he was homosexual.

However, he has since appeared in the film *Flash Gordon* and on television in *Doctor Who*, *Crown Court*, *The Two Ronnies* and *Bulman*.

Most of his recent work has been in the theatre, where he played the King of Siam in *The King and I* and George Bernard Shaw in *Dear Liar*, as well as appearing in London's West End in *Mother Adam* and *Underground*, and at the Old Vic in *Light Up the Sky*.

He directed *Big Toys* in Vienna, *Time and the Conways* and *The Merchant of Venice*, a televised production in which he played Shylock. Peter lives in London.

Mike Yarwood

b. 14 June 1941

FOR three decades, Mike Yarwood was television's top impressionist, mimicking the small screen's other big stars of the moment and some of the more charismatic politicians.

Born Michael Edward Yarwood in Bredbury, Cheshire, the son of an engineering fitter, he was impersonating local shopkeepers, tradesmen and his parish priest by the age of five and, two years later, was cast as a postman in a school concert.

It was Mike's habit of mimicking customers and his boss that led to him being dismissed from his first job, as a dispatch clerk for a mail-order firm in a Manchester warehouse. During the evenings, he played drums in a pop group and impersonated top stars such as Cliff Richard and Adam Faith.

While working as a commercial traveller, he was persuaded to enter a pub talent contest and, although he came third, the landlord offered him work in a pub, The Salvage, in the Manchester suburb of Collyhurst.

He followed it with regular performances in other pubs and Royston Mayoh, later a director of television programmes such as *Opportunity Knocks* and *This is Your Life*, helped to devise his act, with the then new idea of switching from one character to another without any scene changes.

Mike also performed in clubs and summer seasons around the country, as well as warming up audiences for the radio show *Comedy Bandbox*, creating such an impression as to earn himself an eventual slot on the programme. It was his impression of new Labour Party leader Harold Wilson that led to Mike's TV appearance in the classic *Sunday Night at the London Palladium*, in 1964. He impersonated the politician's voice for the Boulting Brothers' 1965 film *Rotten to the Core* and, two years later, joined Lulu on television for two series of *Three of a Kind*, then landed his own ITV series, *Will the Real Mike Yarwood Stand Up?*, in 1968.

Moving back to the BBC, where he had made *Three of a Kind*, the impressionist with something different to offer starred in *Look – Mike Yarwood* and the long-running *Mike Yarwood in Persons*, for 11 years from 1971.

All the leading names of the day figured in his shows, from the flamboyance of Liberace and exuberance of Ken Dodd, to satirised politicians and trade union leaders such as Edward Heath and Arthur Scargill. When the challenge was just a little too much, as with the Princess of Wales, actress Suzanne Danielle stepped in, and although he attempted Margaret Thatcher, he later left her to impressionist Janet Brown.

During the 70s, Mike also had two radio series, *Yarwood Weekly* and *Listen – Mike Yarwood*, and then, tempted by a larger salary and bigger budget, he returned to ITV in 1983 with *Mike Yarwood in Persons*, which ran for four years. However, it proved to be his swansong as the country's leading impressionist, with a new breed of mimic beginning to take over and Rory Bremner eventually assuming his mantle.

At the same time, Mike had drink and marital problems, and his ITV contract was not renewed. In 1988, he attempted to make a new start as an actor, appearing in a tour of *One for the Pot*, but he collapsed from exhaustion and a later chat show for Grampian Television did not provide him with the chance he had been looking for, either.

Mike, who was awarded an OBE in Harold Wilson's 1976 Resignation Honours List, also won the Variety Club of Great Britain's BBC TV Personality of the Year award in 1973, and the Royal Television Society award for outstanding creative achievement in front of the camera five years later.

He has written two autobiographies, *And This is Me* (1974) and *Impressions of My Life*

(1986), and was profiled in two TV programmes, the documentary *Mike Yarwood – And This is Him!* and a *This is Your Life* special.

Mike and his ex-wife, Sandra Burville, who is a former dancer, were divorced in 1987 and have two daughters, Charlotte and Clare.

Jess Yates

b. 20 December 1918
d. 9 April 1993

MAKING popular, quality television on small budgets was *Stars On Sunday* presenter Jess Yates's forté. During his years in television, he did just about everything there was to do, from designing sets and writing, to producing, directing and presenting, but never have the TV authorities dumped anyone as unceremoniously as they did him.

Born Jesse Frederick Joseph Yates in Tyldesley, Manchester, Jess's family later moved to North Wales and he became a cinema organist in Colwyn Bay at the age of 15. On leaving school, he took a job as organist at the then new Odeon cinema in nearby Llandudno. When Rank took over the circuit, he played across the whole country.

After serving in the Army for four years during the Second World War, based at Radcliff, in Lancashire, he went back to organ-playing on the Rank circuit, as the last touring organist in Britain.

Involved in the formation of the Children's Film Foundation as 'Uncle Jess', he made singalong records for children's Odeon Cinema Clubs.

In 1951, Jess formed the Littlewoods and Vernon girls' choirs for both of the pools organisations, moving to television in the same year as a freelance designer for the BBC, which was keen to broadcast from the regions.

He worked on the first *Sooty* show, in 1952, and the first three years of the long-running music-hall show *The Good Old Days* – starting in 1953 at the celebrated City Varieties Theatre, Leeds – as well as *Come Dancing, Top Town* and the Miss World contest.

In 1955, he switched to producing and made *Out of the Blue*, presented by Tyrone Power, wrote and produced *A Boy Named Will*, as a celebration of Shakespeare's birthday, and presented three series of programmes about the film world, *Behind the Scenes, Junior Picture Parade* and *Filmland*.

Moving to Warwick Films in 1957, he wrote and directed documentary shorts on stars such as Joan Crawford, Robert Mitchum, Jack Lemmon, Trevor Howard

and Anna Neagle, for screening on television.

In 1959, a year after his marriage to former dancer and actress Heller Toren (real name Elaine Smith), he gave up showbusiness to buy a seaside hotel in Llandudno. The couple had a daughter Paula, now a successful TV presenter herself, and the wife of Bob Geldof, and Heller subsequently became a best-selling novelist.

But the marriage soon foundered and Jess sold his hotel business, first moving back to Warwick Films, then making a feature film about the Second World War, before joining Yorkshire Television, which became one of the new ITV franchise holders, in 1968.

As Head of Children's Programmes, his first success was the puppet series *Diane's Magic Book*, which he wrote and produced. Other series he masterminded included the children's dramas *The Flaxton Boys* and *Boy Dominic*, featuring Richard Todd and Brian Blessed. He also created and presented *How We Used to Live*, the longest-running schools programme and winner of several BAFTA awards.

One of Jess's greatest successes was *Junior Showtime*, a talent show for children that launched the careers of Bonnie Langford, Joe Longthorne, Keith Chegwin, Mark Curry and Rosemarie Ford.

Jess was also particularly successful with his religious programmes. *Choirs on Sunday* was a forerunner of the hugely popular *Stars on Sunday*, which he created, produced, directed and presented. Its blend of international stars singing well-known hymns and giving Bible readings made it the most popular religious series ever, with regular audiences of more than 15 million.

For a minimum Equity fee of £49, stars such as James Mason, Norman Wisdom, Dames Anna Neagle, Janet Baker and Kiri Te Kanawa, Ken Dodd, Bing Crosby, Eartha Kitt and Johnny Mathis appeared in the programme. Lord Mountbatten, Edward Heath and the Archbishops of Canterbury and York were on the show, too, giving Bible readings.

Jess also persuaded two of the greatest stars of the century to come out of retirement for two Christmas specials. Gracie Fields appeared in *A Gift for Gracie* and Princess Grace of Monaco was in *The Glories of*

Christmas, as well as appearing in *Stars on Sunday* many times.

However, after six years and more than a thousand programmes at Yorkshire Television, Jess's world came crashing down around him with the *News of the World*'s revelation, on 7 July 1974, that he had been having a relationship with actress Anita Kay, more than 30 years his junior, who had appeared in the series *Origami*, which he directed.

Although Jess was still married, he and his wife had been apart for ten years. Heller was in Majorca with another man and Jess and Anita were not even living together, but this was hardly mentioned during the relentless press campaign against him.

He lost his job and never worked in television again – apart from a few appearances as a judge in the talent show *New Faces* – although *Stars on Sunday* carried on for a further five years without him.

Jess, who was divorced from his wife by mutual consent a year after the scandal, lived with Anita until they parted and she subsequently married someone else.

He still hoped that his experience and ideas might enable him to work again, but it was not to be, for he died suddenly of a stroke at the age of 74.

Bernard Youens

b. 28 December 1914
d. 27 August 1984

AS workshy layabout Stan Ogden, Bernard Youens was a *Coronation Street* legend for 20 years. His Laurel and Hardy-style double-act with actress Jean Alexander brought laughs to millions.

Born Bernard Popley in Hove, East Sussex, during the early days of the First World War, the youngster moved with his family to Newcastle upon Tyne at the age of 14 and began his career in the city as an assistant stage manager, at the Players' Theatre, two years later. He subsequently worked in repertory theatre all over Britain.

When the Second World War came, he was called up in 1940, serving in the 1st Batallion, the Loyals Regiment, in North Africa, Egypt and Anzio, in Italy.

After the War, he returned to repertory theatre, but work became scarce and he left acting at one point to become landlord of a rundown Manchester pub with a rough bunch of regulars. He then worked as a bread salesman and a building site labourer, before trying his hand at running another pub, near Preston.

When Granada Television began broadcasting as the ITV company for the North of England in 1956, Bernard returned to showbusiness to become one of its two continuity announcers. The other was Ray Moore, who was to become a Radio 2 disc-jockey.

The velvet-voiced Southerner Bernard could not have been more removed from the character for which he was to become known to the nation. He also found acting work at Granada, appearing in the early ITV drama series *Shadow Squad* and *Knight Errant*.

When *Coronation Street* began, in 1960, he turned down the chance of an audition, preferring the stability of his announcer's job. But, in 1964, with the programme by then a television institution, he joined the cast as Stan Ogden, henpecked husband of Rovers Return cleaner Hilda. His first line, in the pub, was "A pint of mild and 20 fags, missus."

Stan began his screen life as a lorry driver and went through jobs as a chauffeur, coalman, milkman and ice-cream seller, before becoming a window cleaner, but he was more in his element simply staying at home, doing nothing.

The character was so popular that there was even a Stan Ogden Appreciation Society, who dubbed their hero "the greatest living Englishman".

During his later years in the serial, Bernard – a complete professional who never let fame go to his head – suffered a series of heart attacks and a stroke, which left his speech impaired.

With the aid of speech therapy, he battled on bravely, but he suffered more strokes and – having had arthritis of the neck and knees for almost 20 years – had his left leg amputated after gangrene was discovered. Shortly afterwards, in 1984, he died at the age of 69, having appeared in 1200 episodes of *Coronation Street*.

Bernard, who married ballet dancer Edna Swallow – whom he called 'Teddy' – at the age of 18, had two daughters, Ann and Diana, and three sons, Brian, Peter and Michael.

★★★★★★★★★★★★★

Muriel Young

b. 19 June 1928

ONE of the most familiar faces in the early days of ITV was Muriel Young, its first announcer in the London region when the channel began, in 1955, and presenter of children's shows such as *The Five O'Clock Club*, before she turned to producing *Clapperboard* and other programmes for young audiences.

Born in Bishop Middleham, County Durham, Muriel worked briefly as a librarian on leaving school and attended art college, before deciding on acting as a career. She joined a repertory theatre in Henley-on-Thames, where her uncle was directing, and subsequently performed at the Gateway Theatre, London, and Theatre Royal, Chatham.

Trying to get into films, Muriel did photographic modelling for advertisements for products such as toothpaste to earn money until she achieved her ambition. She also studied to be a dental nurse and painted glassware.

She then won parts in the films *The Story of Gilbert and Sullivan* – acting in a segment featuring *The Mikado* – and *The Constant Husband*, which starred Rex Harrison and Kay Kendall.

Later, after she had become a TV announcer, she was cast in the Peter Sellers film *I'm All Right, Jack* as just that, although she was given the role without the director knowing it was her real-life full-time job.

Muriel had, in fact, landed her announcer's job by accident, going along on the day of the announcers', rather than actors', auditions at Associated Rediffusion, one of the two ITV companies set up in London when the channel started. At that time, the job of announcing sometimes entailed ad-libbing for minutes on end because there were not enough commercials to fill the spaces between programmes.

However, her career could easily have taken a different course. Just before joining ITV, she had been touring on stage in a game show called *Double or Drop*, hosted by Eamonn Andrews. Shortly after signing her ITV contract, he told her he had sold the idea to the BBC and it was later used as part of the children's show *Crackerjack!*

As well as announcing, Muriel became a presenter and interviewer for Granada Television's *People and Places* and Southern Television's *Day By Day*, after those ITV regional companies started broadcasting.

Her face was familiar to children as a friend of Pussy Cat Willum in *Small Time* and Ollie Beak and Fred Barker in *Tuesday Rendezvous* and its successor, *The Five O'Clock Club*. Her voice was also heard, for eight years, as a disc-jockey on Radio Luxembourg.

In 1969, she joined Granada Television to set up a children's department and produced programmes such as *Clapperboard*, with presenter Chris Kelly reviewing the latest films, and the pop shows *Lift Off with Ayshea*, *Marc*, with Marc Bolan, *Shang-a-Lang*, with the Bay City Rollers at the height of their teenybop fame, and *Get It Together*.

Changing direction again, in the mid-80s Muriel made two series of *Ladybirds*, a Channel Four programme from Mike Mansfield's independent company, in which she interviewed female singers including Barbara Dickson, Elaine Paige and Kiki Dee, as well as producing the shows. She went as far as Hollywood and Paris to catch Rita Coolidge and Jane Birkin.

Then, in 1986, after more than 30 years, Muriel left television and moved back to her County Durham roots to live in a part of Stanhope Castle with her husband, Cyril Coke, an ITV programme director since the channel's beginning.

She enjoys oil painting and some of her works, mainly landscapes, have been exhibited locally and even at Liberty's, in London.